The Woven Coverlets of Norway

The Woven Coverlets of Norway

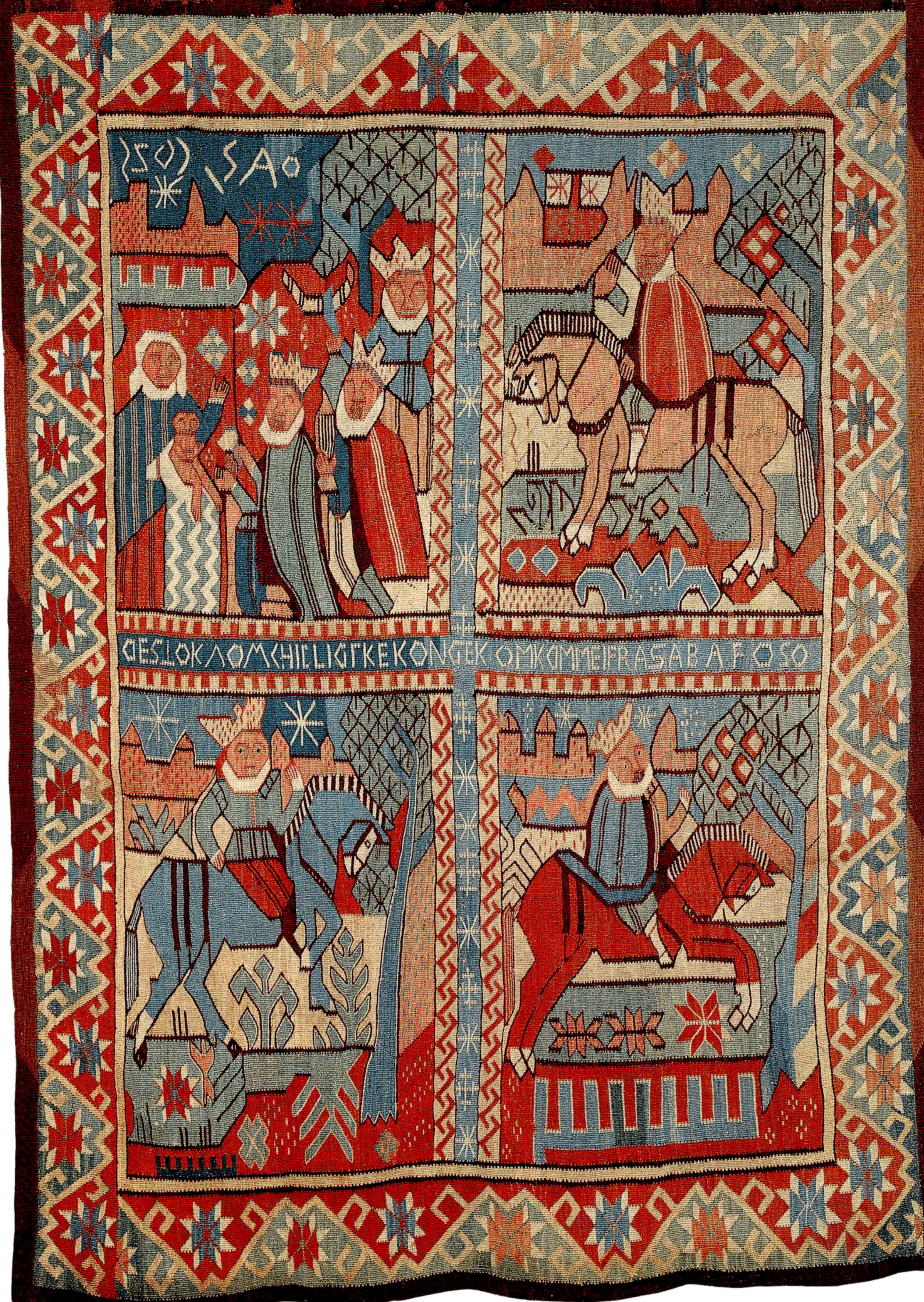
1520
DES LOKAOM CHIELLIGFKE KONGER OMKOMMEFRASABA FÖSO

THE WOVEN COVERLETS OF NORWAY

KATHERINE LARSON

UNIVERSITY OF WASHINGTON PRESS   SEATTLE & LONDON

IN ASSOCIATION WITH THE NORDIC HERITAGE MUSEUM   SEATTLE

This book is published in conjunction with the exhibition "Woven Treasure: The Coverlets of Norway," organized by the Nordic Heritage Museum in association with the Vesterheim Norwegian-American Museum.

EXHIBITION SCHEDULE

The Nordic Heritage Museum, Seattle, Washington
September 13–November 11, 2001

The Plains Art Museum, Fargo, North Dakota
May 16–July 14, 2002

West Vancouver Museum and Archives,
West Vancouver, British Columbia
August–October 2002

The book and exhibition were made possible by generous support from the National Endowment for the Arts, a federal agency, and the American-Scandinavian Foundation.

p. ii: The Norwegian tapestry coverlets lent a mark of distinction to homes in Norway's relatively wealthy eastern valleys. "The Magi and the Adoration" was a well-known motif. *Verterheim Norwegian-American Museum.*

p. vi: Time-honored motifs and lively colors characterized the square weave coverlets of Norway's western and southern districts. *Photo: Mark Frey. Nordic Heritage Museum.*

Copyright © 2001 by the University of Washington Press
Printed in Canada
Designed by Audrey S. Meyer

LIBRARY OF CONGRESS CATALOGING-IN-PUBLICATION DATA
Larson, Katherine, 1951-
    The woven coverlets of Norway / Katherine Larson.
        p. cm.
    "In association with the Nordic Heritage Society Museum, Seattle."
    Includes bibliographical references and index.
    ISBN 0-295-98130-X (cloth : alk. paper) — ISBN 0-295-98131-8 (alk. paper)
    1. Coverlets—Norway. 2. Hand weaving—Norway. I. Title.
NK8960.A1 L37 2001
746.9'7'09481—DC21   2001018835

In memory of my parents,

Gene and Gertrude Larson

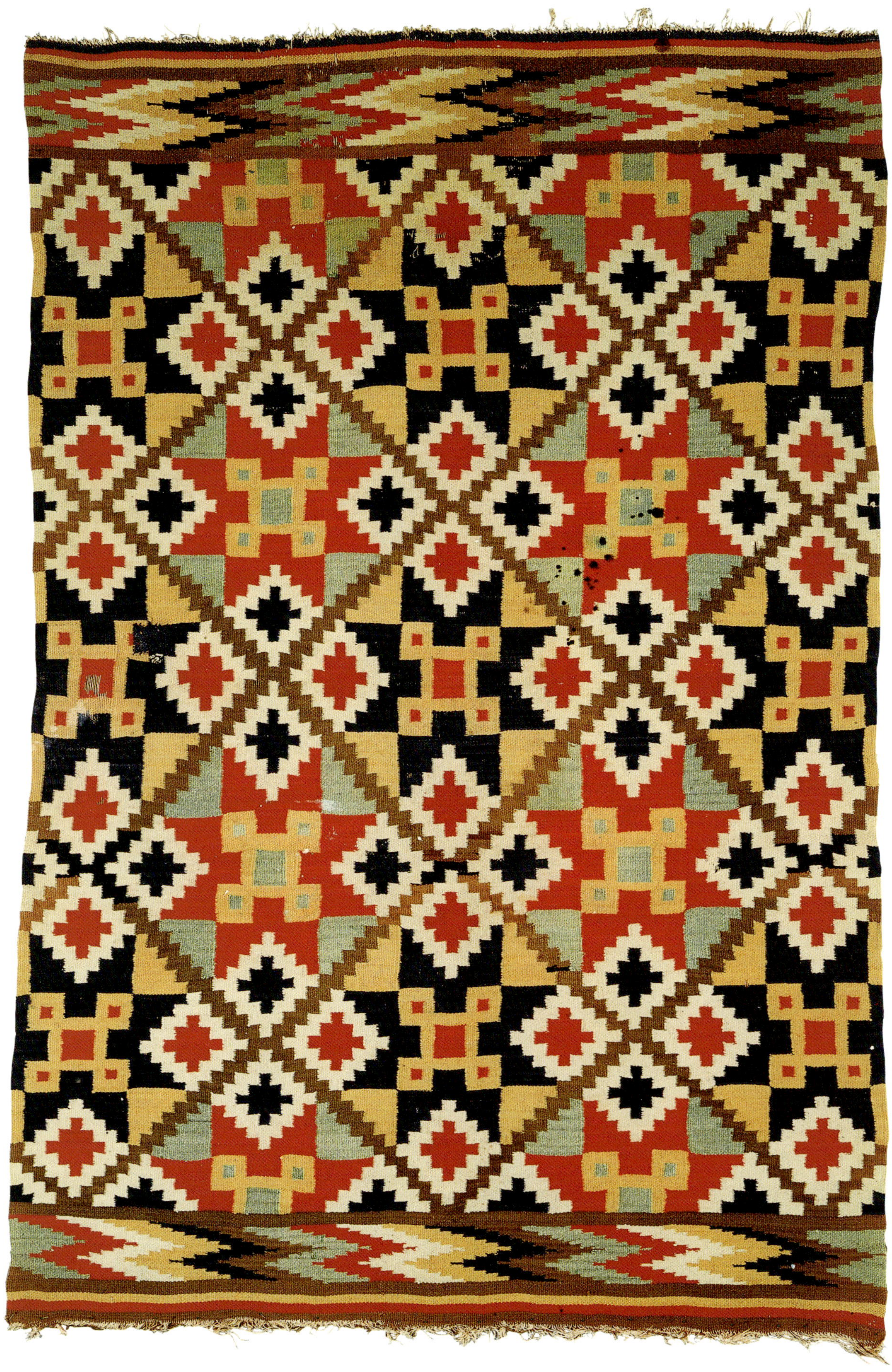

Contents

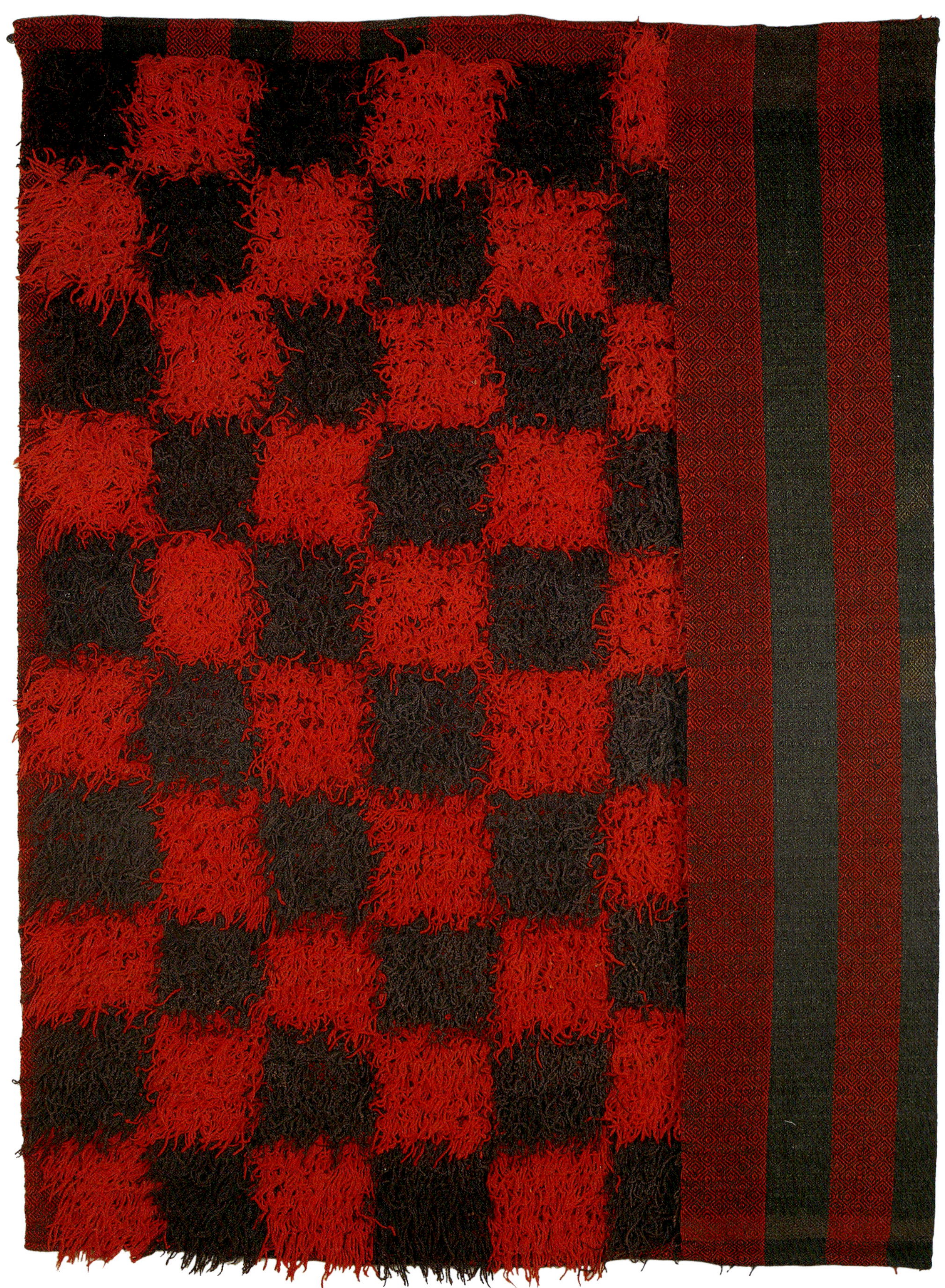

Preface

The thick pile of a *rya* provided a warm cover at night. Knotted-pile coverlets were particularly valued in coastal areas, where they were considered essential equipment by Norwegian mariners. *Photo: Mark Frey. Nordic Heritage Museum.*

THIS IS A BOOK ABOUT WEAVING, ABOUT TECHNIQUES and patterns, tools and materials. As such, I hope there will be much to interest textile enthusiasts within its pages. But it is also a book about emigration and cultural heritage, about the the decision to start a new life and the things that inevitably were left behind, and this is a history shared by many Americans.

Like most children in our ethnically diverse country, I spent my youth in blissful ignorance of my cultural heritage. The one notable exception was the dreaded Christmas lutefisk feast at Great-uncle Olav's house. Of course, with grandfathers named Lars Larson and Peter Peterson, there was never any doubt that Norwegians made up a sizable portion of my family tree, but apart from a Scandinavian surname, a pair of blue eyes, and the unfortunate yearly encounters with lye-soaked fish, the thousands of years my forebears had spent in another part of the world might never have been real to me. All of this changed during a year of schooling in Norway.

As a college student I went to the land of my ancestors searching for my lost cultural heritage. To my surprise, I found that most Norwegians spoke English with ease, putting to shame my own halting attempts at their language. My fellow students were also considerably more advanced than I in matters of style and social attitudes, and decidedly modern cars and trucks thundered past my dorm-room window on a busy national highway. This was not the land of my ancestors. This was the twentieth century with a foreign accent!

Purely by chance I stumbled onto what I was looking for. Assigned to the home-arts section at my *folkehøgskole*, or folk high school, I spent the year alternating between two weeks in the kitchen and two weeks in the weaving studio. With the clear vision sometimes granted to twenty-year-olds, I quickly determined that cooking would be of little use in my future life (!), but weaving began to exert its magical influence from the moment I stepped into the studio. Rows of looms, cupboards full of yarn, huge warping mills, delicate umbrella swifts—all were equally intriguing. But it was not simply the satisfying process of throwing a shuttle and beating the weft into place that drew me on. In most Norwegian homes I observed textiles on display, either hanging on the wall, draped over the back of a chair, or peeping from beneath the goodies that always appeared on the coffee table. Many of these weavings were originally coverlets or smaller decorative pieces woven in coverlet techniques. Through further study I learned that the elaborate patterns and painstaking methods evident in these weavings were the result of centuries of tradition, years in which the creation of textiles played an important part in the everyday life of the family. This was the link with the past for which I had been searching. By studying the steps of preparation, the techniques of weaving, and the combinations of patterns from which these coverlets were made, I was learning the skills that my grandmothers of generations past had spent a good part of their lives pursuing.

Perhaps more than our immigrant ancestors realized, the momentous decision to come to a new country meant the gradual abandonment of their cultural heritage. With each generation the memories were destined to grow dimmer, until the few revered relics that remain to us today—the painted chest, the delicate brooch, the woven coverlet—are often an enigma to their owners, a distant, indistinct echo of the past. I would like to make a part of that heritage come alive, to introduce Americans to the Norwegian weavers of the past, to show their surroundings, the seasons of their work, their tools and materials. And finally, I would like to present the prized creations of these generations of weavers: the Norwegian coverlets.

I have relied on a number of institutions, met a host of new people, and renewed many old acquaintances during the course of my research.

To begin at the beginning, I would like to thank Sigrid Hansen, my home-arts teacher of thirty years ago at Romerike folkehøgskole, who recognized my interest in weaving and went out of her way to satisfy my curiosity. She later offered every support and encouragement during the course of my research, including the gracious offer of extended lodgings. I am also indebted to the memory of Torbjørg Gauslaa, respected author and Husflid Consultant for Oppland, who encouraged my work and offered much useful advice.

For over fifteen years the Nordic Heritage Museum in Seattle, Washington, has supported my attempts to enhance the appreciation of traditional Norwegian weaving in this country. I would like to express my deepest gratitude to Director Marianne Forssblad, who has encouraged my efforts from the day I appeared in her office, toddler in tow, with a proposal for a weaving course. Her continued support has proven invaluable in the development of this book and its accompanying exhibition.

I have endeavored to make the information in this book as accurate as possible, and in this attempt I am indebted to Anne Kjellberg, Textile Curator at the Oslo Museum of Applied Art, for her careful reading of the manuscript and her many cogent comments. I would also like to thank Lila Nelson, retired Textile Curator, and Laurann Gilbertson, current Textile Curator at Vesterheim Norwegian-American Museum in Decorah, Iowa, for their timely reviews, helpful suggestions, and sage advice. Any mistakes that remain are purely of my own making.

Research for this project would literally never have gotten off the ground without the generous financial support of the American-Scandinavian Foundation, which contributed to my initial research tour of Norway. In addition, funding granted by the National Endowment for the Arts, the Sons of Norway Foundation, the Daughters of Norway, and Inger Osberg, Lisa Garbrick, and Kimberley and Alan Lippman helped defray the cost of the many illustrations essential to the presentation of this subject.

For help in finding the many photographs included in this book, I have relied heavily on the staff at several institutions. I would particularly like to thank the Norwegian Folk Museum; the Oslo Museum of Applied Art; the Historical Museum, University of Bergen; the Trøndelag Folk Museum; the National Museum of Decorative Arts; Vesterheim Norwegian-American Museum; and the Nordic Heritage Museum. I am also grateful to a number of other institutions who allowed me to view their textile collections and provided me with assistance in locating photographs. These include Vestfold County Museum; Vest-Agder County Museum; Stavanger Museum; the Heiberg Collection; Valdres Folk Museum; Voss Folk Museum; Maihaugen, the Sandvig Collection; Nordland Museum; Rana Museum; and Tromsø Museum.

In the course of my research, I have been able to make good use of the University of Washington Libraries, and I would like to extend special thanks to Laura Barnard of the Seattle Public Library for her help in acquiring many resources through the Interlibrary Loan Program. I would also like to thank Ed Egerdahl, Director of the Scandinavian Language Institute, for checking my translations of old Norwegian verse, Karen Diadick Casselman, for reviewing the portion of the manuscript dealing with natural dyes, and Sue Mohr, for her excellent organizational advice and general moral support. I am grateful to my copyeditor, Mary Ribesky, and to Marilyn Trueblood and Audrey Meyer of the University of Washington Press for their careful attention to detail in the creation of this book. What began as a vision became a reality through their efforts, despite the interruption of a major earthquake during which we huddled together in an unsteady building.

I think I could happily spend the rest of my life visiting museums, but nothing can replace the privilege and pleasure of being a guest of the people whose traditions I have endeavored to study. I would therefore like to offer my gratitude to distant relatives in southern Norway, the Nysteds, Henriksens, and Eiks, who have hosted an apparently unending stream of American relatives, myself included, all bent on discovering their roots; and to Torger Flatestøl, who graciously invited me and my family to visit the ancestral farm and see the many old weaving and household implements carefully preserved by his family. I would also like to thank my relatives in northern Norway (unknown to me before research for this book led me to their district), particularly Molvin Vilmo for filling in many gaps in the family history, and Sissel Aanes, who was kind enough to entertain her never-before-heard-of fourth cousin and at the same time reveal another treasure trove of antique implements stored in the family's old homestead.

It would be impossible to conclude without acknowledging the support of my parents. My father always encouraged an interest in the family's Norwegian ancestry, of which he was very proud. The eight-harness floor loom that he built from cryptic drawings I brought home from Norway helped to set me on my way. And my mother, frequently consulted for her wisdom and ready support, was instrumental in getting this project under way by being my companion on a lengthy, but by no means leisurely, research trip that encompassed most of Norway.

Most of all I would like to offer a heartfelt thank-you to my husband, Tracy Collier, whose great patience, sound advice, and constant encouragement have made this project possible, and to my children, Sarah and Christopher, who have grown up with *The Woven Coverlets of Norway*.

Introduction

"There Lies a Land Near the Eternal Snow . . ."

"Der ligger et land mot den evige sne . . ."

NORWAY LIES AT THE EXTREME NORTHWEST corner of Europe, "near the eternal snow," in the words of poet Bjørnstjerne Bjørnson. Because of its historical involvement in shipping and trade and the early far-reaching exploits of the Vikings, Norway was not completely excluded from the mainstream of European events. But to some extent the country has suffered from (or some might say benefited from) a certain amount of isolation. This is particularly true in the area of textiles. Although much of western Europe witnessed the birth of the textile industry in the Middle Ages and the subsequent transformation of a home-oriented craft into a business run by professionals, in Norway the art of weaving remained firmly in the home. The challenging climate and difficult terrain of this rugged northern land fostered a hard life in which things of value were carefully preserved, and the natural conservatism of a farming culture impeded the acceptance of new methods. Thus certain weaving tools and techniques that had largely disappeared centuries ago from the homelife of France or England were still to be found in the early part of the twentieth century in Norway, preserved within the folk art of its farming community.

Not everyone in Norway lived on a family farm, of course. A small portion of the populace were city dwellers (roughly 9 percent in 1800), either employed by the church or engaged in commerce, government service, or a professional trade. While most of the remainder made their living through farming, it should be noted that not all farm situations were the

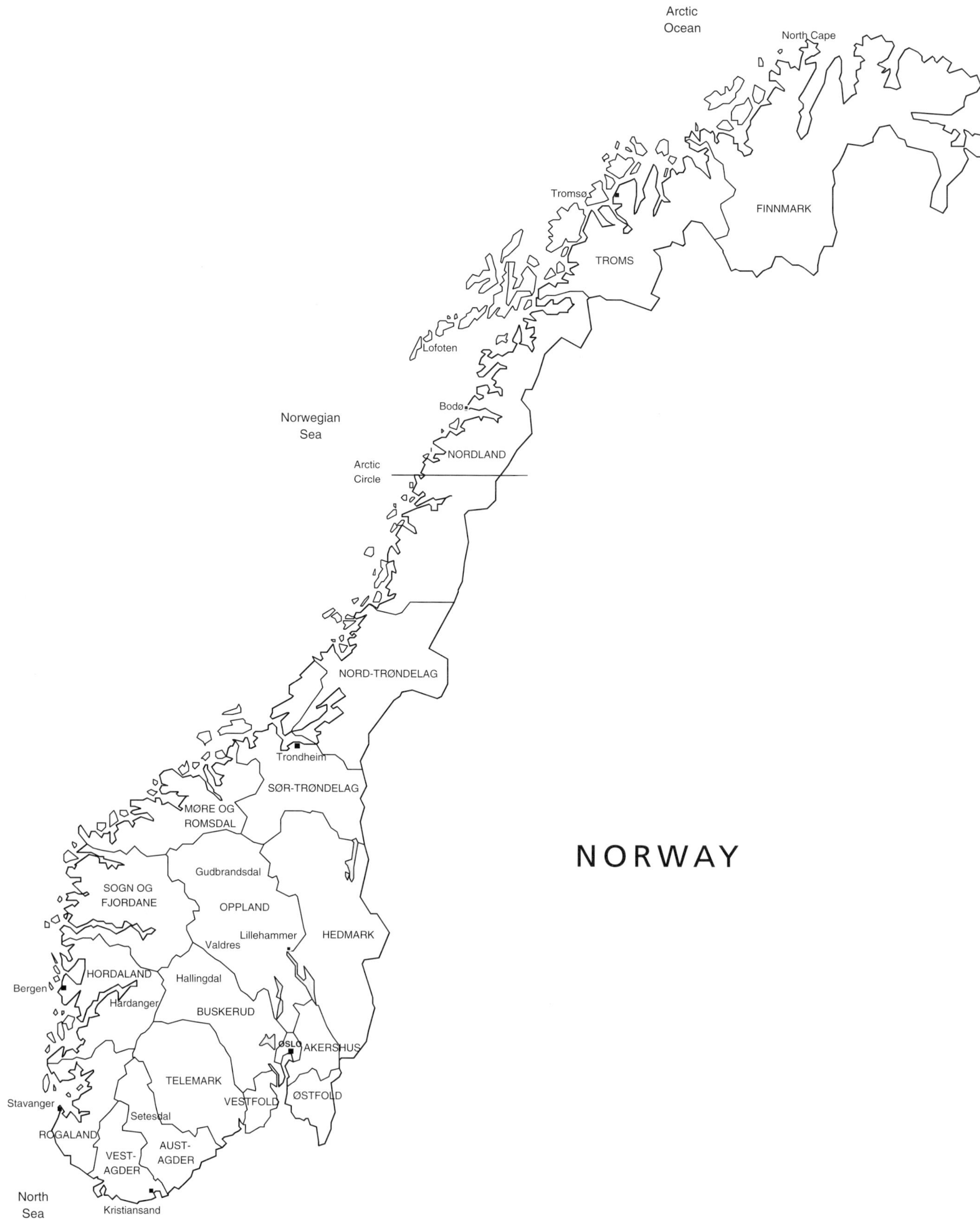

Arctic
Ocean
North Cape
FINNMARK
Tromsø
TROMS
Lofoten
Norwegian
Sea
Bodø
NORDLAND
Arctic
Circle
NORD-TRØNDELAG
Trondheim
SØR-TRØNDELAG
MØRE OG
ROMSDAL
NORWAY
Gudbrandsdal
SOGN OG
FJORDANE
OPPLAND
Lillehammer
HEDMARK
Valdres
HORDALAND
Hallingdal
Bergen
Hardanger
BUSKERUD
OSLO
AKERSHUS
TELEMARK
VESTFOLD
ØSTFOLD
Stavanger
Setesdal
ROGALAND
AUST-
AGDER
VEST-
AGDER
North
Sea
Kristiansand

A family pauses on the steep path to Bykle, Setesdal. Communities located in remote mountain regions of Norway were often isolated by difficult and dangerous traveling conditions, especially during the winter months. *Norwegian Folk Museum.*

same. Individual holdings varied in size, from substantial farms owned by affluent landowners and wealthy civil servants, to modest homesteads that provided a comfortable livelihood for the owner or renter, to tiny marginal parcels often inhabited by a tenant farmer/laborer and his family. At the bottom of the economic and social ladder were the hired domestic and farm laborers who supplemented the workforce on many holdings. The prosperity of a farm also depended on its location: those situated in the eastern and southern valleys generally fared better than those clinging to mountainsides in the western fjord country or struggling in the harsher conditions of northern districts; and farms located along important trade routes benefited from the passing flow of goods and ideas unavailable to holdings isolated in steep mountain valleys. Yet despite this range of position and prosperity, a stable culture of families engaged in working the land formed the backbone of Norway's rural population. Within this environment, the art of weaving flourished.

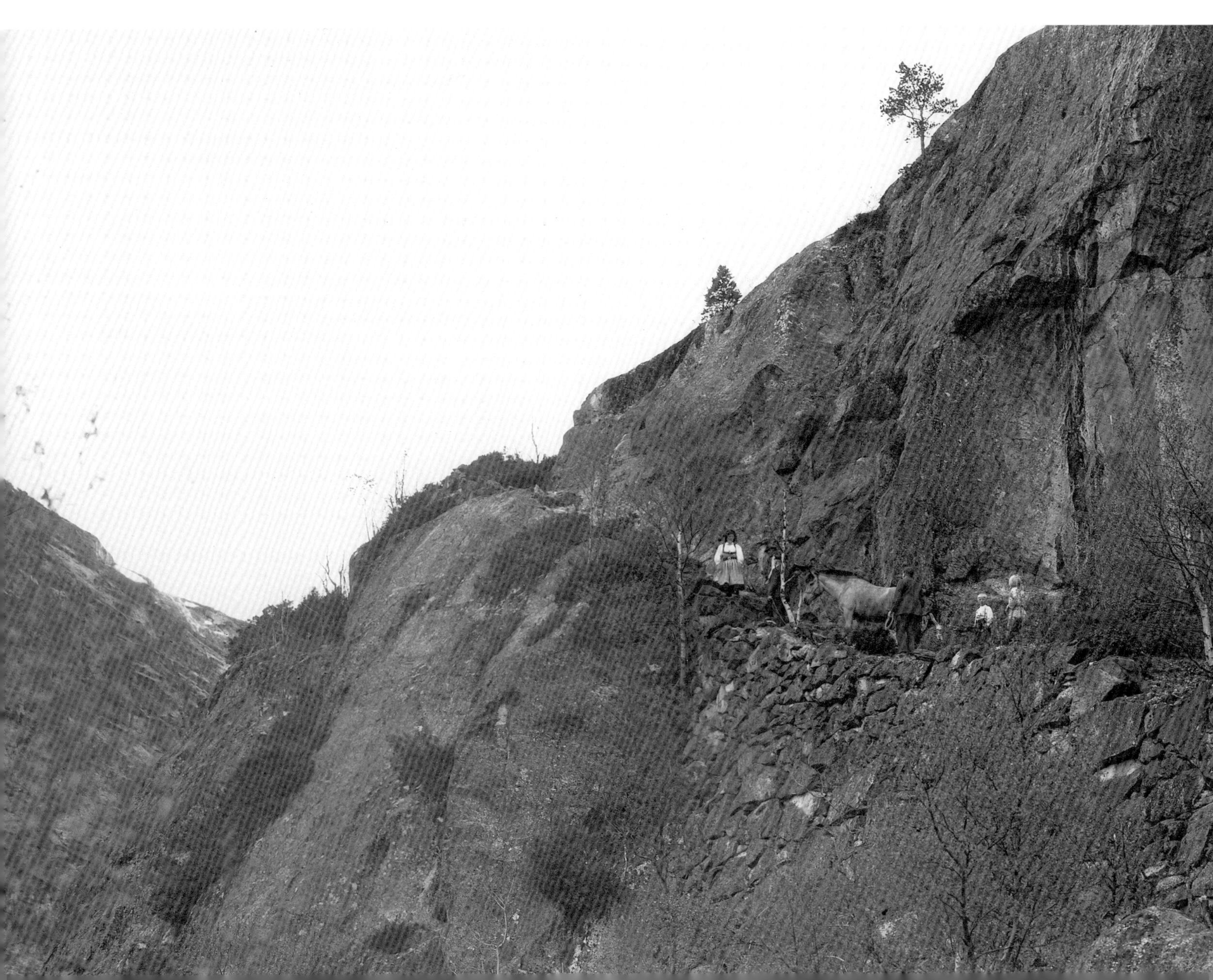

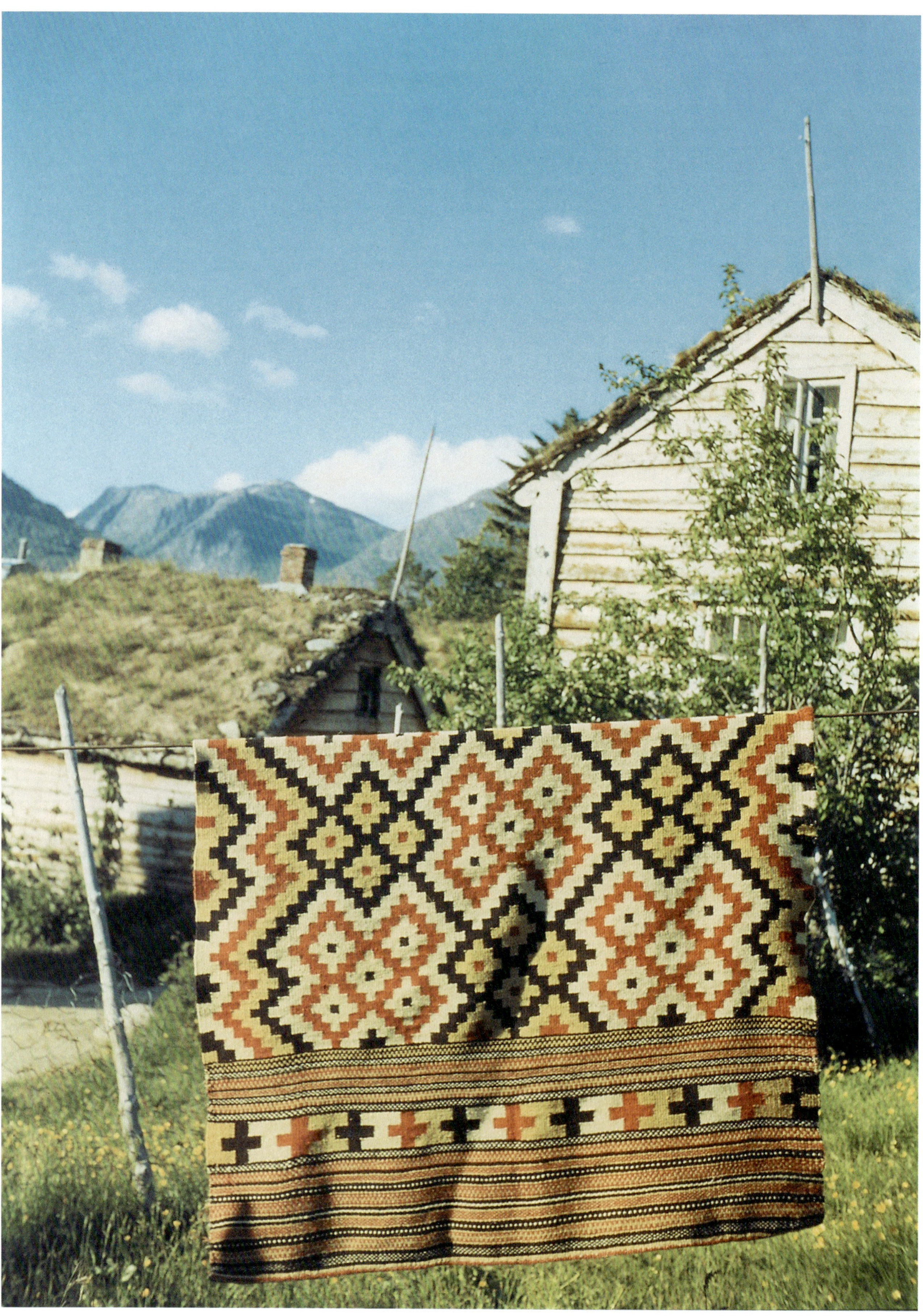

Weaving as a Part of Norwegian Folk Life

A square-weave coverlet hangs outdoors beside a farmhouse
in rural Norway. *Norwegian Folk Museum.*

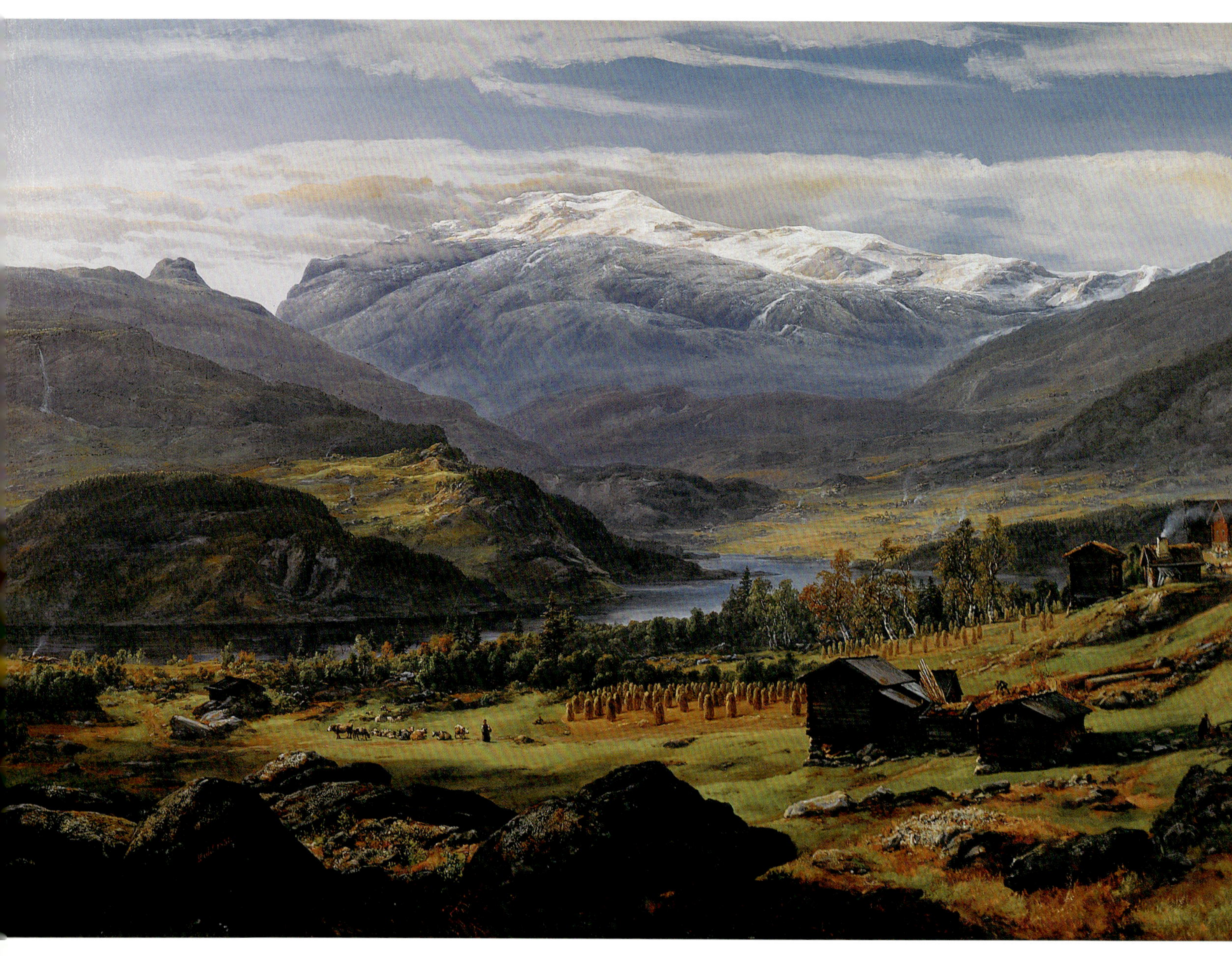

1.1 During the long days of summer, everyone on the farm worked outside
tending the crops and animals. *Fra Hjelle i Valdres, by J. C. Dahl, 1851.
Photo: O. Væring. National Gallery.*

1 / *The Yearly Cycle of Textile Production*

1.2 The *primstav*, a flat stick with the days of summer recorded on one side *(top)* and the days of winter on the other *(bottom)*, served as a primitive calendar on some Norwegian farms into the eighteenth century. This calendar stick from Telemark is dated 1711. *Drawing: Brit Hegenhougen, in Alver 1970. Collection of the Norwegian Folk Museum.*

A Time to Every Purpose

SUMMER AND WINTER. DAYS FILLED WITH LIGHT AND days of unending night. For centuries the pattern of life in rural Norway followed the unchanging rhythm of the sun. People adhered to the ways of their ancestors because they knew the old ways worked. To stray from the established pattern was to risk privation, if not outright disaster. Each change of the seasons brought its own series of familiar tasks that were repeated year after year. Every step in the ancient rhythm was followed with care, and each child was taught the skills he or she would need, with survival being the ultimate measure of success.

To keep track of the passage of days and the appointed yearly tasks, many families had a primitive calendar know as a *primstav*. This was a long flat stick with notches on both sides to mark the days (fig. 1.2). The year was divided into two parts, the light days of summer recorded on one side of the calendar stick and the dark days of winter on the other. On each farm it was known that if the crops were not in the ground by a certain date they might not fully ripen, or that by such a date the ice on the lake was no longer safe to walk upon.

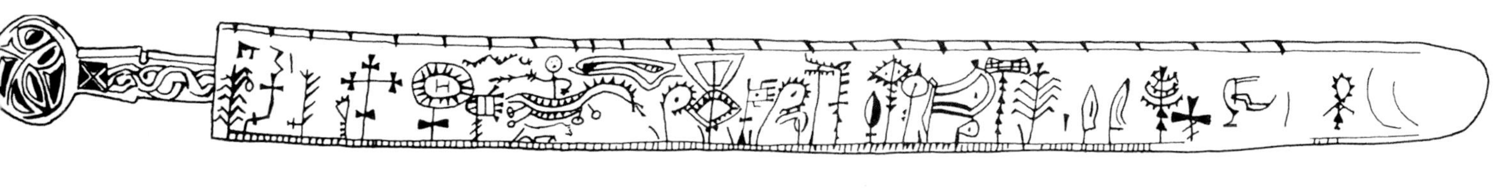

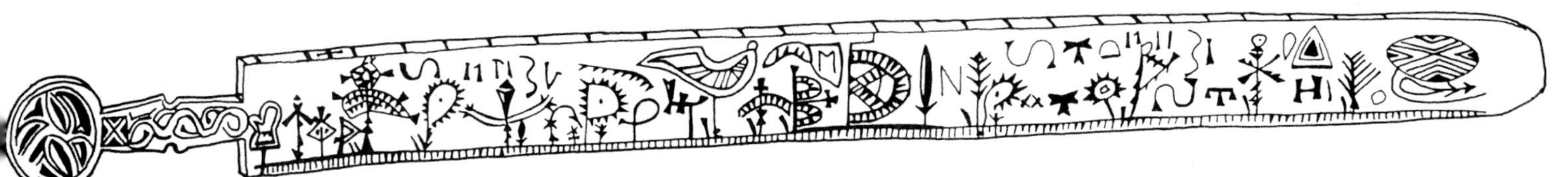

The light days began in mid-April, and with them came the time for working outdoors. The animals were let out of the barn after their long winter of confinement to follow the greening leaves up the mountainsides. Planting was begun, sheep were sheared, and all the clothing and bedding were gathered for the biggest washday of the year.

During the summer, children tended the animals grazing in the mountain meadows and helped their mother make cheese from rich goats' milk, and everyone on the farm helped with whatever tasks the crops demanded (fig. 1.1). As the summer waned, crops were harvested, sheep were sheared again, and those animals that could not be fed through the winter were set aside for slaughter. All was made ready for the winter, when short days and bitter cold would keep outdoor work to a minimum.

In the middle of October, the calendar stick was turned over as the dark days of winter began. Although some outdoor chores still required attention during the short hours of daylight—chopping firewood, hauling sleds loaded with fodder from the seters (mountain dairy cabins), bringing in water, caring for the animals in the barn—the focus of daily life was indoors. For the men of the household, winter was a time to repair farming and fishing equipment in preparation for the next season and to make any household implements that were required. For the women, it was the season for transforming mounds of raw wool and flax into yarn, and yarn into woven or knitted clothing, a job that occupied every available minute and required the help of children and grandparents as well.

In the evenings as the family gathered around the hearth to mend fishing nets or wind balls of yarn, stories were passed from one generation to the next. Kings and heroes marched through the sagas of the past, and trolls roamed the mountains and forests of the darkened countryside. Beside the fire, source of heat and light during the long winter nights, beliefs and fears that sustained a way of life were renewed while every hand was busy with the tasks that would insure the family's survival (fig. 1.3).

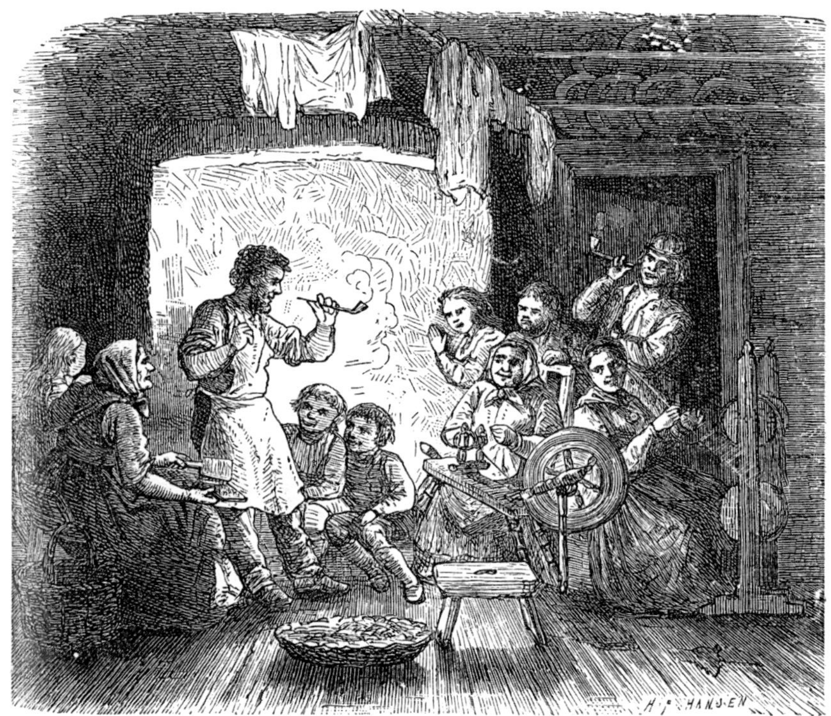

1.3 Gathered around the hearth on winter evenings, family members kept their hands busy with household tasks. In this illustration by Adolph Tidemand, women card, spin, and wind balls of yarn while listening to the tales of a storyteller. *In Asbjørnsen 1940.*

Gradually the dark days passed, and with the return of the light days another cycle of the ancient pattern was complete.

Woman's Work Is Never Done

Every member of the household made a contribution to the prosperity of the farm in his or her own way. Responsibilities were generally divided along traditional lines, the menfolk working the fields, the forests, and the fishing grounds while the women cared for the children, handled all food preparation, and provided clothing for the family. Milking and sheepshearing were tasks that also fell within a woman's purview, and along with everyone else she helped as needed in the fields. In coastal areas where husbands and sons were often away fishing for months at a time, a woman's responsibilities could even extend to caring for the entire farm, but her work in the home was of paramount importance. In the joint effort between husband and wife that went into making a successful farm, a woman who could "decisively and authoritatively . . . organize the large household and insure that at all times there was enough food and clothing for everyone on the farm" was highly valued.[1]

Of the housewife's traditional duties, cooking and childcare have changed but little over the centuries. Where today an electric range may replace an open hearth and diaper service thankfully takes the place of chapped fingers, these are only changes by degree to jobs that are still essentially the same. However, the task of clothing the family has altered so drastically over the past several hundred years that a woman of today, transported back through time, might not even recognize the required tools, let alone know how to use them. Certainly many women still sew clothes for themselves and their families, but even this has become a hobby rather than a necessity. Every other step of the procedure, from raising the fibers to weaving the cloth, has disappeared from our everyday lives, so that learning about these skills is a bit like studying a foreign language. It comes as a revelation to discover the commitment of time and energy that our grandmothers devoted to these tasks to which we have become strangers.

For the Norwegian housewife, clothing the family was a yearlong process. Beginning with sheepshearing and the cultivation of flax, it encompassed the transformation of these fibers into yarn through carding and spinning, the collection of plants for making colorful dyes, weaving or knitting the yarns into cloth, sewing new clothes and mending used clothing, and even unraveling rags to make the yarns available for use again. Not only were members of the family outfitted, but the hired help needed clothing as well, often considered a part of their yearly payment. The home periodically needed new bedding and kitchen linens, ships had to be outfitted with new sails, and fishermen had to be supplied with special equipment, from warm, sturdy stockings and mittens to thick pile coverlets. It was the housewife's responsibility to direct the work of her daughters and the family's domestic help so that

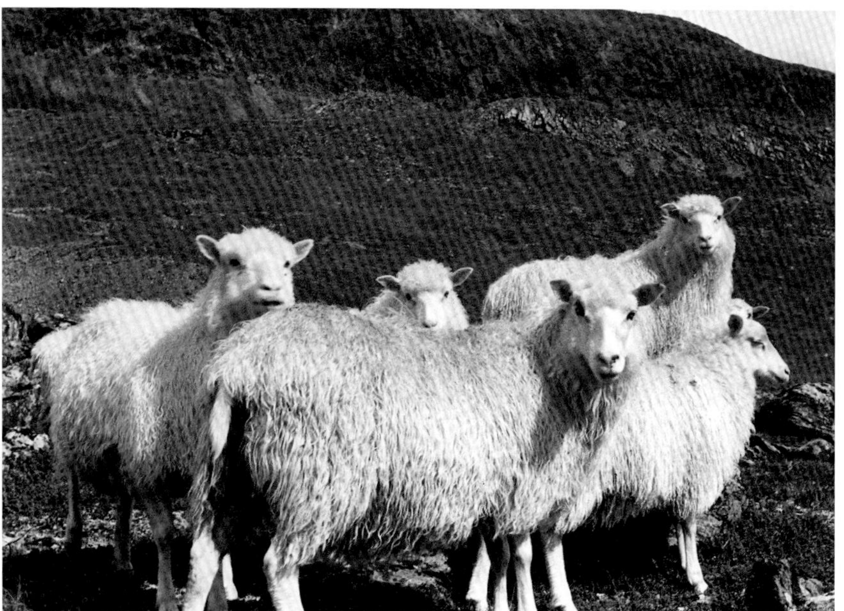

1.4 The *spælsau* is a descendant of the ancient breed of short-tailed sheep native to northern Europe. *Photo: P. A. Røstad. Courtesy of the Norwegian Association of Sheep and Goat Breeders.*

1.5 The fleece of a *spælsau* is composed of long guard hairs and short underwool: a lock of *spælsau* fleece with both guard hair and underwool *(left)*; a lock of *spælsau* fleece from which the underwool *(top center)* has been removed from the guard hair *(right)*. Modern breeds of sheep no longer have guard hair in their fleece: a lock of Romney wool *(bottom center)*. *Photo: T. Roubal.*

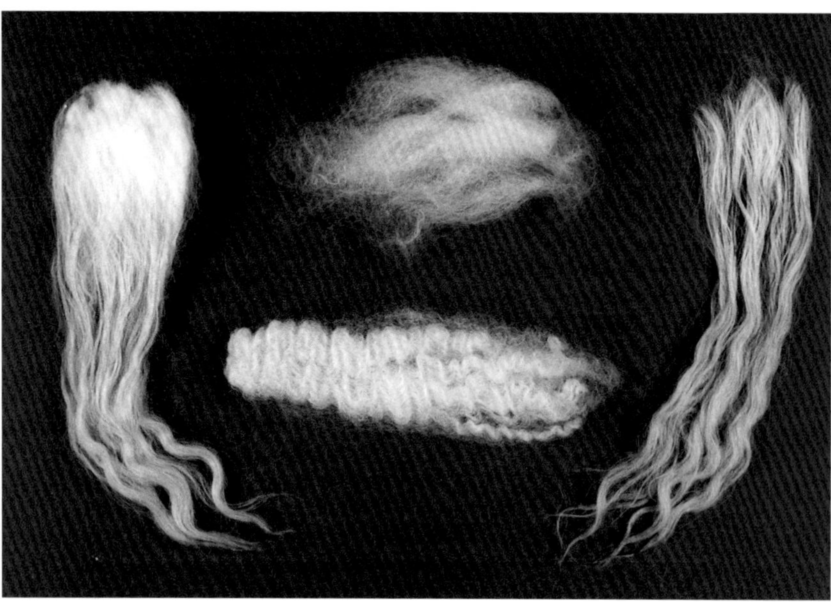

Today our thoughts about the fibers we wear are usually limited to checking the fiber content of a new article of clothing. (Will it need ironing? Will it shrink when it inevitably ends up in the dryer?) In the past, however, fibers were not just names on labels. They were familiar materials that were grown, harvested, and prepared with great care by the family, for they were the beginning of the cloth-making process. In Norway there were two fibers of significance, the indispensable sheep's wool, produced every year on most farms, and the fibers of the flax plant.

Since its domestication in Mesopotamia at least 4,000 years ago, the sheep has provided man with the fibers of its wonderfully soft warm coat. Wool's insulating qualities combined with its durability, elasticity, and the relative ease with which it is prepared and spun made it the dominant clothing fiber in the Middle East and Europe for thousands of years. The added capacity for holding warmth even when wet made this marvelous fiber doubly useful to the mariners of the far north.

The breed of sheep native to Norway is a variant of the ancient northern European race of short-tailed sheep. A descendant that probably closely resembles this old breed survives in very limited numbers today in Norway's coastal regions. Known as the *utgangarsau* (primitive or wild sheep), it winters outside in the relatively mild maritime climate and sheds its fleece around mid-summer. A direct descendant of the older breed is also found in the *spælsau*, a slightly larger animal that is brought in for the winter months and whose fleece must be sheared (fig. 1.4). Both of these sheep are relatively small and have a fleece composed of two layers, an outer coat of long, smooth guard hairs and an inner layer of short, soft wool (fig. 1.5). Beginning in the eighteenth century and continuing into the nineteenth, farmers in Norway began to experiment with sheep breeds from other parts of Europe that were larger and provided finer wool. With the advent of commercially spun yarns late in the nineteenth century, for which the two-layered fleece was not acceptable, the numbers of the older breeds began to decline. Today, the *spælsau* represents about one fourth of Norway's sheep production, and only a limited amount of carefully sorted *spælsau* wool is produced for use by art weavers.

Flax *(linum usitatissimum)* is an herbaceous plant whose inner fibers can be processed into a strong, slightly stiff thread known as linen (fig. 1.6). Of less importance in Norway than wool and often imported as a semi-processed product into areas where arable land was limited, flax was still sown and harvested on many farms into the nineteenth century. Flax was used by the Egyptians as early as 6,000 B.C. and was cultivated throughout the Mediterranean region, where it provided a basic source of fiber for spinning and weaving. Flax has been grown in Norway since at least the Migration period (fourth to sixth centuries), although clear evidence for spinning flax into linen is not present until the Middle Ages. Although not as easy to prepare as wool, flax fibers have the advantage of being smooth and comfortable when worn close to the skin. They also produce a fine fabric well suited for use in household textiles.

Two other plant fibers also used in Norway and processed in a fashion similar to flax were hemp, suitable for coarse uses such as sacking, rope, and fishing line; and nettles, which produced a soft grayish yarn sometimes used in place of linen.

each part of the mammoth cloth-making process was completed at the appointed time in the yearly calendar. To oversee all these tasks in addition to the preparation of daily meals and the responsibilities of childcare was no small accomplishment. Is it any wonder that the housewife was often the first one up in the morning and the last one to bed at night?

Textile Production during the Light Days of Summer

On a sunny spring day soon after the animals were let out of the barn, the housewife washed the sheep to remove as much dirt and straw from the wool as possible (fig. 1.7). Once the wool was dry it was the housewife's job to shear the sheep of their heavy winter coats. At one time this was accomplished by simply plucking out tufts of the shedding wool (a characteristic of the older breed of Norwegian sheep), but evidence of sheared wool from the Oseberg Viking–ship find indicates that wool shears may have been in use as early as the ninth century (figs. 1.8–1.9). Since farm work required all of the women's time during the summer, the newly shorn wool was packed away in large baskets and stored in the loft for later use (fig. 1.10).

In districts where arable land was plentiful, spring was also the time for the housewife to plant her flax crop. Seeds saved from the previous year's harvest were often sown close to the house in a small fenced field called the *linåker*, or flax field. A densely sown crop produced the best fibers, as plants developed stems that were straight and tall. Early in the summer the young plants were carefully weeded, with extra precautions taken to avoid trampling the stems.

In late spring and early summer, a variety of leaves, bark, and mosses was gathered to replenish the housewife's supply of dye stuffs. It was important to collect dye plants at the right time of year, usually early in the summer before flowering, so that the coloring properties would be at their strongest. Children were often sent to collect baskets of birch leaves, heathers, lichen, and club moss to be dried for later use in the dye pot.

Working outdoors with the crops and the animals required most of the family's efforts during the summer months. Whenever the women of the farm had a few minutes to spare, however, whether walking to and from the fields or while minding the cheese-making at the mountain seters, they had their balls of yarn and knitting needles close at hand so not a minute would be wasted (fig. 1.11).

Late in summer the flax plants were pulled up by their roots and dried. They were then drawn through a coarse comb known as a ripple to remove the seed pods (fig. 1.12). On some farms further processing was put off until the following spring, but usually flax preparation continued into the fall.

Textile Production during the Dark Days of Winter

Several steps and a lot of hard work were required to turn flax plants into fine fibers suitable for spinning. First the plants were set out in the dew of

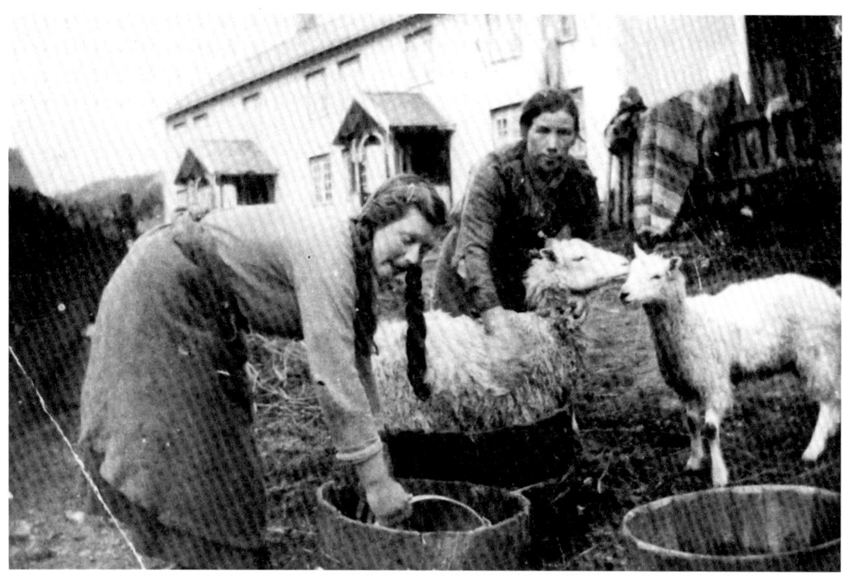

1.7 Two women from Kvam, Oppland, wash sheep before they are to be sheared. *Kvam Historical Association.*

1.8 Shearing sheep in Åfjord, Sør-Trøndelag, 1910. *Fosen Picture Archive.*

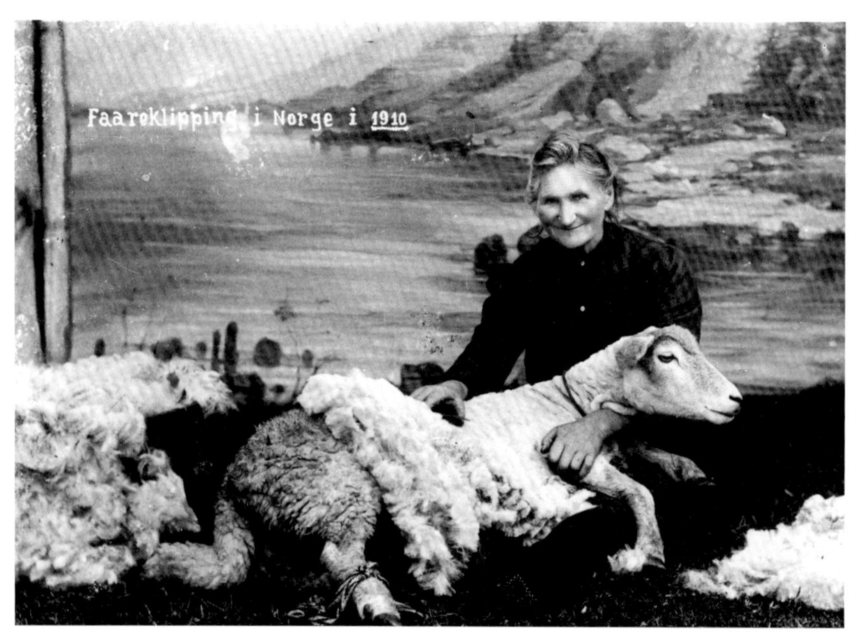

1.6 The flax plant, an annual with slender upright growth and pale blue flowers, contains fibers that are spun into linen. *La Botanique mise a la portée de tout le monde,* 1774, in *Huxley 1984.*

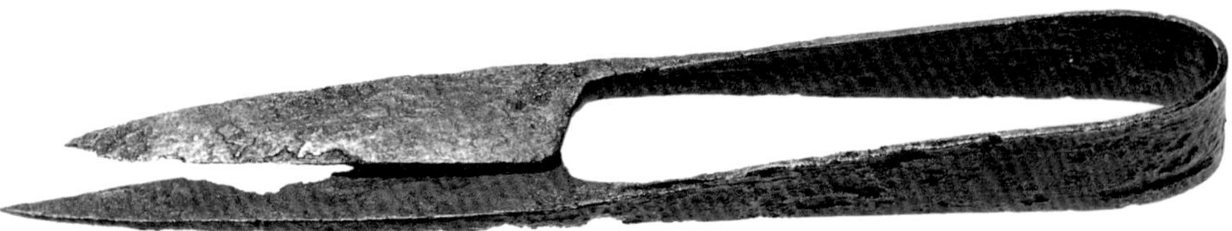

1.9 An early pair of sheep shears. The design of sheep shears has changed little over the years. *University of Trondheim, Museum of Natural History and Archeology.*

1.10 A carved basket of medieval design
used for storing wool. Probably sixteenth
century. Seljord, Telemark. *Norwegian
Folk Museum.*

1.11 Walking to and from the mountain
seter was not a time for idle hands. *Seter
Girl, by Hans Dahl. Private collection.
Photo courtesy of the Heiberg Collection.*

1.12 Bundles of dried flax plants are drawn
through a ripple to remove the seed pods.
Vestmarka, Hedmark. *Norwegian Folk
Museum.*

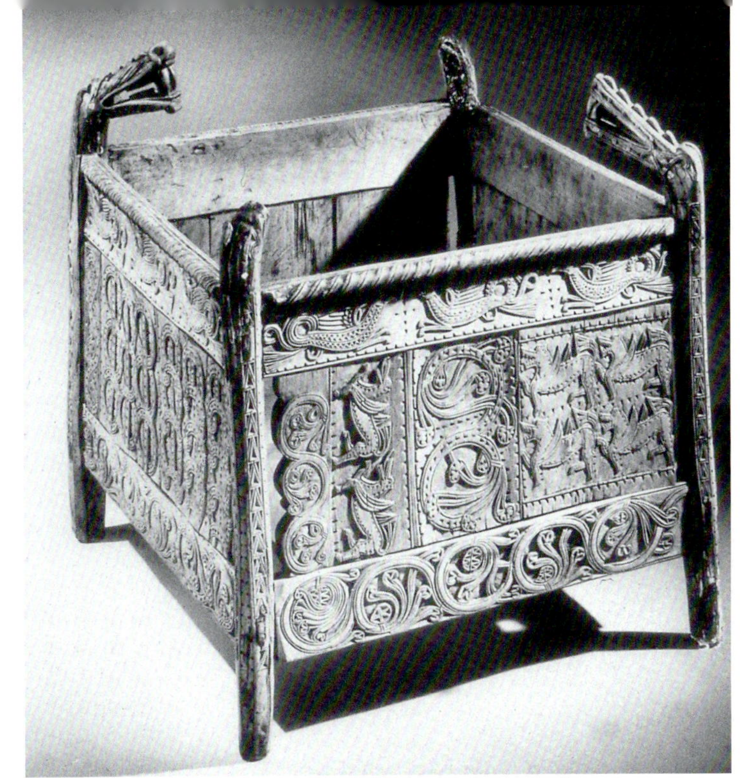

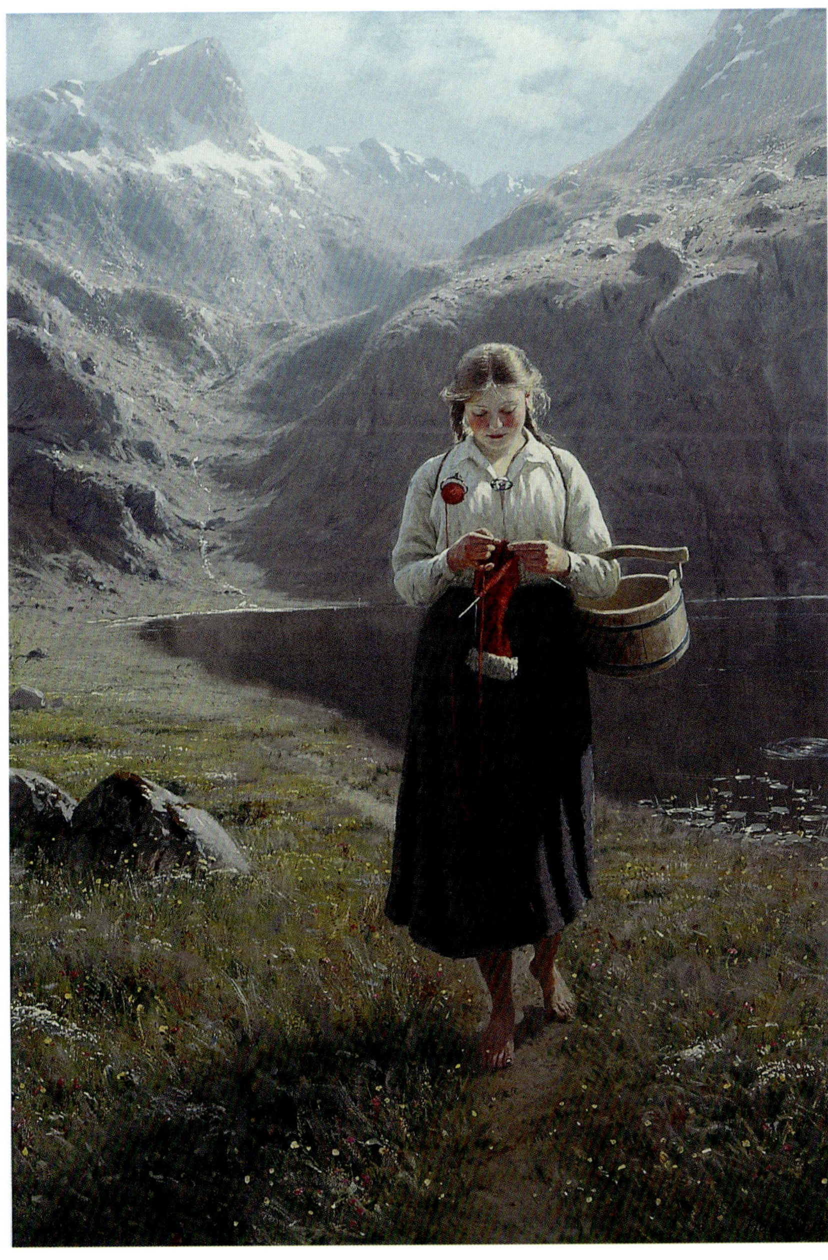

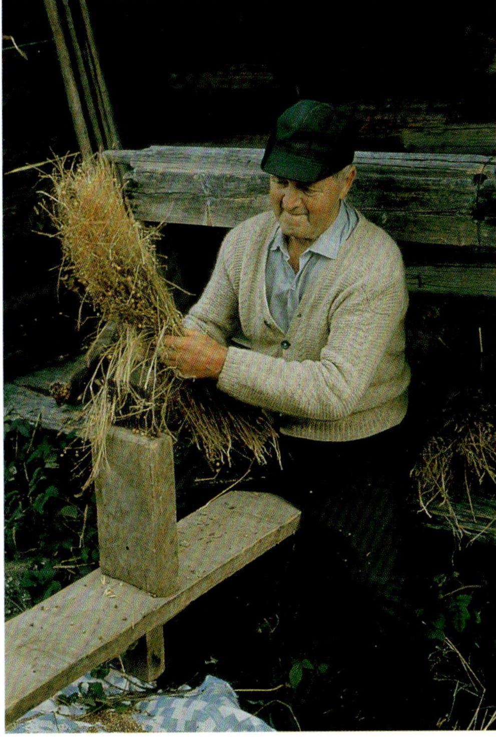

a meadow or in a stream for several weeks. This process, known as retting, allowed the outermost layer of the flax plant to rot off while loosening the remaining fibers. Bundles of flax were then hung up to dry in preparation for the next step.

In the process known as breaking, the flax bundles were beaten using a flax brake (or on some farms a wooden club) to break up the woodiness in the stems. Bundles placed in the brake were beaten along their entire length as the bundle was pulled forward a bit after each stroke (fig. 1.13). In the next step, called scutching, the fibers were loosened from one another as remaining bits of plant material were scraped away. In some districts this was accomplished by placing the fibers atop a special stand with a sharp edge on top and hacking at them with a wooden "knife." In other districts, the flax fibers were freed of extraneous material as they were drawn through the jaws of two sticks that were hinged together (figs. 1.14–1.15). Frequently scutching became a community party as women from surrounding farms gathered early in the morning with all their children, their bundles of flax, and their scutching equipment and worked late into the night, exchanging gossip and news of everything that had happened on their farms over the summer (fig. 1.16).

Hackling was the last step in the lengthy process of linen preparation. Groups of fibers were drawn over a board fixed with large iron spikes, which combed the flax and drew out those fibers that were short or of poor quality (figs. 1.17–1.18). The shorter tow fibers, used for coarse materials like work clothes and sacks, and the fine flax fibers were now ready to be spun.

1.13 A woman from Meldal, Sør-Trøndelag, uses a flax brake to break up the woodiness in a bundle of flax stems. Leaning against the wall next to the flax brake are, *from far left*, a ripple, a hackle, and a hinged instrument for scutching the flax. Dedekam, 1914. *Norwegian Folk Museum.*

1.14 Flax is scutched using a stand and a wooden knife in Vestmarka, Hedmark. *Norwegian Folk Museum.*

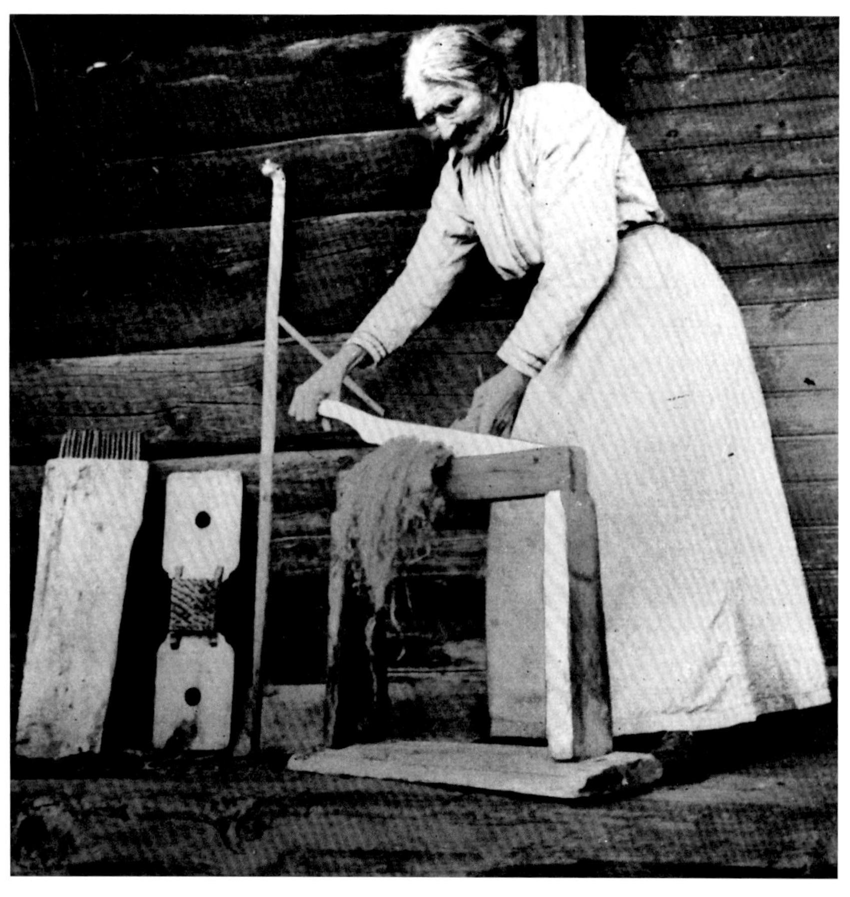

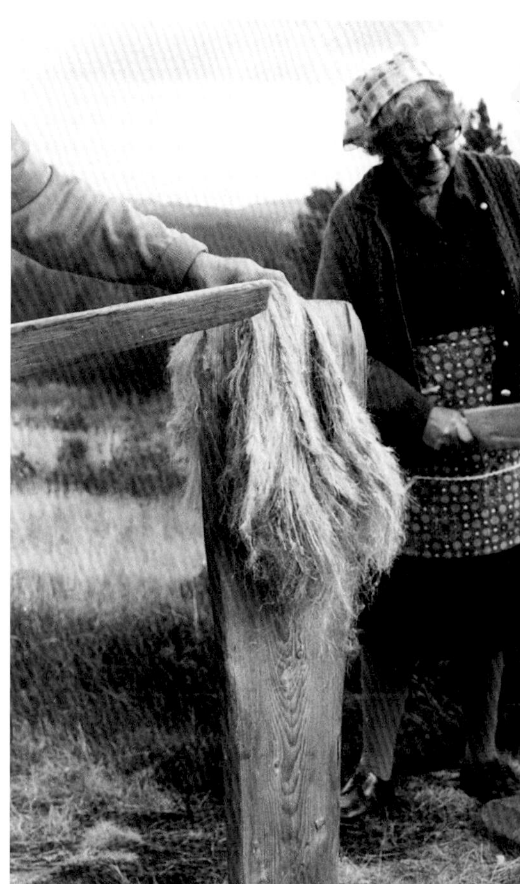

1.15 Woman scutching flax in Sør-Trøndelag.
An alternate method for scutching flax,
using a wooden hinged device known variously as a *garm* or a *klammer*, was common
in Trøndelag. Dedekam, 1914. *Norwegian
Folk Museum.*

1.16 Women often gathered in a group to
scutch their flax. Piles of processed flax lie
in the foreground. *County Conservator,
Nord-Trøndelag.*

1.17 Two hackles from the Steinkjer
Museum, Nord-Trøndelag.

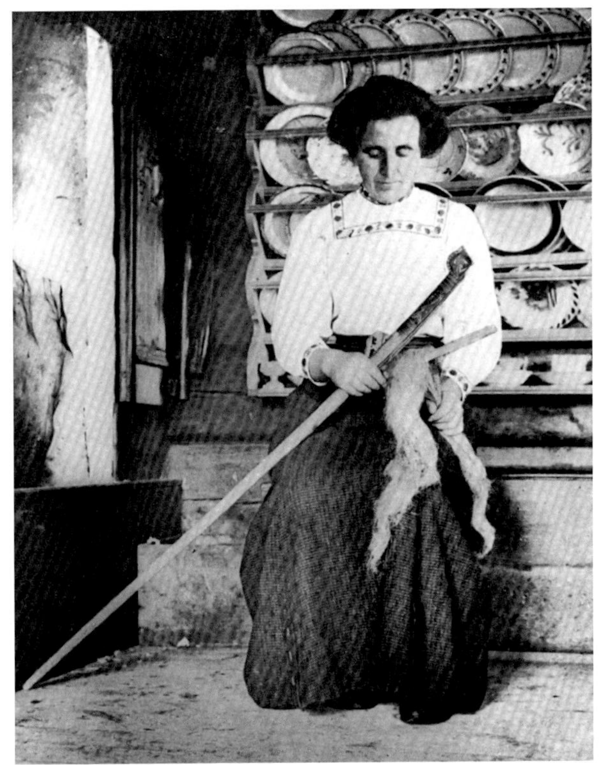

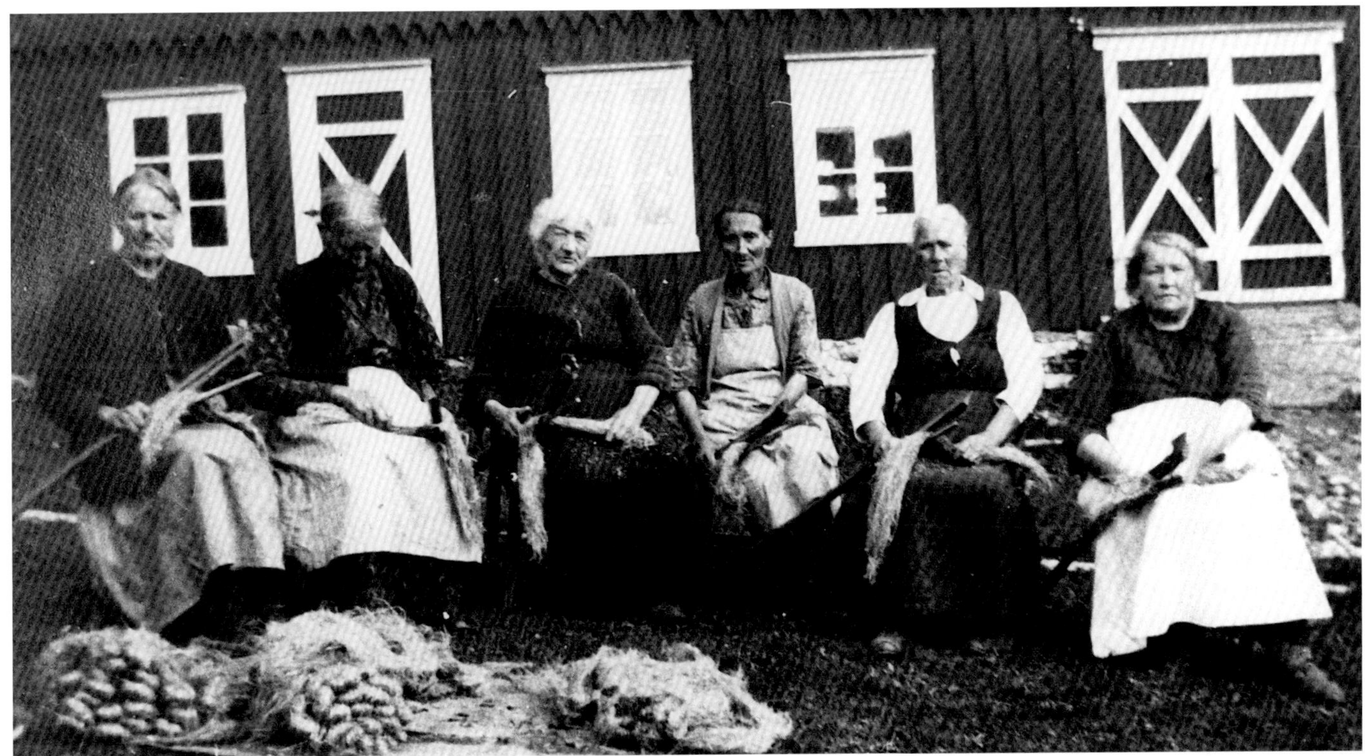

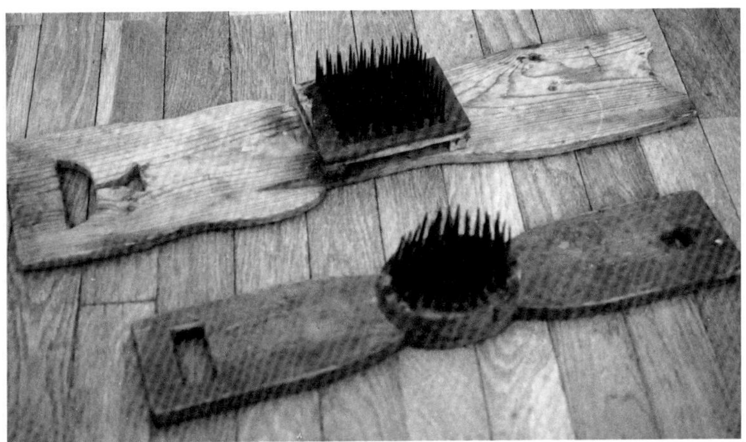

One of the Norwegian housewife's last jobs in the fall was to wash and shear the sheep before they were confined to the barn for the long winter. The freshly sheared raw wool was combined with the baskets of spring wool from the storage loft, and both were carefully sorted according to quality, a job that required skill and experience. The underlayer of wool was pulled from the longer guard hairs, and those areas of the fleece with fibers that were coarse or matted were separated from those that were of finer quality. Fleeces sheared in the fall after a full summer of grazing were generally considered to be of better quality than those sheared in the spring, with the result that fall wool was often selected for the more stressful process of weaving, while spring wool was set aside for knitting. The extra length and strength of the guard hairs made them well suited for spinning tightly twisted warp thread, and the lustrous sheen they displayed upon dyeing was particularly prized for the weft yarns of decorative weavings. The softer, shorter underwool was reserved for knitted clothing and the weft of other woven articles.

Before the wool could be spun into yarn, the fibers needed to be separated from one another and transformed into an even, fluffy mass. Originally this was accomplished with the use of two long-toothed combs (figs. 1.19–1.20). These were particularly effective for combing the long guard hairs parallel once the underwool was removed. Wool combs disappeared from household use in Norway sometime before the eighteenth century, to be replaced by wool cards, an innovation probably introduced during the late Middle Ages. These small rectangles of wood set with short spikes were used in pairs, the wool fibers being drawn apart as one card was pulled against the other. Cards with coarsely set spikes, one mounted on a bench and the other held in the hand, made the first processing of tangled wool easier. Hand cards with finer, more closely set spikes were then used as the wool was carded a second and sometimes a third time, allowing any remaining irregularities in the wool quality to be evened out in a thorough blending of the fibers (figs. 1.21–1.22).

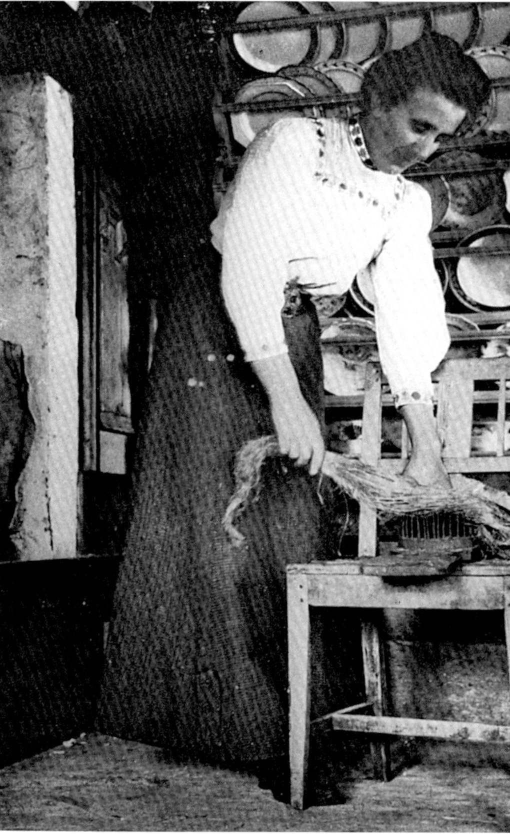

1.18 Flax fibers received a final combing and the short tow fibers were removed with the use of a hackle. Nord-Trøndelag. Dedekam, 1914. *Norwegian Folk Museum.*

1.19 Wool combs discovered in a Viking Age grave in Hordaland. Such combs were used to arrange the long guard hairs of the primitive two-layered fleeces into parallel order for spinning. *Årbok for foreningen til norske fortidsminnesmerkers bevaring, 1892, in Hoffmann 1991.*

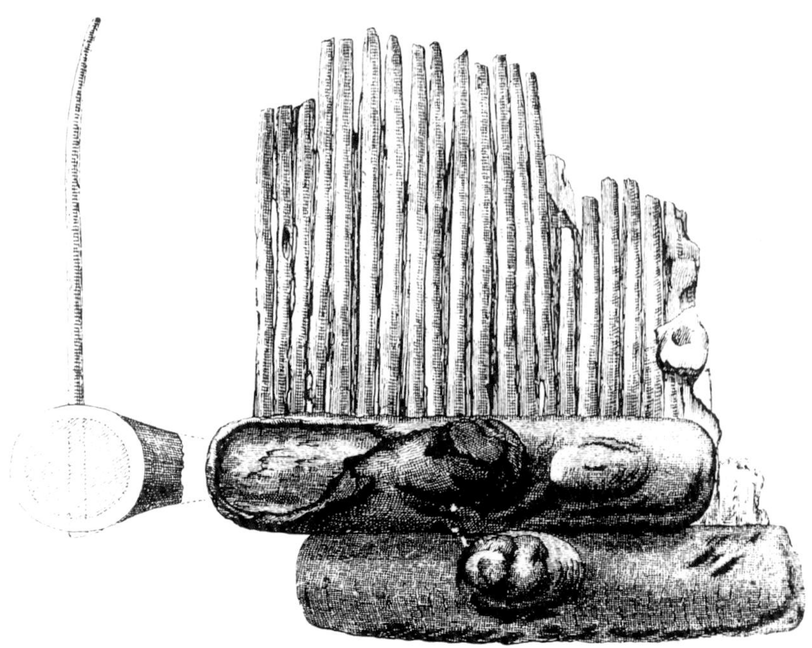

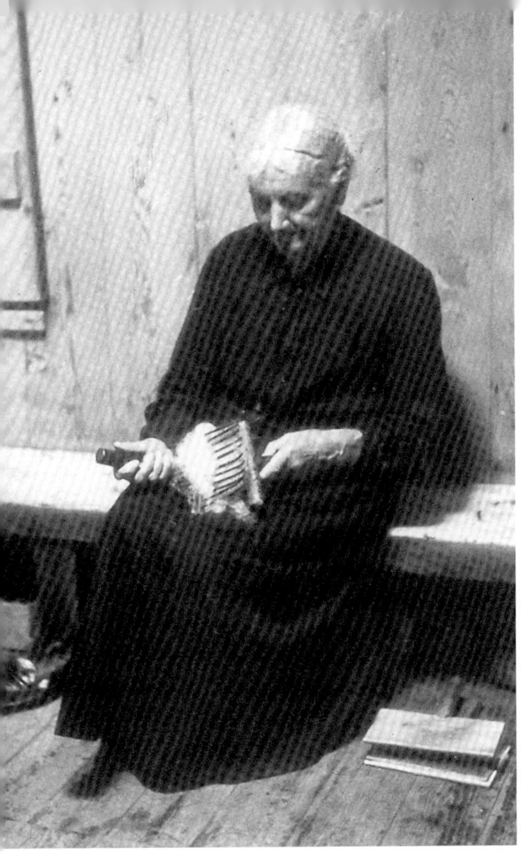

1.20 A woman using wool combs in the Færoes, ca. 1947. Wool combs disappeared from household use in Norway prior to the eighteenth century. *Nationalmuseet, Nyere Tid, Brede, Denmark.*

1.21 Separating wool fibers in preparation for spinning was accomplished with wool cards. One card was often attached to a bench to make the initial coarse carding easier. A bench card from Sør-Trøndelag. *Norwegian Folk Museum.*

1.22 Carding wool with hand-held cards in Valle, Setesdal. *Norwegian Folk Museum.*

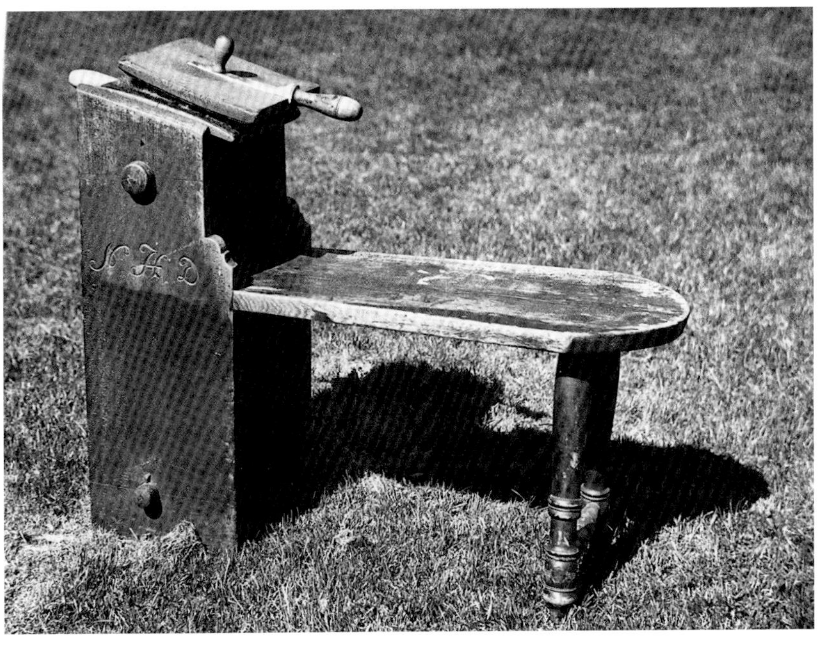

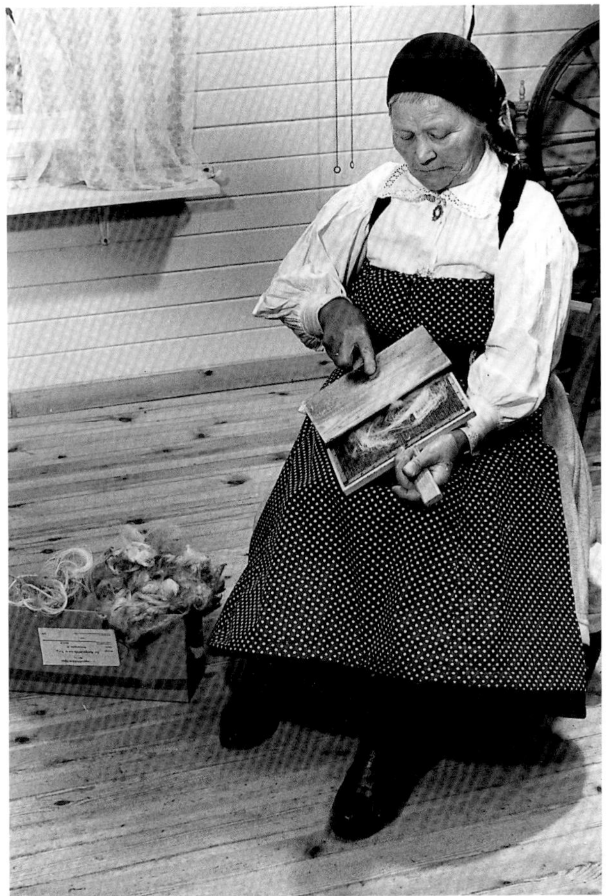

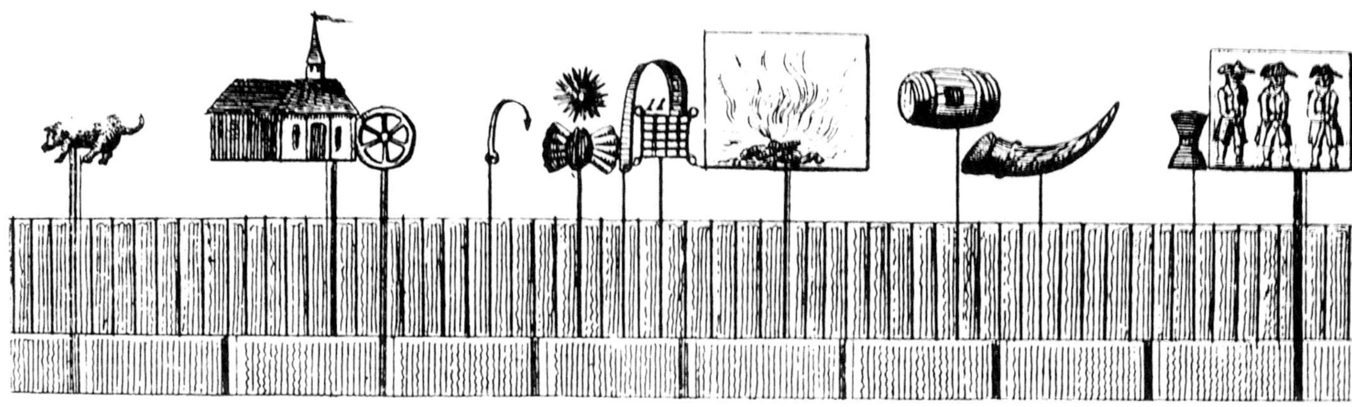

Although the creation of clothing was a year-long process and each season had its appointed tasks, wintertime truly was dominated by the need to produce cloth. November 25 was marked by a wheel on many calendar sticks in honor of Saint Catherine and as a reminder that spinning should now begin (1.23). The spinning wheels that were brought out and set into motion at this time were seldom idle until after Christmas. From early morning, when most housewives spun at least one bobbin-full of yarn before attending to their barnyard chores, until late evening when the family gathered around the fireside, the gentle whirring of the wheels could be heard as the womenfolk worked to transform flax and wool fibers into yarn. Every woman in the household had a spinning wheel, often the one she had received as a child. Young girls began their "education" as early as six years of age, gradually learning to spin fine, even strands and ply two strands into a sturdy yarn (fig. 1.24).

1.23 A wheel *(third figure from left)* marks Saint Catherine's Day, November 25, on this calendar stick from Seljord, Telemark. Wille, 1786. *Norwegian Folk Museum.*

1.24 A mother and daughter card and spin in Setesdal. *Photo: A. B. Wilse. Norwegian Folk Museum.*

1.25 Carded wool fibers are teased out of soft rolls as they are spun. Nord-Troms. *Norwegian Folk Museum.*

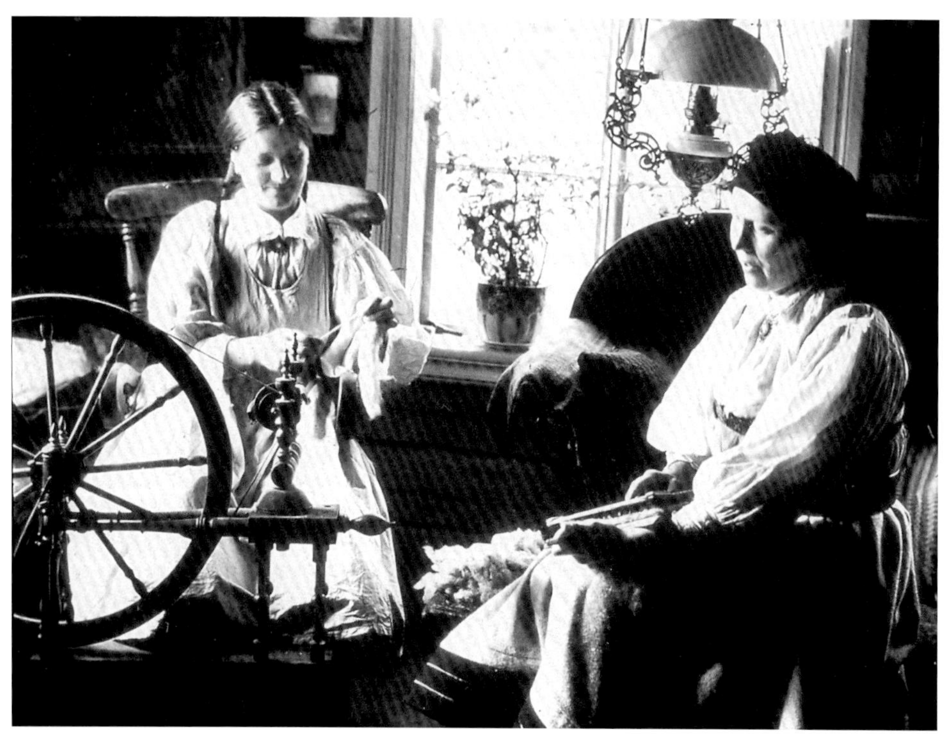

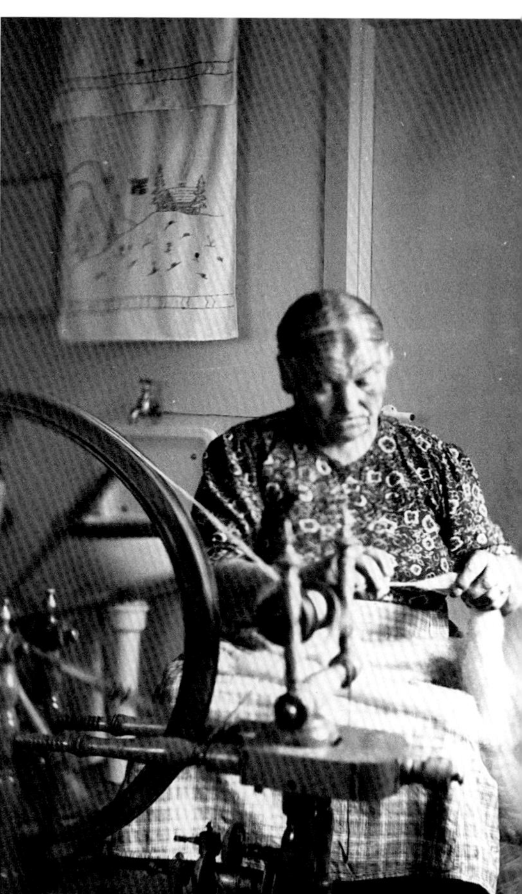

14

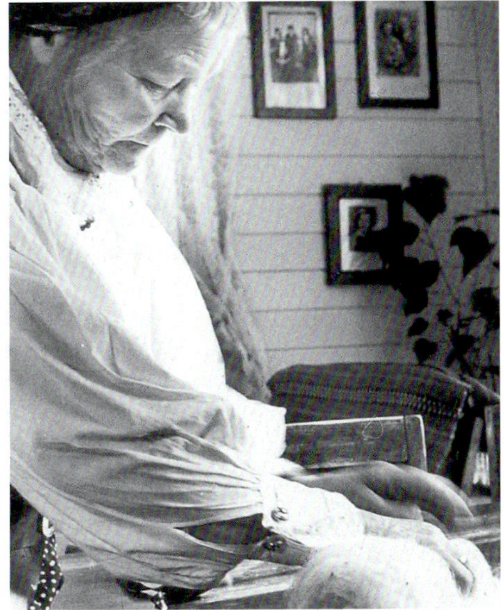

1.26 Long-fibered guard hair combed parallel is rolled onto a distaff for spinning. Valle, Setesdal. *Norwegian Folk Museum.*

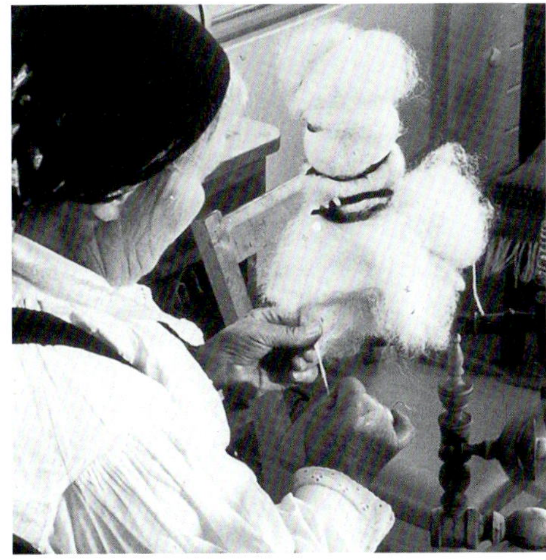

1.27 *(Above)* A criss-crossing band holds combed guard hair fibers to the distaff from which they are drawn for spinning. Valle, Setesdal. *Norwegian Folk Museum.*

1. 28 Flax fibers are swept onto a distaff for spinning. Hedmark. *Norwegian Folk Museum.*

1.29 *(Far right)* Flax fibers are gradually drawn off the distaff to be spun into linen. Hedmark. *Norwegian Folk Museum.*

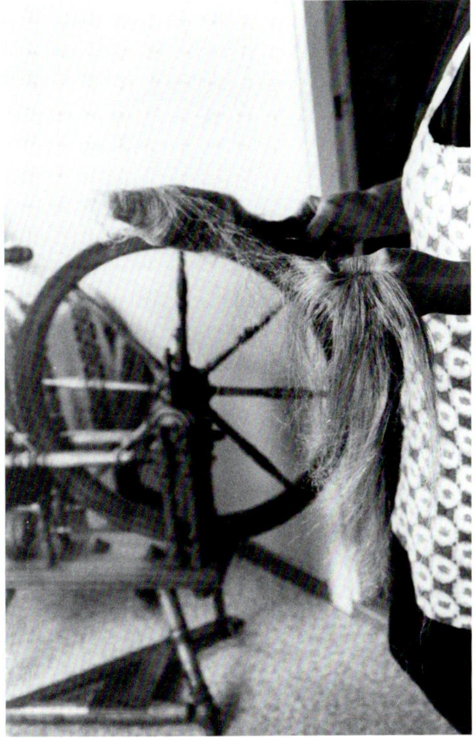

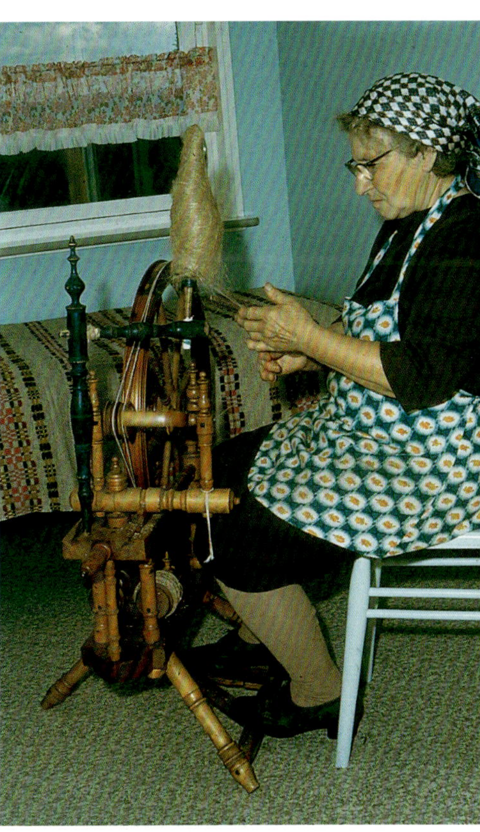

The short inner layer of wool was carded into soft, smooth rolls that were held by the spinner while she teased out the fibers to be spun. The guard hairs were spun from groups of fibers, combed parallel with wool cards, and then wound onto the distaff and tied loosely with a crisscrossing band (figs. 1.25–1.27). Combed flax fibers were also wound onto a distaff in preparation for spinning, although in some cases they were draped over a distaff with a serrated top (figs. 1.28–1.30). Winding the finished yarn off the bobbin of a spinning wheel was an easy but repetitive task that was frequently assigned to children. For some uses, such as knitting and warping, balls of yarn were most appropriate, and a ball winder in the form of a small carved stick was used. Yarn could also be wound into skeins on a reel that in earlier times was hand held, but was largely replaced by the eighteenth century with a rotary version (figs. 1.31–1.34). Skeins provided a simple method for calculating amounts of yarn and, of equal importance, allowed the yarn to freely absorb color in the dyebath. A swift could then be used to draw yarn smoothly from the skein for further use. (fig. 1.35).

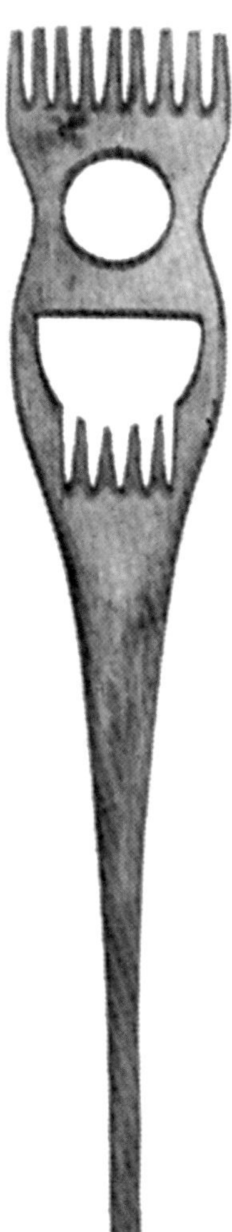

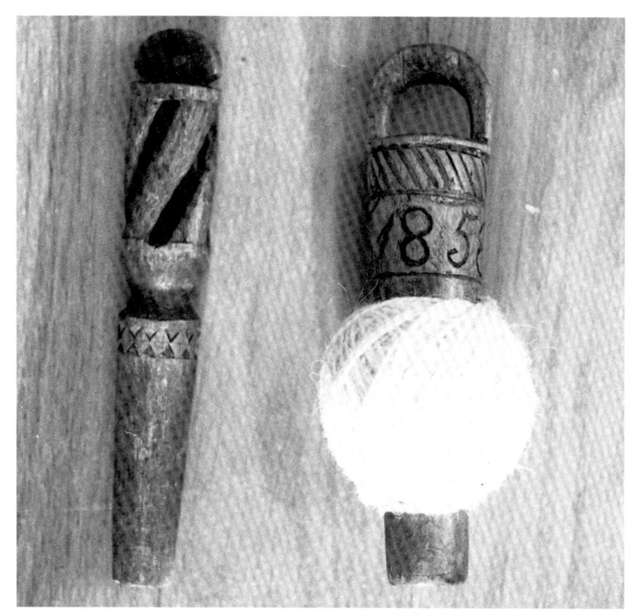

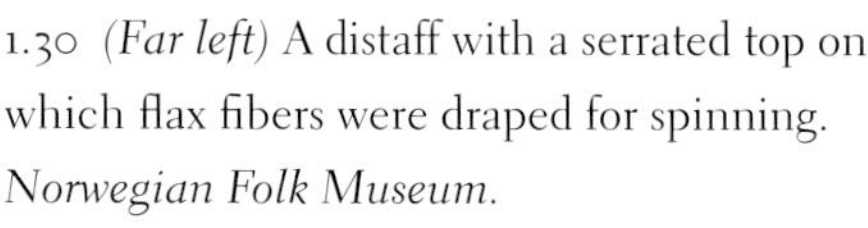

1.30 *(Far left)* A distaff with a serrated top on which flax fibers were draped for spinning. *Norwegian Folk Museum.*

1.31 Small carved sticks, sometimes hollowed out with wooden beads inside, were used as ball winders. When not in use they frequently served as baby rattles. *Steinkjer Museum.*

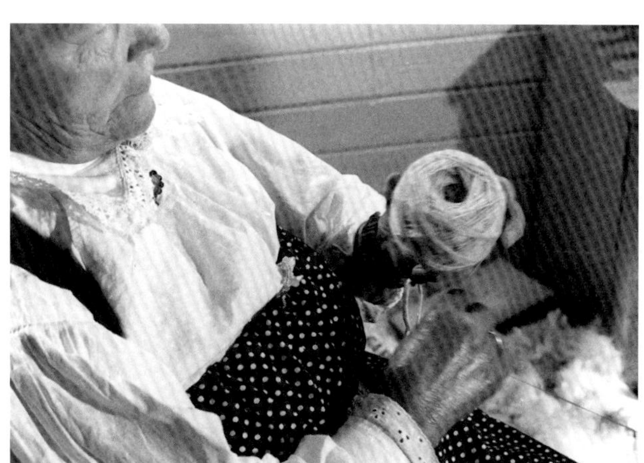

1.32 Yarn is wound from the spinning wheel onto a ball winder. Valle, Setesdal. *Norwegian Folk Museum.*

1.33 *(Below left)* Two hand-held skein-winding reels from the ninth-century Oseberg Viking ship. *University Museum of National Antiquities, Oslo.*

1.34 *(Below right)* Yarn is wound from the bobbin of a spinning wheel onto a rotary reel. Hedmark. *Norwegian Folk Museum.*

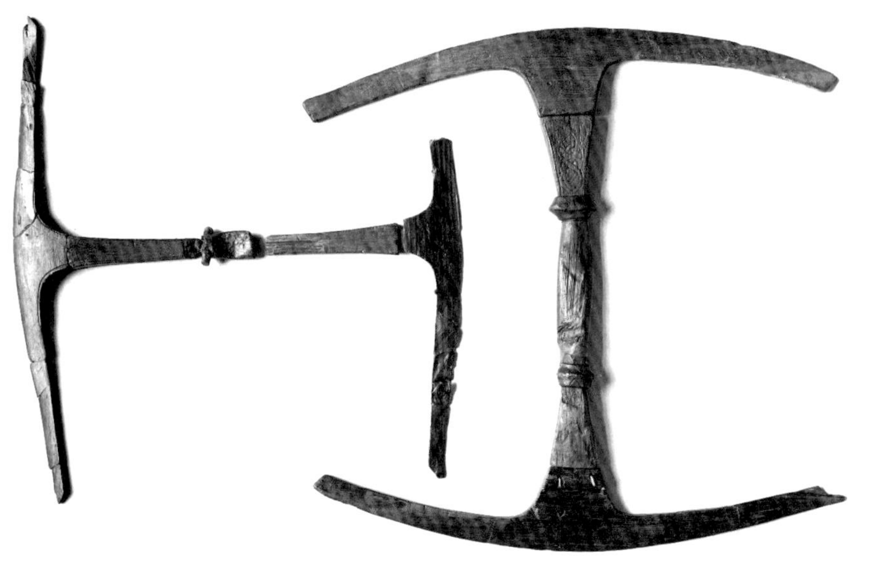

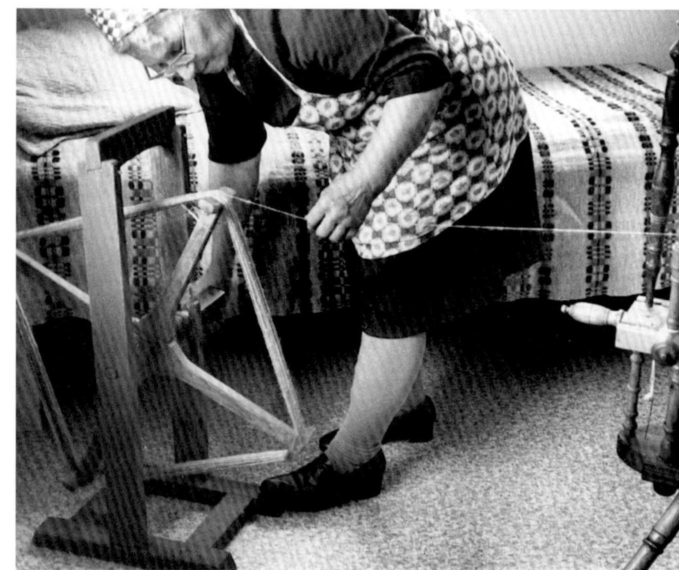

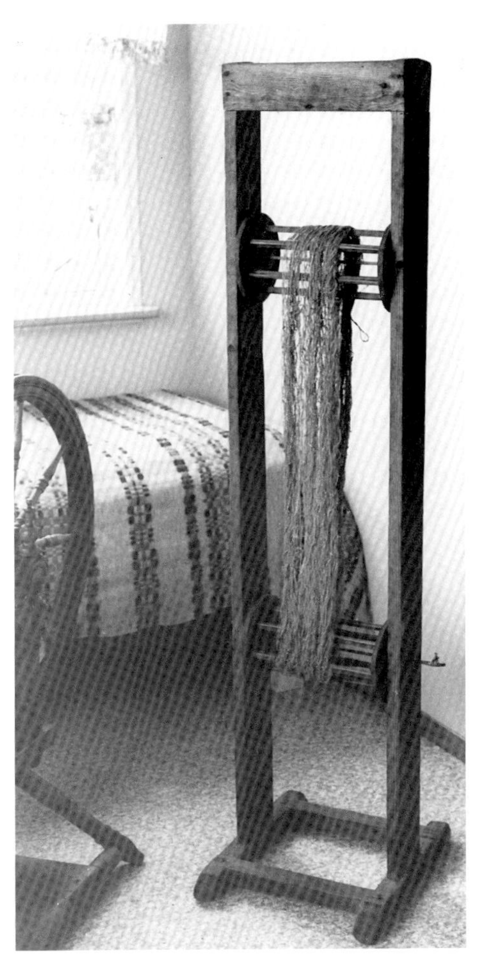

Producing a technically correct piece of weaving was a skill that most capable housewives were able to achieve, but imbuing that weaving with pleasing colors was not a simple task. Recipes for vegetable dyes were handed down from mother to daughter, but there were many variables in the process of producing a desired color. The time of year that the dye plants were collected greatly influenced their coloring properties; the chemical content of the water could vary with the seasons, which caused the dye pot to react with slight differences; and the blending of two separate elements to achieve one color was often difficult to repeat. Obtaining yarn of the desired color in the proper amounts for the intended use was a challenging job that required knowledge, experience, and good judgement. Most dyeing was done in the *eldhus*, a separate farm building with an open hearth used for baking, brewing, and washing (fig. 1.36). Here the housewife soaked skeins of yarn in dye vats containing concoctions of leaves, bark, or moss. The skeins of brightly colored yarn were then hung to dry in preparation for the next step in the cloth-making process.

1.35 An adjustable barrel swift allows yarn to be drawn from skeins of different size. Hedmark. *Norwegian Folk Museum.*

1.36 Dyeing, baking, brewing, and washing were done over the hearth in a separate farm building known as the *eldhus. Open-Hearth Room at Voss, by Adolph Tidemand. National Gallery.*

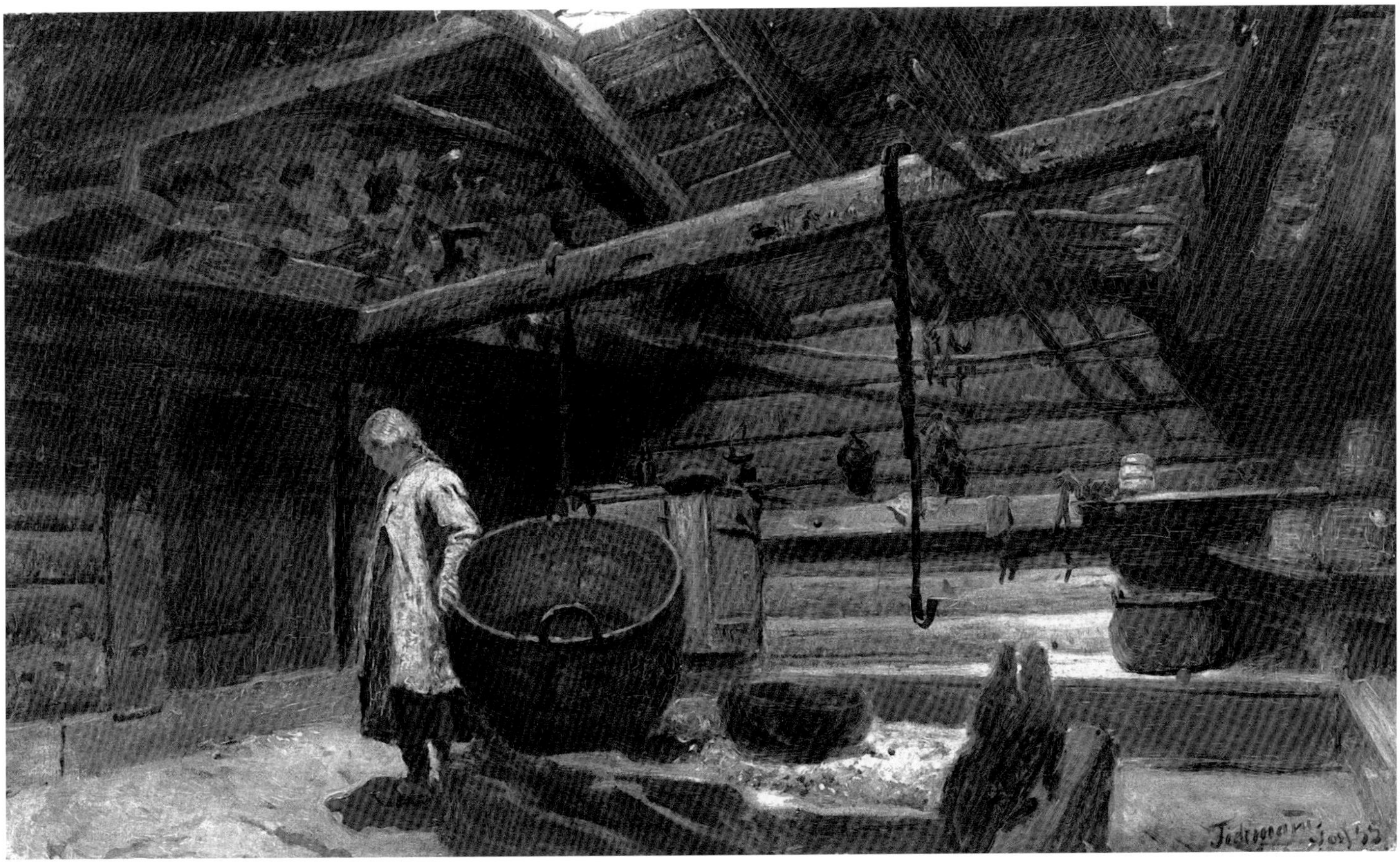

A variety of plants found in Norway, in addition to some imported dyestuffs, provided a good range of options to the dyer (fig. 1.37). Unfortunately, many beautiful dyes that were commonly used were not lightfast, with the result that colors often faded beyond recognition over the years. Effective natural dyes were possible, however, to those experienced or lucky enough to collect the right dye plants and apply them correctly. Their expertise is evident in the many older textiles that still retain their original lively color schemes.

Of most importance to the dyer were the primary colors (yellow, blue, and red), since other colors could be derived from blending these three. Sources for yellow were abundant in Norway, but many of these, particularly the commonly used birch leaves (*Betula spp.*) and heather (*Calluna vulgaris*) were subject to fading. Plants that offered a more stable yellow were club moss (*Lycopodium complanatum*) and several species of willow (*Salix phylicifolia* and *S. pentandra*). Paler shades of yellow were obtained from bearberry (*Arctostaphylos uva-ursi*) and blueberry (*Caccinium myrtillus*), and shades of gold from a lichen known as Iceland moss (*Cetraria islandica*).

Reds ranging from clear red to shades of golden red were derived from the roots of several species of bedstraw, the most important of these being northern bedstraw (*Galium boreale*). Madder root (*Rubia tinctorum*), a superior source of red dye grown in more temperate regions and used throughout Europe and the Middle East, was imported into Norway by the early nineteenth century. A red or red-violet dye was extracted from a lichen (*Ochrolechia tartarea*) known variously as k*vitlav* (white lichen), *kvitkork* (white cork), or simply *korkje* (pronounced kor-sheh). Korkje was in use in Norway before the tenth century.

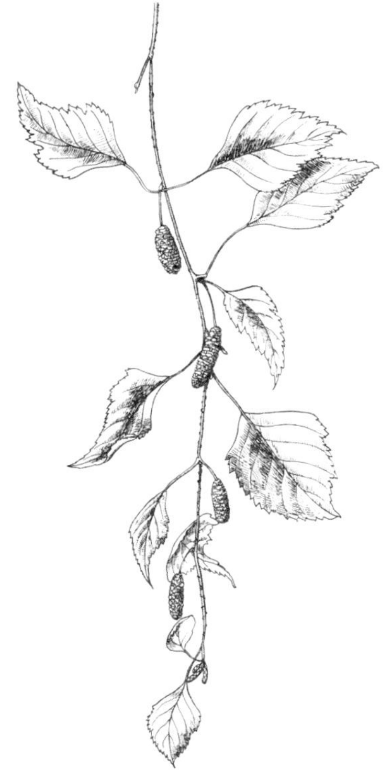

1.37 Natural dye plants

Birch leaves, *bjerkeløv (Betula verrucossa)*. *Nordhaugen 1970.*

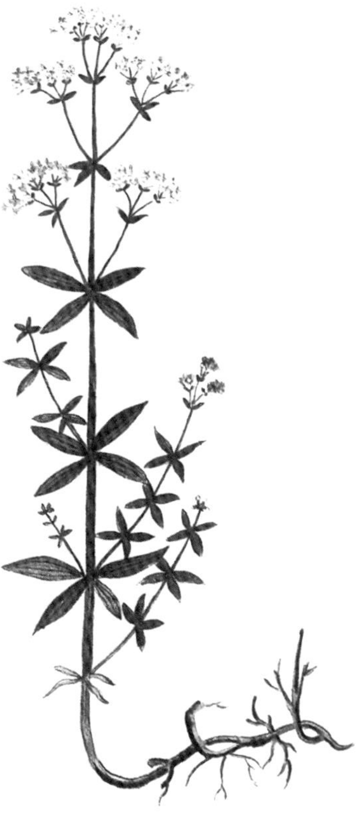

Northern bedstraw, *kvitmaure (Galium boreale). I. A. Heltzen 1834. Original illustration in University of Bergen Library, Ms. 315.*

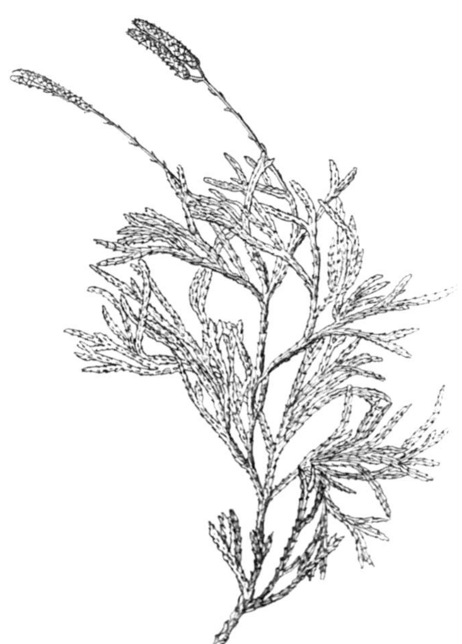

Club moss, *jamne (Lycopodium complanatum). Nordhaugen 1970.*

It was also collected and processed into round dry cakes that were exported to other parts of Europe during the Middle Ages. Like many other dyestuffs, korkje was subject to fading unless carefully prepared, a particular problem since the more complex process of lichen dyeing was often not fully understood.

A source of blue dye found in Norway as early as Viking times was woad *(Isatis tinctoria)*. Extracting a dye from woad involved several steps, and although it was cultivated to some extent in Norway, it was also imported from areas of Europe that specialized in its processing. The tropical indigo plant *(Indigofera tinctoria)*, a much stronger source of the same blue dye, eventually replaced woad throughout Europe. Indigo was imported into Norway and widely used from about the eighteenth century on, but its use was often governed by extreme frugality as it had to be purchased. It was not unusual for a housewife to soak worn-out blue garments in a fermenting agent (usually a pot of urine) to draw out as much of the blue dye as possible before consigning the clothes to the ragbag.

As a secondary color, green could be obtained by blending blue and yellow. Some sources of green dye were also used, the most important of these reportedly blue scabious leaves *(Succisa pratensis)*. Most dyers in Norway today agree, however, that there are no native lightfast plant sources for green dye.

Shades of brown and black could, of course, be taken from the natural wool of black sheep, but good browns were available from several species of lichen (notably *Parmelia spp.* and *Xanthoparmelia spp.*). Varying shades of brown could also be obtained from the bark of alder *(Alnus spp.)*, birch *(Betula spp.)*, oak *(Qurecus spp.)*, and buckthorn *(Rhamnus frangula)*. When a black or grey dye was desired, a tannin-rich dyestuff such as alder or oak bark was mixed with iron, either from iron filings or from the iron of the dye kettle.

Most plant dyes required either a period of fermentation to extract the dye colorants (as with indigo and korkje) or the presence of a fixing agent known as a mordant. Iron or copper from the dye pot could provide the mordant for some dyestuffs, and mordanting chemicals such as alum were used in Norway by the late eighteenth century, but some natural fixing agents were available to the dyer from plants. Club moss, a natural source of alum, and tree bark, containing tannin, were often used in conjunction with other dye plants as mordanting agents.

By the late nineteenth century, synthetic dyes based on coal-tar products were introduced into Norway, and the use of natural dyes became less common. In place of the muted colors available from nature, people began to experiment with a wider range of strong, clear colors (often with less than harmonious results), and much of the knowledge of natural plant dyeing was lost.

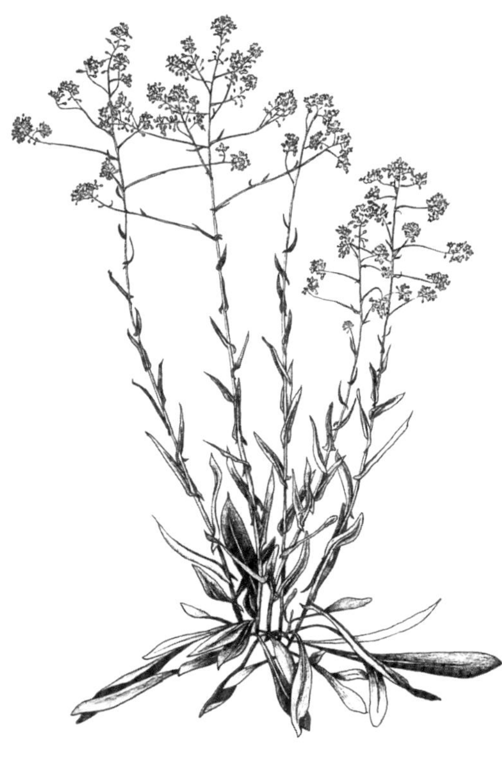

Woad, *vaid (Isatis tinctoria)*. *Nordhaugen, 1970.*

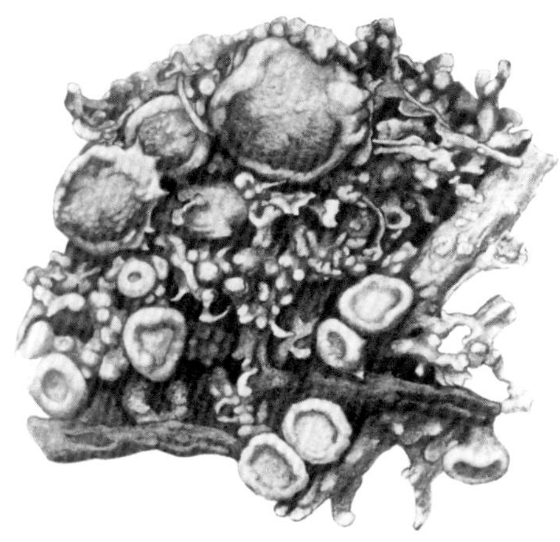

White lichen, *korkje (Ochrolechia tartarea)*. *Galløe, 1936.*

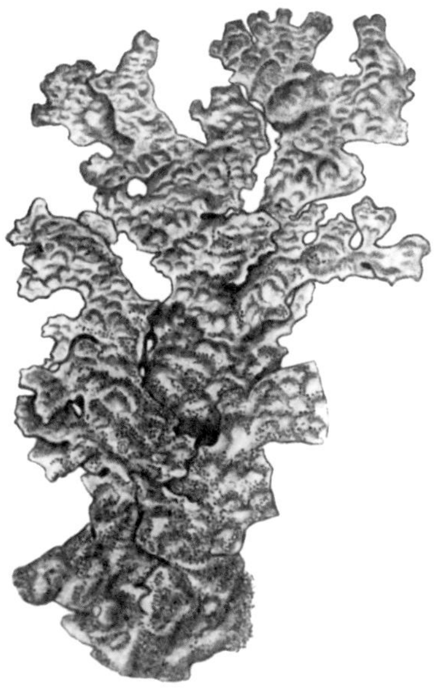

Lichen, *fargelav (Paramelia saxatilis)*. *Galløe, 1947.*

Several weeks after Christmas when most of the yarn that would be needed for the year had been spun, the loom was brought out of storage and assembled. The loom was a fairly large piece of equipment that could be taken apart and stored for most of the year, but when it was set up for use, it filled a large part of the main room of the house. On some farms, the loom was simply too big for the house and was set up in a separate storage building. In such cases, the women often waited until the days lengthened and the weather grew warmer before beginning their weaving.

Warping the loom was the first step in the weaving process. This involved stringing a number of threads of equal length on the loom, putting them under tension, and arranging a device for raising and lowering selected numbers of warp threads to form a shed, or opening, for inserting the weft. Methods for measuring out the yards of warp threads varied from home to home, but usually the housewife relied on pegs inserted into the loom, the walls, or the furniture. By the late nineteenth century, warping mills came into use for this purpose (figs. 1.38–1.39). After the required number of warp threads were measured out, they were wound onto the back beam of the loom, a job that often required the help of several women. Next, each thread was passed though its own heddle, a part of the harness system which allowed threads to be raised and lowered with the use of foot treadles. The warp was then threaded through slots in the reed, a comb-like device in the beater that both spaced the warp threads and packed the weft threads into place during weaving. Finally the warp threads were attached to a beam at the front of the loom (fig. 1.40).

1.38 A bench turned on its side with pegs inserted near the ends served as a frame for measuring the warp threads in this home. A warp-weighted loom, background, will receive the warp. Hordaland. *Norwegian Folk Museum.*

1.39 A warping mill provided an easy method for measuring lengthy warp threads. Hå, Rogaland. *Photo: Jon Vold. State Archive in Stavanger.*

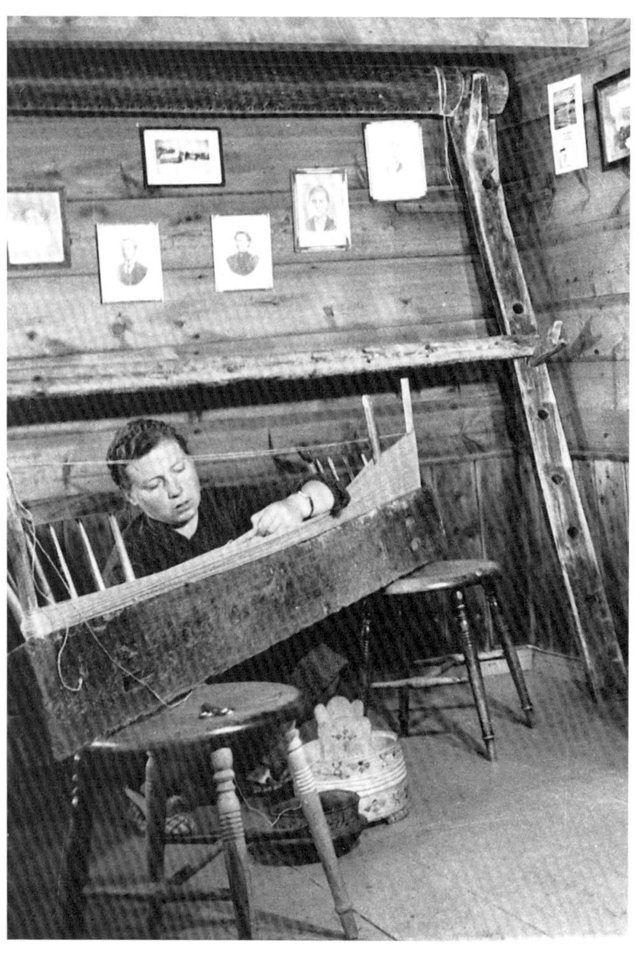

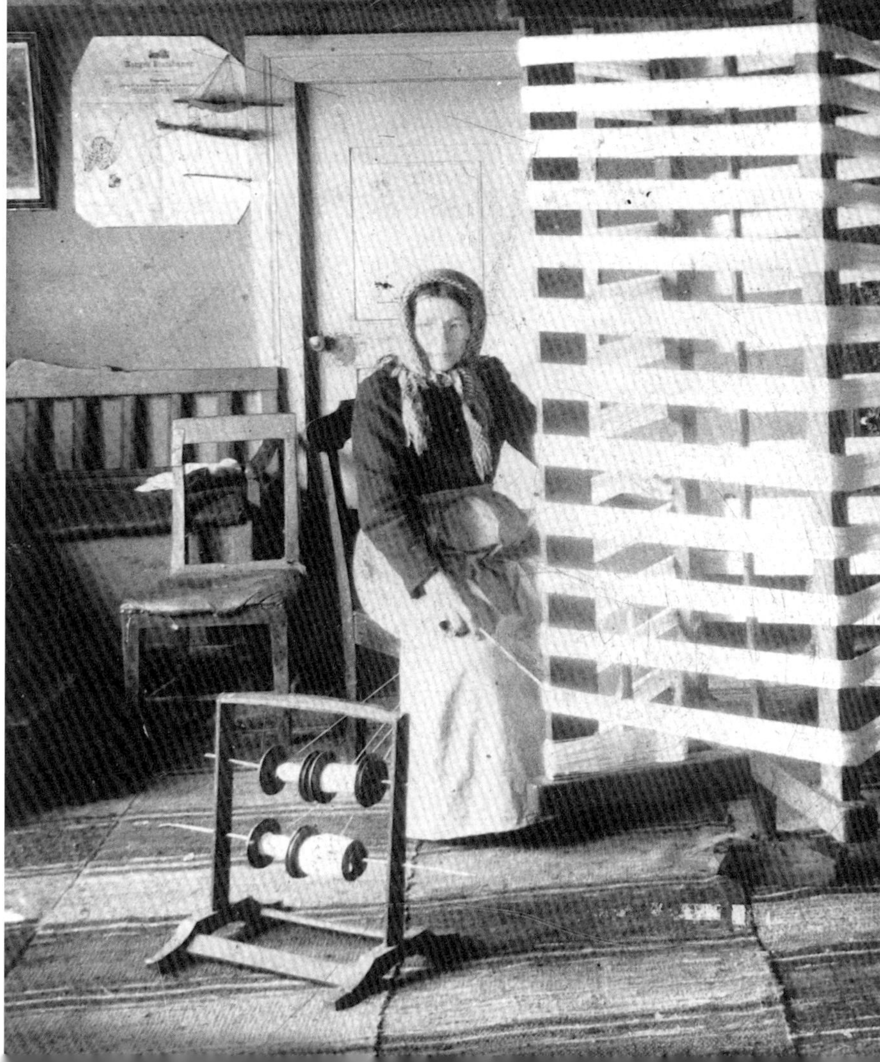

1.40 The parts of a floor loom:

(a) frame   (f) harnesses
(b) cloth beam   (g) treadles
(c) breast beam   (h) heddles
(d) warp beam   (i) reed
(e) beater   (k) pulley

Drawing: Ingrid Lowzow, University of Oslo, for Norwegian Folk Museum; in Hoffmann 1989.

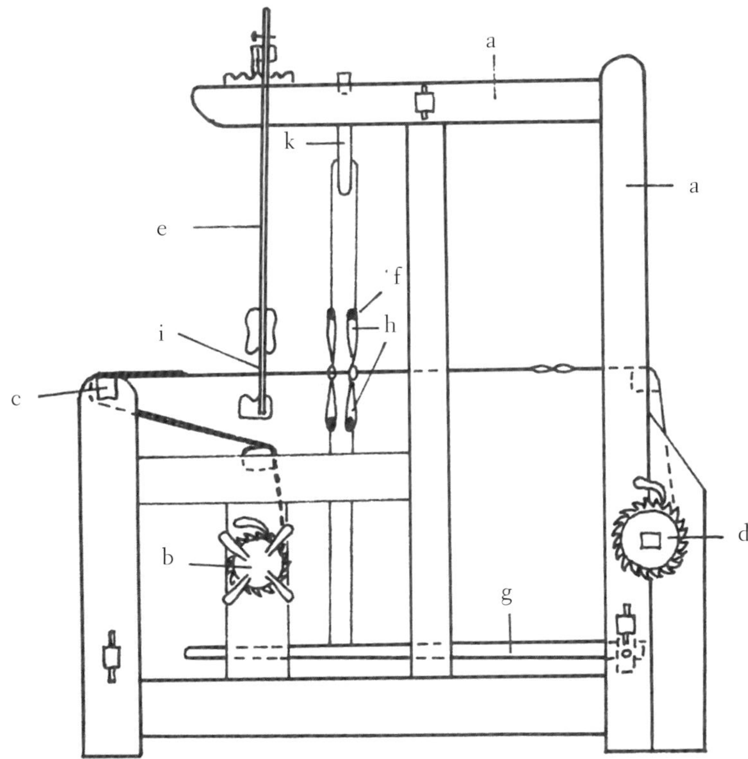

With warping complete, the loom was ready for weaving. Now the housewife and her daughters were working against time, for each day the sun rose higher in the sky, bringing with it the light days of summer when indoor work would be put aside. Yard by yard the newly woven fabric was wound onto the cloth beam of the loom as the treadles pulled the harnesses up and down, the shuttle flashed back and forth, and the swing of the beater set the weft in place. If the weaver grew tired, someone was always ready to pick up the rhythm, for the loom must not stand idle if the work was to be finished (fig. 1.41).

In planning her yearly weaving, the housewife needed to estimate how much of each type of cloth she would need in order to determine the kind and length of each warp. To minimize the number of times the loom was threaded, it was desirable to plan one warp, often thirty to forty yards in length, for each type of fabric. The following list is a Nordfjord housewife's estimate of what a year's weaving in the early 1900s should include:

1 warp of grey wadmal [a woolen cloth]—clothes for the men
1 warp of white wadmal—underclothes and cloth for dyeing
1 warp of plain weave—underclothes, dresses, children's clothes
1 warp of wool twill for bedding
1 warp for the grandparents living on the farm
1 warp for the hired help's clothing*
1 warp for a coverlet (if time allowed)[2]

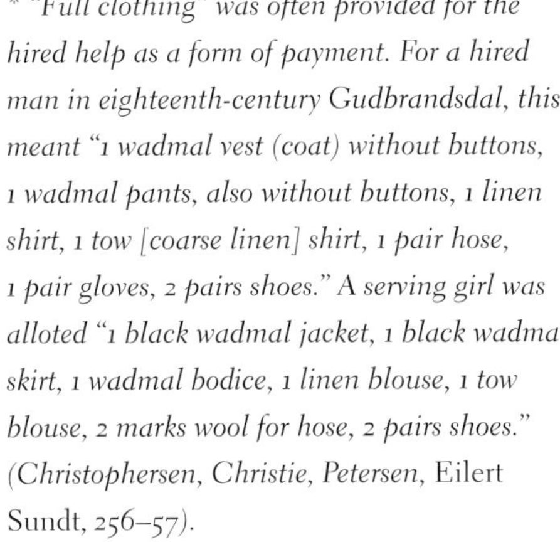

* *"Full clothing" was often provided for the hired help as a form of payment. For a hired man in eighteenth-century Gudbrandsdal, this meant "1 wadmal vest (coat) without buttons, 1 wadmal pants, also without buttons, 1 linen shirt, 1 tow [coarse linen] shirt, 1 pair hose, 1 pair gloves, 2 pairs shoes." A serving girl was alloted "1 black wadmal jacket, 1 black wadmal skirt, 1 wadmal bodice, 1 linen blouse, 1 tow blouse, 2 marks wool for hose, 2 pairs shoes." (Christophersen, Christie, Petersen, Eilert Sundt, 256–57).*

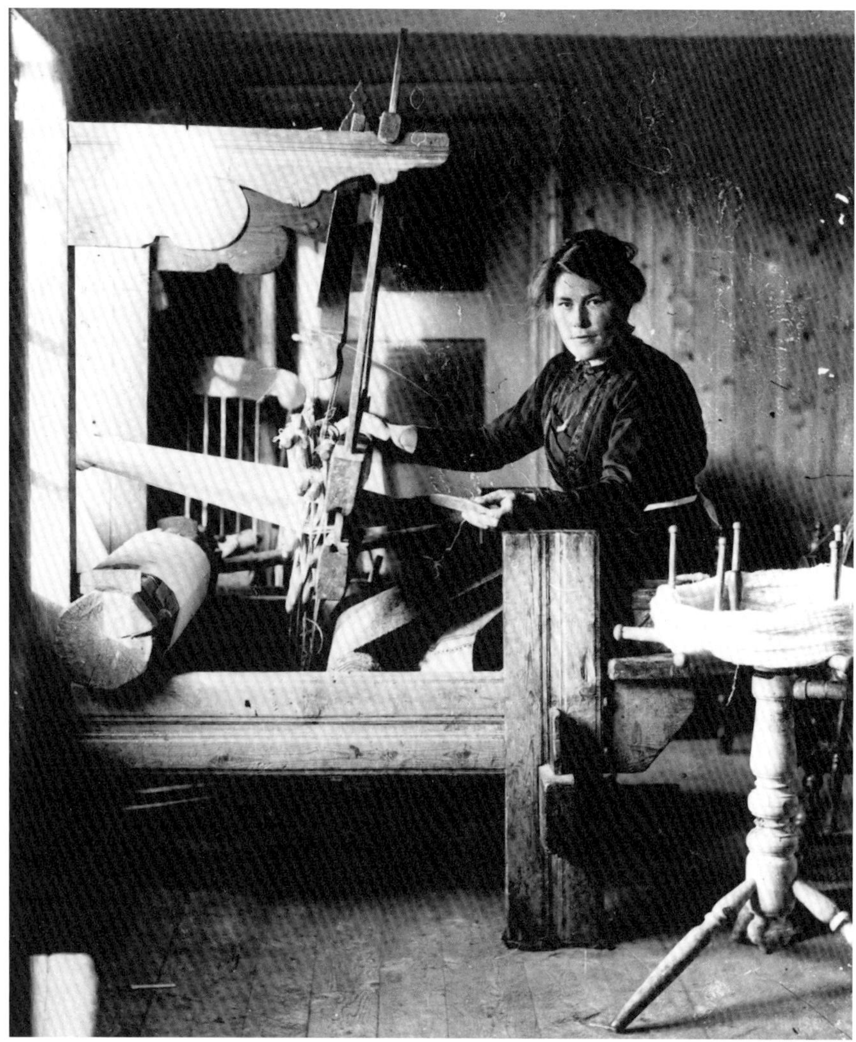

1.41 The steady beat of the loom was heard from morning until night in the early months of the year. *Fosen Picture Archive.*

Aside from providing the basics of clothing for the family and the hired help, many housewives needed to prepare their menfolk for the sea. Fishing boats were active all year up and down the coast of Norway, and the Lofoten fishery in the north drew a great many Norwegians from January through April (fig. 1.42). Whether they went to sea as fishermen, traders, or in earlier times as Vikings, these sailors needed chests of warm sturdy clothing and bedding. They also needed sails, a community responsibility enforced with a stiff fine during the Viking period. Sails were made from wadmal (Norwegian: *vadmel*), a woolen twill fabric woven in the home for many purposes and considered a standard form of payment during the Middle Ages (a piece of wadmal six ells in length, approximately one yard by three yards, had a value of one øre[3]). After fulling, a process that shrinks and thickens the fabric, lengths of wadmal were sewn together in vertical strips that were impregnated with a mixture of sheep tallow, fish oil, and tar, which made a windtight and water-repellant sail. That a tremendous amount of this cloth was required is evident from the advice of a thirteenth-century mariner to his son: one should never put to sea without "two or three hundred ells of wadmal [about 100 to 150 yards] of a sort suitable for mending sails. . . ."[4]

If possible during the busy weaving schedule, time was set aside for more
artistic pursuits. The mother and her daughters might make additions to
each girl's hope chest, which would include fine clothing for the daughter's
wedding day and household linens and bedding for her new life as a housewife. Time was also found for making the fancier touches to the home's
decor—an exquisitely decorated hand towel, a pillow cover, or a coverlet
for the bed. Although not an essential part of the yearly cycle, these artistic
creations allowed the housewife to demonstrate not only her skill at weaving
but also her ability to run the household with such efficiency that there was
time to spare for such refined pursuits.

Sewing clothes from yards of woven cloth was the last step in the year-
long cycle of cloth production. With the coming of spring, the fibers that
had been carefully nurtured through the previous spring and summer, gathered and prepared in the fall, and spun, dyed, woven, and sewn during the
winter, were now put into use. It was time for the cycle to begin anew.

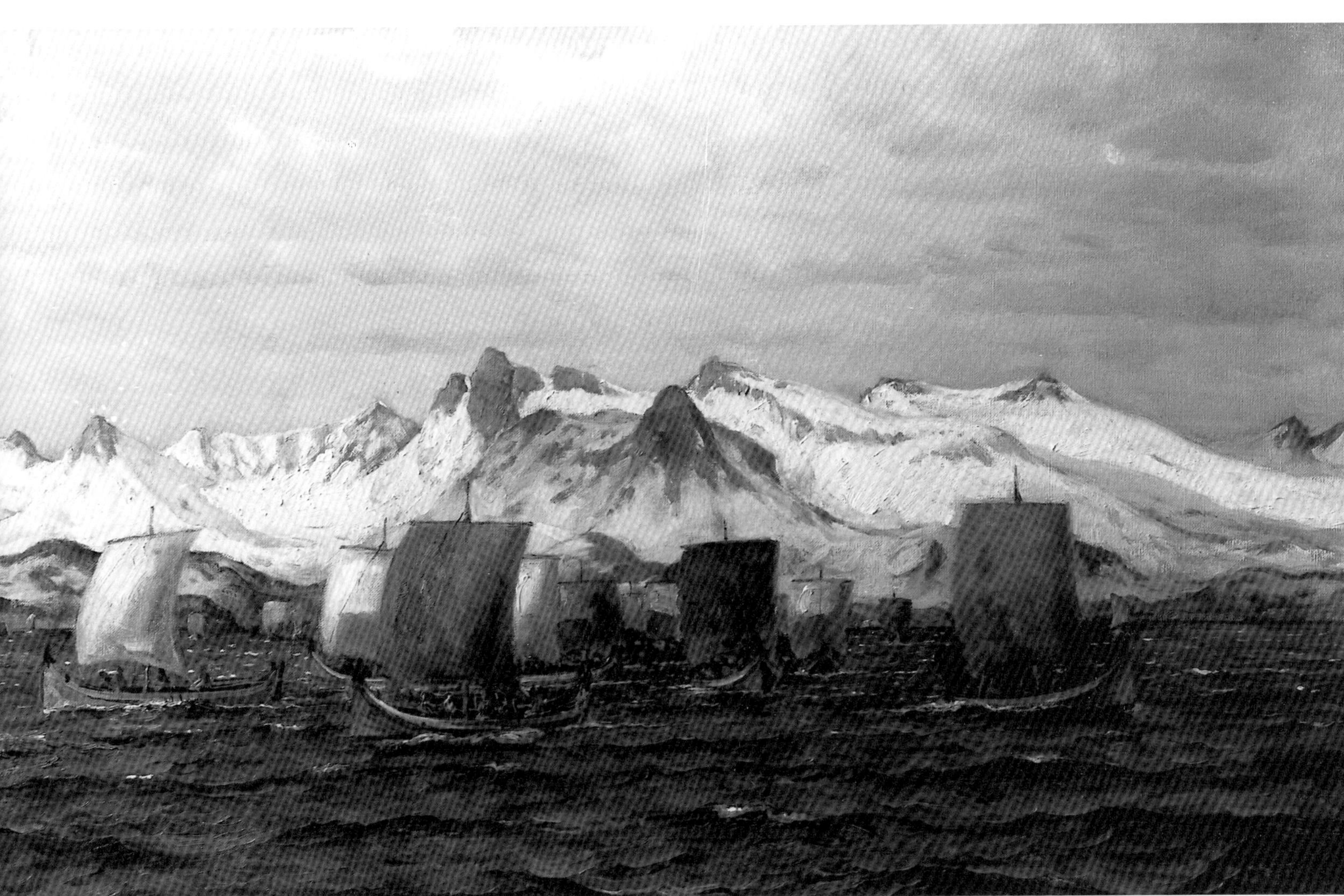

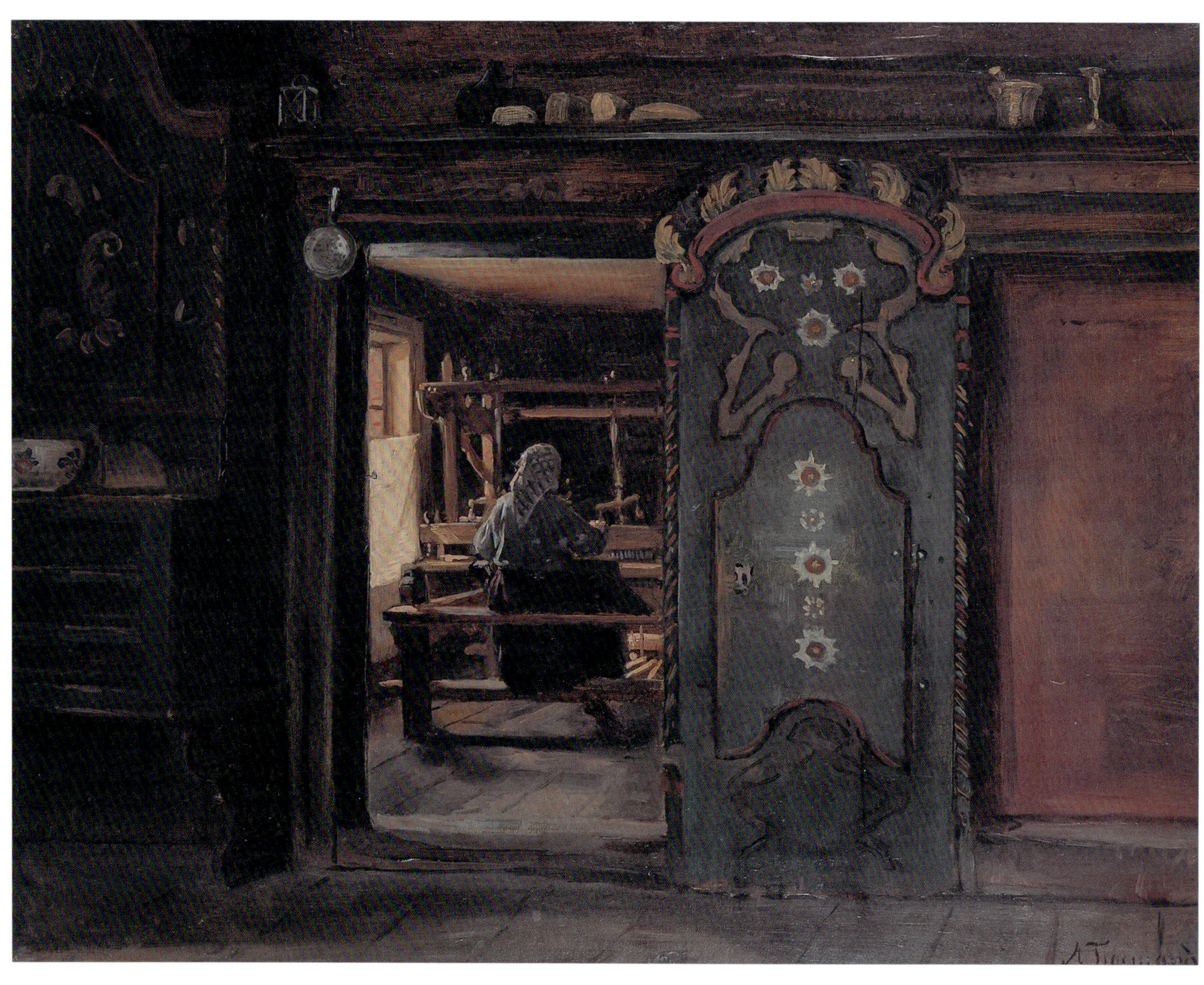

2.1 Interior of a Norwegian home in the nineteenth century.
Woman at the Loom, Gulsvik, by Adolph Tidemand.
Photo: O. Væring. National Gallery.

2 / Of Spinning Wheels and Looms

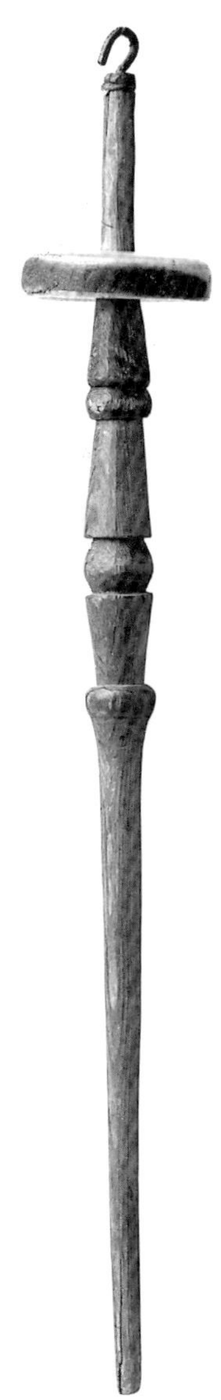

2.2 The drop spindle, a stick weighted with a disk of wood, stone, clay, or bone, was a slow but effective method for spinning fibers. Skaun, Sør-Trøndelag. *University of Trondheim, Museum of Natural History and Archeology.*

TODAY WE ARE SO BOMBARDED BY NEW DEVELOPMENTS in technology that it is difficult to imagine a time when whole generations lived their lives completely untouched by change. In times past, advances in technology were few and far between, and although a new implement might be invented in one area of the world, it could take hundreds of years for that idea to spread. During the seventeenth and eighteenth centuries several major improvements reached the remote country of Norway, transforming the lives of its inhabitants and no doubt leaving them gasping at the accelerating pace of change.

Before you are introduced to these watershed transformations, take a moment to consult your imagination. Very likely you have formed a picture of the Norwegian housewife going about her daily chores in a bright and cheery wooden home. You can see her sitting at her spinning wheel or perhaps before her loom. Logs crackle in the fireplace, intricate painted designs decorate cupboards, trunks, and even the walls of the home, and daylight streams into the house through the wavering panes of old window glass (fig. 2.1). What you have imagined is, in fact, correct, but only for the past 300 to 400 years. In the centuries prior to that time, home life was considerably different. Up until the seventeenth century, and well into the eighteenth century in some cases, the house had no chimney or glass windows, and the housewife had no spinning wheel or horizontal loom. Returning to your mental image, erase the cheery interior and replace it with a dark, sooty room. Daylight filters in through a smoke hole in the roof, and there are few decorations except occasional designs carved into the wooden walls or furniture (see fig. 3.1). A whirling spindle rises and falls from the housewife's hands as she slowly draws out the yards and yards of thread needed for weaving. And instead of sitting comfortably at her loom to weave, the housewife stands before a huge three-sided frame that leans against the wall. For the many generations of housewives who lived prior to the seventeenth century, this is the picture to keep in mind.

The changes that came about in the seventeenth and eighteenth centuries were truly dramatic. As one authority on Norwegian folk culture comments,

"Few things have brought with them such a thorough change to the farmers' homelife, over large parts of our country, as the introduction of the fireplace and chimney."[1] This was certainly true for the family in general. Smoke holes were shut off, and the space under the roof, finally free of smoke, could be used for sleeping lofts and storage. The addition of window glass soon afterward further improved the interior, with sunshine highlighting the now soot-free and newly decorated walls. For the housewife, however, more significant still was the introduction of the spinning wheel and the horizontal loom, for they improved her working conditions and made her work considerably less time consuming.

Drop Spindles and Spinning Wheels

For thousands of years, people solved the problem of spinning fibers into yarn through the use of the simple drop spindle. Egyptian tomb paintings from the twentieth century B.C. show women spinning fine linen thread with a drop spindle, and in Europe its use can be traced to the Stone Age.[2] The drop spindle consists of a stick fitted near one end with a whorl, or weighted disk (fig. 2.2). Spinning begins with a short piece of yarn attached to the spindle. To this yarn the spinner joins loosely combed fibers, drawing them out to the correct thickness and allowing them to be spun by the dropping, whirling motion of the weighted spindle. The newly spun length of yarn is then wound onto the spindle, providing the basis for the next length of yarn that will be spun from more carefully drawn-out fibers (figs. 2.3–2.4). Although offering only a slow means of production, the drop spindle served as an effective spinning implement until the emergence of the spinning wheel.

The spinning wheel, developed in the East (possibly in India, Persia, or China), arrived in Europe during the Middle Ages and went through several stages of development. The first wheels were turned by hand as the spinner alternately drew out the fibers being spun and then wound the spun length of yarn onto the spindle. Known as the high wheel or great wheel, this early development was largely superseded by the treadle wheel. This smaller, more efficient version initially had a flyer for winding the yarn onto a bobbin as it was spun; a foot treadle was added later for turning the wheel. Both types of spinning wheels were known in Norway, although the great wheel was never as widely used. The treadle wheel was the version commonly used in Norway after its introduction in the early seventeenth century, and it closely resembles the wheel used by most handspinners today (figs. 2.5–2.7).

A spinning wheel can spin yarn so much faster than a drop spindle that it must have seemed to a generation of housewives as if there were suddenly more hours in the day. This did not mean that the old way of doing things was completely abandoned, however. The drop spindle, more portable than the spinning wheel, continued to be a useful tool as it could be brought along anywhere to fill spare moments with spinning.

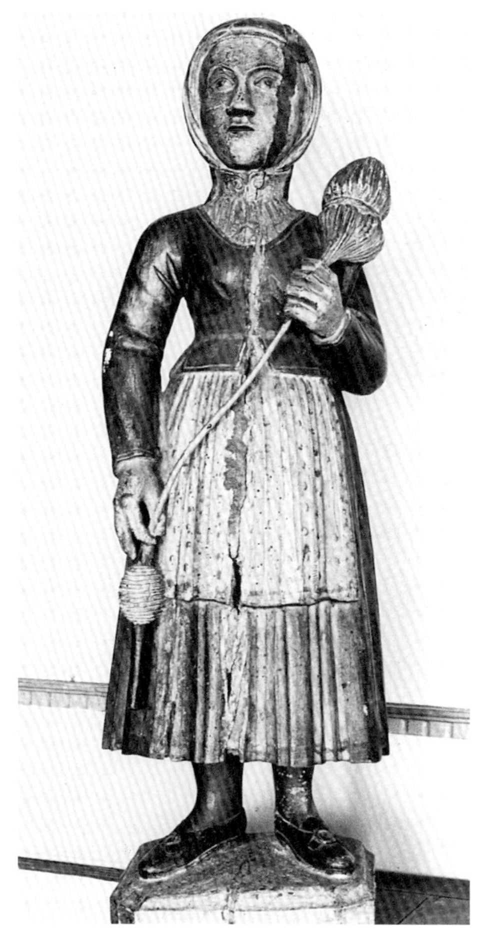

2.3 When manipulating a drop spindle, the spinner could stand with the distaff tucked into her belt or held under one arm, as seen in this wooden carving from Lista, Vest-Agder. *Norwegian Folk Museum.*

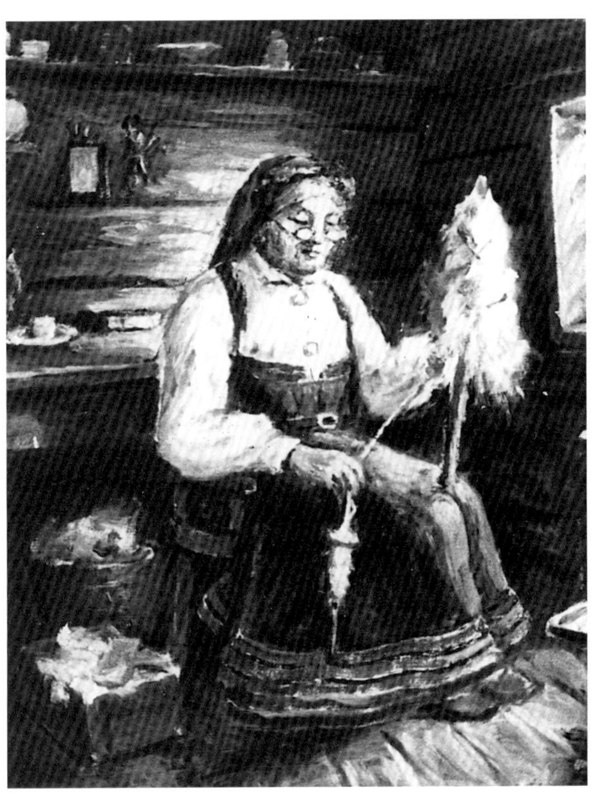

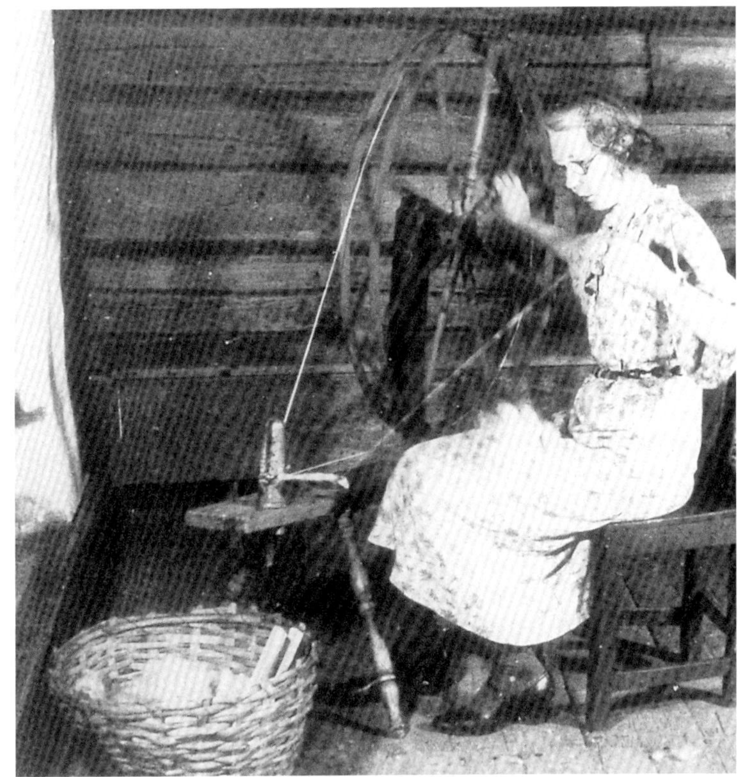

2.4 A drop spindle could be used while sitting, with the distaff held between the knees or under the arm. *Painting of a woman from Setesdal, Aust-Agder, by Lars Osa. Photo: Norwegian Folk Museum, private collection.*

2.5 *(Upper right)* The great wheel was an early version of the spinning wheel. The spinner turns the wheel by hand. After each length of fiber is drawn out and spun, it is wound onto the spindle. Akershus. *Norwegian Folk Museum.*

2.6 The spinning wheel commonly used in Norway. The spinner turns the wheel with a foot treadle, which leaves her hands free to manipulate the fibers to be spun. Yarn is wound automatically onto the bobbin by the whirling flyer. *Photo: A. B. Wilse. Norwegian Folk Museum.*

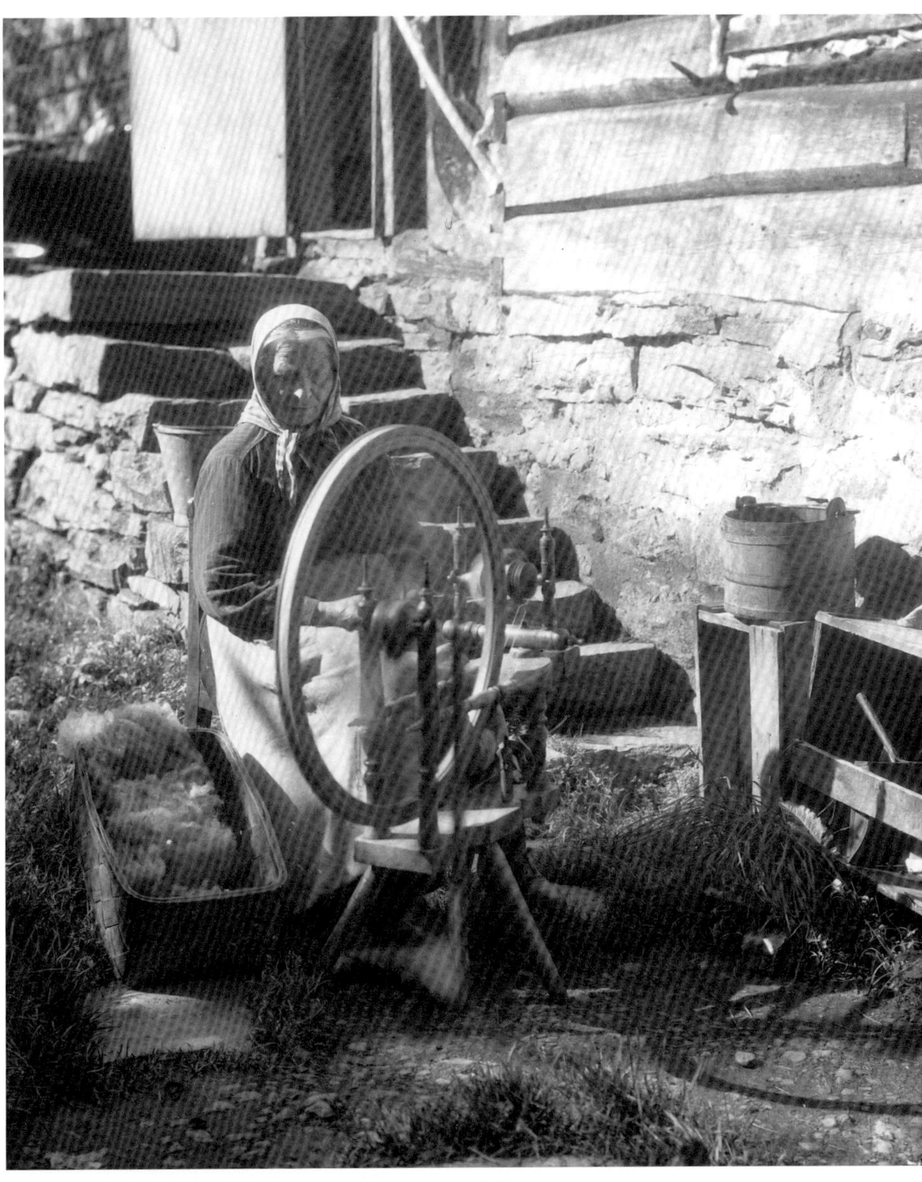

The loom that was in use throughout Norway until the fifteenth or early sixteenth century was an ancient piece of weaving equipment known as the warp-weighted loom. Like the drop spindle, the warp-weighted loom was a primitive but effective tool that had been in use for thousands of years in countries north of the Mediterranean Sea (fig. 2.8). The discovery in Hungary of what appear to be loom weights from the sixth millennium B.C. gives evidence of the warp-weighted loom's great antiquity.[3]

Extremely simple in design, the warp-weighted loom consists of a top beam supported by two posts that lean against a wall. The warp threads hang from the beam and are tensioned by a series of weights attached to bundles of warp threads near the floor. Weaving progresses from the top down, and the weaver stands with her arms raised to insert the weft and beat it into place with a sword beater (figs. 2.9–2.10). Although this may seem awkward to us today, it was so common in areas north of the Mediterranean that the Greek historian Heroditus, writing of his travels in the fifth century B.C., was struck by the unusual methods of the Egyptians, noting that in "weaving, while other people push the woof [weft] upward, the Egyptians push it down."[4]

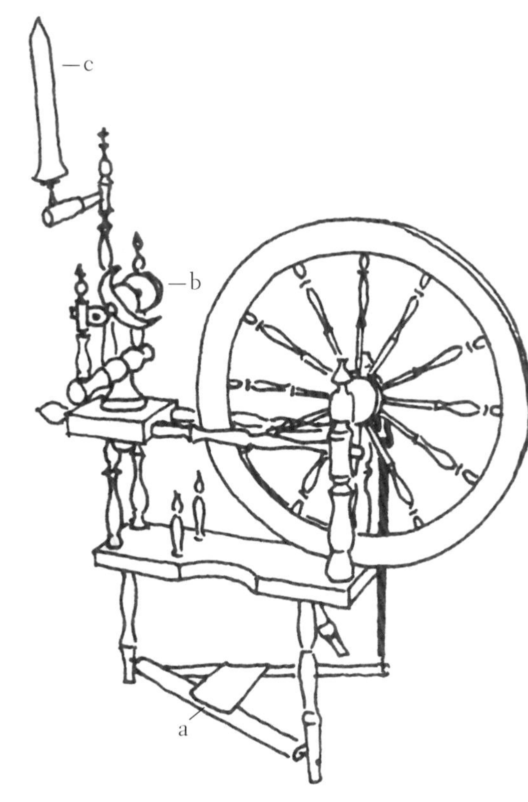

2.7 Parts of the spinning wheel: *(a)* foot treadle; *(b)* flyer, spindle, and bobbin assembly; *(c)* distaff. *Drawing: Ingrid Lowzow, University of Oslo, for Norwegian Folk Museum; in Hoffmann 1989.*

2.8 Two women weaving on a warp-weighted loom. Detail of an illustration on a Greek vase, sixth century B.C. *The Metropolitan Museum of Art, Fletcher Fund, 1931 (31.11.10).*

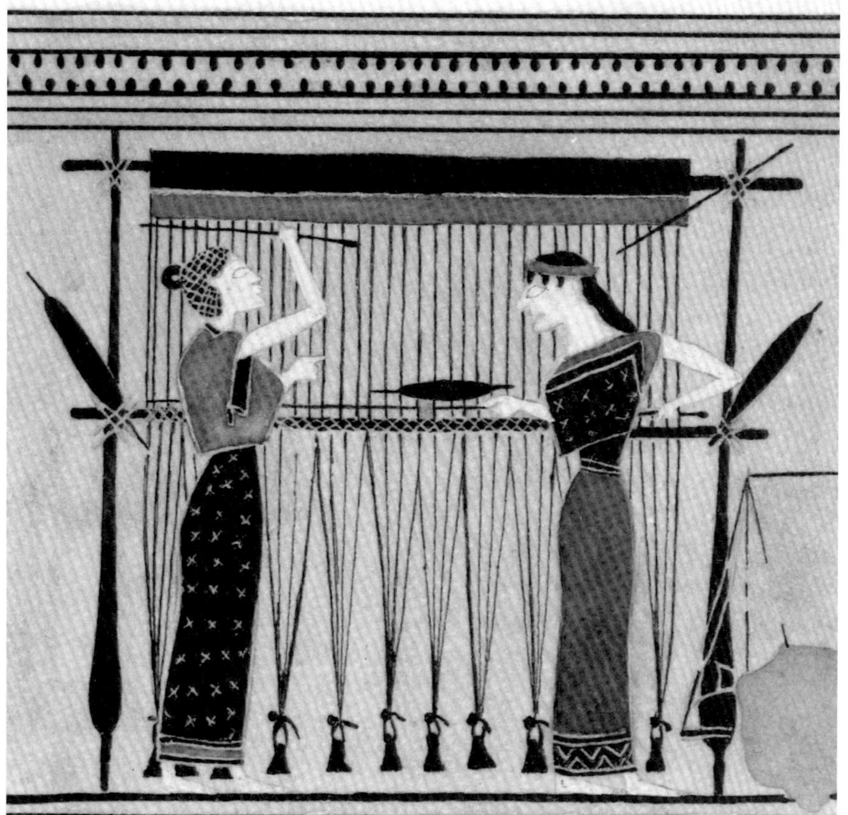

2.9 The warp-weighted loom:

I . Warp threads hang from the top beam, and weights are attached to bundles of warp threads near the floor. *(a)* upright; *(b)* beam; *(c)* heddle rod; *(d)* shed rod; *(e)* heddle rod supports; *(f)* supports for beam; *(g)* hole for nailing upright to wall or beam; *(h)* forward threads; *(i)* back threads; *(k)* chained spacing cord; *(l)* loom weights.

II. Half the threads hang straight to the floor while the other half pass over the shed rod forming a natural shed.

III. The second shed is created when the heddle rod is placed in the Y-shaped heddle rod supports, drawing the back layer of warp forward. *Drawing: Unni Fürst, Norwegian Folk Museum, in Hoffmann 1964.*

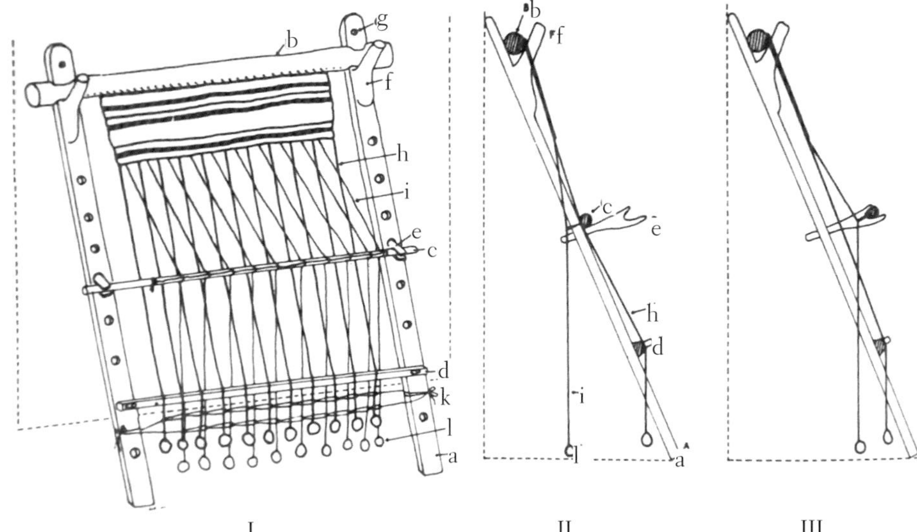

2.10 A sword beater is used to beat the weft into place on a warp-weighted loom. Sword beaters were made of wood, iron, or whale bone. Hordaland. *Norwegian Folk Museum.*

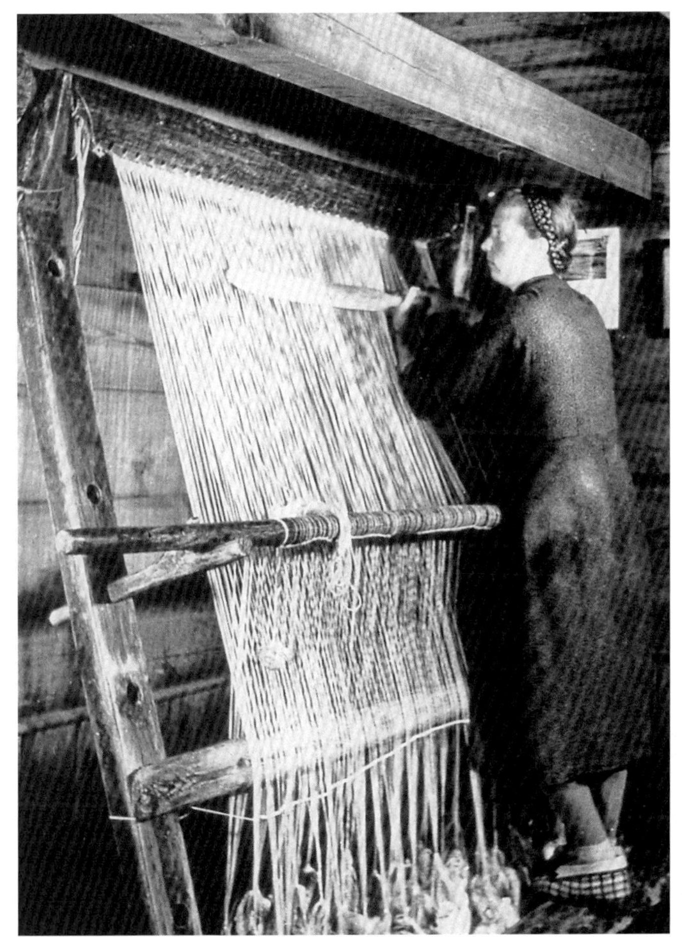

By about 1000 A.D., the warp-weighted loom was replaced in most of
Europe by the more versatile horizontal loom. The chief advantage of this
loom (aside from the fact that the weaver could finally sit down!) was a system of harnesses that were raised and lowered by treadles, allowing a variety
of fabric structures to be woven. Although the warp-weighted loom could be
fitted with three harnesses, such a system was more cumbersome than the
treadle system of the horizontal loom, which could weave easily with eight
or more harnesses. The new horizontal loom was also equipped with front
and back beams, which allowed lengthy warps to be handled more efficiently
(fig. 2.11). The one advantage that the warp-weighted loom had over the horizontal loom was the width of the woven piece. On the older loom, weaving
width was merely limited by the length of the top beam, a dimension that
had very little impact on the total amount of space occupied by the loom.
The horizontal loom, however, with its cube-like structure, presented obvious space problems when enlarged.*

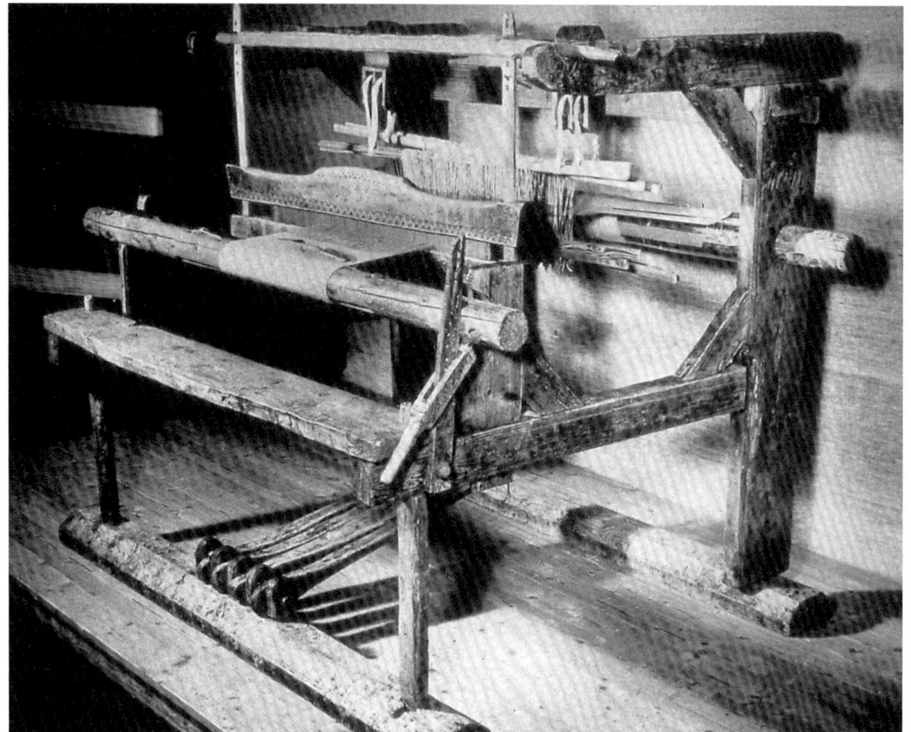

2.11 A horizontal loom from Setesdal with the
year 1668 carved into the beater. The harness
and treadle system and front and back beams
of the horizontal loom made it a great
improvement over the warp-weighted loom.
Note that in this early version of the horizontal loom, the functions of the breast beam and
the cloth beam are combined. Valle, Setesdal.
Norwegian Folk Museum.

The oldest known horizontal loom preserved in Norway dates from 1668, although this innovation was probably introduced by professional weavers sometime during the Middle Ages and came into widespread use by the fifteenth or early sixteenth century. It did not immediately replace the older loom, however, and it is likely that the problem of loom size versus the desired weaving width contributed to the warp-weighted loom's survival. The weaving of yardage for clothing and household use was readily transferred to the newer looms, but when a housewife set out to reproduce a coverlet of the same size as that woven by her grandmother, the warp-weighted loom was often the loom of choice. Although many districts eventually adapted even their coverlet techniques to the newer loom, the older loom still did not die out entirely. During the 1950s, when the warp-weighted loom had been gone from most of Europe for almost a thousand years and had become an intriguing museum piece even in Scandinavia, textile authority Marta Hoffmann was able to find a family in western Norway and another in the far north who still wove coverlets in the way of their ancestors, the last link in a tradition that had passed from culture to culture and generation to generation for eight thousand years (fig. 2.12).[5]

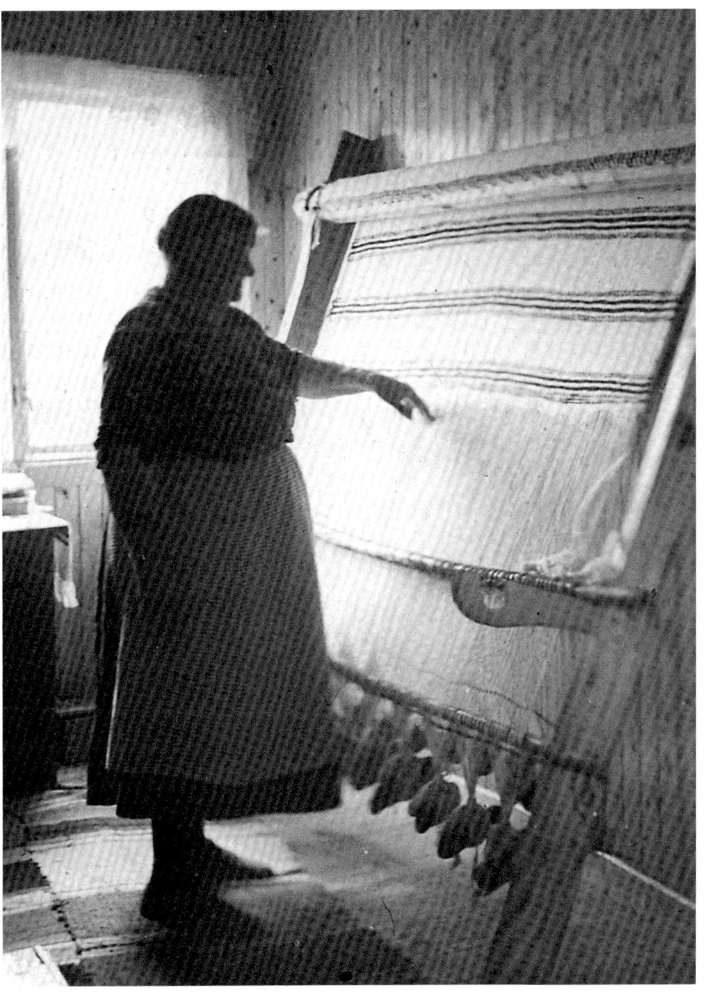

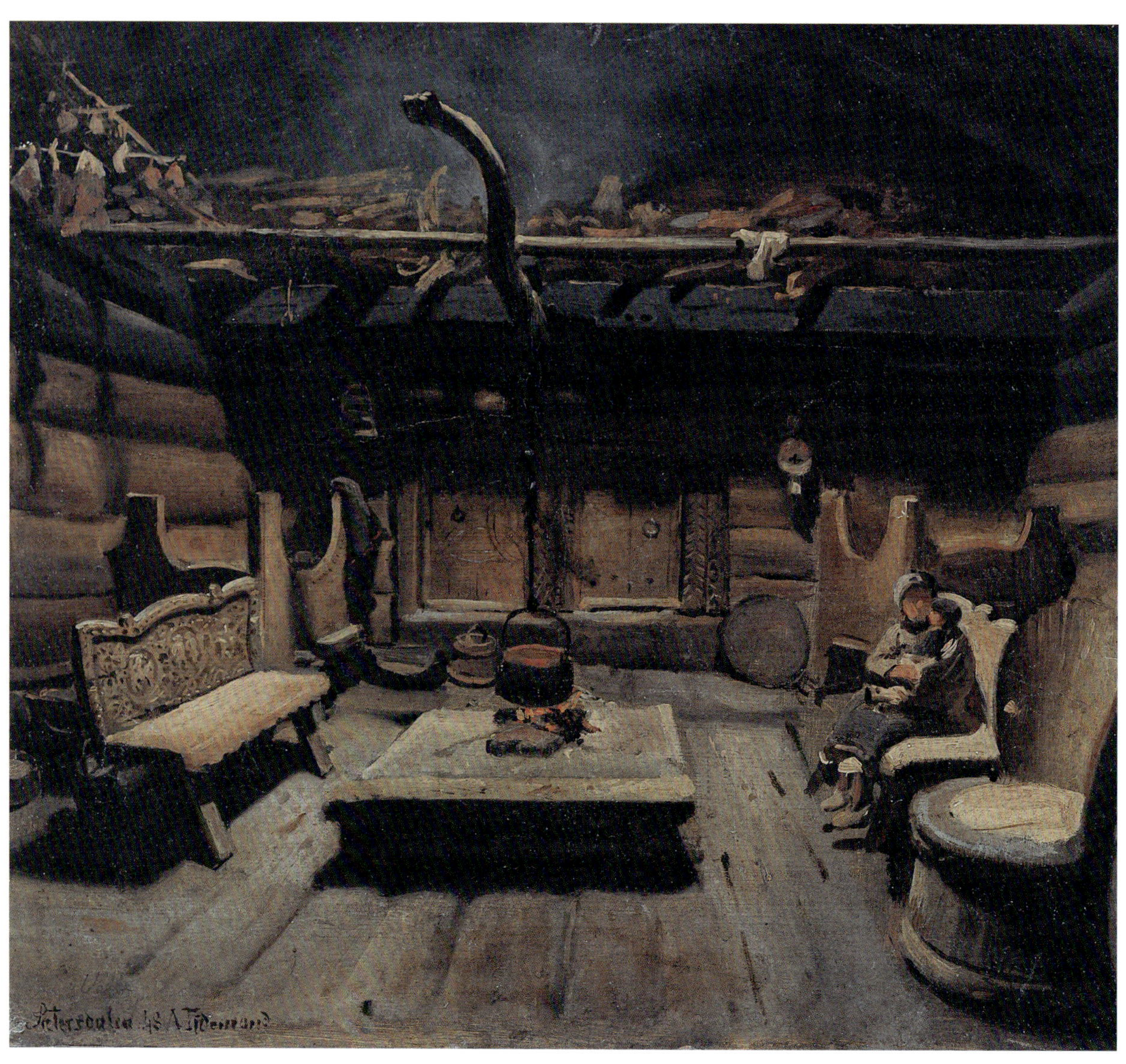

3.1 Interior of an old log home with a central hearth. Note the boxlike beds in the corners. *Open-Hearth Room at the Farm Sogneskar in Valle, Setesdal, by Adolph Tidemand. Photo: O. Væring. National Gallery.*

3 / More Than Just a Cover for the Bed

A WARM AND COMFORTING COVER AT NIGHT HAS BEEN an essential part of human existence ever since our ancestors wrapped themselves in furs and huddled around a fire. Providing us with that warmth on the long road from bearskins to bedspreads has been the primary purpose of the coverlet. In Norway, this final and often decorative covering for the bed is known as an *åkle* (pronounced "oh-kleh.") Although today the traditional åkle is usually replaced by a modern down-filled comforter, these treasured keepsakes can still be seen brightening the walls in many homes, serving as a reminder that in times past the handwoven coverlet had a more important role to play in daily life.

In Norway, where keeping out the cold can be described as a national pastime for at least half the year, coverlets were sometimes so densely woven or so thick with pile that simply throwing back the covers to get out of bed in the morning must have required an unusually robust nature. Of course, not all of the Norwegian coverlets were quite this weighty—some were remarkably lightweight—and merely providing for the family's warmth does not explain the inordinate amount of time and effort that went into the making of these heirloom creations. Clearly, the simple matter of keeping warm at night was not the only object. It had to be done with style.

Imagine decorating the walls and ceiling of your home in dark brown and black, and you will readily appreciate the Norwegian housewife's desire to add a burst of color and design to the furnishings of her home. In the soot-covered interior of the older Norwegian homesteads (fig. 3.1), decorating the walls with textiles or paintings was impractical except during festive occasions. The family bedsteads, however, conveniently situated in the corners of the typically one-roomed homes, were the perfect place for a colorful display, transforming the coverlet into an integral part of the household decor. This was true long after the introduction of the chimney allowed decorations

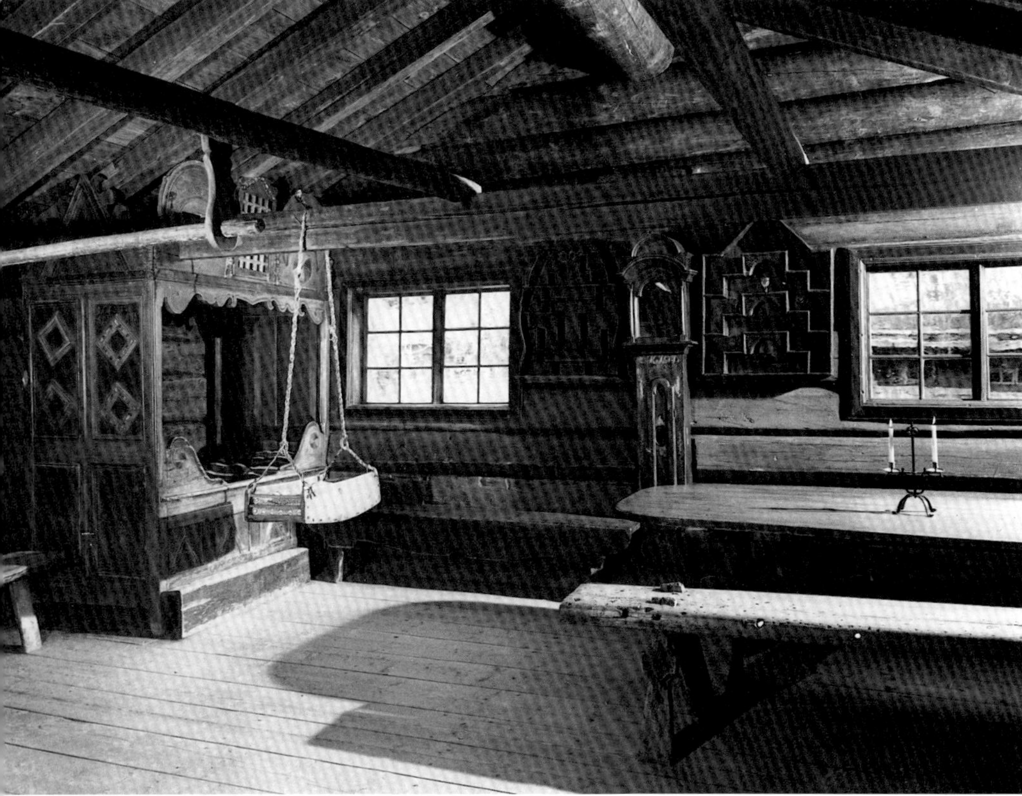

to be added to the soot-free walls, for the bedstead remained a part of the furnishings in the main room of many Norwegian homes well into the nineteenth century (fig. 3.2).

The prominent location of the bedstead also made the coverlet a perfect showcase for the housewife's handwork capabilities. Well-sorted wool and an experienced hand at the spinning wheel resulted in yarns of a fine, even quality; skill and good judgment at the dye pot gave vibrant colors in sufficient quantities; and a thoughtful selection of pattern and color combined with a steady hand at the loom produced a coverlet that was sure to be admired. To a practiced eye (and the eyes of visiting housewives were all well practiced), these factors were readily apparent in a finished coverlet. As a result, only the best efforts could be displayed on the family's bedsteads.

Apart from its eye-catching appeal, the coverlet had another, more solemn role to play. Birth, marriage, death—the passages of a person's life— all revolved around the family bed, and the coverlet assumed its proper place in these ceremonious occasions. A finely woven coverlet wrapped the family's newest member on his or her first trip to church for christening. The hopes and dreams of a young bride were woven into the coverlet she placed upon the marriage bed. And finally, a last offering of comfort was symbolized by the coverlet that draped a loved one's coffin on the final ride to the church yard for burial. From birth to death, the coverlet provided a constant and reassuring presence (fig. 3.3).

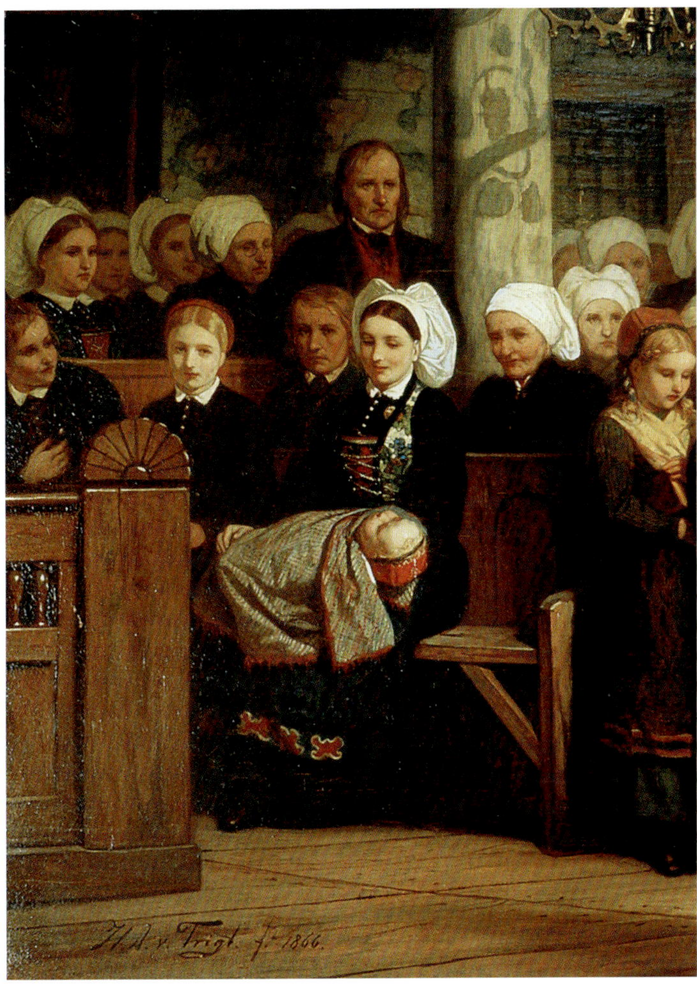

What were the bedsteads like for which these coverlets were woven? Certainly they do not conform to our modern idea of comfort. Giving the appearance of a shallow wooden box attached to the wall on one or two sides and supported by posts at the outside corners, a typical bed might measure only four by five feet (fig. 3.4). Even taking into consideration the smaller stature of most people centuries ago, this left little room to stretch out. In fact, people slept in these beds in a semi-sitting position, often reclining on large pillows. A pile of straw served as a mattress, covered either by an impervious layer of woven rags, a fulled or matted wool blanket, or even an old pelt. Several thin woolen blankets served as sheets, and these were topped by the coverlet as a final layer. Sheepskin was used as a bedcover from earliest times and was often added to the pile of coverings for warmth. Sheepskin blankets, sewn together from the pelts of several sheep, were used with the wool side down. When a coverlet was of a relatively lightweight weave, it was a common practice to sew the coverlet to the skin side of a pelt blanket, making a decorative finish for the top of the bed (fig. 3.5).

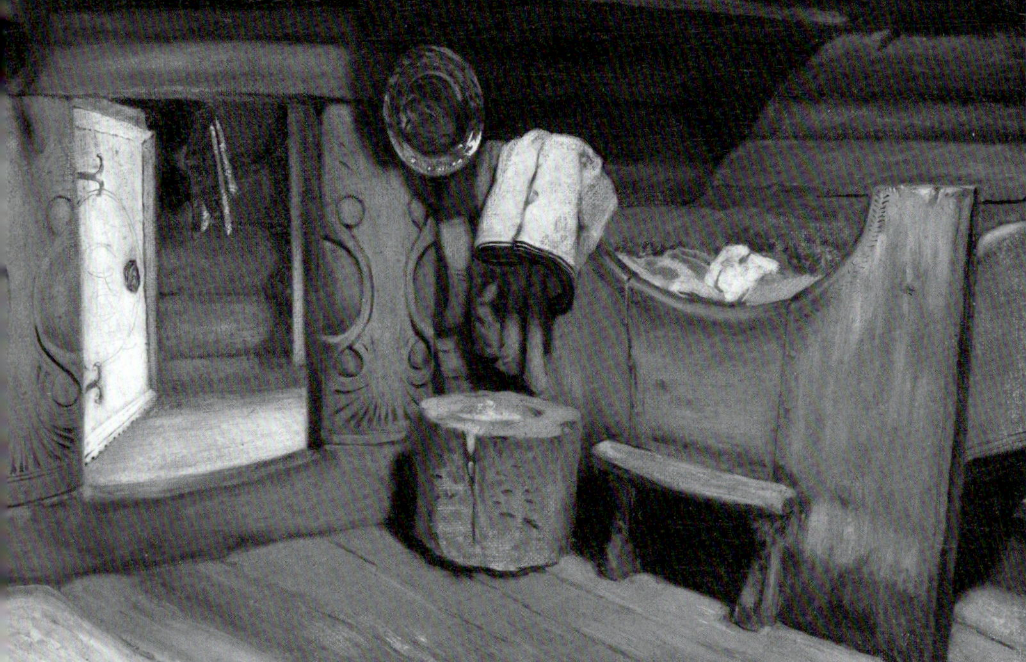

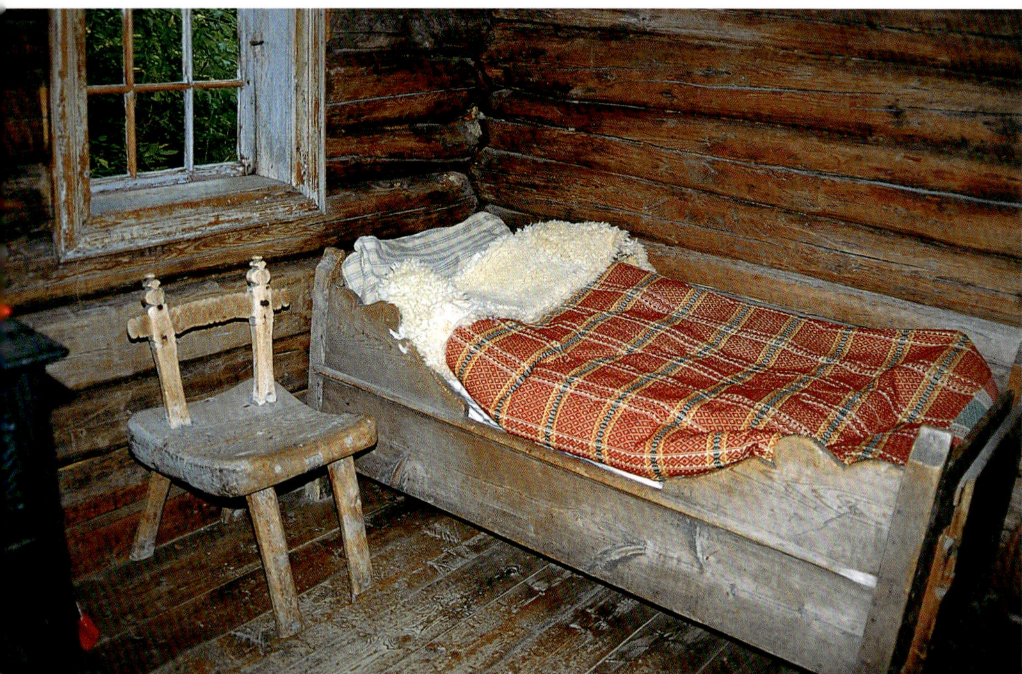

3.4 Beds were usually set in the corner of the room, supported on two sides by the walls of the house. *Interior from Setesdal, by Olaf Isaachsen. National Gallery.*

3.5 Lightweight coverlets were often sewn to the skin side of sheepskin blankets to make a warm and decorative covering for the bed. Nordland's weave coverlet sewn to a sheepskin blanket. *Photo: Dino Makridis. Trøndelag Folk Museum.*

3.6 Plain weaves: (*a*) balanced plain weave; (*b*) weft-faced plain weave; (*c*) warp-faced plain weave.

The simplest form of weaving, and the one that serves as the basis for most of the Norwegian coverlet weaves, is known as plain weave (also referred to as tabby). In this weave structure the weft thread travels over one warp thread and under one warp thread across the width of the fabric; on its return trip, the weft travels over and under the opposite warp threads (fig. 3.6 [a]). Plain weave serves as the foundation for a variety of weave structures, including tapestry, brocading, double weave and, in some cases, pile weave.

A departure from the basic plain-weave structure is seen in the twill weaves. In a twill, the weft thread travels over and under more than one warp thread at a time, and this over-and-under sequence shifts one or more threads to the right or left with each new row of weaving. The diagonal lines formed by the shifting interlacement of the warp and weft threads is characteristic of twill weaves

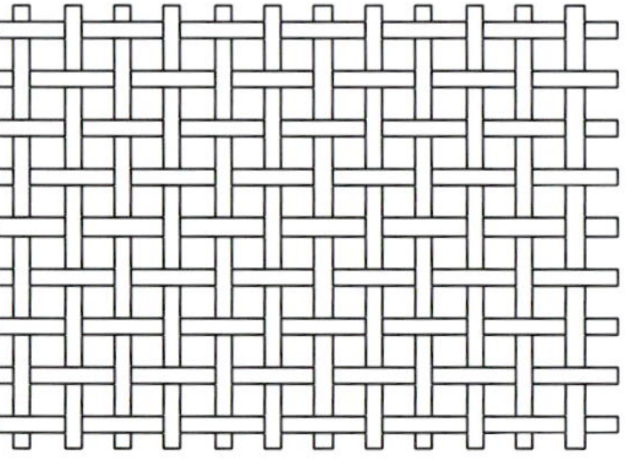

a

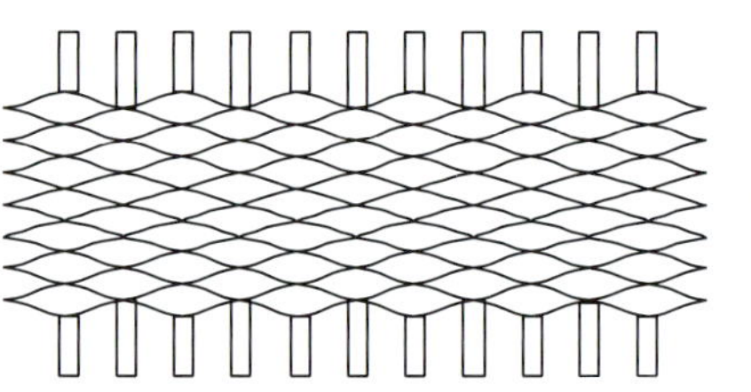

b

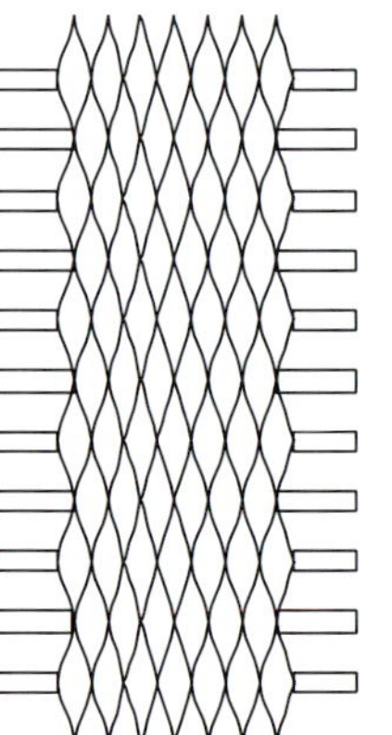

c

(fig. 3.7[a]). The basic over and under sequence of a twill can vary, as in the over two, under two of a 2/2 twill, or the over one, under two of a 1/2 twill; and the diagonal lines can be arranged into subtle patterns, such as points, diamonds, and zigzags. Twill weave can also serve as the foundation for other weave structures, notably pile weave in the Norwegian coverlets.

The character of a fabric is controlled not only by the sequence in which the warp and weft threads are interlaced, but also by the proportions in which they appear on the surface. A weaving in which the warp and weft threads appear in equal proportions on the surface of the fabric is called a balanced weave (figs. 3.6 [a], and 3.7 [a]). In a plain weave, if the spacing between the warp threads is increased so that the weft threads pack down and cover the warps completely, a weft-faced weave results (fig. 3.6 [b]). On the other hand, if the warp threads are spaced so closely that the weft threads are no longer visible, a warp-faced weave is created (fig. 3.6 [c]). In a twill, when the weft threads travel over more warp threads than they travel under, a weft-faced weave results, while the opposite relationship creates a warp-faced weave (figs. 3.7 [b] and [c].)

The basic need for a coverlet was interpreted in a variety of ways throughout Norway, hardly surprising when over a thousand miles of mountains, valleys, and fjords separate Kristiansand in the south from North Cape well above the Arctic Circle in the north. Six major types of coverlets and several minor variations were known in different and often overlapping parts of Norway. Some forms of coverlet weaving encompassed large areas of the country, others were practiced only in small districts, and still others of limited distribution in recent memory were more widespread in the past.

In the following chapters, the Norwegian coverlet weaves are presented in detail. The history of each technique, the materials and looms with which the coverlets were woven, and the designs and colors that made them uniquely Norwegian are discussed, all the while recognizing that there is nothing new under the sun, and that Norway is a part (if the farthest-flung part) of the Old World. Concluding each chapter is a brief description of weaving techniques, designed to give the non-weaver a good grasp of how the coverlets were made.

The first four types of coverlets presented, tapestry, square weave, *krokbragd*, and a catch-all of minor varieties, are all weft-faced weaves. This means that they have the same "face," or surface, one in which the weft threads completely cover the warp threads (see "Weaving Primer," opposite). These coverlets also share the same warp and weft materials, and although they represent several distinct weave structures, the techniques are often found mixed with one another in individual coverlets. The remaining three coverlet types differ considerably from one another in structure. The two layers of the double-weave coverlets, the thick pile of knotted-pile coverlets, and the lightweight ground weave with supplementary pattern wefts of the overshot coverlets form three distinct classes that were rarely combined within the same coverlet.

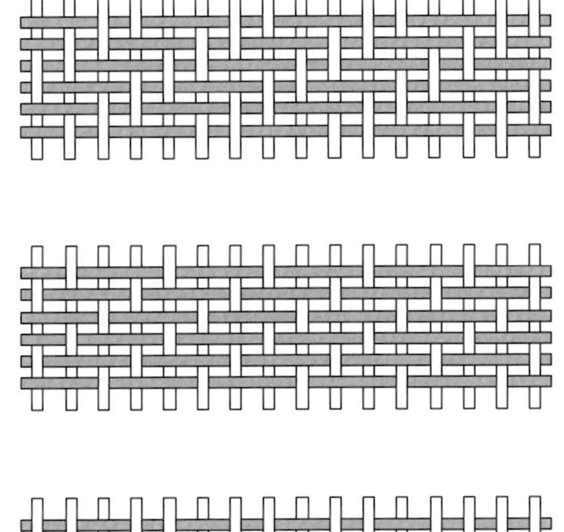

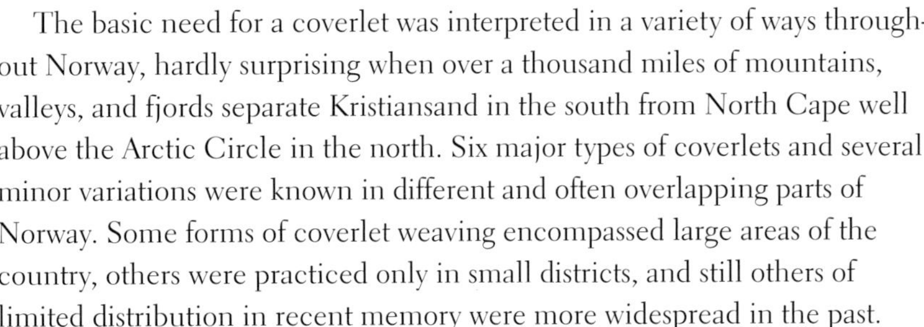

3.7 Twill weaves:

(a) balanced 2/2 twill;

(b) weft-faced 2/1 twill;

(c) warp-faced 1/2 twill.

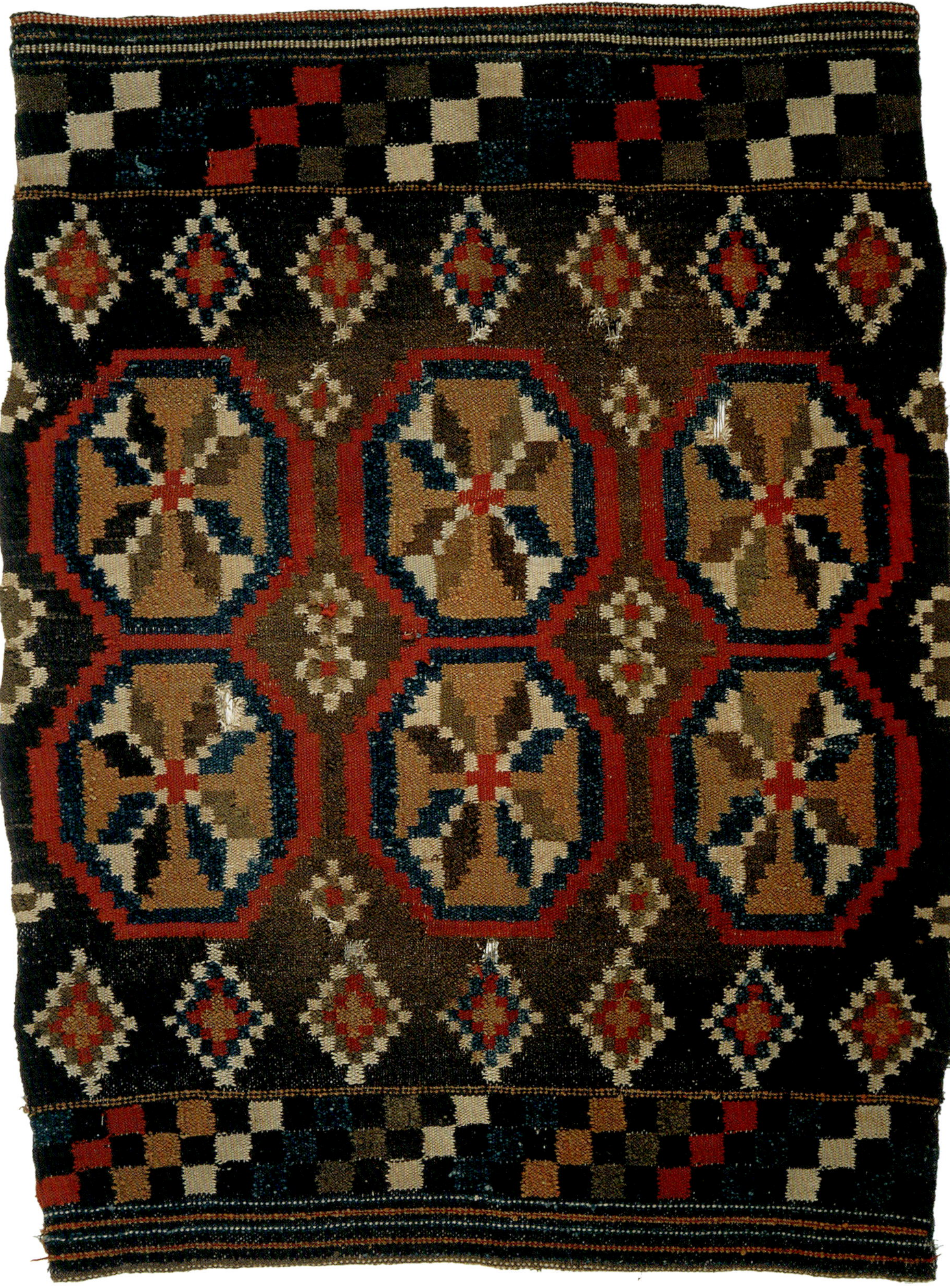

The Coverlets

Traditional motifs and subtle colors impart a timeless quality to this
square weave coverlet. *Historical Museum, University of Bergen.*

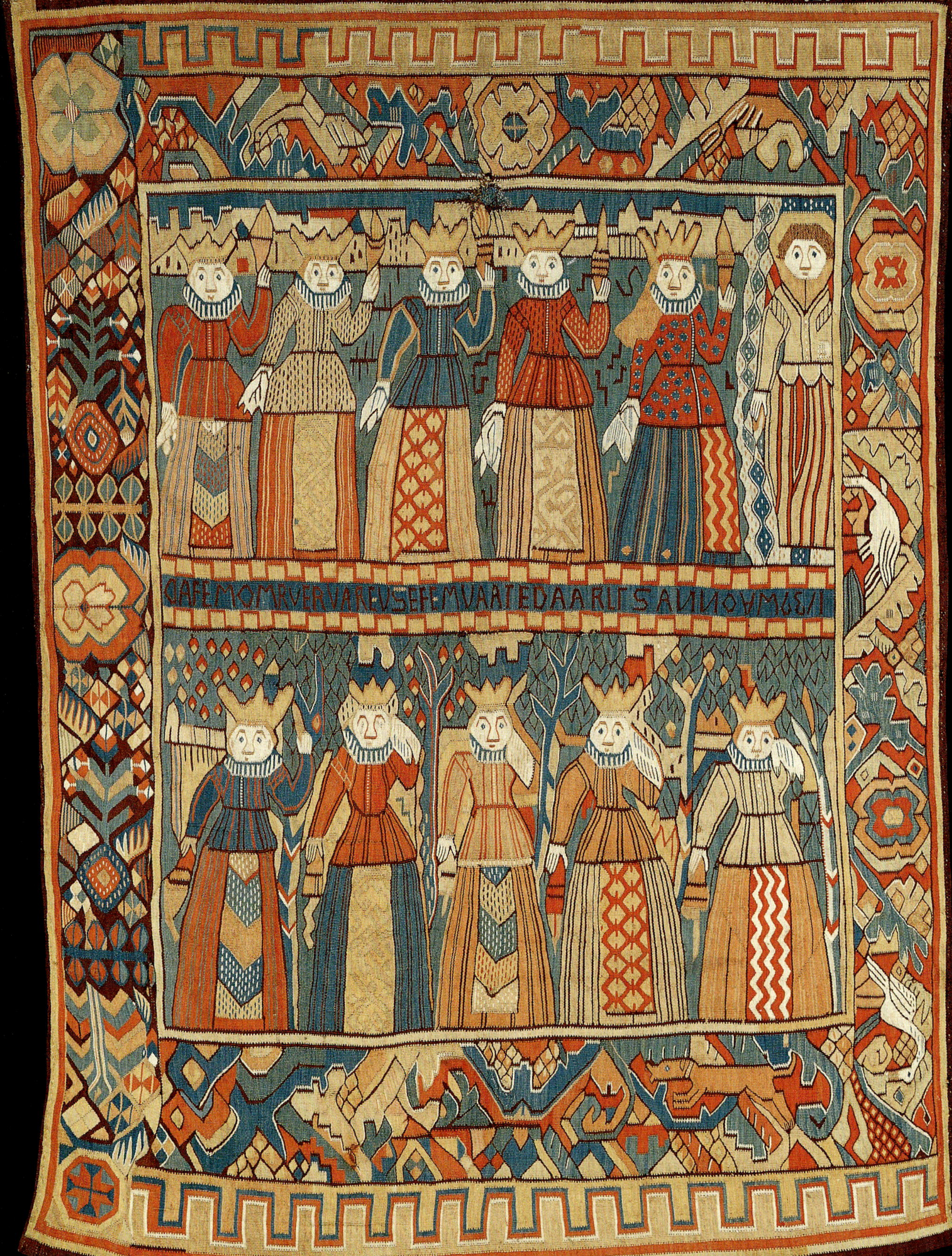
DAFEMOMRVERVAREVSEFEMVAATEDAARLISAVNOVMDSVI

4 / Tapestry Coverlets: Billedvev

AN ECHO OF AGES PAST IS EVIDENT IN THE ARCHAIC, two-dimensional figures of the Norwegian *billedvev* (picture weave), or tapestry coverlets. Religious figures, bridal couples, and mythical animals peering out of a framework of vines and flowers must have brought life into any room graced by these splendid weavings (fig. 4.1). In Gudbrandsdal and other eastern valleys of Norway, a tapestry coverlet on the family bed was considered the height of luxury. In later years such finery might be displayed on the wall, perhaps to dignify the seat of the head of the household, but such use was never widespread. In Norway, tapestries were chiefly prized as an elegant cover for the bed.

Origins

Tapestry developed as an art form in Europe during the Middle Ages, probably as a result of contact with the Middle East, where the craft was well established before the birth of Christ. Supported by royal and noble patrons, tapestry weaving flourished through the Renaissance in France and the Low Countries, where monumental pieces depicting Biblical, mythical, and romantic scenes were produced.

In Norway, a form of pictorial weaving was practiced as early as the Viking Age. The Oseberg "tapestry," an intriguing fragment unearthed in 1904 in the burial ship of a ninth-century Viking queen, consists of small figures brocaded onto a probable ground weave of linen, long since rotted away (fig. 4.2). This fragment is similar to Viking Age weavings discovered elsewhere in Scandinavia, but because these pictorial weavings were created through the use of brocading, they are not considered to be true tapestry weaves (see "Brocaded Coverlets of Vestfold," chapter 7).

4.1 The Five Wise and Five Foolish Virgins were a popular subject in Norwegian tapestry coverlets. *The Minneapolis Institute of Arts.*

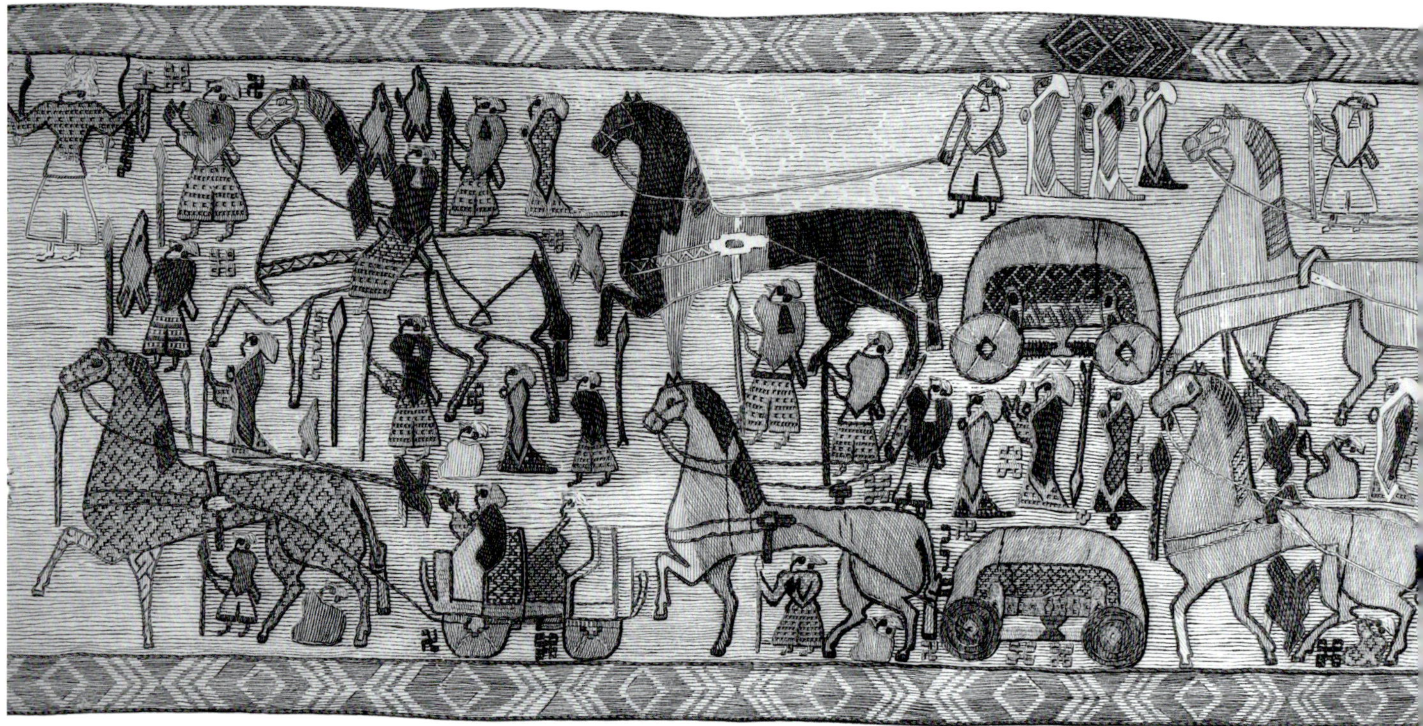

4.2 A procession of people, horses, and wagons is seen in the Oseberg tapestry, discovered in the burial ship of a ninth-century Viking queen. The small knot motif under the wagons (*at bottom*) and the horse (*at bottom right*) is found in coverlets from later periods. *Drawing: M. Strom. University Museum of National Antiquities, Oslo.*

4.3 The twelfth-century Baldishol tapestry was discovered following the demolition of Baldishol Church in Hedmark. Probably a fragment of a larger piece, the month of April is depicted by a man standing next to a tree, and the month of May by a horseman in armor. Approximately 4 x 7 ft. *Oslo Museum of Applied Art.*

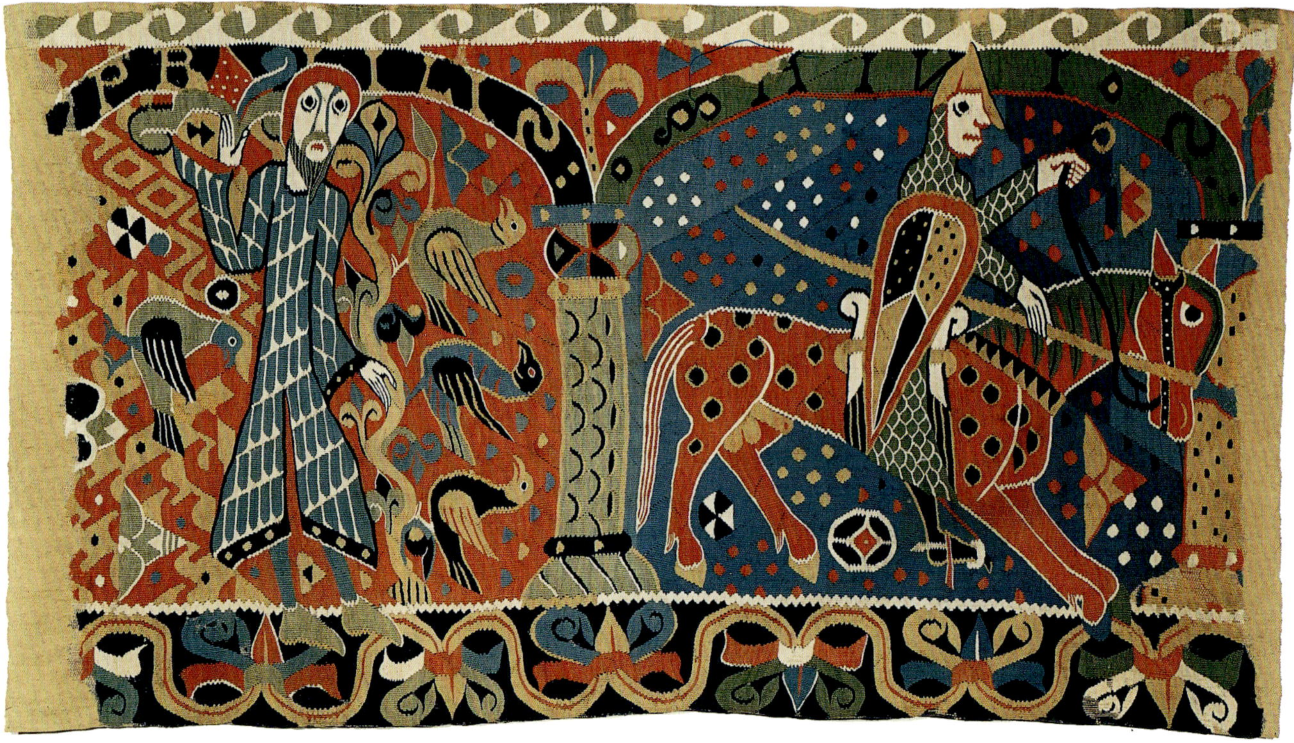

The first representation of standard tapestry techniques in Norway is found in the twelfth-century Baldishol tapestry (fig. 4.3). This sizable fragment depicting two months of the year appears to have been part of a much larger piece, possibly designed for the walls of a church. The figures of birds and flowers surrounding a man standing near a tree (representing April) and a fully armored rider on horseback (representing May) have retained their color surprisingly well considering the weaving's seven-hundred-year history: after the demolition of Baldishol Church in the late 1870s, this unique tapestry came to light in the shape of a tattered old rag covered with the dirt of its final use—protecting the feet of the church sexton from drafts. As the woman who finally recognized its worth remarked, "Surely no other sexton, past or present, has ever had such a priceless rug at his feet!"[1]

The Baldishol tapestry shows strong similarities to the tapestry traditions of the continent (fig. 4.4) and in fact is one of the few pieces of tapestry work to have survived from the early Middle Ages in all of Europe. Whether the fragment found in Baldishol Church was actually woven in Norway or created at another weaving center in northern Europe is unknown; however, its basis in the European tapestry tradition seems clear. Unfortunately, there is no other evidence of tapestry work in Norway from the twelfth century until the end of the sixteenth century, but given the precarious circumstances through which the Baldishol tapestry survived, it is possible that other tapestry work simply perished.

4.4 A strong stylistic relationship is evident between the twelfth-century Baldishol tapestry and the renowned eleventh-century Bayeux Tapestry, an embroidery on linen probably created in England. Compare the rider's mail, helmet, shield, and saddle with those of the rider in figure 4.3. *By special permission of the City of Bayeux.*

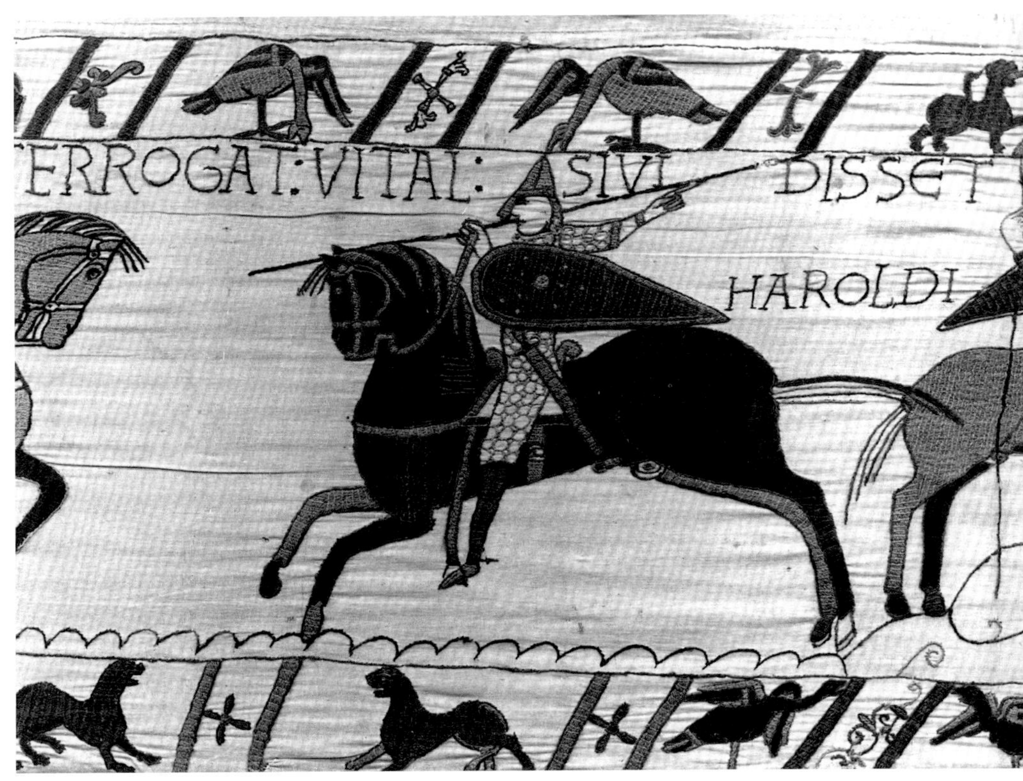

Almost all of the Norwegian tapestries that have been preserved date from the seventeenth century or later. Beginning in the seventeenth century and increasing in the eighteenth century, Norway experienced a growth in prosperity that permitted a flowering in all the folk arts. The migration of professional tapestry weavers into Scandinavia during the late sixteenth century combined with this prosperity to stimulate a flurry of tapestry production. Initially, the work of these immigrant professionals was in much demand by the upper classes in Norway's coastal cities. Although it is uncertain exactly how knowledge of the tapestry technique spread inland, by the time these coverlets were no longer fashionable in the cities, the technique had taken root in the countryside. The thriving valley of Gudbrandsdal, well situated on the major internal route of commerce, soon became a center of cultural development and of tapestry weaving. Other eastern regions such as Valdres, Hedmark, Telemark, and Sør-Trøndelag produced tapestries, and to a limited extent less sophisticated works were woven in the western fjord country, but Gudbrandsdal was the acknowledged center of tapestry weaving in Norway, both in stylistic influence and in volume of weavings.

Although tapestry coverlets were considered extremely desirable, the technique was time consuming and required skill and experience. While a well-born lady might have filled her leisure hours with such pursuits, these distinctive weavings were not produced by the average housewife. Instead, some women developed sufficient skill to establish themselves as specialists, weaving coverlets for others in their district while supplementing the income of their own farm or supporting themselves and their children if they were widowed. For a family with sufficient means, a coverlet might be commissioned from one of these specialists, but even in the homes of less wealthy families one might find a pillow in the tapestry technique or a cover for the long benches built into the walls of earlier homes. In fact, the majority of tapestry work registered in Norway consists of such smaller pieces of weaving which were more likely to be within the reach of the average farm family (fig. 4.5; and see 4.18).

Design and Color

The Norwegian tapestries offer a distinctive expression of Renaissance styles simplified over time by provincial artisans. The professional weavers who migrated to Scandinavia brought with them the realism and perspective typical of Renaissance tapestry work on the continent. The use of light and shadow, the subtle blending of colors, and the differentiation between objects in the foreground and background all appeared for a brief time in the Norwegian tapestries (fig. 4.6). But gradually the efforts of less sophisticated local artisans resulted in a flat, two-dimensional style. Subjects in the background were placed above those in the foreground with little regard to relative size, and colors were bright and strong, without nuance or shadow to lend realism. A tendency to fill intervening areas with small geometric or

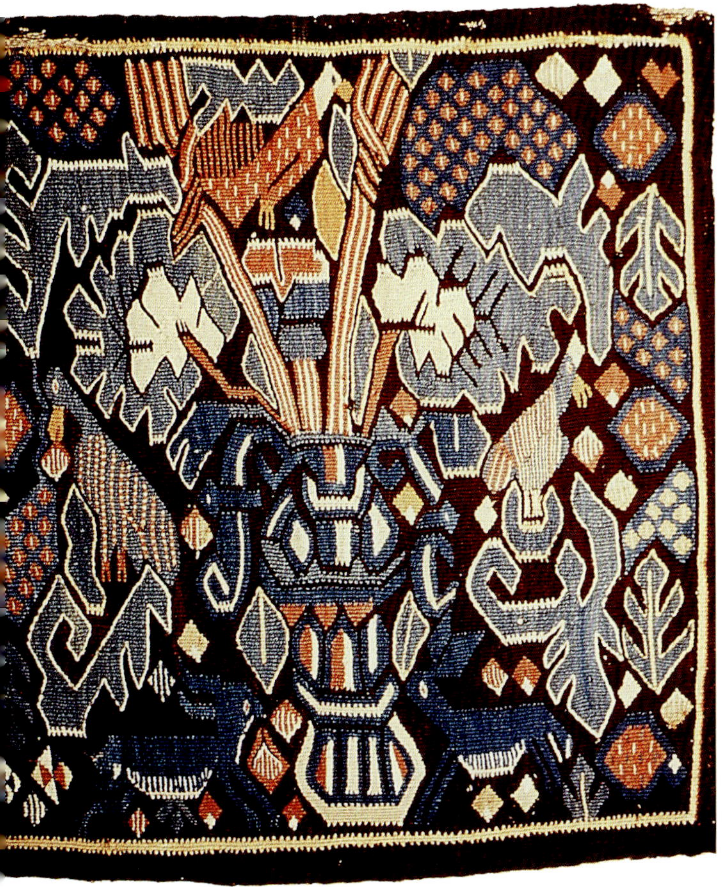

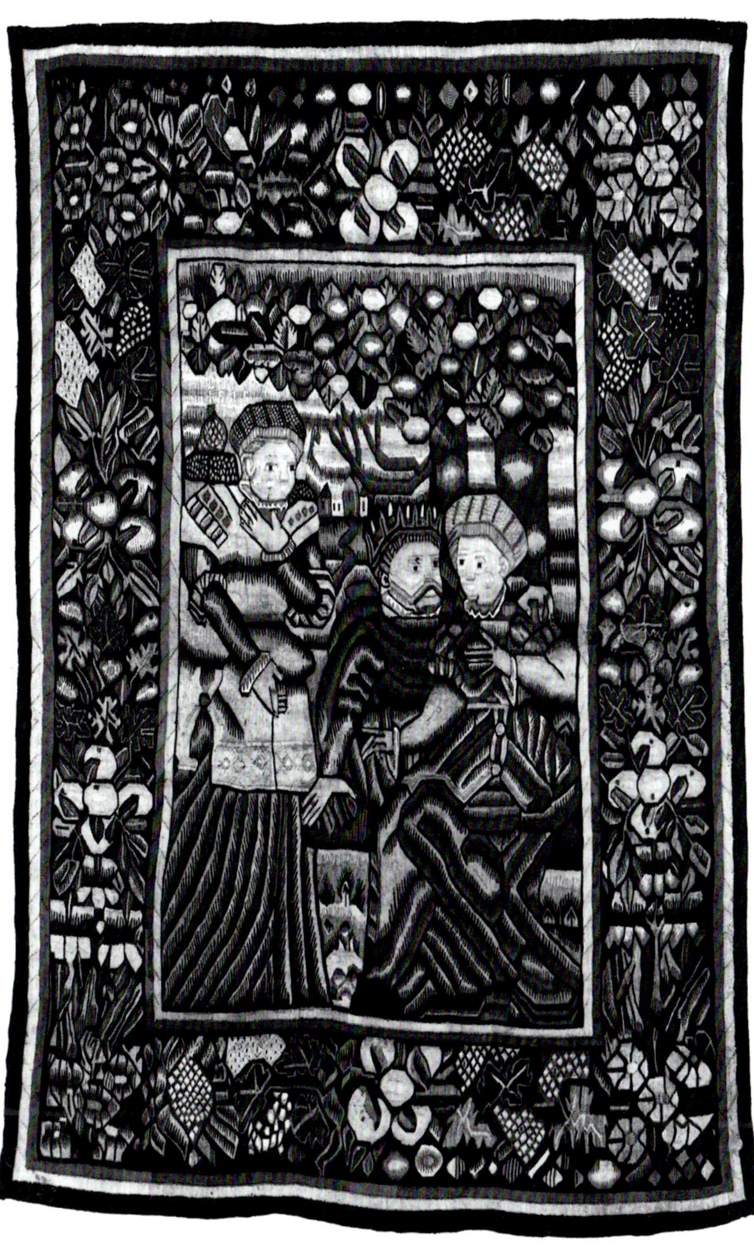

4.5 Pillow cover from Gudbrandsdal with a vase of flowers, birds, and animals. *Oslo Museum of Applied Art.*

4.6 "Lot and His Daughters," a tapestry from Heddal, Telemark. Note the frame of fruit and flowers, the low horizon, and the realistic perspective in the presentation of the figures. *Norwegian Folk Museum.*

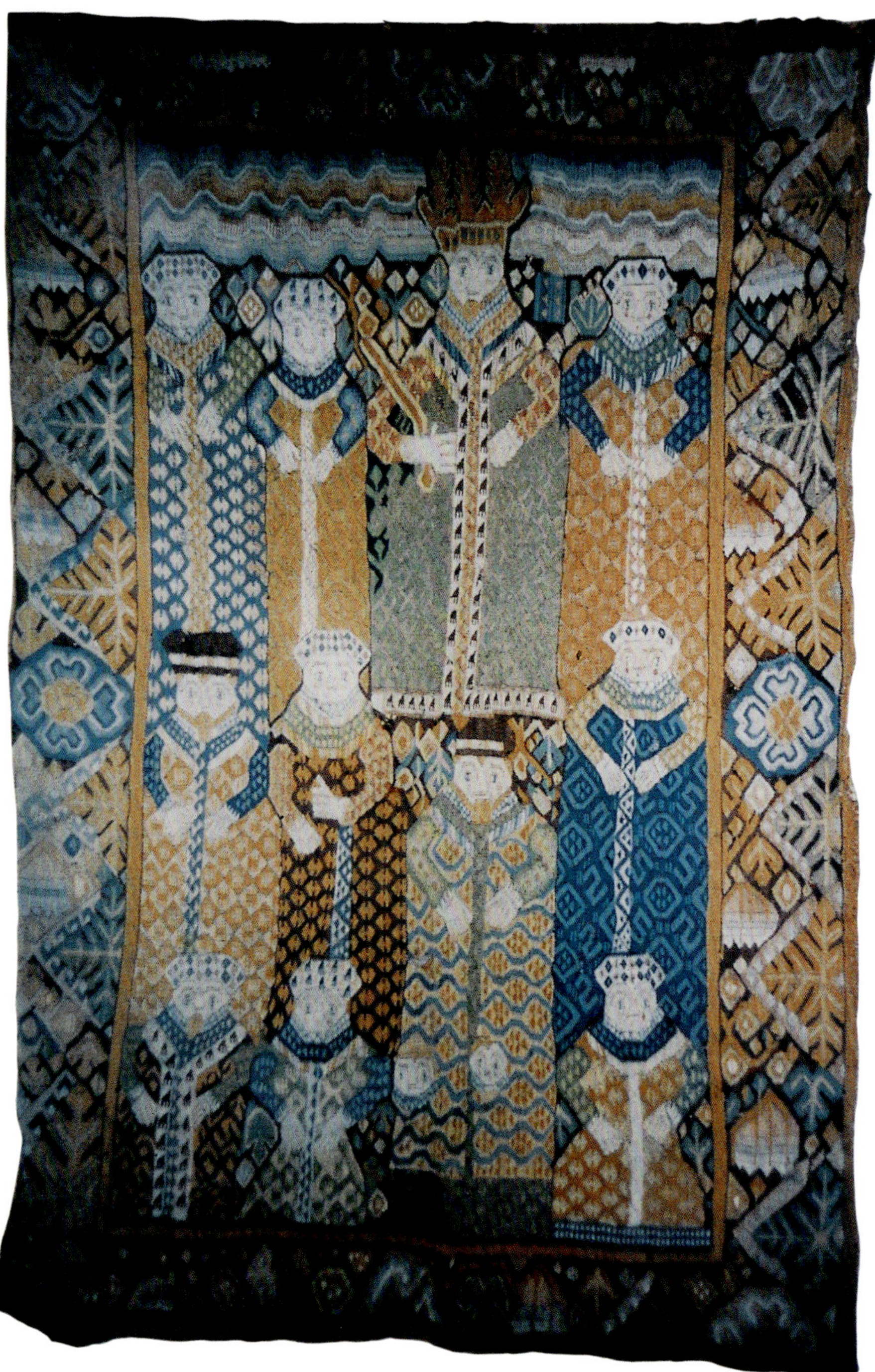

4.7 "Solomon's Wisdom," a seventeenth-century tapestry. Compare the placement of figures and the implied horizon with the tapestry seen in figure 4.6. Note also the lack of shading between colors, and the simplified presentation of fruit and flowers in the border. The realism and perspective brought to Norway by professional tapestry weavers in the late sixteenth century devolved into a less sophisticated style in later tapestries such as this. Solomon, with crown and scepter, stands in the middle *(top)* surrounded by courtiers and the Queen of Sheba. The two small heads at bottom are possibly remnants of a row of children seen in earlier renditions of this theme, a reference to Solomon's ability to distinguish between a boy and a girl by observing how they caught an apple. *Oslo Museum of Applied Art.*

floral patterns appeared, while the dovetailing technique, largely discarded
by continental weavers for more refined methods, remained an integral part
of Norwegian weavings. Some influences of the Renaissance were more last-
ing, chiefly the transition from the time-honored frieze of medieval weavings
(such as the Baldishol tapestry) to the upright, rectangular presentation of
a subject. The newly formatted tapestries were also given floral borders typical of European tapestries of the period, and the architecture and clothing
depicted in the Norwegian weavings represent the styles of the Renaissance
(fig. 4.7).

While the tapestry centers of Europe continued to perfect the realism
of their art, the Norwegian tapestry weavers, far removed from such professional influences, continued on their rather provincial path. However unin-
tentional it may have been, the gradual devolution into a less sophisticated
style resulted in tapestries with a powerful artistic effect. As noted by Thor
Kielland, former Director of the Oslo Museum of Applied Arts and author
of the three-volume *Norsk Billedvev,* "Paradoxically enough it may be said
of the development of European tapestry weaving, that the greater the tech-
nical efficiency of the craftsman, the worse his art. Once the plastic illusion
is introduced the true nature of weaving is undermined."[2] Kielland believed
that the strength and character inherent in the mixture of fiber and color,
and warp and weft, was diminished through the avid pursuit of realism. He
continued, with understandable national pride, "[Today] weaving sheds can
reproduce on their looms anything they want to, but in this very perfection
of technique is a danger; and I think it would do artists, about to work on
some monumental textile work, a lot of good to study at frequent intervals
the Gudbrandsdal tapestries with their austere poise."[3]

Although time has faded the colors in many tapestries, in some cases
completely distorting the intended design, their original color schemes can
sometimes be seen on the reverse side or between the threads. In general,
tapestries that were a product of the earlier, more sophisticated period
show a relatively natural, subtle use of color. Later tapestries exhibit fewer
nuances, with brighter, stronger hues. In both periods, prominent subjects
were projected through the use of outlining.

Biblical motifs were the subject of the majority of Norwegian tapestries.
This was a common practice throughout Europe, where the great continental
weaving sheds worked from cartoons drawn by masters such as Rubens and
Raphael. The early Norwegian tapestries were usually either copies of such
European work or patterned on illustrations found in the Bible, and the
somewhat limited number of motifs selected for translation into tapestry by
Norwegian weavers were copied over and over again. Professionally trained
weavers of the early period possibly worked from cartoons, but it is likely that
later weavers used an existing tapestry as a model, or they may have worked
from memory. After many renditions of the same motif it is not surprising that
the initial purpose of the weaving became obscured or even lost: details that
originally contributed to the intent of the subject were gradually simplified

into symbolic figures or were deleted entirely, and borders that had once been flowers and fruit became simplified frames of zigzags, stylized eight-petaled roses, and repetitive geometric shapes. When a weaver could not read, inscriptions might be unknowingly reversed or words or letters left out, and the dates and initials which were often woven into a tapestry might be faithfully copied from one weaving to the next, posing interesting questions for the textile historian trying to determine the date of a particular tapestry (see fig. 4.10).

The parable of the Wise and Foolish Virgins was the most popular motif represented in Norwegian tapestry. Although the virgins were a well-known theme in Medieval Europe, they were rarely the subject of tapestries except in Norway. The parable was represented by two rows of women wearing bridal crowns, the wise virgins in the top row with their lamps full and burning brightly, ready to light the way for Christ, the foolish virgins in the lower row with their empty lanterns, holding handkerchiefs to signify sorrow at missing the wedding. Through time the virgins lost many of their identifying characteristics, such as the lanterns and handkerchiefs, and simply became two rows of women wearing bridal crowns (figs. 4.1 and 4.8–4.9).

The Three Magi and the Adoration was another motif commonly found in Norwegian tapestries. Again, the subject was well known throughout Europe, but its representation in tapestry was little known outside of Norway. The three kings were shown mounted on horseback individually, and then as a group around Mary and the baby Jesus. Early renditions placed each of the three riders in their own quarter of the picture, with the adoration occupying the final quarter. Later tapestries place the three kings and the nativity scene within an oval frame (figs. 4.10–4.11).

Other biblical themes appeared in Norwegian tapestries but with less frequency. Notable among these were interpretations of The Feast of Herod, The Wisdom of Solomon, and Lot and His Daughters (see figs. 4.6–4.7).

The number of non-Biblical subjects was limited, probably due to the lack of good sources for illustrations. Books other than the Bible were rare, as were artists who might draw cartoons of well-known secular themes for the early professional craftsmen to copy. A few non-Biblical subjects did find their way into tapestry work, however, including the coat of arms of Christian IV, King of Denmark and Norway; legends and myths, such as the Saga of Guimar and the Shield of Medusa; and popular Renaissance themes, such as the fountain of life, the tree of life, and intertwining fruit and flowers (figs. 4.12–4.13). A notable exception to the pictorial themes was the abstract *skybragd*, or cloud design, a pattern consisting of palmette shapes in alternating shades of red and blue (fig. 4.14).

Western Norway was dominated by other weaving techniques, but there were some examples of tapestries from this area. The bridal couple, set on a dark background and surrounded by foliage and animals, was a theme unique to the western districts. A less sophisticated version of the Wise and Foolish Virgins was also found, and there were a number of coverlets with pictorial subjects woven in the resident square-weave technique (figs. 4.15–4.17).

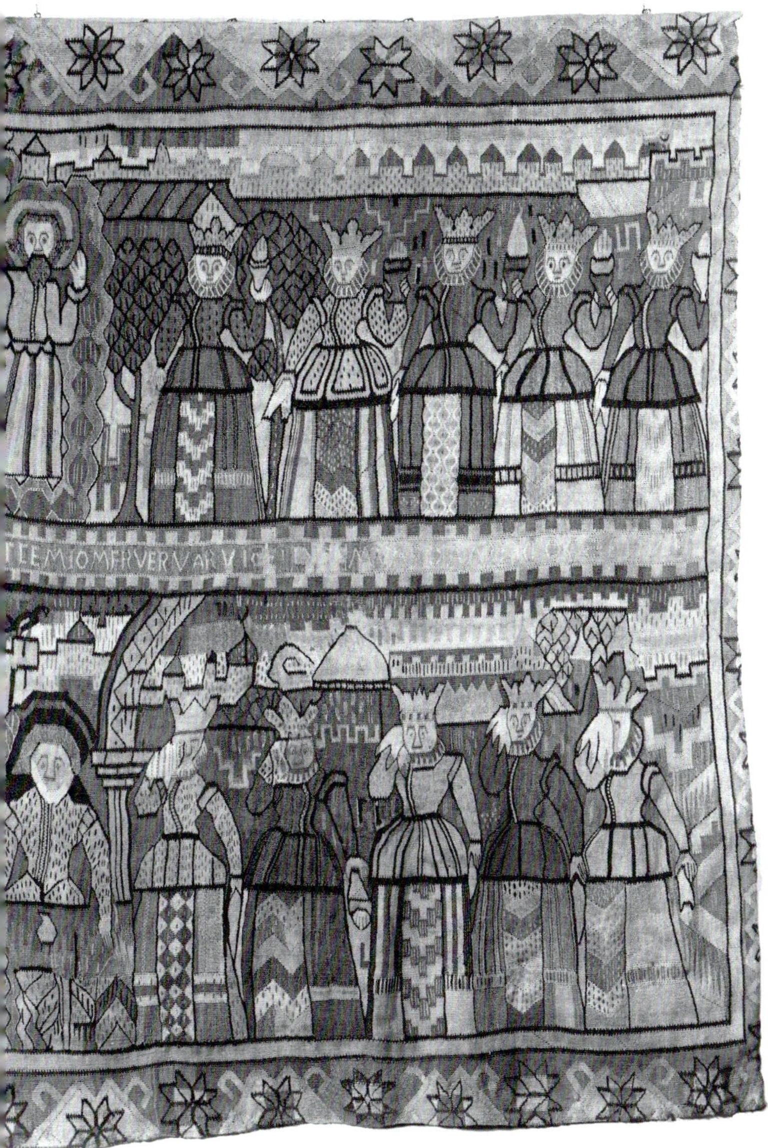

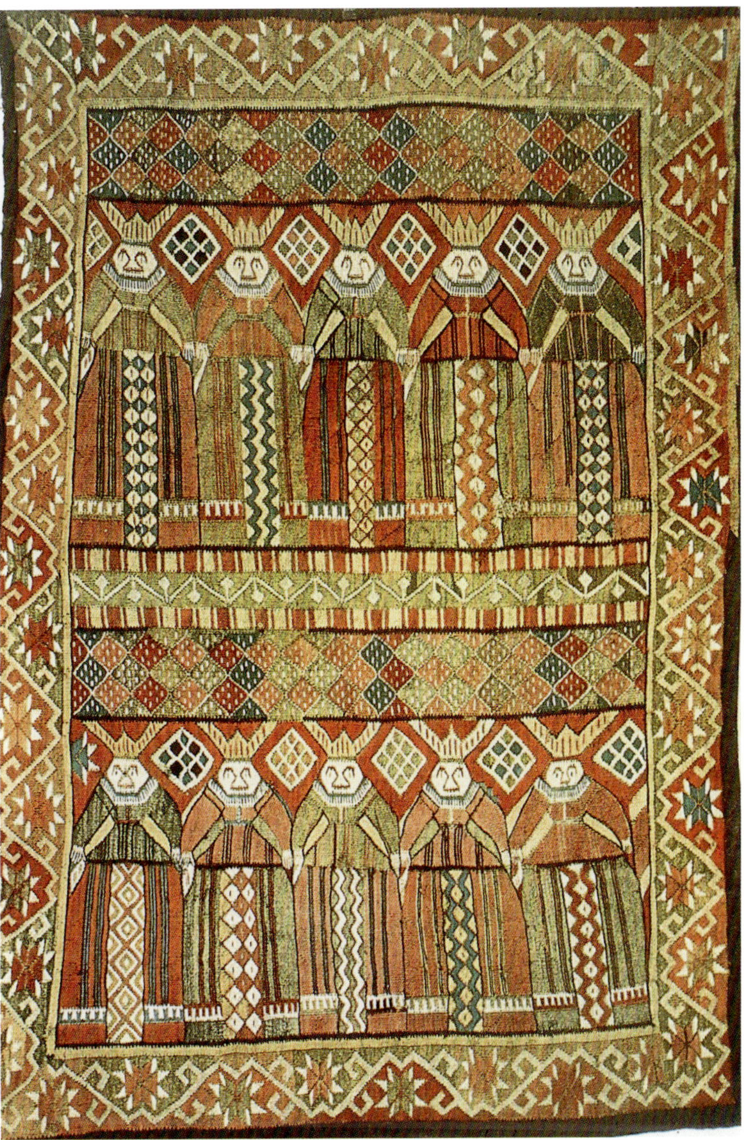

4.8 An early version of the "Wise and Foolish Virgins" tapestry. The wise virgins in the upper row hold their brightly burning lanterns high, and Christ stands to the left. The foolish virgins in the lower row hold their empty lanterns in one hand and a handkerchief in the other, and an oil seller appears behind his table on the left. The skyline of a city can be seen in the background, and between the two rows is an inscription: DE FEM IOMFRVER VAR VISE DE FEM VAR DAARLIG (Five Virgins Were Wise, Five Were Foolish). Gudbrandsdal or Valdres, seventeenth century. *Courtesy of The Brooklyn Museum. Gift of Frank L. Babbott.*

4.9 A later version of the "Wise and Foolish Virgins" tapestry. The figures of Christ and the oil seller have disappeared, and the virgins' lanterns and handkerchiefs have been discarded or become unrecognizable. The absence of the city skyline in the background has removed any sense of depth, and the inscription, usually placed between the two rows of figures, has been replaced with a row of pattern. *Oslo Museum of Applied Art.*

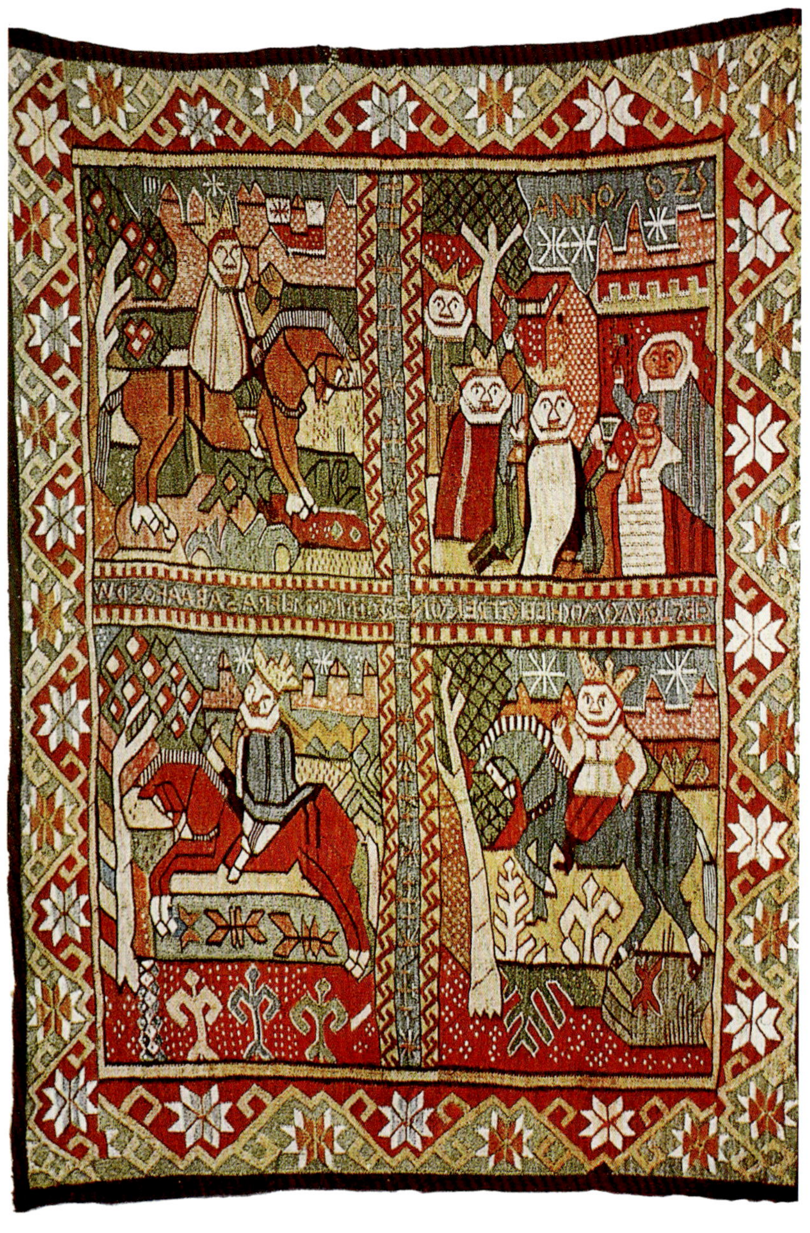

4.10 The "Magi and the Adoration" tapestry in a square format. The three kings appear individually in three of the squares, and the fourth square presents the Adoration with the three kings grouped around the Mother and Child. The year (ANNO 1625) woven into the upper right corner is probably copied from an earlier tapestry and does not reflect the year that this tapestry was woven. *Oslo Museum of Applied Art.*

4.11 The "Magi and the Adoration" tapestry in an oval format. The Magi on horseback and the Adoration appear surrounded by a frame of animals. An angel looks on from each corner. *Oslo Museum of Applied Art.*

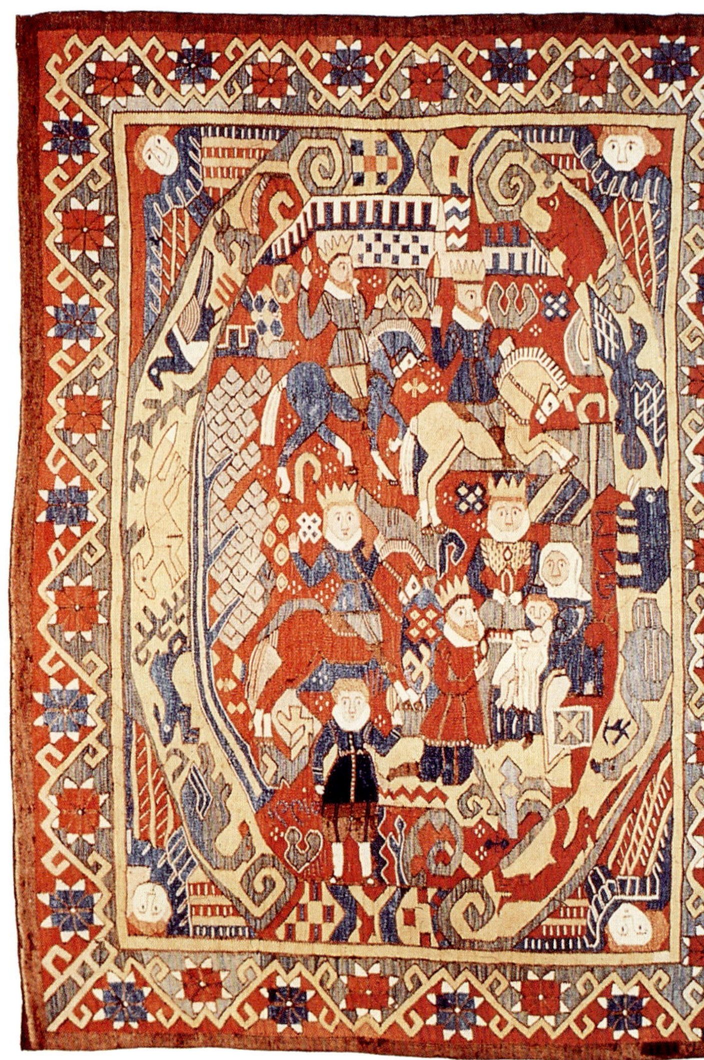

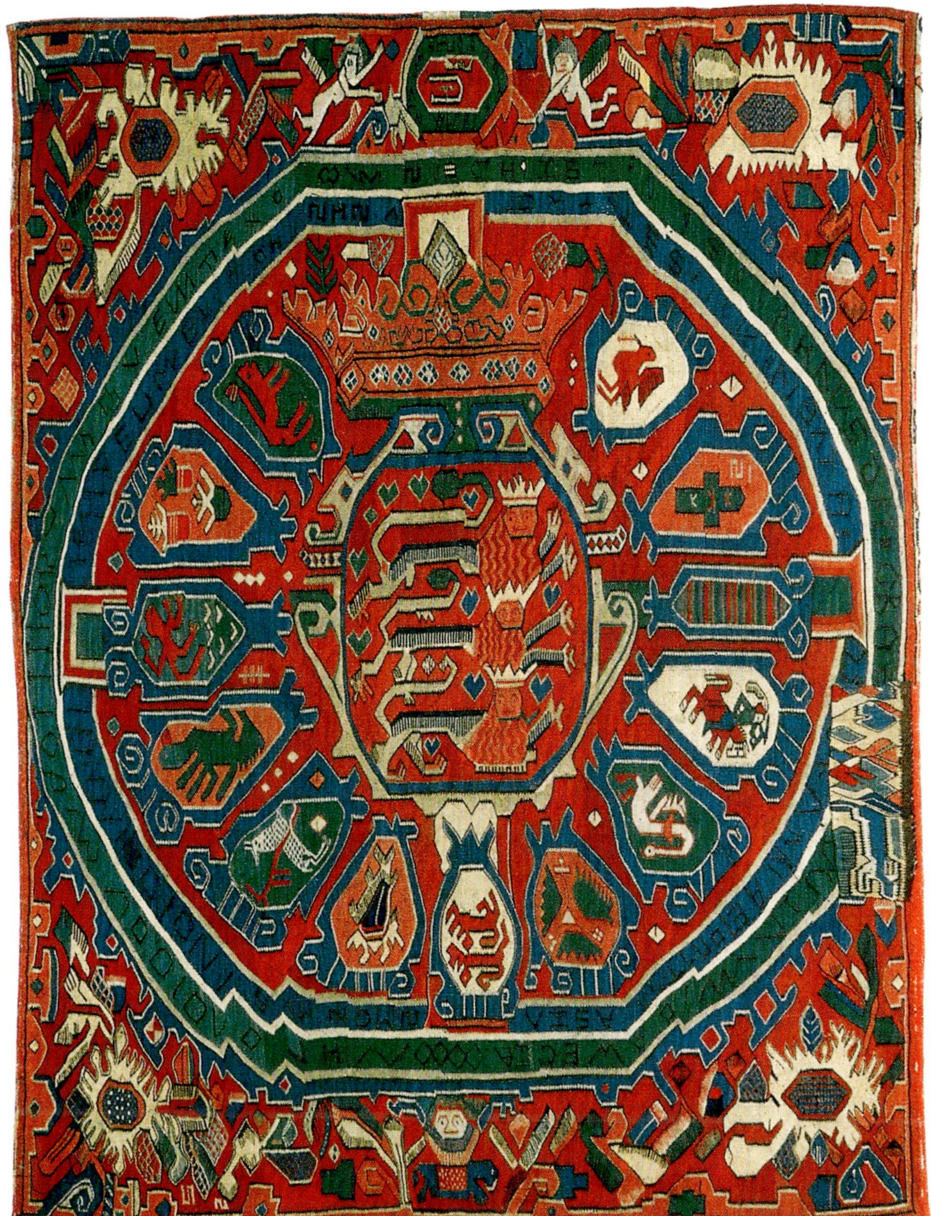

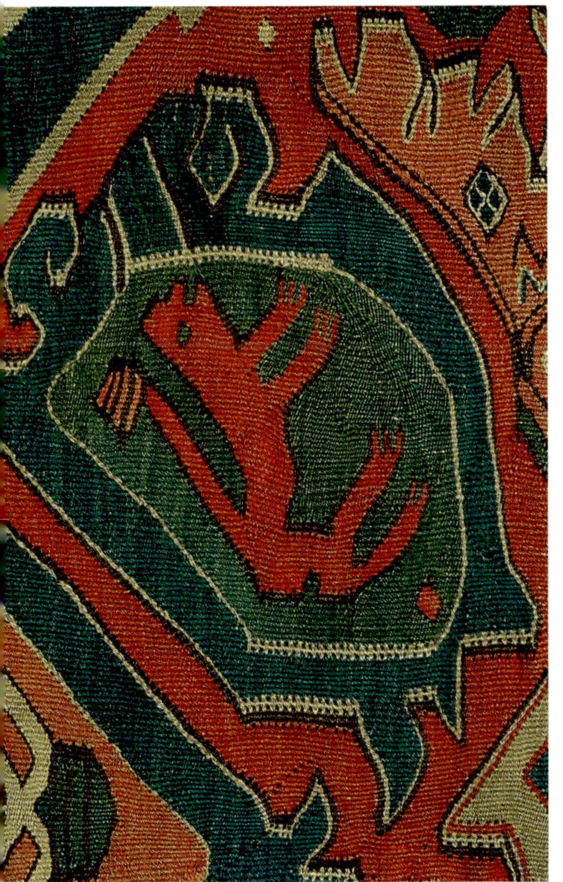

4.12 The coat of arms of King Christian IV surrounded by escutcheons
of the thirteen provinces under Danish rule. The Norwegian lion is seen
to the left of the crown and in detailed view. Probably Gudbrandsdal.
Norwegian Folk Museum.

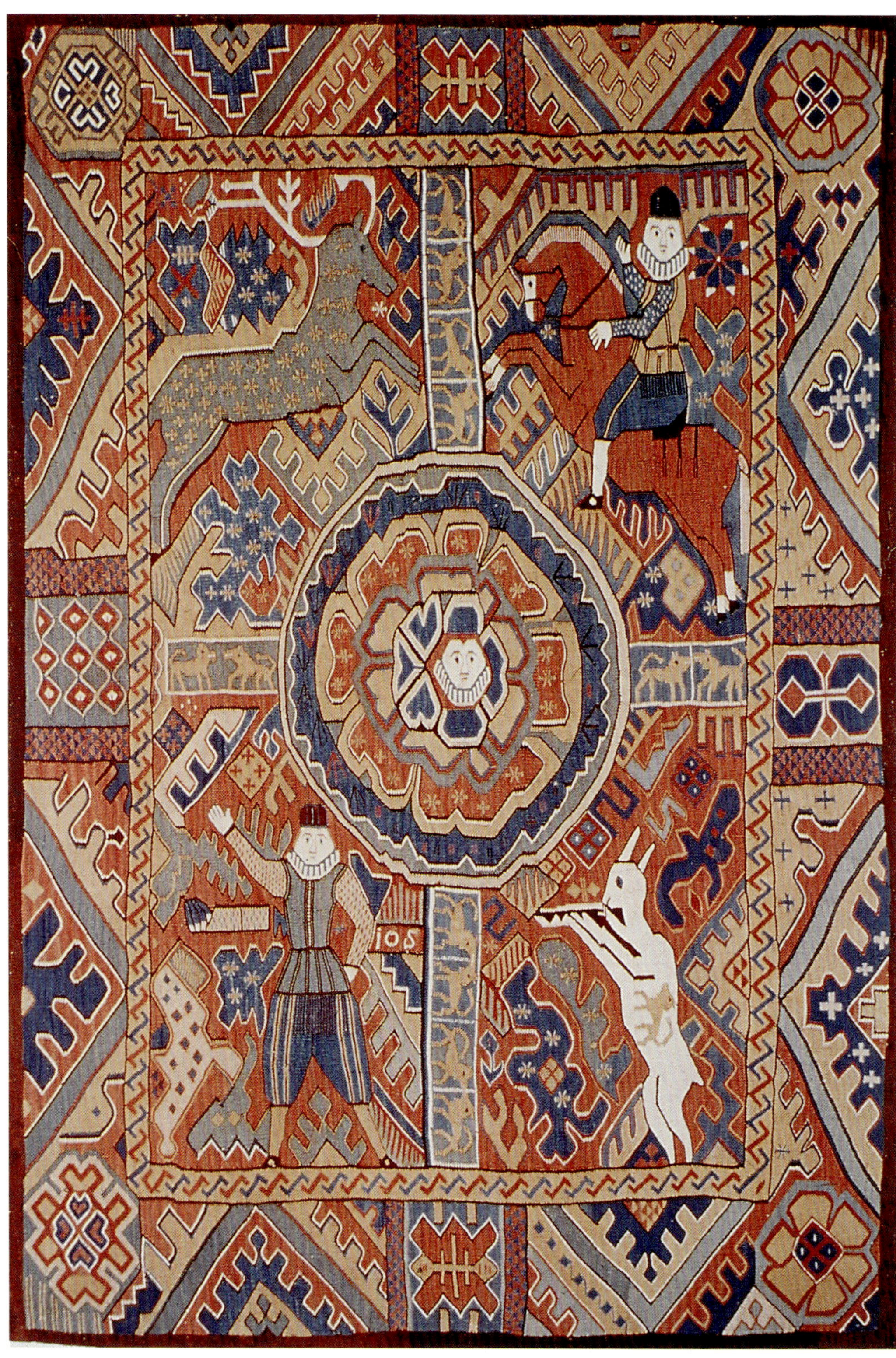

4.13 A tapestry possibly representing the Saga of
Guimar, a Breton legend of a knight who discovers
a magical white deer. *Oslo Museum of Applied Art.*

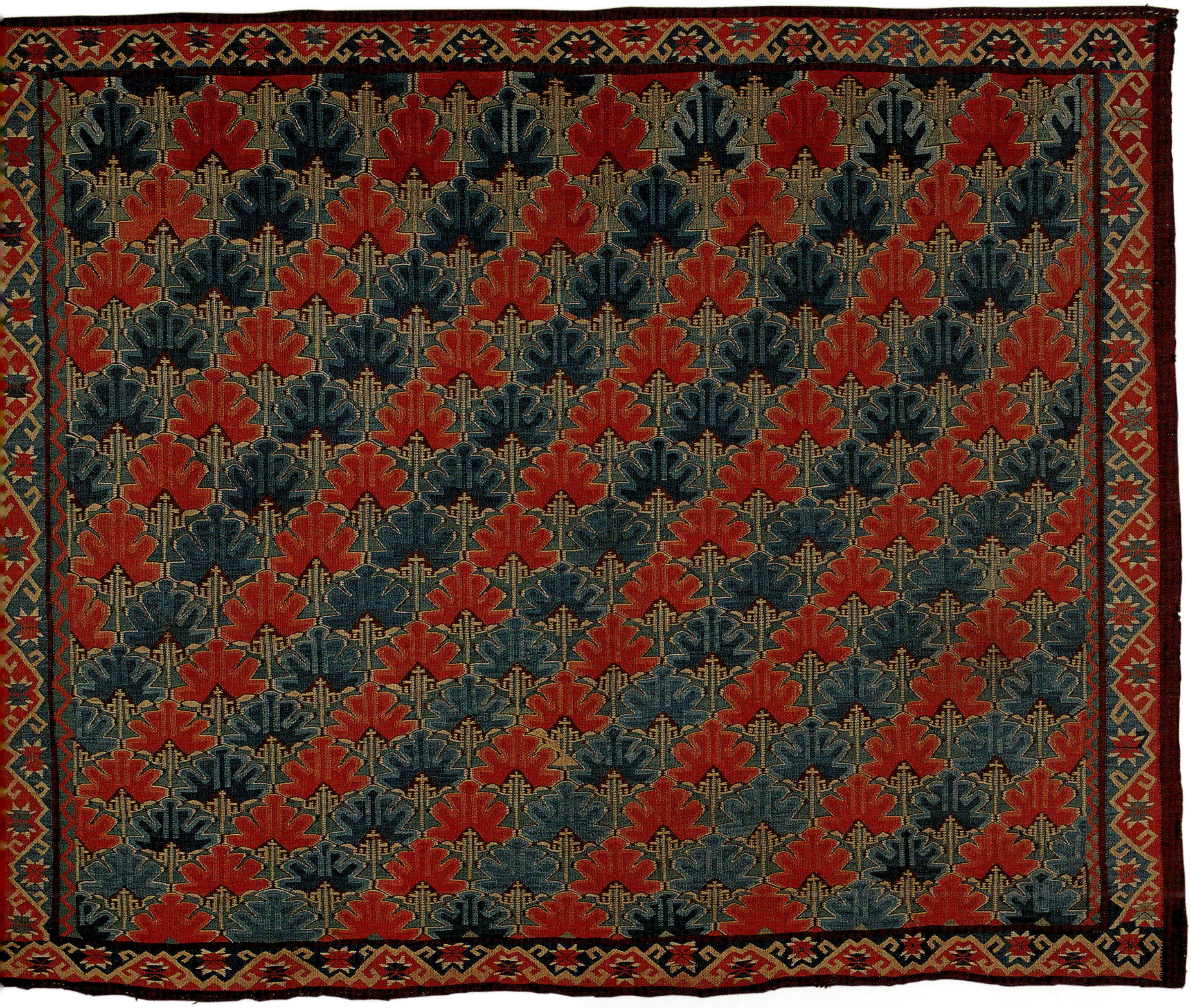

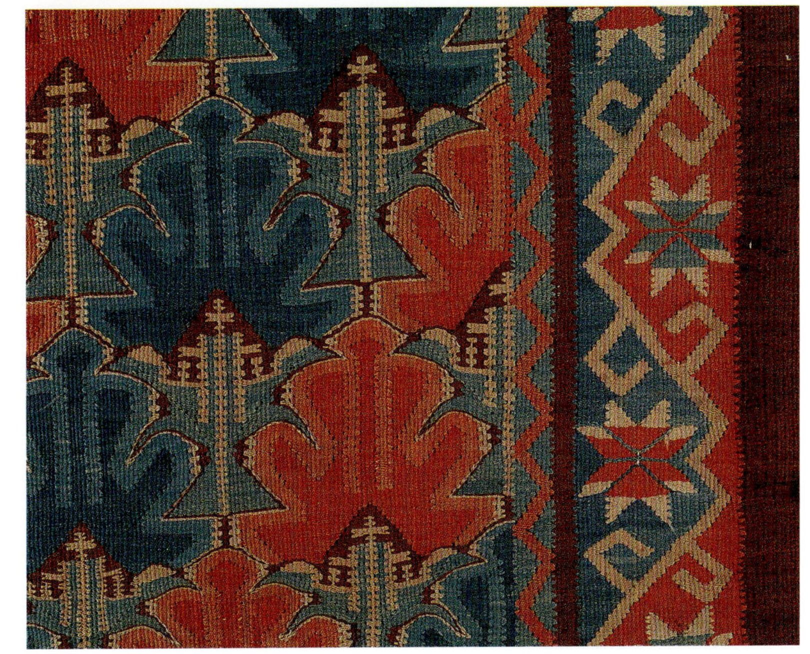

4.14 The *skybragd*, or cloud pattern, a series of
palmette shapes woven in alternating rows of red
and blue. Gudbrandsdal. *Norwegian Folk Museum.*

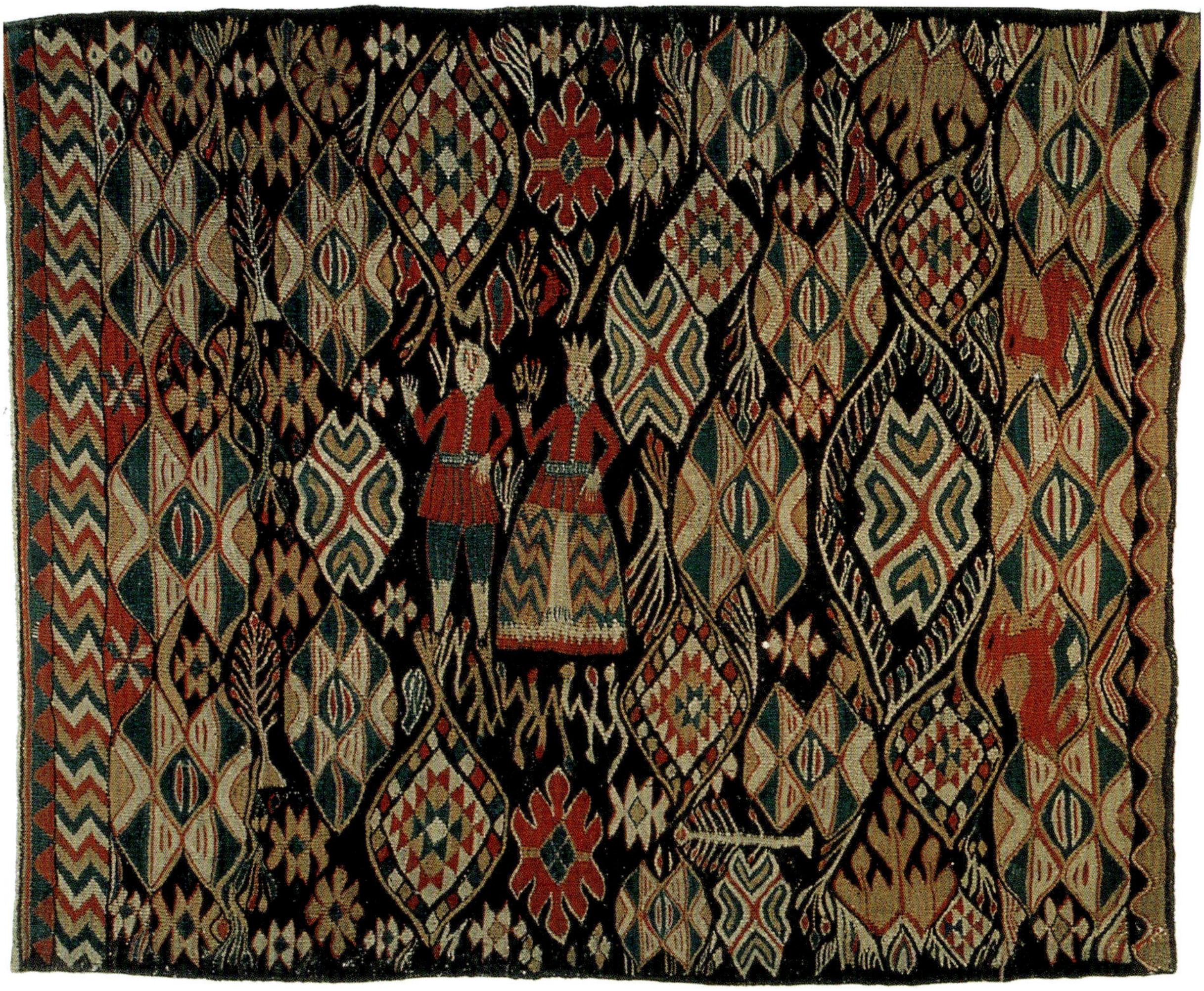

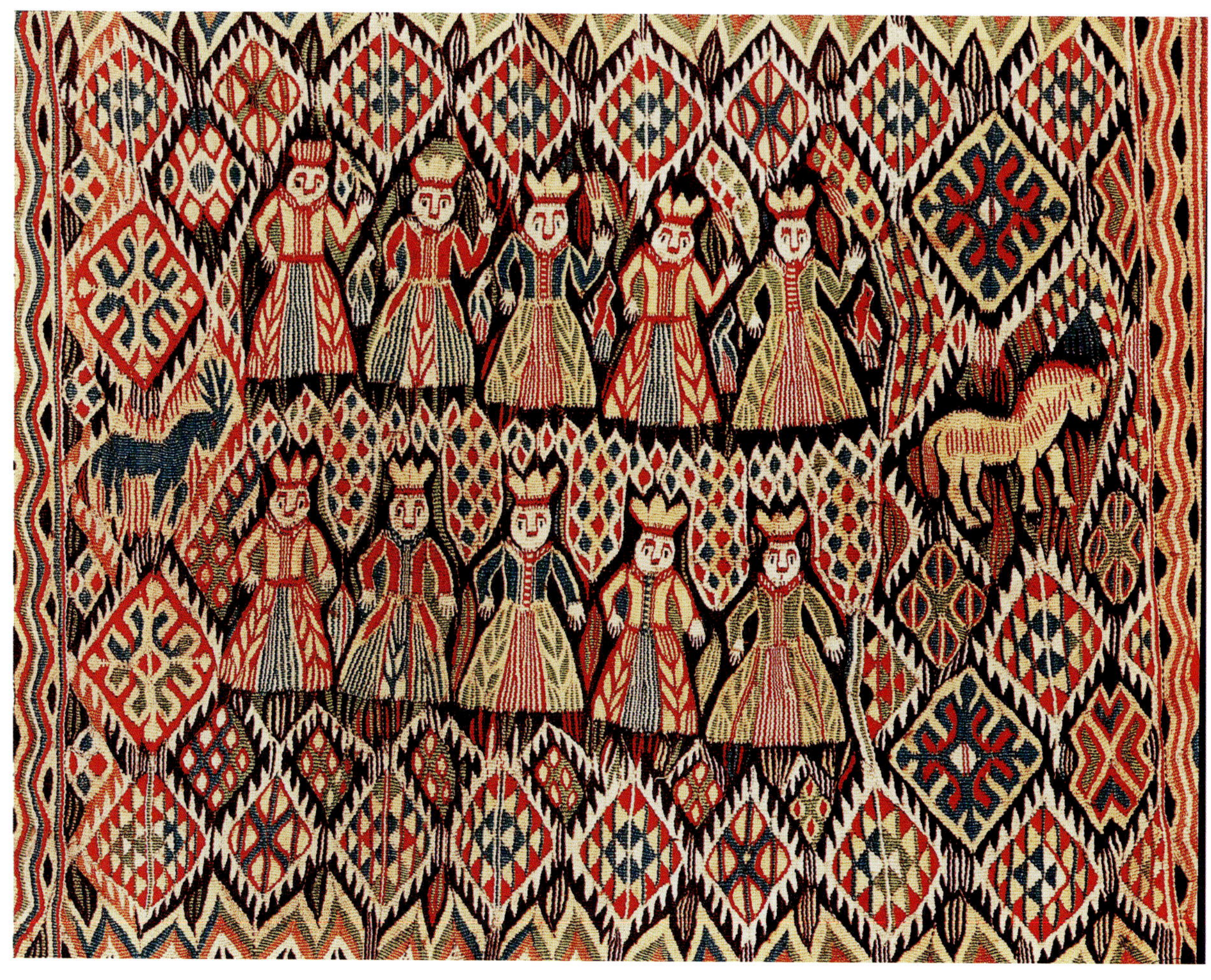

4.15 The bridal couple was a tapestry theme found in the western districts. Sogn and Fjordane. *Norwegian Folk Museum.*

4.16 A simplified version of the "Wise and Foolish Virgins" was found in west-coast tapestries. *Historical Museum, University of Bergen.*

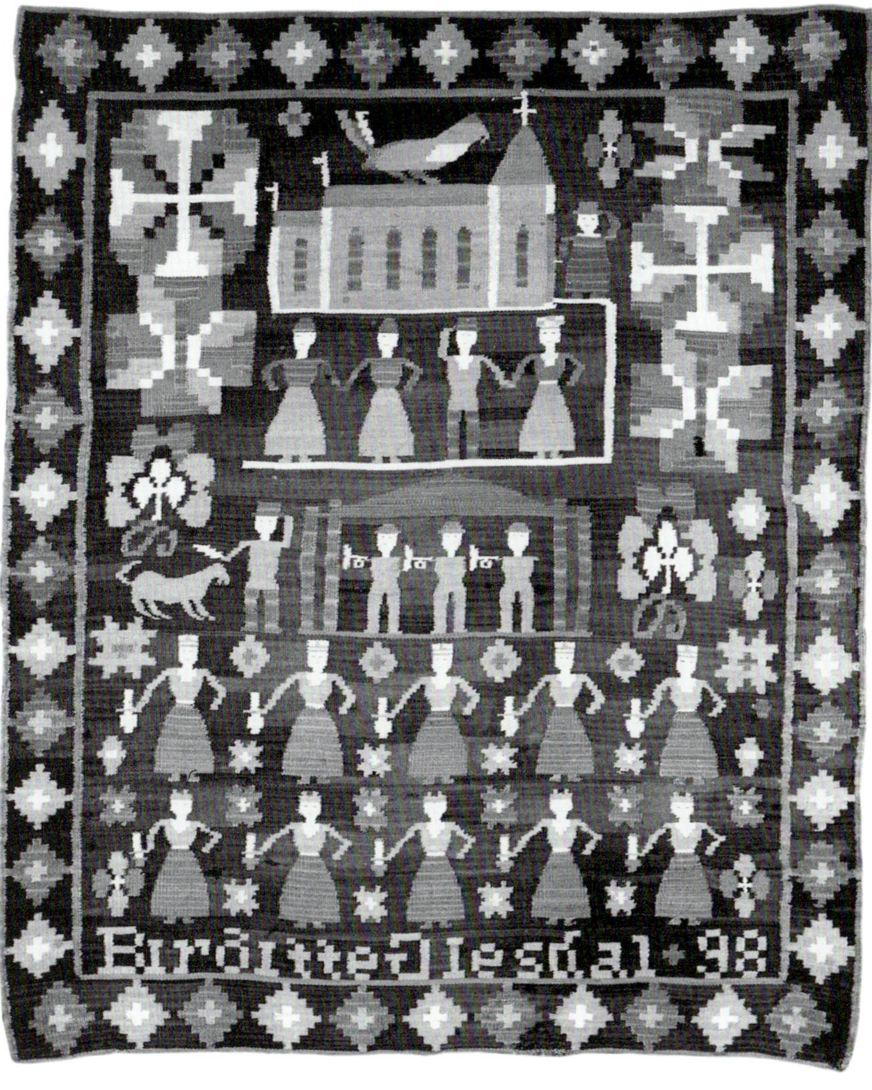

4.17 A pictorial coverlet woven in the square-weave technique with inscription "Birgitte Glesdal 98." The bridal couple appears under the church and in detailed view *(bottom).* Sunnfjord. *Historical Museum, University of Bergen.*

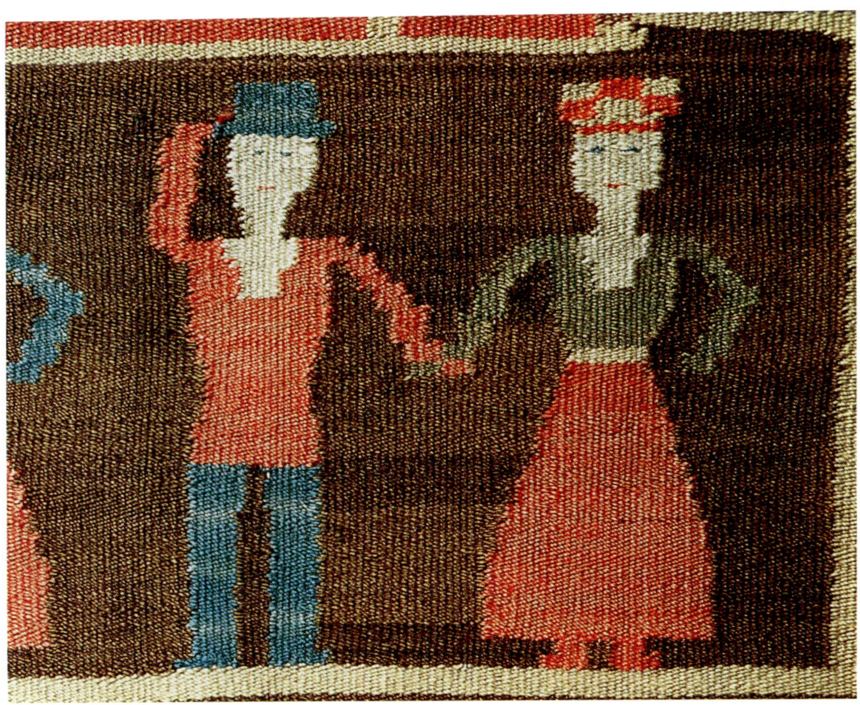

A broader range of motifs was used in the smaller, more "affordable" pillow and bench covers woven in the tapestry technique. Elements from larger tapestries, such as a pair of women from the Five Wise and Five Foolish Virgins or a single rider from the Three Magi, were popular subjects. Parrots, ducks, and stags were also common, as were mythical creatures. Other designs included the cloud pattern and stylized motifs, such as the tree of life, the eight-petaled rose, the heart rosette, the cross, the lily, and the pomegranate, many of which appear in geometric form in the double-weave coverlets (fig. 4.18; and see fig. 4.5).

Materials and Looms

A two-ply yarn of *spælsau* guard hair (noted for its brilliance, especially when dyed) was the weft material of choice in the Norwegian tapestries. Occasionally this weft material was supplemented by the use of linen, silk, or even decorative metal thread. Warp threads were usually a two-ply linen, although in the western pictorial work a warp of tightly spun wool was common. The warp threads could be spaced as widely as six ends per inch or as closely as ten ends per inch.

The size of a tapestry varied from six by eight feet for a monumental piece to a modest four by five feet suitable for a bed cover. Pillow covers were usually square, from eighteen to twenty-four inches in dimension, while the rectangular bench covers, similar in width to the pillow covers, varied greatly in length. The longer bench covers, which could measure as much as sixteen feet in length, were intended for built-in benches that ran along the walls of older homes.

The standard tapestry loom, an upright frame with beams at the top and bottom between which the warp threads were tightly strung, was probably introduced into Norway in the late sixteenth century by immigrant tapestry weavers from the continent (fig. 4.19). Although older looms of this type have not survived in eastern Norway, it is probable that some version of the two-beamed upright loom was used by tapestry weavers in the area. The survival of a two-beamed loom in the western districts, possibly inspired in design by an early tapestry loom, offers support for this theory. A two-beamed variation of the warp-weighted loom, surviving in a single instance, may also have been an offshoot of the early tapestry loom (see figs. 5.29–5.31).

Weaving Techniques

Although any textile used as a wall decoration can be referred to as a tapestry, the coverlets were woven in a true tapestry technique. In the weft-faced plain weave of a tapestry coverlet, individual bobbins of weft yarn traveled back and forth in their own area of the warp, independently building up small portions of the pattern. This differed from most other forms of weaving in which a single weft thread traveled the entire distance from selvage to

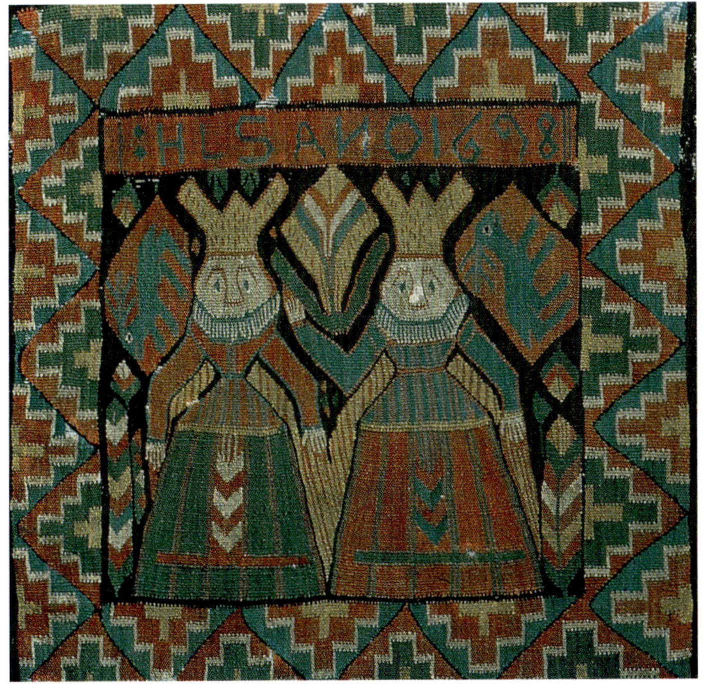

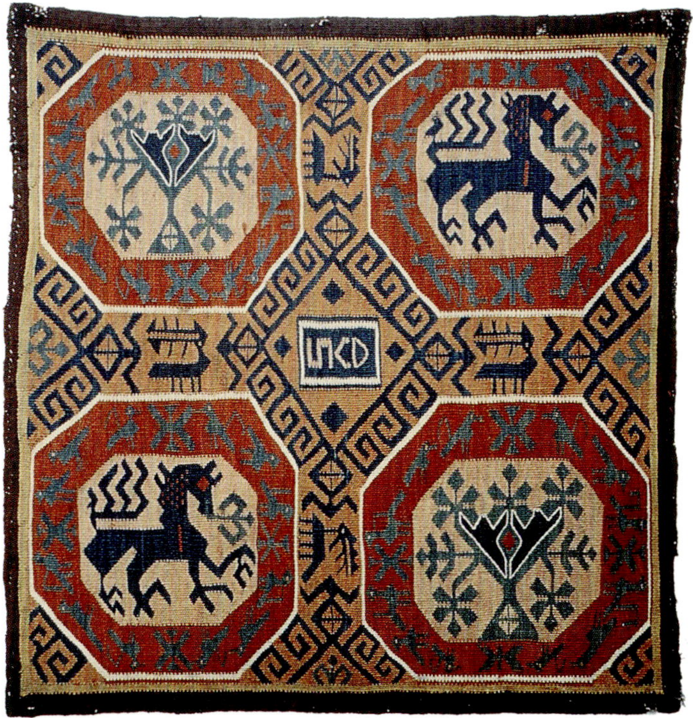

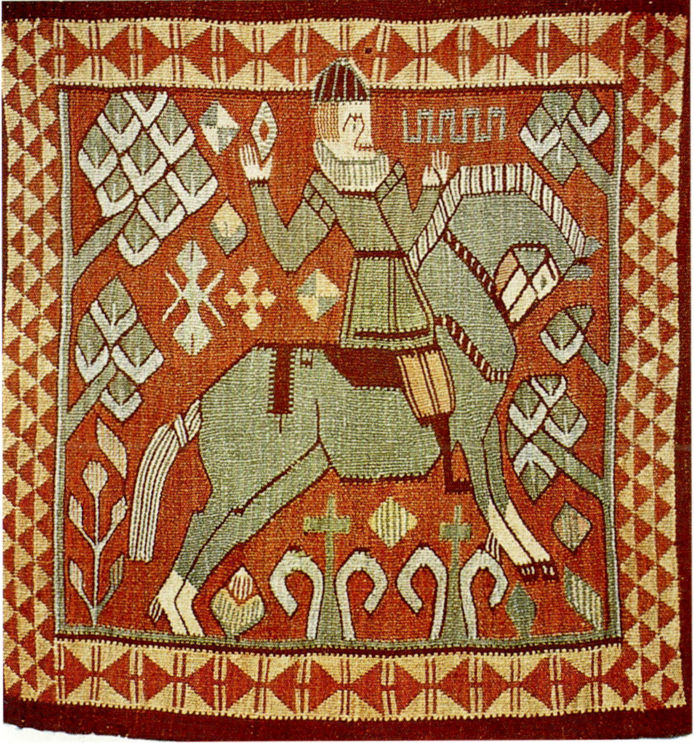

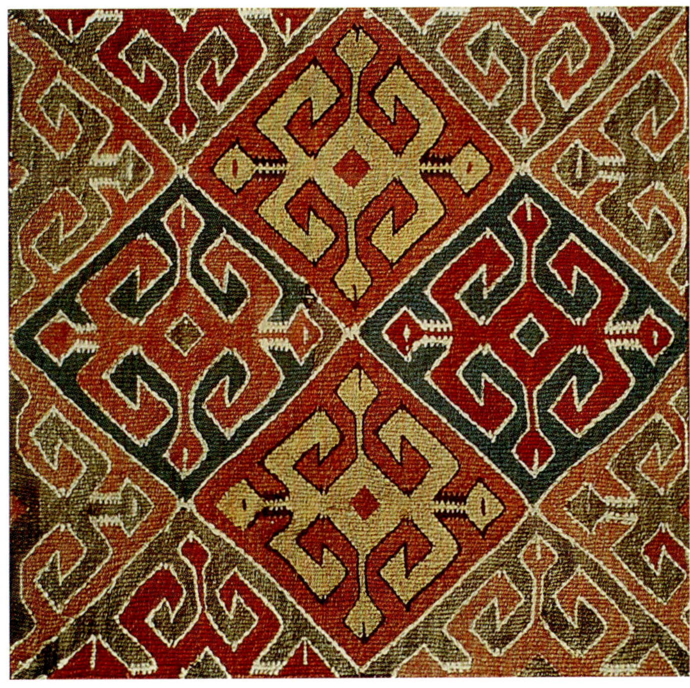

4.18 Pillow covers in the tapestry technique: *(top left)* two women wearing crowns, a detail from the "Wise and Foolish Virgins" tapestries, Norwegian Folk Museum; *(bottom left)* a single rider, similar to those in the "Magi and the Adoration" tapestries; *(top right)* mythical animals and trees; *(bottom right)* a simplification of the lily cross motif. *Oslo Museum of Applied Art.*

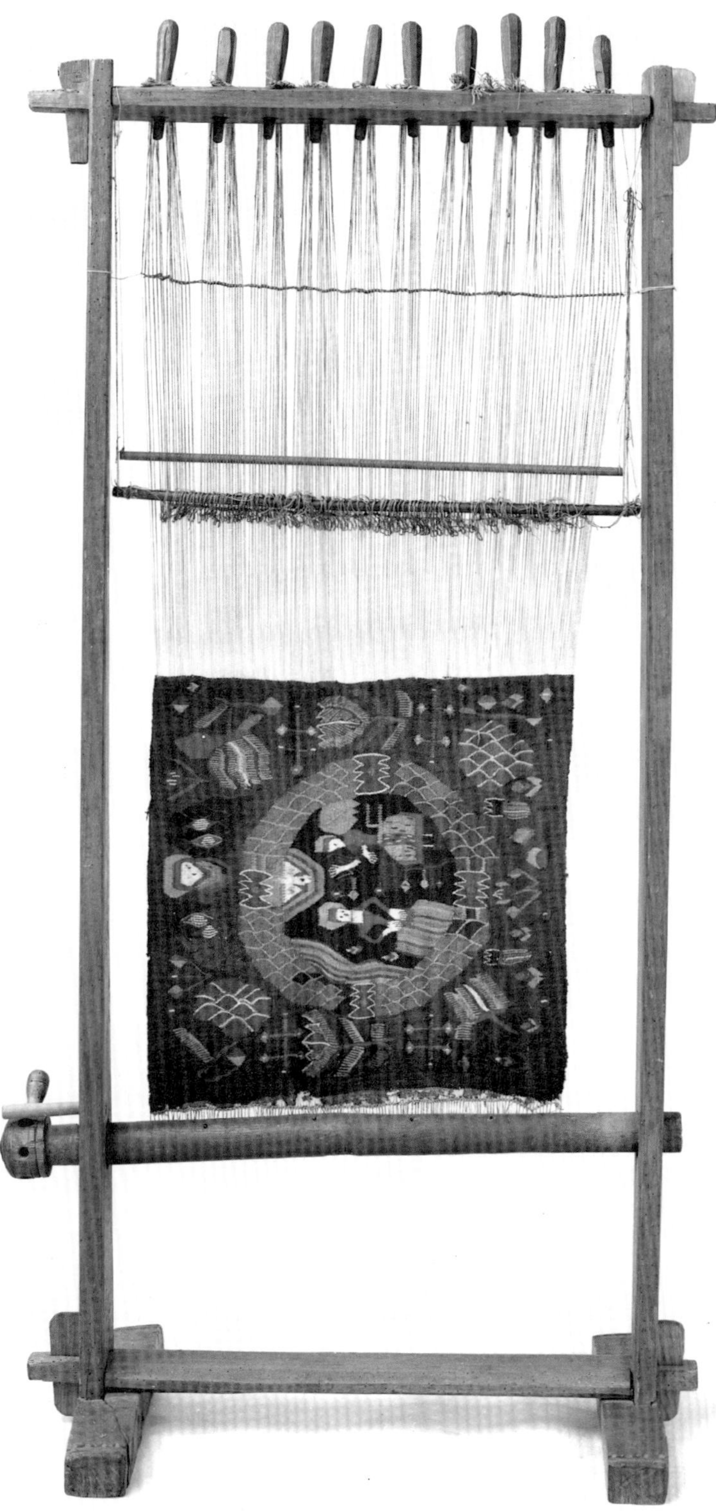

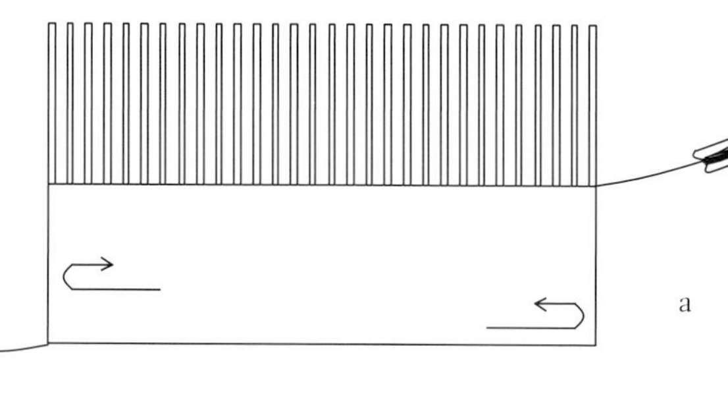
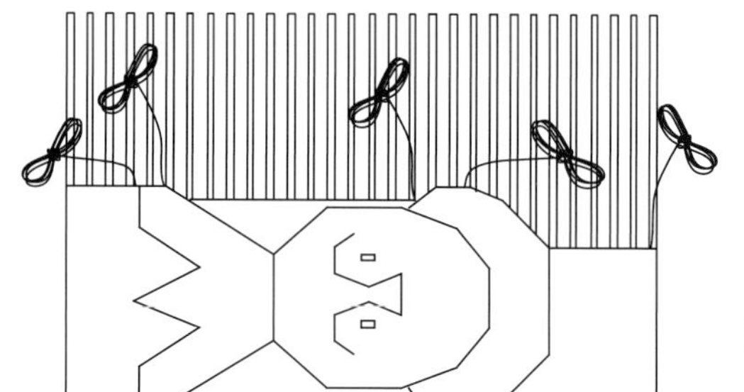

4.20 Tapestry technique: *(a)* The weft travels from selvage to selvage in most types of weaving. *(b)* In a tapestry weave, many weft threads travel back and forth in their own small area of the warp, and individual areas are built up at different rates.

4.19 A small tapestry loom with rotating lower beam and pegs for fastening warp threads to the fixed upper beam. *Nordic Museum, Stockholm.*

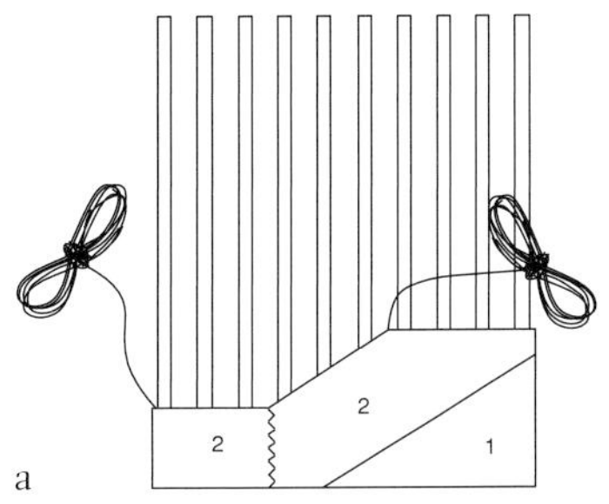

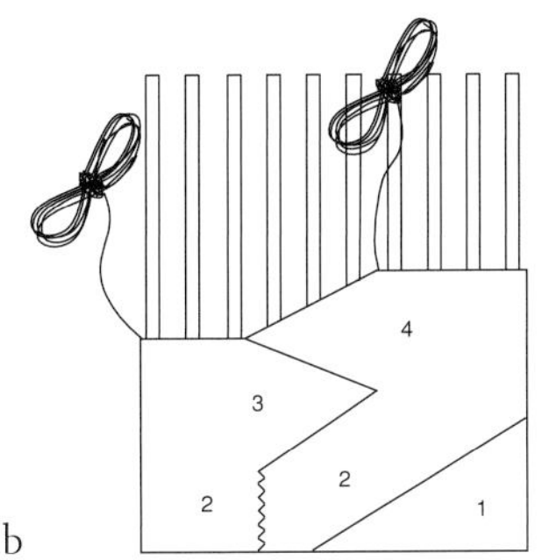

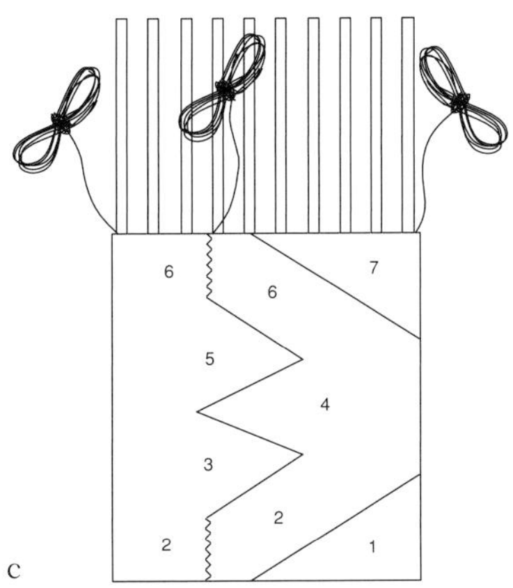

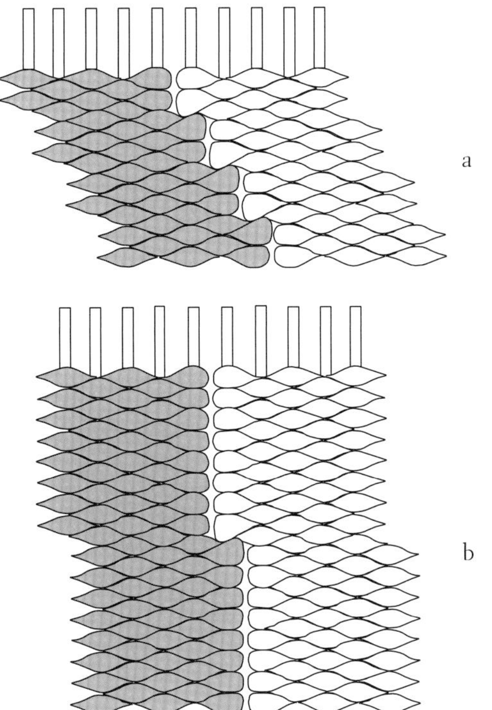

4.22 Sloping lines: *(a)* Noticeable slits do not appear when weaving gently sloping lines. *(b)* Slits appear at a point where vertical or steeply sloping lines are woven.

4.23 *(Below)* The dovetailing technique allows vertical lines to be woven without a slit. Neighboring weft threads take turns weaving around a common warp thread: *(a)* square dovetailing; *(b)* pointed dovetailing.

4.21 Like a game of pickup sticks in reverse, underlying areas must be woven first in tapestry: *(a)* Area 1 underlies its neighbors and therefore is woven first. Area 2 includes both sides of a line of dovetailing, which are woven at the same time (see fig. 4.23). The right side of area 2 continues at an angle to prepare for area 3. *(b)* Area 3 expands into a wedge before area 4 is woven. *(c)* Area 5 is woven, followed by another line of dovetailing in area 6 that requires two sections to be woven at the same time. Area 7 is woven last.

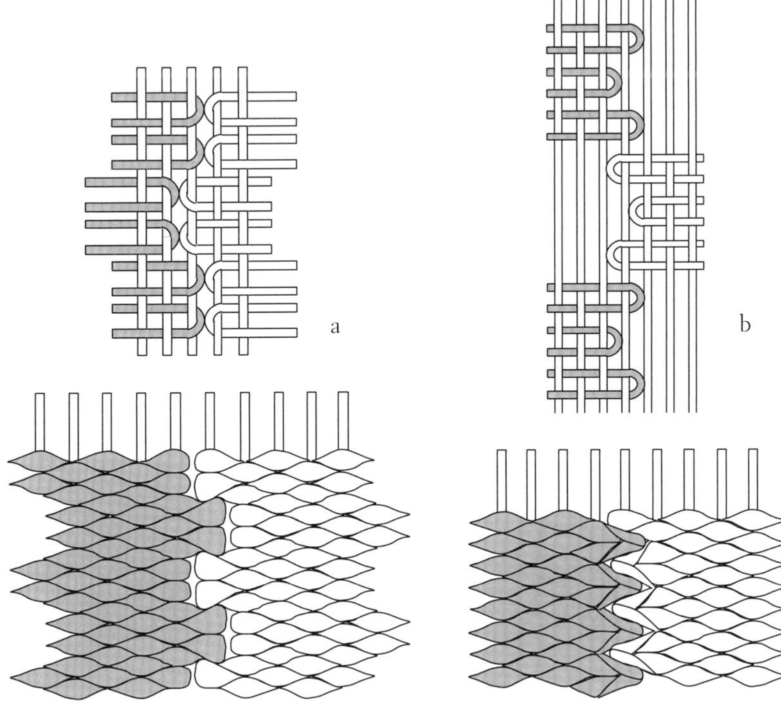

selvage (fig. 4.20). Tapestry weaving progressed rather slowly, as all the weft threads were laid into the warp by hand as opposed to being thrown through an open shed on a shuttle, but the weaver was relatively free to create pictures or designs at will.

It took years of experience to perfect the tapestry technique, but for the most part the weaver filled in small sections of a design following the basic rule that underlying areas must be woven first (fig. 4.21). Proper treatment of vertical lines or lines that were steeply sloped was the main challenge facing the weaver. This was due to the small vertical slit that formed when two adjacent areas of weaving met. In a gently sloping line, the interface between the two areas was constantly moving so that noticeable slits never developed. In a vertical line, however, or a steeply sloping line (which was actually a series of small vertical lines), the slits became more pronounced (fig. 4.22). This was especially troublesome in a tapestry designed to hang on its side. Long slits could be sewn together from the back when weaving was complete, a custom eventually adopted by most continental tapestry workshops, but the Norwegian tapestry weavers retained the earlier practice of weaving vertical closures with overlapping notches. The *hakketeknikk* or dovetailing technique required neighboring areas of the weave to alternately share a common warp thread and gave the line of interface a somewhat jagged appearance (fig. 4.23). Since the dovetailing solution presented the weaver with a fairly complex puzzle in balancing the progress of many interrelated weft threads, tapestries were normally woven on their side (with the bottom and top of the weaving becoming the sides of the finished tapestry) to reduce the number of vertical lines. This was particularly helpful when human figures were a part of the design, as a brief study of the number of vertical and horizontal lines required by such a subject will reveal. Coverlets that were woven with figures "standing," as was occasionally attempted by the less sophisticated tapestry weavers of the western districts, demonstrate the difficulties involved (fig. 4.24).

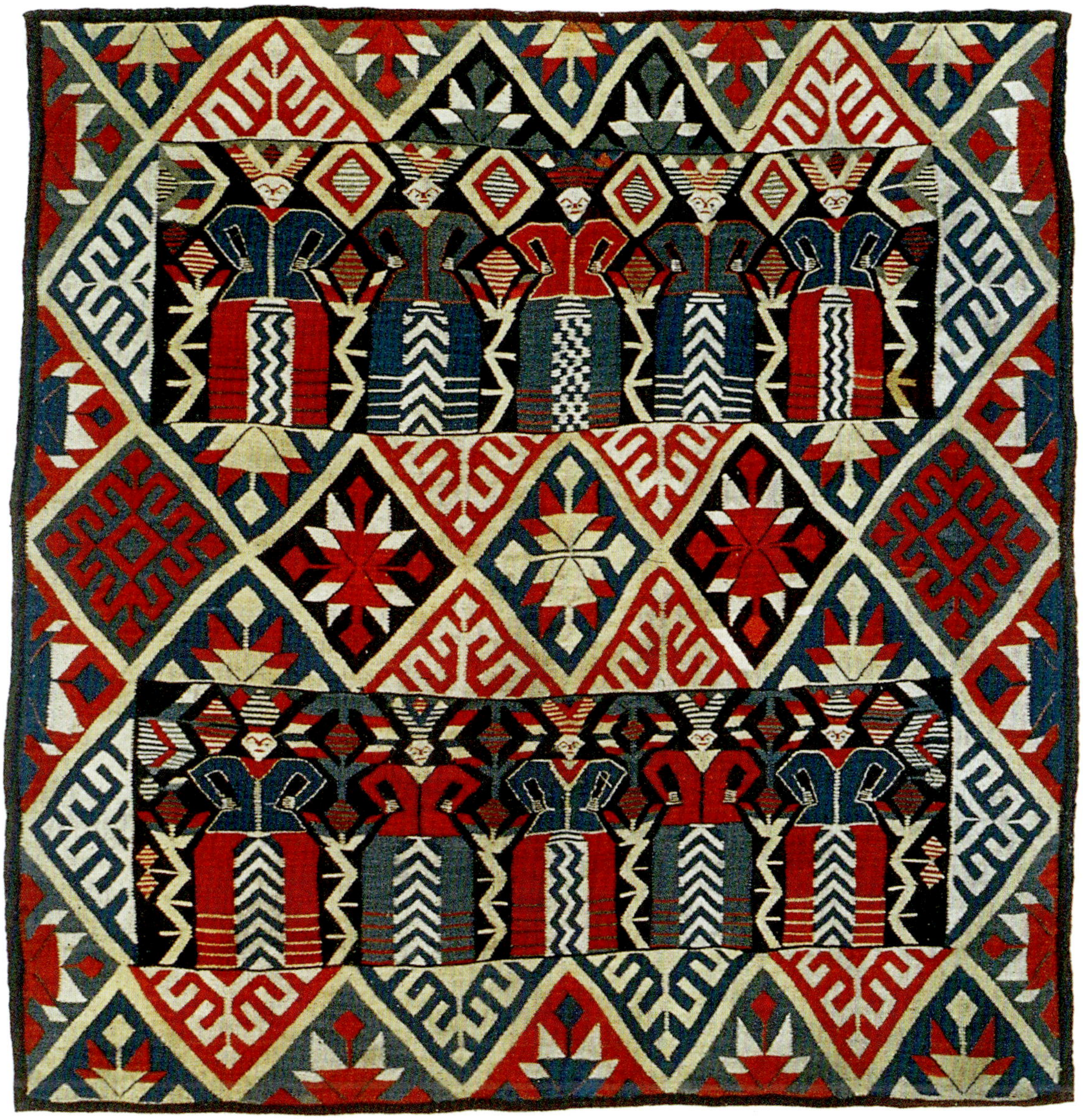

4.24 Figures that are "standing" in the loom
are more difficult to weave. Two rows of
women, a simplified version of the "Wise and
Foolish Virgins," appear in this eighteenth-
century coverlet from Voss or Sogn. Figures
placed horizontally for weaving often gave
better results. Compare the faces in the
detailed view with those in figure 4.1.
Norwegian Folk Museum.

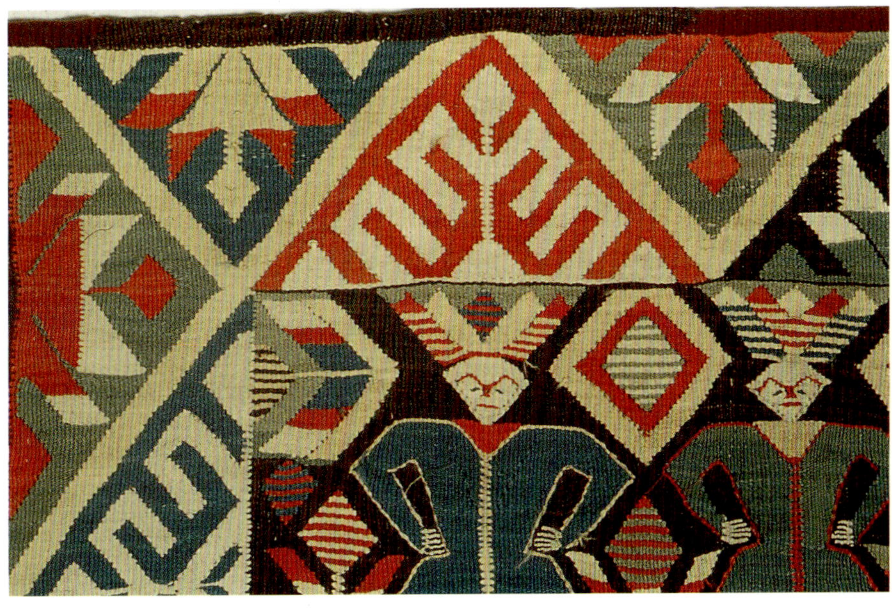

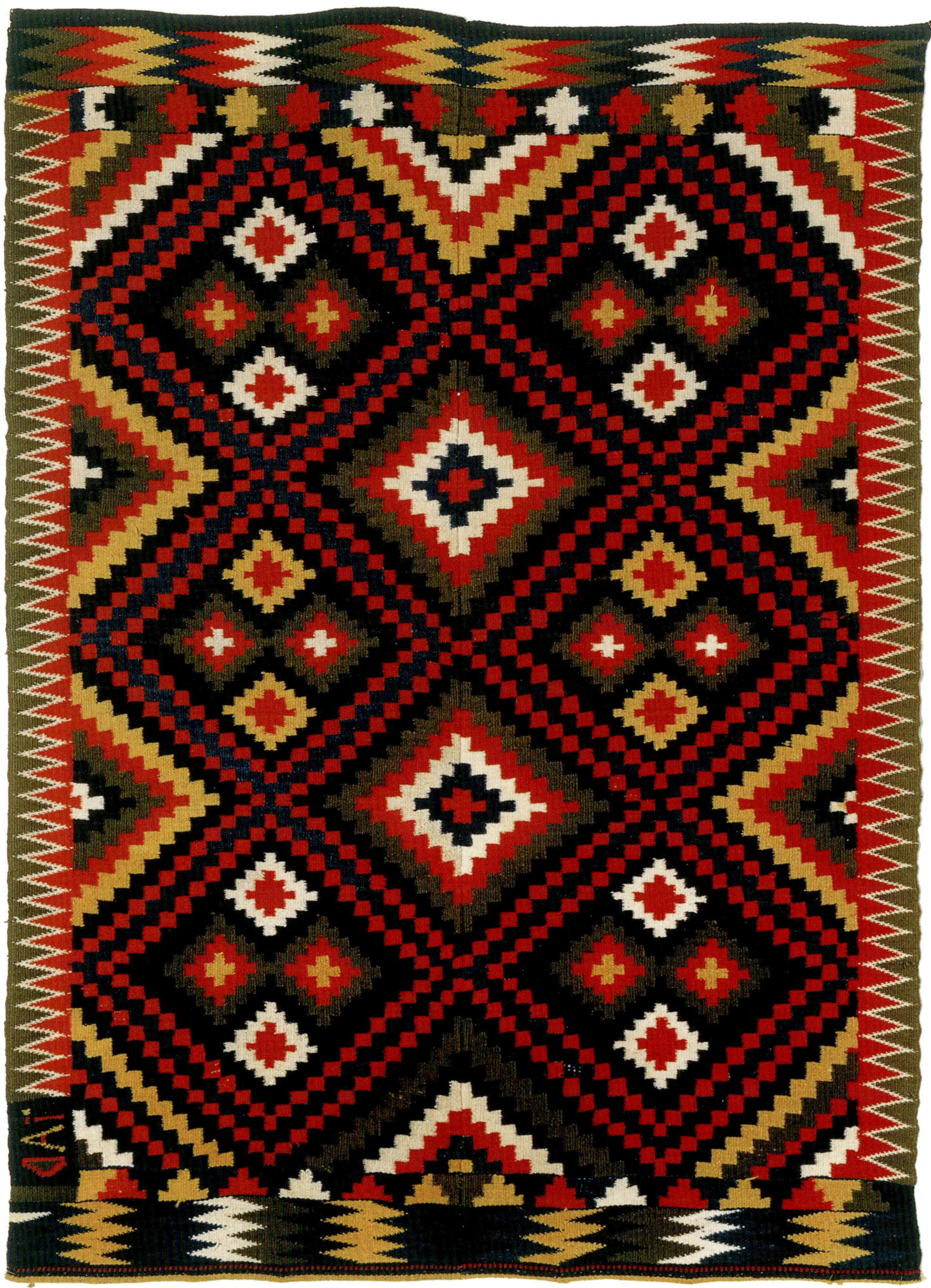

5 / Square-Weave Coverlets: Rutevev

A SENSE OF BALANCE EMANATES FROM THE RHYTHMIC repetition of pattern in the *rutevev,* or square-weave coverlets. Stylized flowers, tiers of diamonds, convoluted knots, elaborate crosses: all the time-honored patterns set in orderly array must have suggested the presence of a similar orderliness in the pattern of one's life. Far from being a luxury for the rich, the straightforward designs of this geometric cousin of the tapestry coverlets could be produced with relative ease. Throughout the fjord and mountain country of western and southern Norway, the square-weave coverlet reigned supreme (fig. 5.1).

Origins

Square weave, also known as geometric tapestry or by the Swedish term, *rölakan,* is a variation of the tapestry technique found in many parts of the world. Cultures that encompass India, the Middle East, north Africa, and eastern Europe in the eastern hemisphere, and the native populations of Peru, Mexico, and the southwestern United States in the western hemisphere, all have geometric tapestry traditions. In many cases, the durable and decorative saddle blankets, rugs, bags, wall hangings, and coverlets created from this weave show a remarkable similarity, even in geographically diverse areas. Some similarities of pattern can be explained by the constraints of the technique itself, especially where little or no cultural contact has existed. This is presumably the case between the New World and the Old, but it is probable that a good deal of cultural borrowing accounts for the similarities to be found within the square-weave traditions of the Old World.

The earliest examples of square-weave coverlets in Norway date from the seventeenth century, but it appears that these weavings are based on a much older tradition. Traces of similar weavings from the eighth and ninth centuries have been found in neighboring Sweden, and the square-weave technique is known to have existed in continental Europe since prehistoric times.[1] Whether the technique developed spontaneously in Scandinavia or whether it spread from other areas to this remote part of Europe is impossible to tell. Some of the similarities between the Norwegian weavings and those of the Middle East and eastern Europe are truly striking, however, and possibly result from a more direct form of contact. While it is known that rugs from the Middle East were imported into Scandinavia during the Middle Ages, it is also true that a host of Scandinavians descended on coastal Europe, western Russia, and the Mediterranean during the tenth century, "borrowing" from other peoples while disseminating healthy doses of their own customs. These representatives, also known as Vikings, were primarily noted for their ability to transfer wealth, but they served as effective tools in the transfer of culture as well. This was especially true of textiles, which, intrinsic beauty aside, provided a handy way to gather up valuables. Whether through medieval trade or through contact of a more abrupt nature, it is a distinct possibility that the textiles of Europe and the Middle East provided inspiration for local Norwegian weaving traditions (figs. 5.2–5.3).

Design and Color

A square-weave coverlet usually consisted of a central pattern area bracketed by borders above and below. One motif repeated in a regular array, or several motifs combined in a repetitive design, generally dominated the central pattern area. These motifs varied in size from small, frequently repeated forms to larger versions requiring fewer repetitions. A single rendition of one motif occasionally filled the entire area (figs. 5.4–5.7). Additionally, the figures of a man or woman, the initials of the weaver, or the date might become a part of the pattern (figs. 5.7 and 5.9).

Borders at the top and bottom of the coverlets in many cases showed a lack of symmetry in size and design and were often composed of techniques other than square weave. Horizontal bands of the simple pick-and-pick technique formed the basis of most border designs. Supplementary weft patterning was often combined with pick-and-pick to create more elaborate patterns, and brocading and a tapestry weave composed of zigzag stripes known as lightning weave were also used (fig. 5.8). (These techniques are discussed in greater detail in chapter 7, "Other Weft-Faced Coverlets.") Occasionally the central pattern area of a coverlet was divided by vertical and horizontal borders, and in some southern districts it was common to frame the entire coverlet with a fairly uniform border (figs. 5.9–5.10; and see figs. 5.2–5.3).

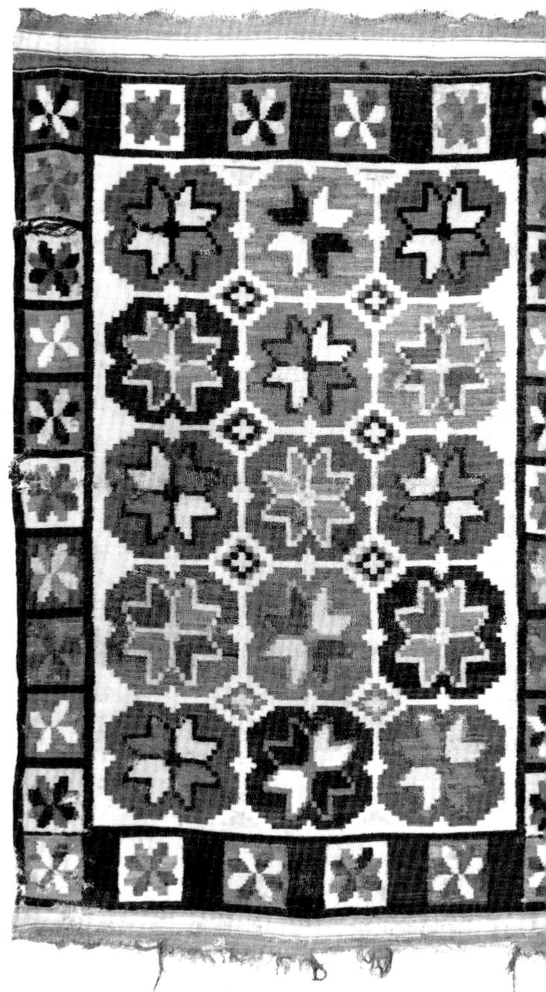

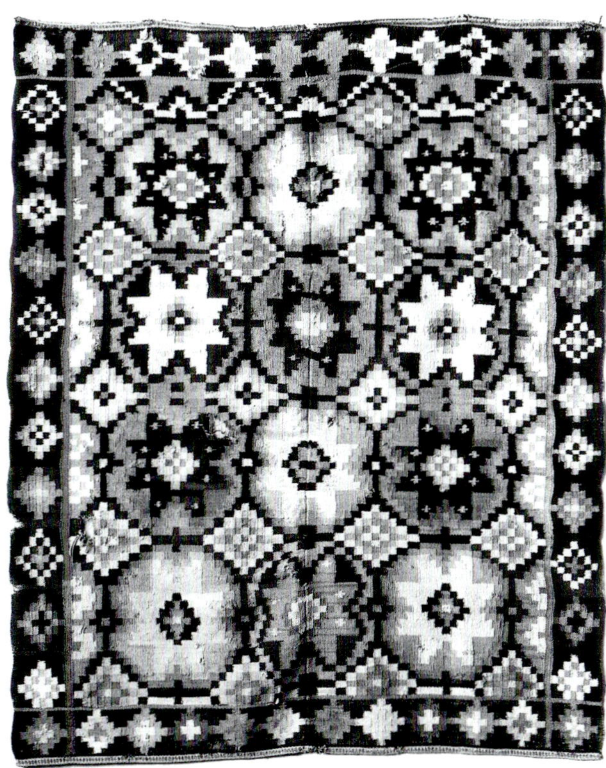

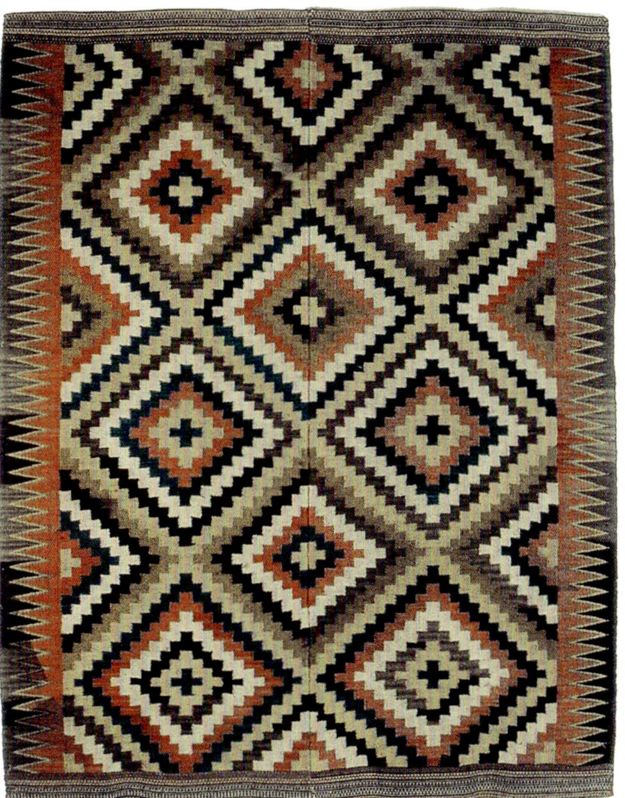

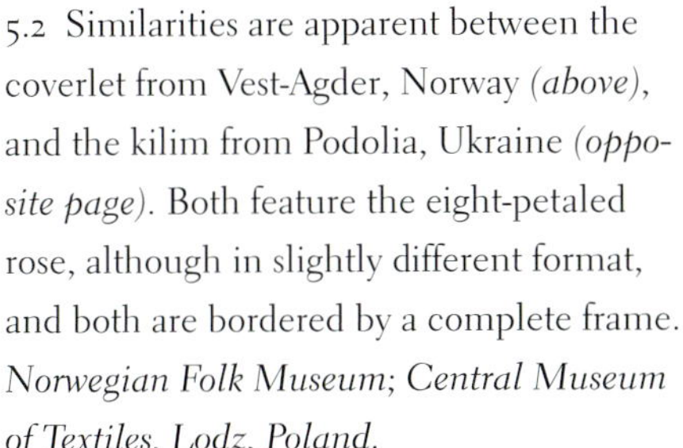

5.2 Similarities are apparent between the coverlet from Vest-Agder, Norway *(above)*, and the kilim from Podolia, Ukraine *(opposite page)*. Both feature the eight-petaled rose, although in slightly different format, and both are bordered by a complete frame. *Norwegian Folk Museum; Central Museum of Textiles, Lodz, Poland.*

5.3 Although lacking a complete framing border of zigzags, the Norwegian coverlet from Vest-Agder *(top right)* shows a striking similarity to the kilim from South Persia *(bottom right)* in the use of diamond motif and border patterns. *Norwegian Folk Museum; Textile Museum, Washington, D.C.*

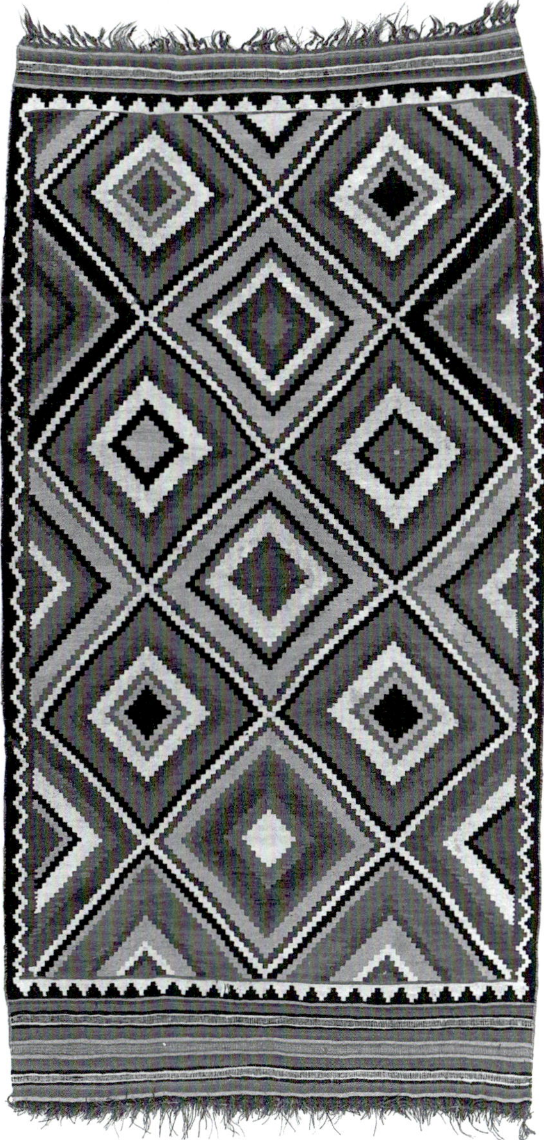

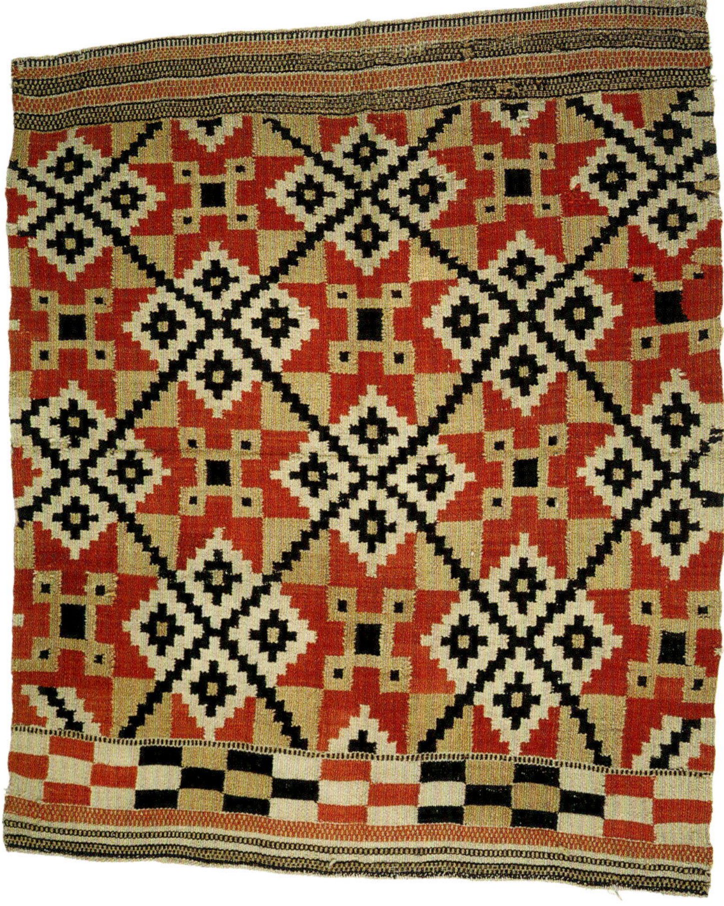

5.4 The eight-petaled rose, knot, and diamond motifs are combined in the design of this coverlet. Sogn and Fjordane. *Historical Museum, University of Bergen.*

5.5 The central pattern area of this coverlet is dominated by four large renditions of the eight-petaled rose. *Historical Museum, University of Bergen.*

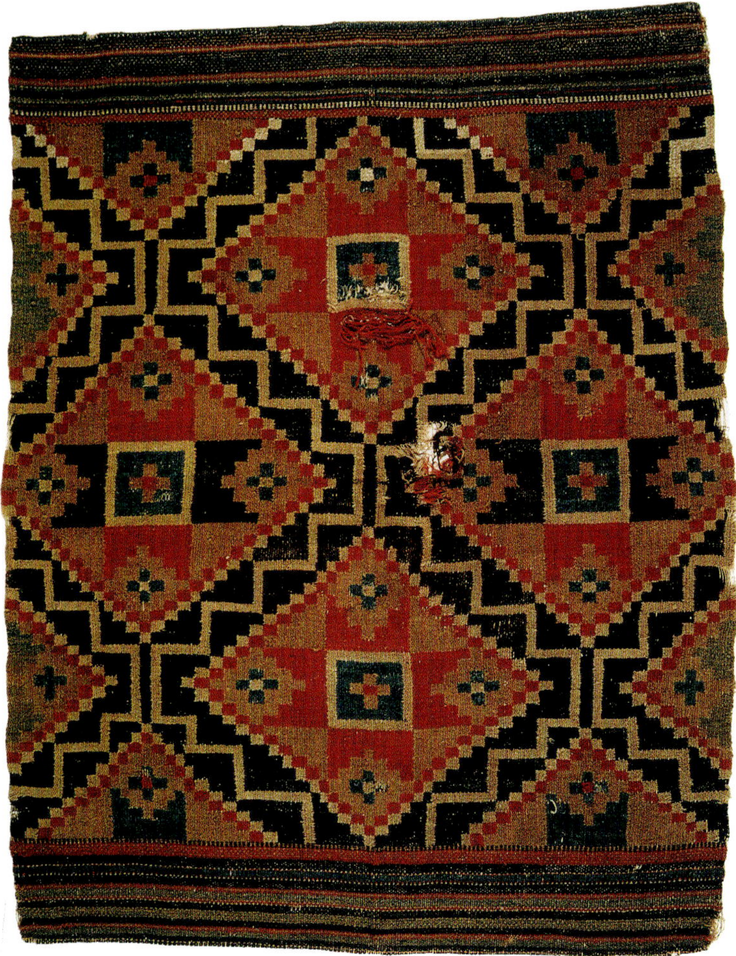

5.6 Frequent repetitions of relatively small eight-petaled roses fill the central pattern area of this coverlet. Hardanger. *Historical Museum, University of Bergen.*

5.7 A single rendition of the large cross with elements of the lily motif. Note the initials and date, "TISH 1875," woven into the border. Sogn and Fjordane. *Historical Museum, University of Bergen.*

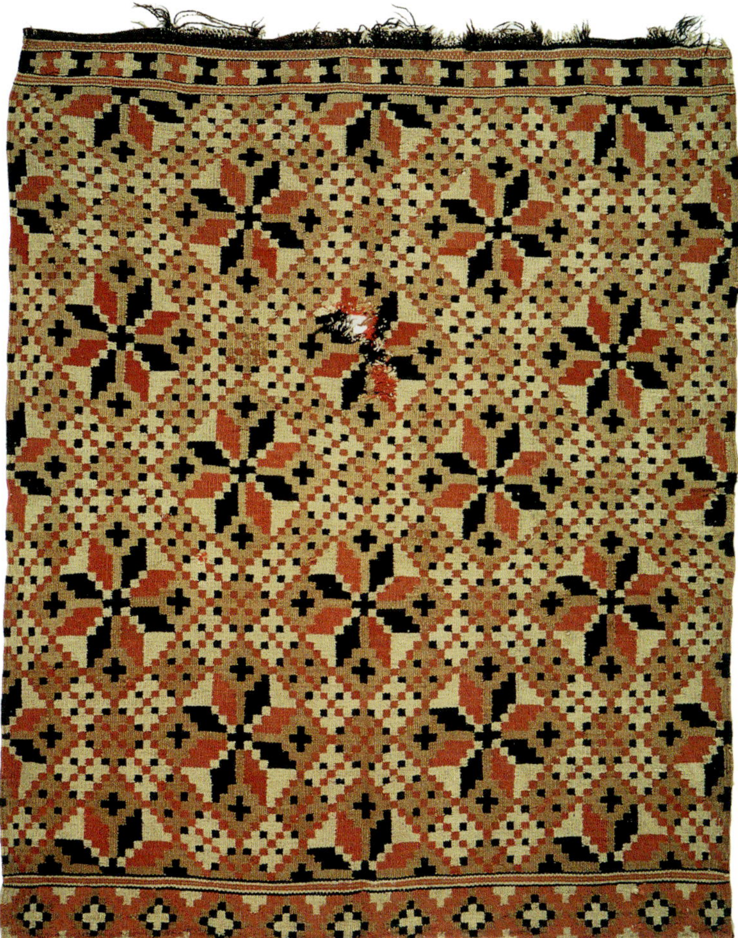

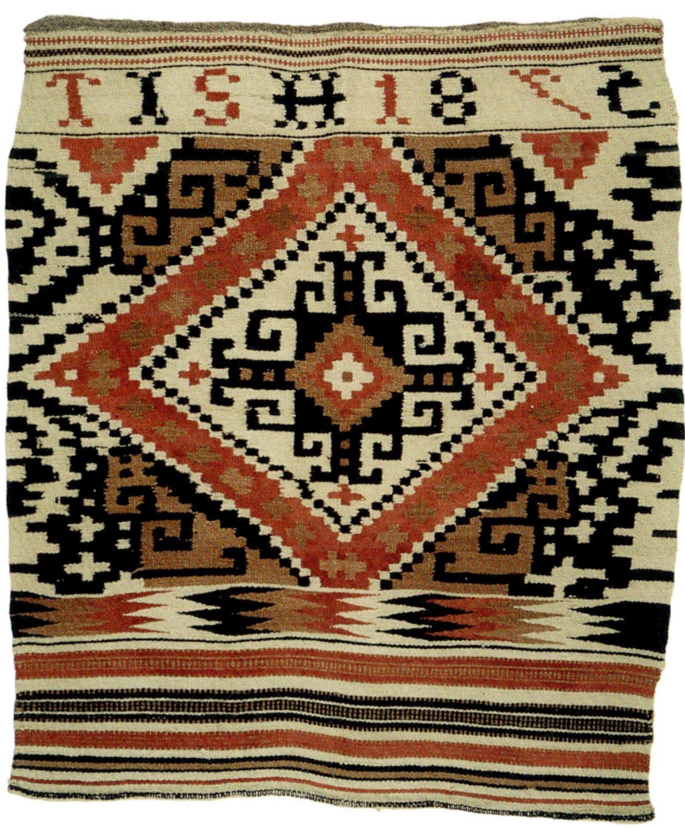

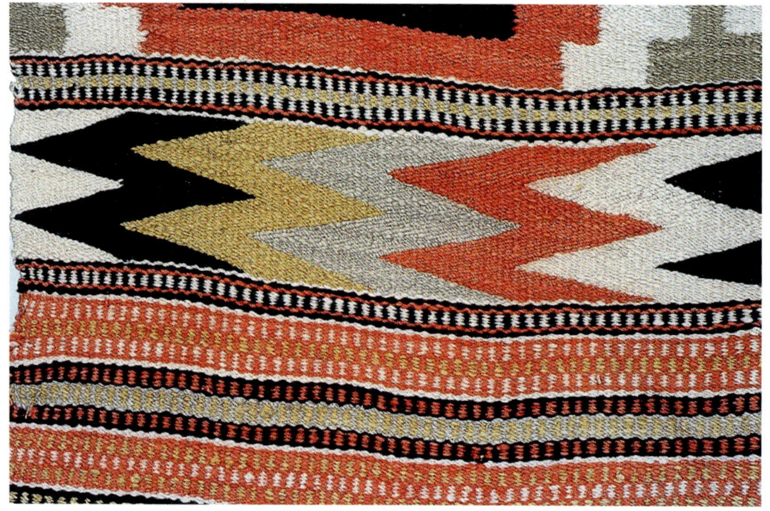

a

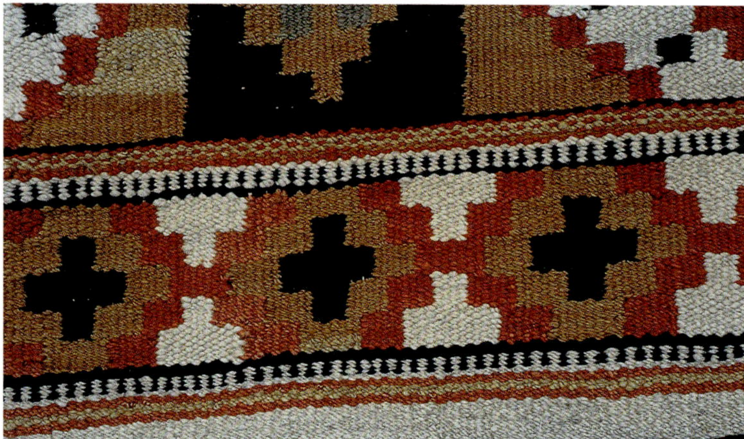

b

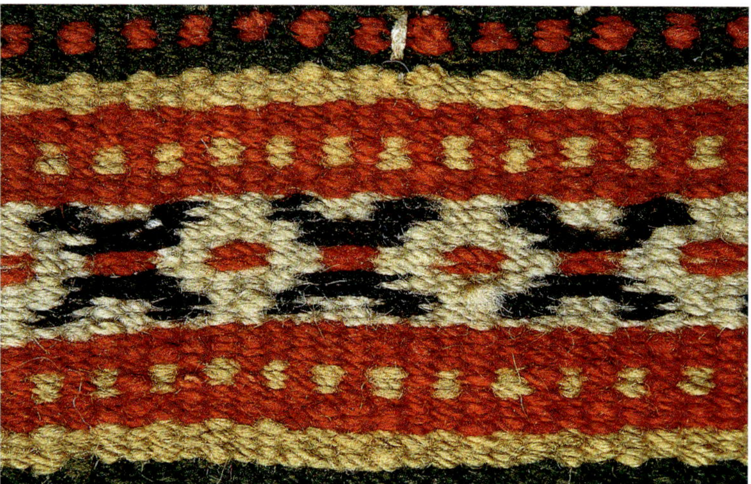

c

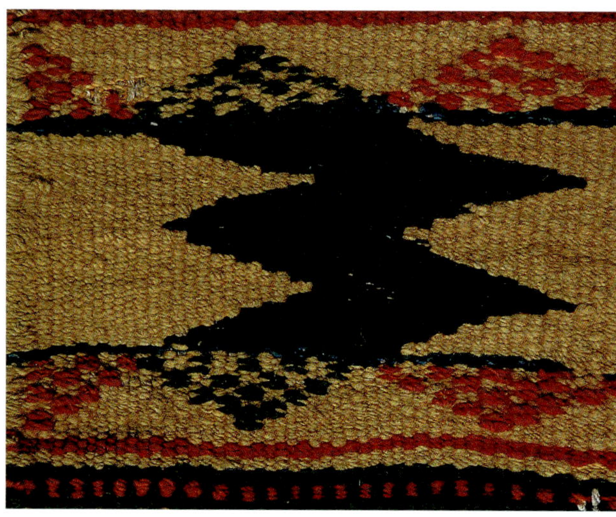

d

5.8 Borders of the square-weave coverlets included: *(a)* horizontal bands of dots in the pick-and-pick technique and the zigzag lightning-weave border; *(b)* small square-weave patterns; *(c)* supplementary weft patterning such as Xs shuttled in from selvage to selvage; and *(d)* small brocaded patterns such as the triangles appearing above and below the lightning weave. *(a)* and *(b)*: *Vesterheim Norwegian-American Museum; (c)* and *(d): Luther College Collection, Norwegian-American Museum.*

5.9 A variety of motifs, including the figures of two pipe-smoking men, are divided into four quarters by a border of diamonds. Sogn and Fjordane. *Norwegian Folk Museum.*

5.10 The popular color scheme of red, black, gold, and white is used in this lively coverlet. Initials and year, "RASH 1848," are embroidered on the top border. *Historical Museum, University of Bergen.*

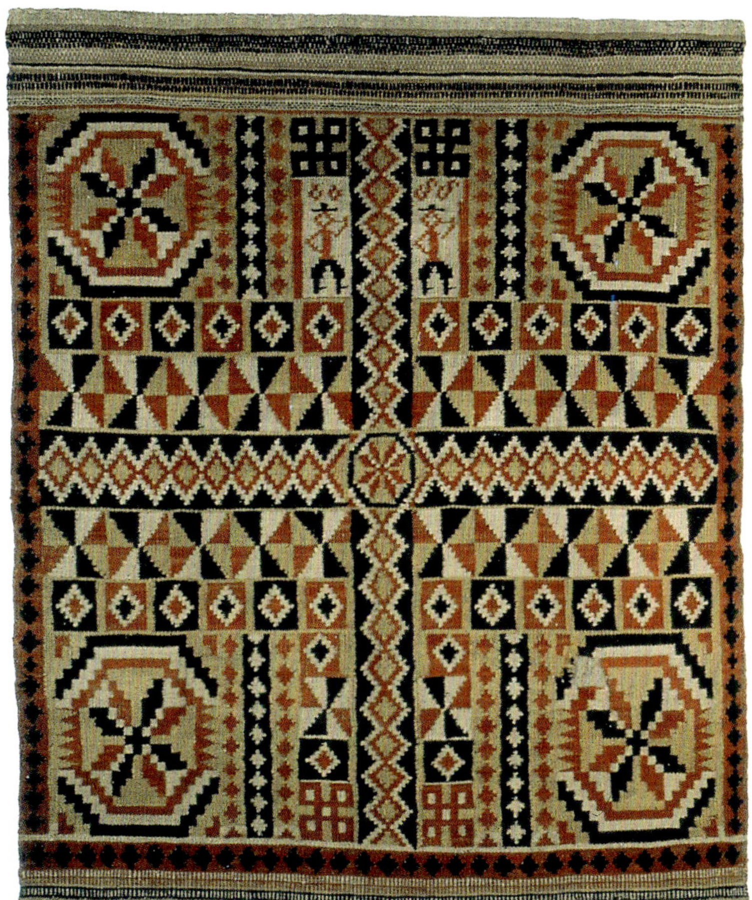

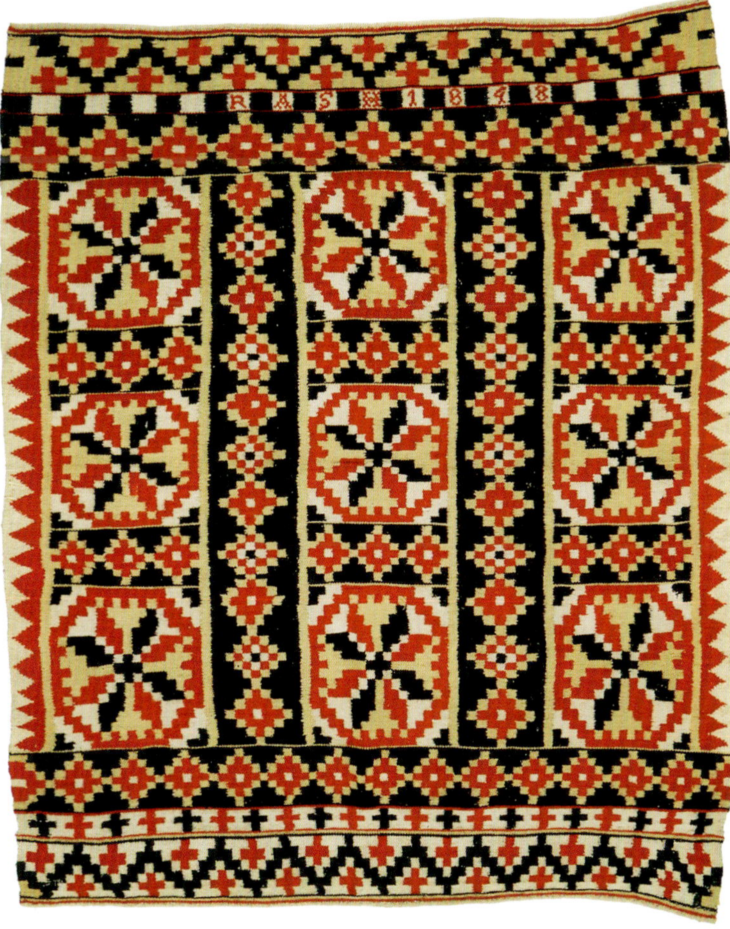

Square-weave coverlets were commonly designed with combinations of four or five colors. A vibrant arrangement of red, black, white, and gold, typical of the folk artist's love of strong colors, was one of the most popular combinations. Although fading has often reduced the gold to a light beige, the original color scheme is still visible in some coverlets (figs. 5.10 and 5.23–5.24). Blue and/or green were often used as balancing dark tones in place of black. An emphasis on darker colors, such as blue, green, and brown, was fairly common in coverlets from the southern districts (fig. 5.22, and see fig. 5.1).

Within the wide variety of patterns found in the square-weave coverlets, five major motifs emerge. All stem from the Middle Ages if not earlier, and most can be found in one form or another in the folk arts of other cultures from Europe to the Middle East (fig. 5.11).

Eight-Petaled Rose A motif of universal popularity throughout Scandinavia, the eight-petaled rose was prevalent in weavings from the Middle East, northern Africa, and Europe. In general the motif consists of a stylized flower with eight petals and owes its distinctive appearance to the ninety-degree angles formed between the tips of each pair of petals. In Norwegian square-weave coverlets, individual flowers could be separated into distinct petals that often alternated in color, or the petals could be joined together in solid form, usually with another motif, such as a diamond, cross, or square placed in the center. In a further variation, the points of the eight petals were smoothed into a "rosette." When used as the major motif of a coverlet, the eight-petaled rose was often placed within octagons arranged in rows and columns. It could also be set in either a diagonal or a square grid, sometimes alternating with other motifs, such as the cross or the diamond (figs. 5.12–5.15).

Knot Knotwork designs are found in cultures as diverse as Turkey, Ethiopia, and China. In Norway, the knot motif has been known in textile art since Viking times, as cloth fragments from the ninth-century Oseberg ship indicate (see fig. 4.2). It is likely that the motif, referred to as *valknute* in Norwegian, was associated with the powerful Norse god, Odin, or Valfader (father of the battle-slain), who presided over the mythical Valhalla and the Valkyrie.[2] Folk belief held that magical properties inherent in the intricate knotwork designs would provide protection from evil powers.

In geometric form the knot motif consists of a varying number of hollow squares that intersect at their corners. Simple knots have a large central square with smaller squares at each corner and sometimes along the sides. A more complex version has twenty small squares radiating out from the central square. In the square-weave coverlets, the simplest form of the knot motif was often arranged side by side in bands of pattern, or used as the center of another motif. The more complex variation was placed in a regular array that filled the entire pattern area of the coverlet (figs. 5.16–5.18).

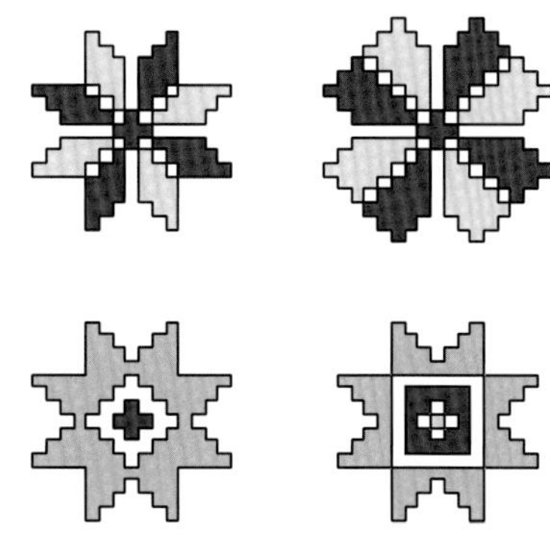
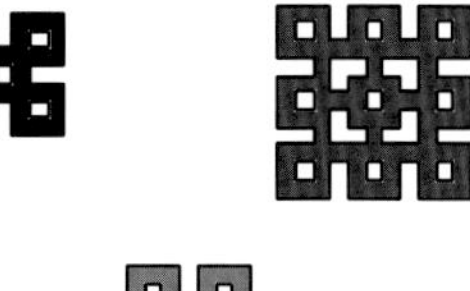
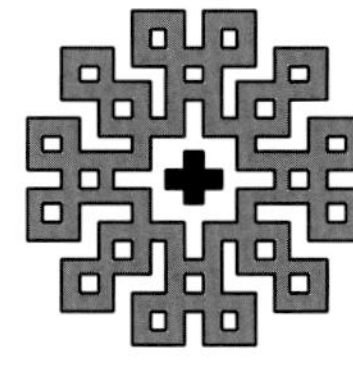
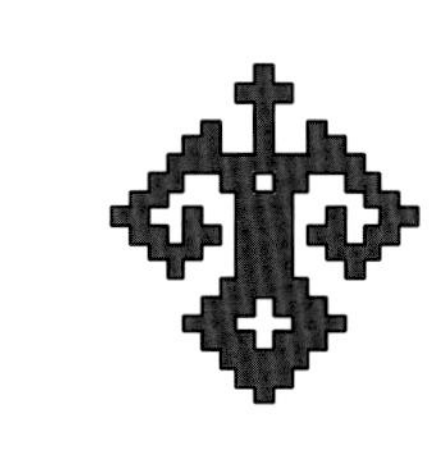
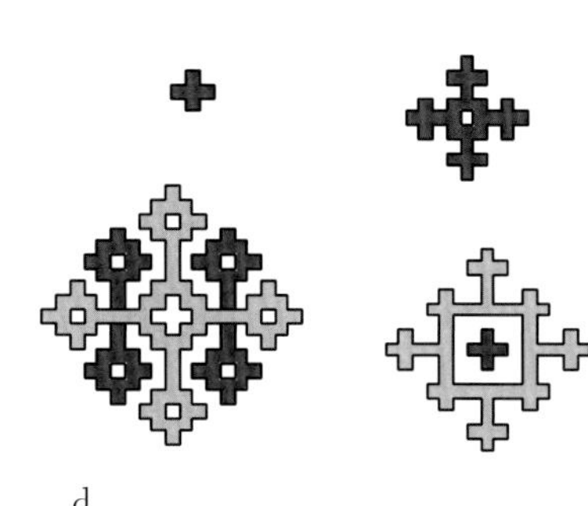

5.11 Square weave motifs: *(a)* eight-petaled rose; *(b)* knot; *(c)* lily; *(d)* cross; and *(e)* diamond.

a

b

c

d

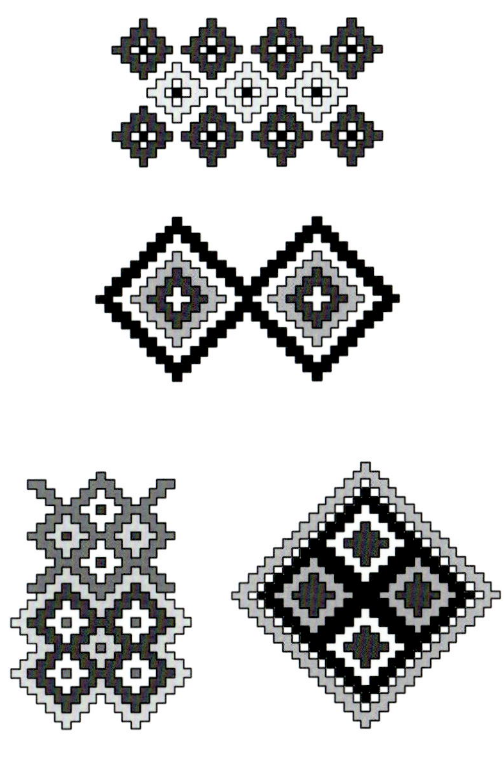

e

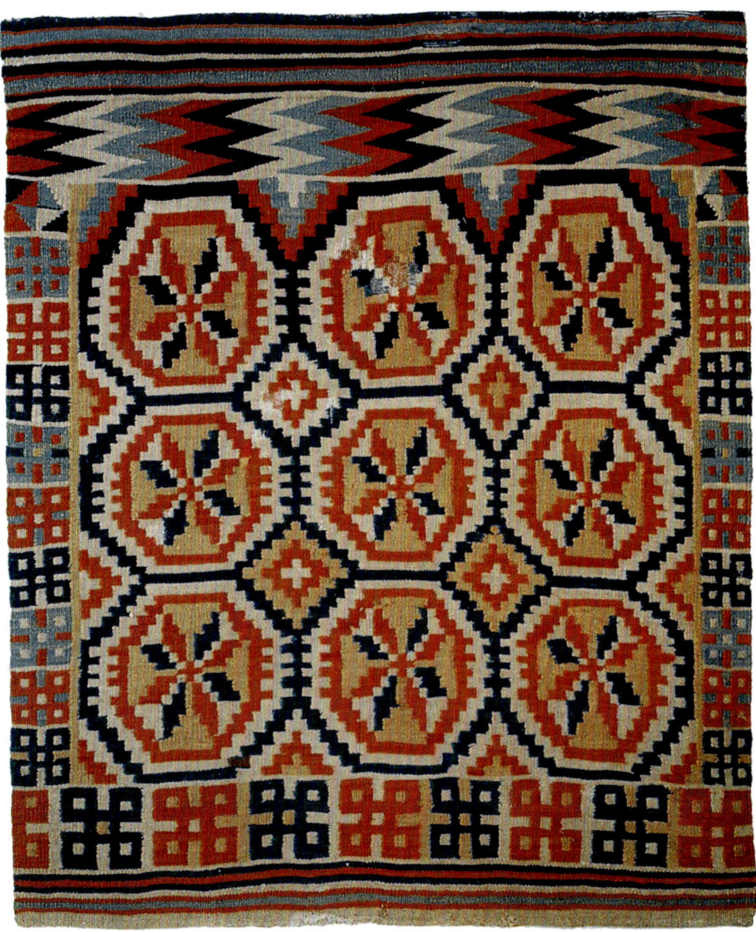

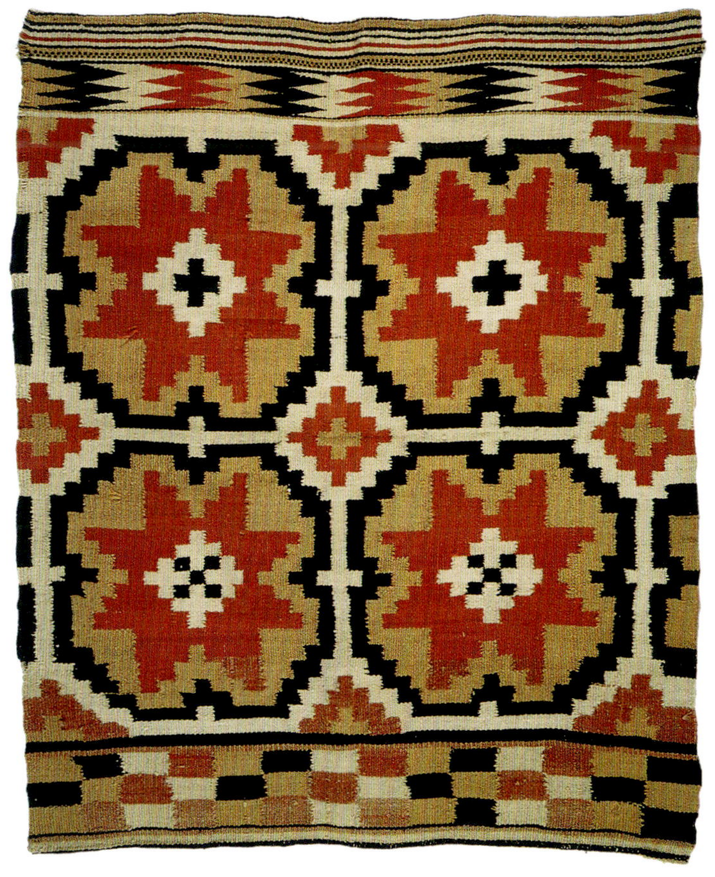

5.12 *(Top right)* The eight-petaled rose was often placed in an array of octagons. Note the three-sided border of simple knots. Rogaland. *Norwegian Folk Museum.*

5.13 *(Bottom right)* Four large eight-petaled roses with joined petals. Sogn. *Historical Museum, University of Bergen.*

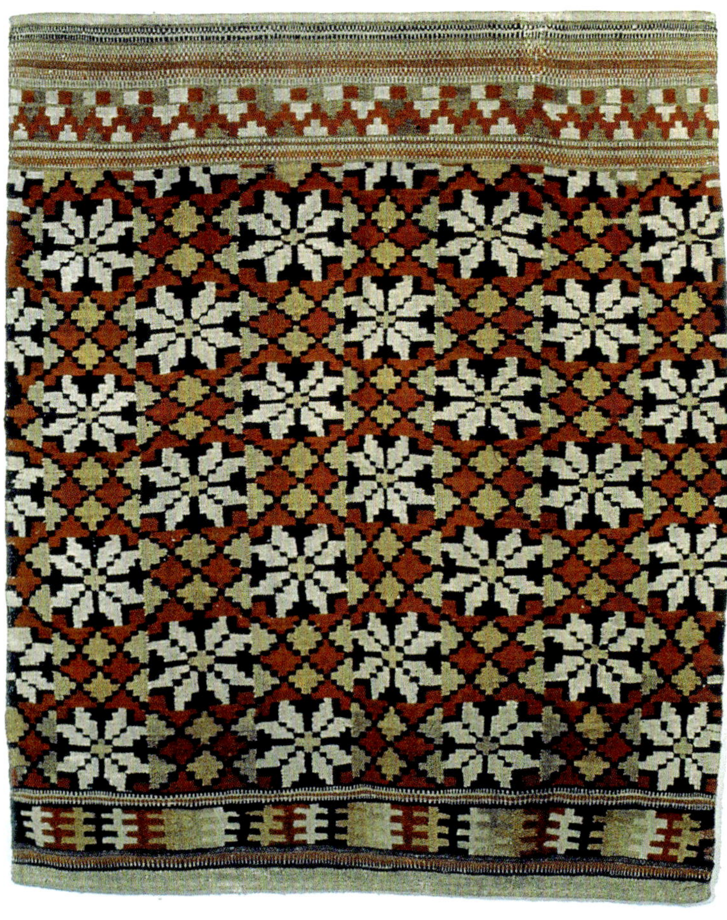

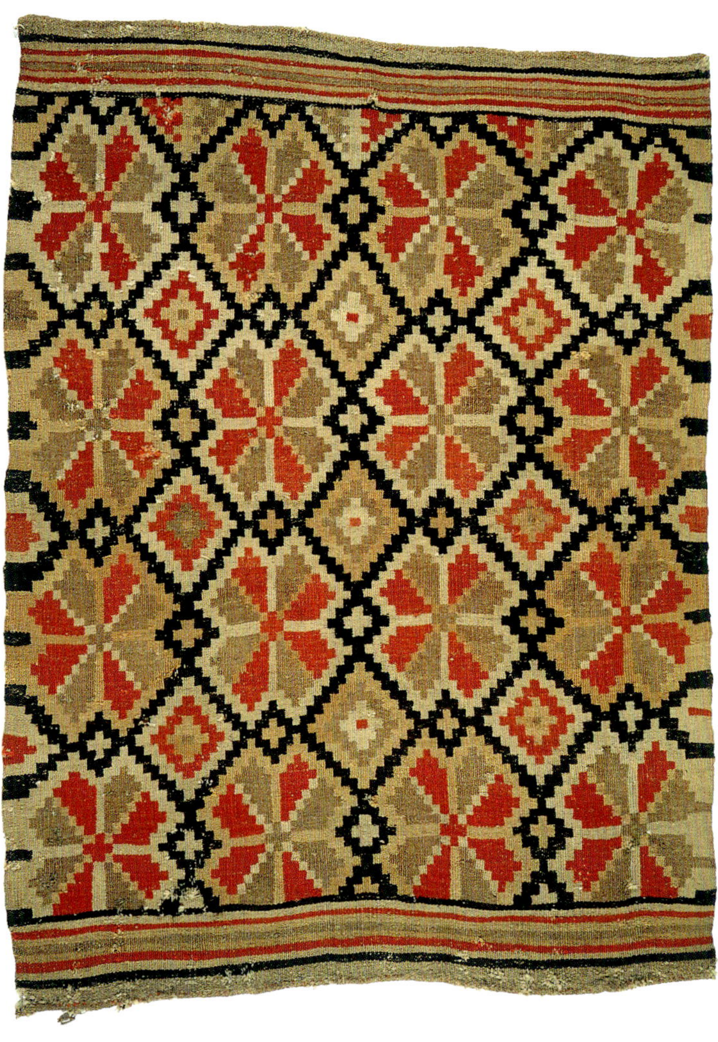

5.14 Eight-petaled roses of a single color set in a background of squares alternate with a gridwork of diamonds. Sogn and Fjordane. *Norwegian Folk Museum.*

5.15 The smooth-sided rosette version of the eight-petaled rose combined with the diamond motif. Voss. *Historical Museum, University of Bergen.*

5.16 Plain horizontal stripes in the pick-and-pick technique are enlivened by several rows of square-weave pattern, including a row of the simple knot motif, bottom. *Historical Museum, University of Bergen.*

5.17 Square-weave patterns, including a version of the knot motif, alternate with pick-and-pick and supplementary weft patterning. *Historical Museum, University of Bergen.*

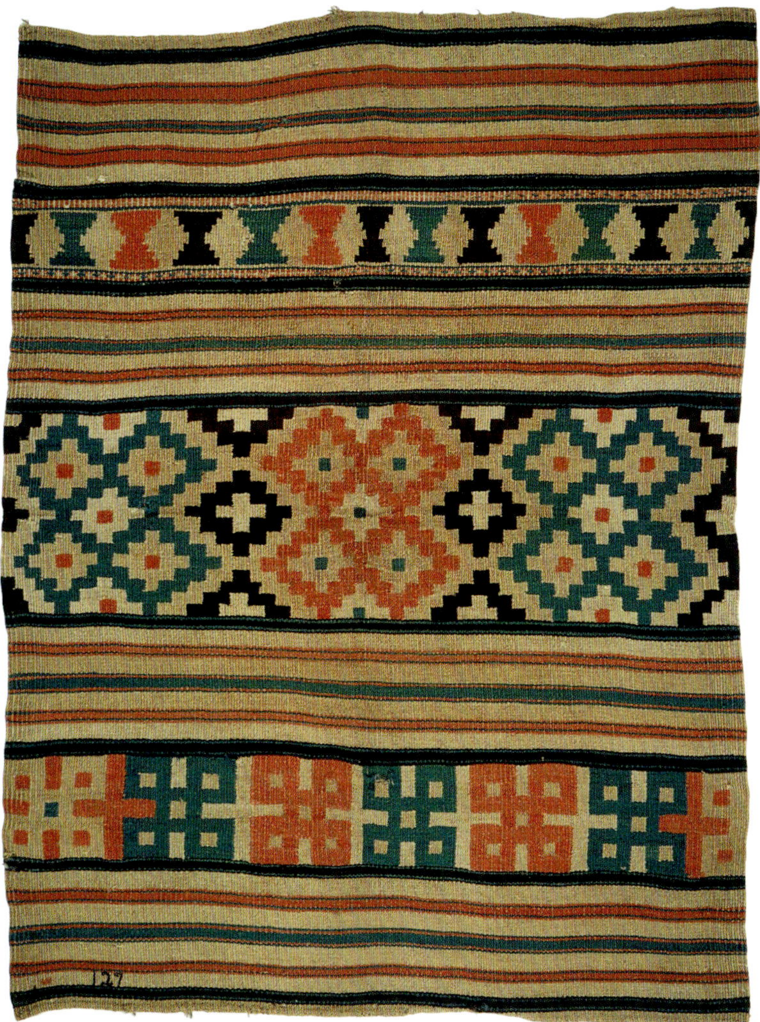

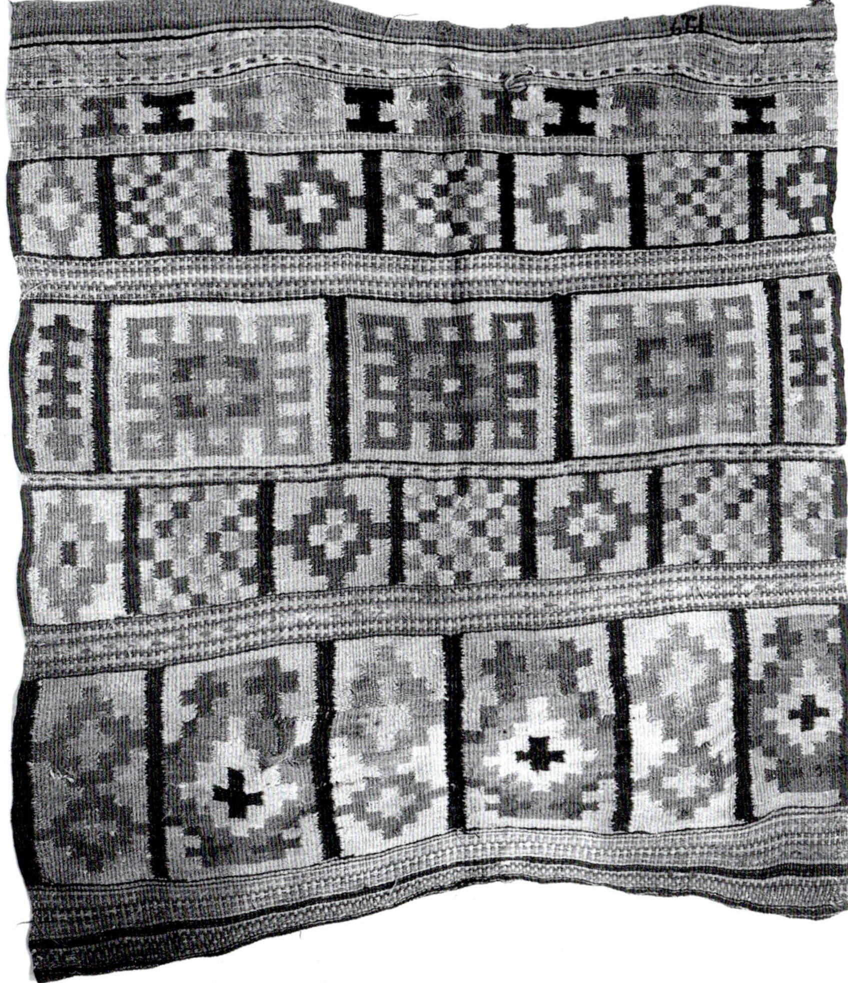

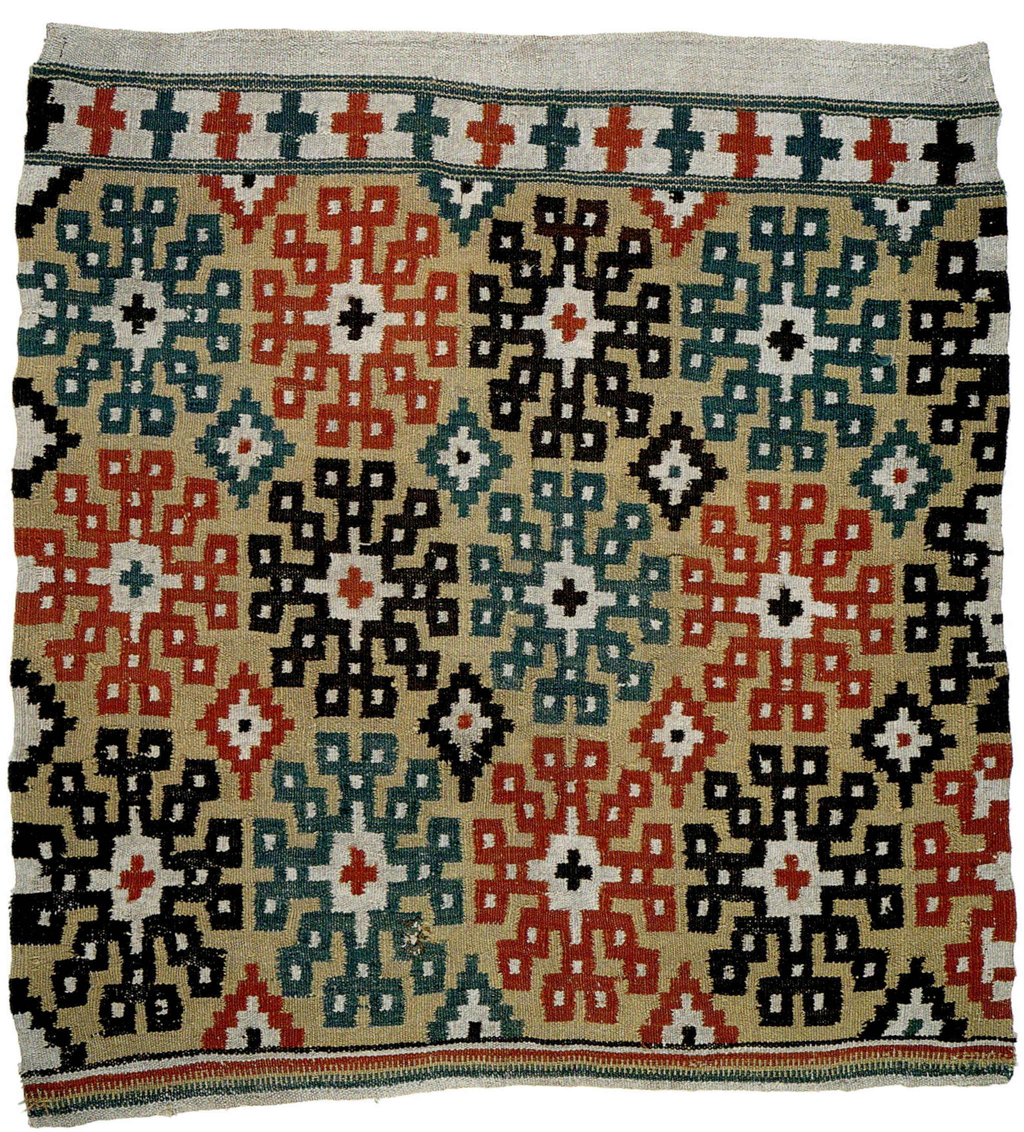

5.18 The complex knot motif in a regular
array. Sogn and Fjordane. *Historical Museum,
University of Bergen.*

Lily The lily motif is probably a derivation of the stylized palmette of the Middle East.[3] In Europe the lily was associated symbolically with the Virgin Mary, and was adopted by the Bourbons of France in the form of the fleur-de-lis in the twelfth century. It has been used in Norwegian folk art since the Middle Ages, if not earlier. In square-weave coverlets, the lily usually appeared in a diagonal grid, although elements of the lily motif can be seen in a version of the large-cross motif (figs. 5.19 and 5.7).

Diamond The diamond motif is a basic design element found in geometric patterns from many cultures. Most square-weave coverlets had small versions of the diamond serving as the center of another motif or filling in the intervening spaces in the design. When used as the major motif of a coverlet, the diamond was often arranged in varying numbers of concentric rings, sometimes placed in rows that alternated in color. Alternating groups of four and five diamonds formed another popular arrangement (figs. 5.20–5.23).

Cross The simple cross motif was used by many cultures in their geometric designs even before the advent of Christianity gave the symbol added significance. Like the diamond, the simple cross was commonly used in square-weave designs to fill the empty spaces between other motifs or as a small central pattern within a larger motif. More complicated versions of the cross motif, created by placing additional crosses on or between the arms of a larger cross or by enlarging the center of the motif into a square, were used as the main design in some coverlets and were often set in a diagonal grid or an array of octagons (figs. 5.24–5.26).

Not all of the square-weave coverlets fit conveniently into the five major categories described above. Some coverlets show a blending of motifs into almost unrecognizable form, such as those combining parts of the eight-petaled rose with the small cross (fig. 5.27). Others display variations on basic geometric shapes, such as a division of squares into triangles of alternating color (fig. 5.28). But the tendency to reproduce a successful design from the past is a strong element of most folk cultures, and this fact is well demonstrated by the patterns in the majority of square-weave coverlets.

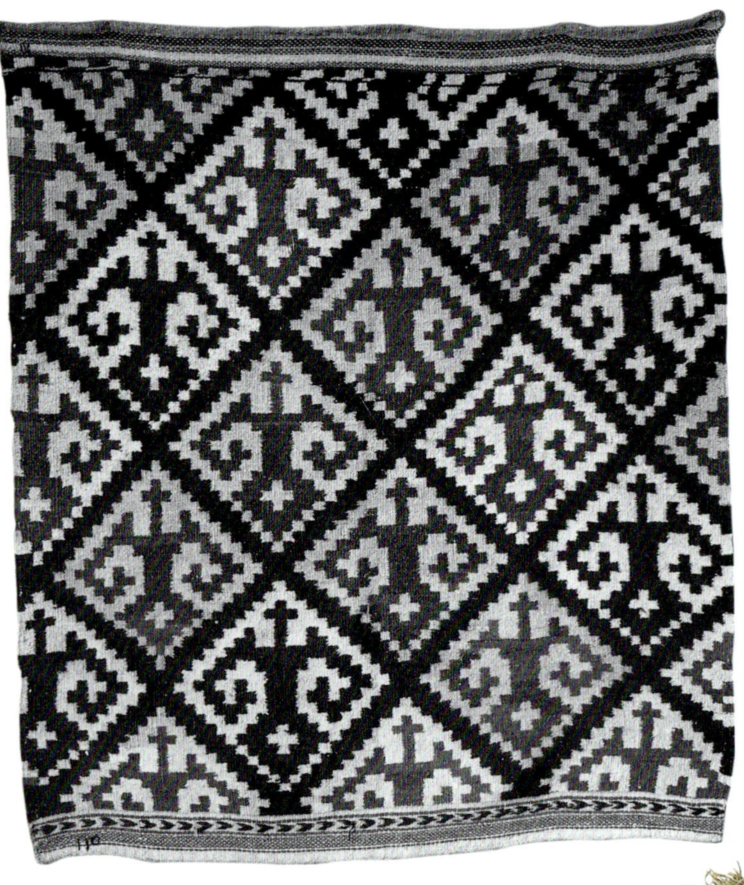

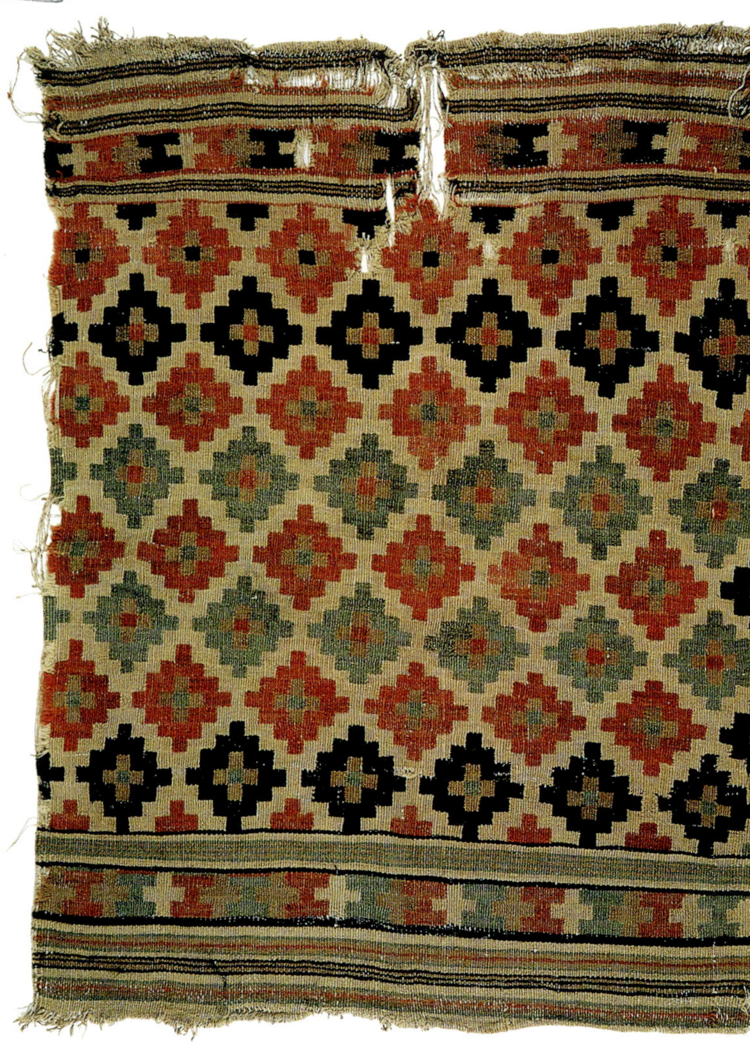

5.19 The lily motif was commonly placed in a diagonal grid. Sogn and Fjordane. *Historical Museum, University of Bergen.*

5.20 Diamonds were often arranged in rows of alternating color. Sunnmøre. *Historical Museum, University of Bergen.*

5.21 Concentric rings of diamonds in a
regular array. Hardanger. *Historical Museum,*
University of Bergen.

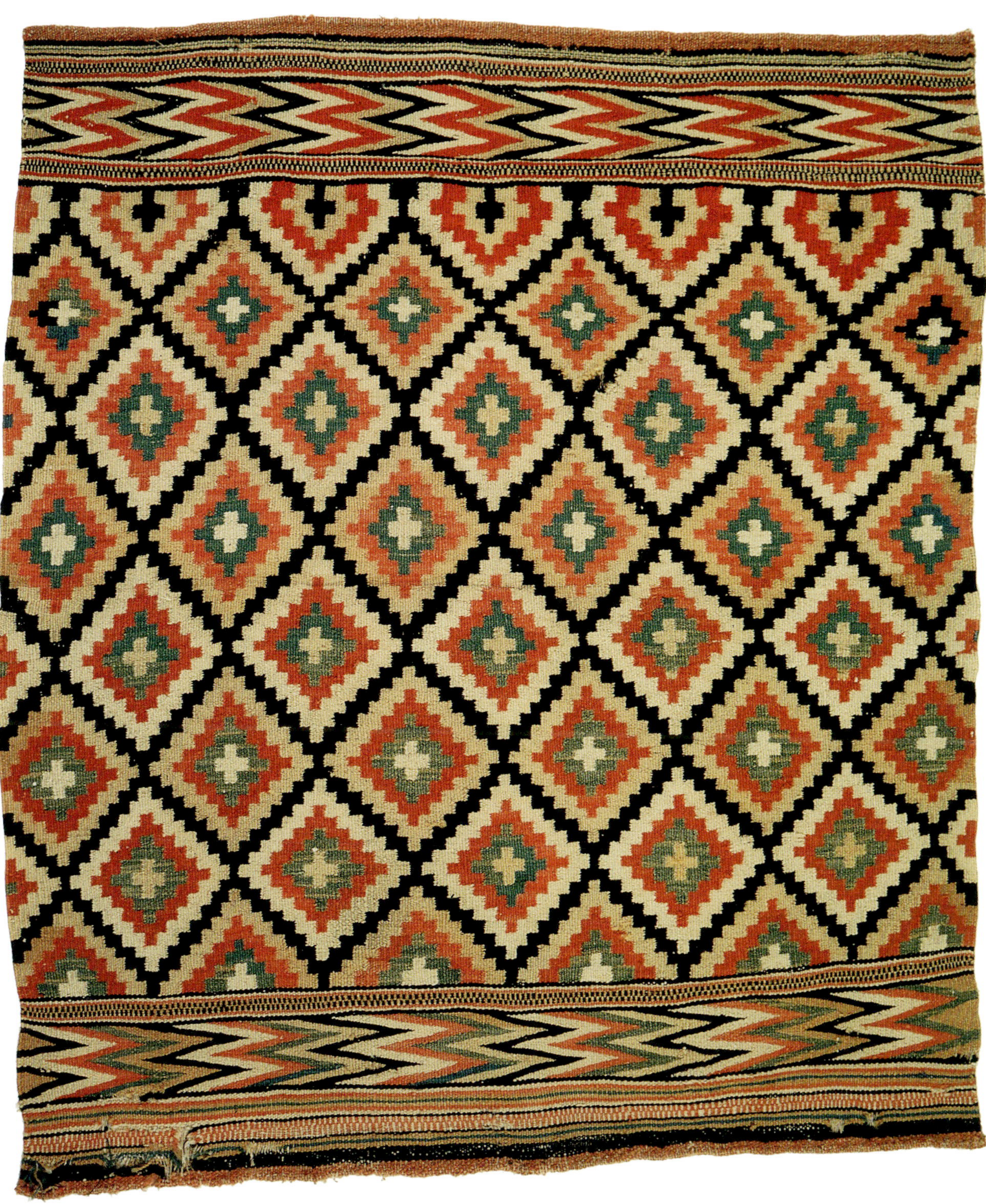

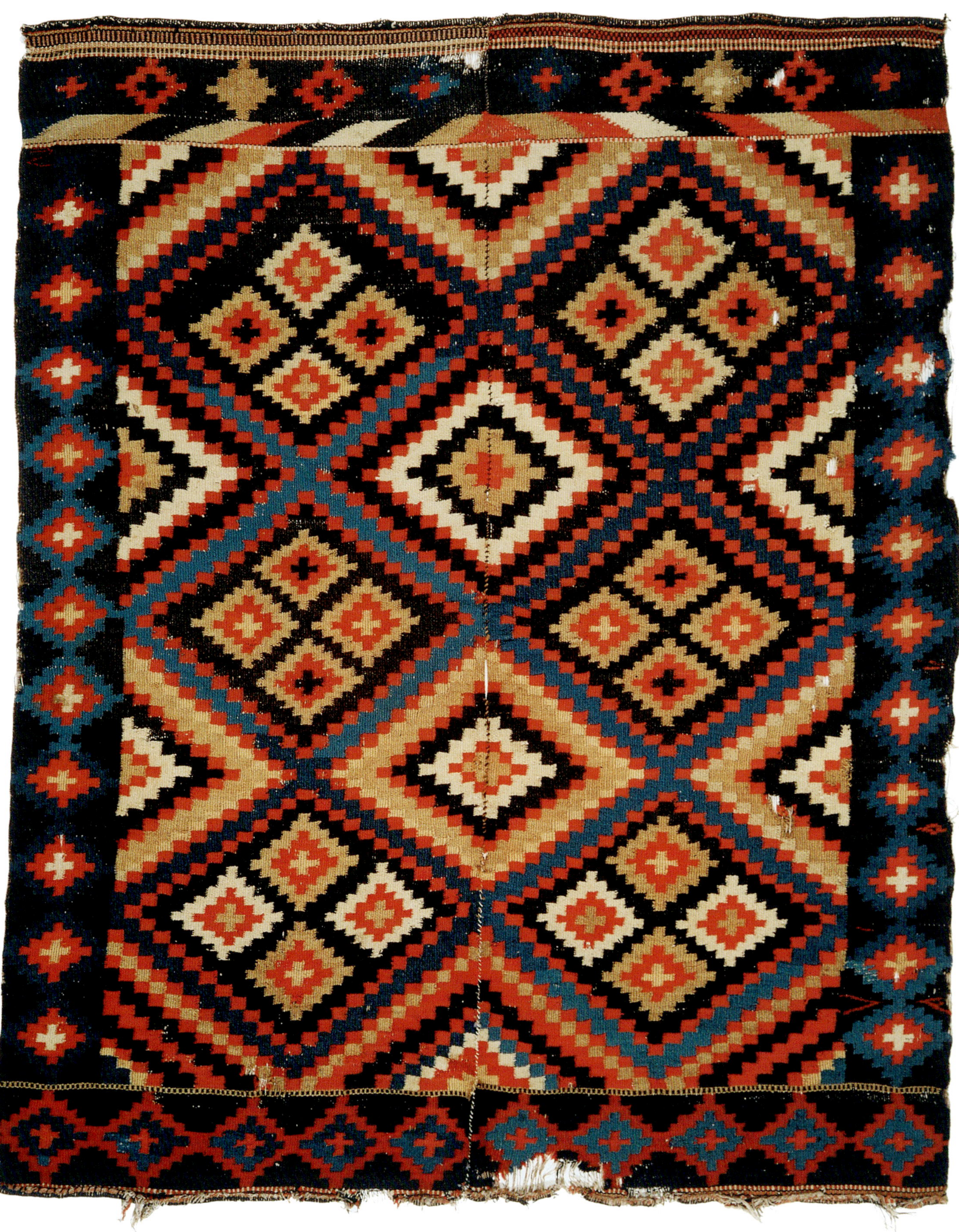

5.22 *(Opposite)* Vest-Agder coverlets were
often filled with concentric rings of diamonds,
sometimes with smaller groupings of four
diamonds. The use of darker colors was also
typical of coverlets from southern districts.
Historical Museum, University of Bergen.

5.23 A combination of diamonds arranged
in groups of fours and fives. *Norwegian Folk
Museum.*

5.24 *(Below)* The five cross in a diagonal array.
Norwegian Folk Museum.

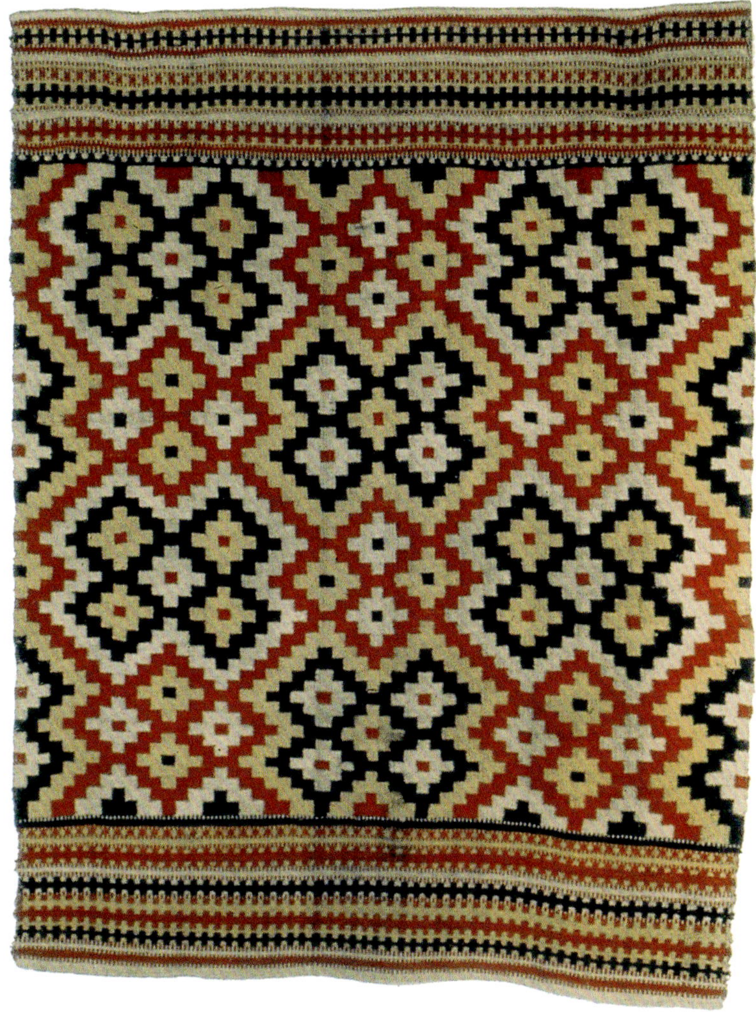

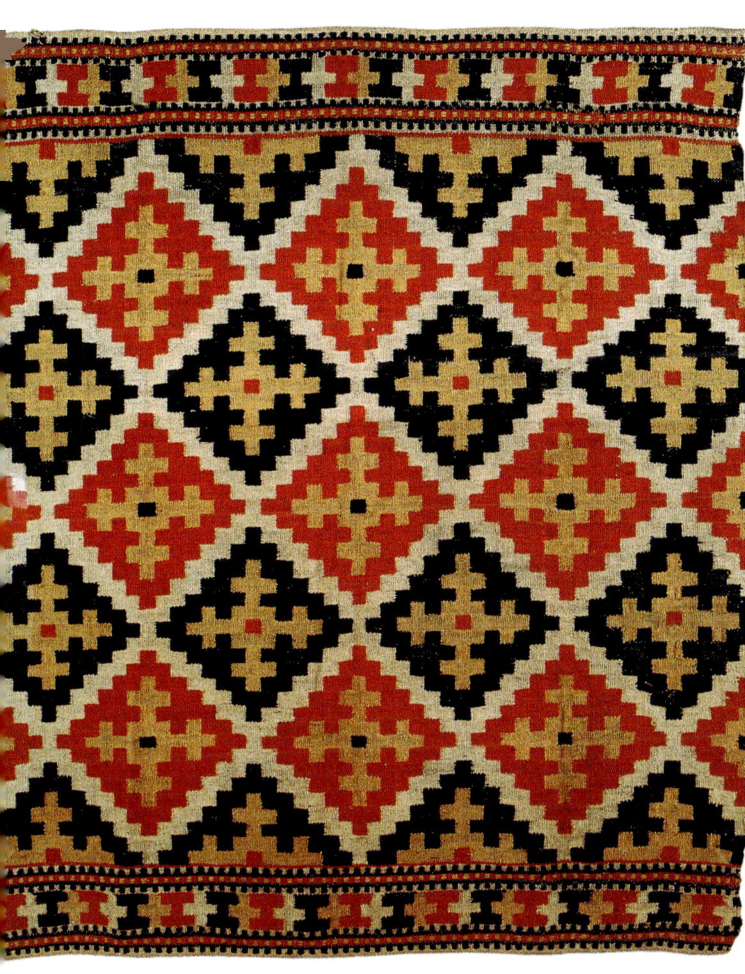

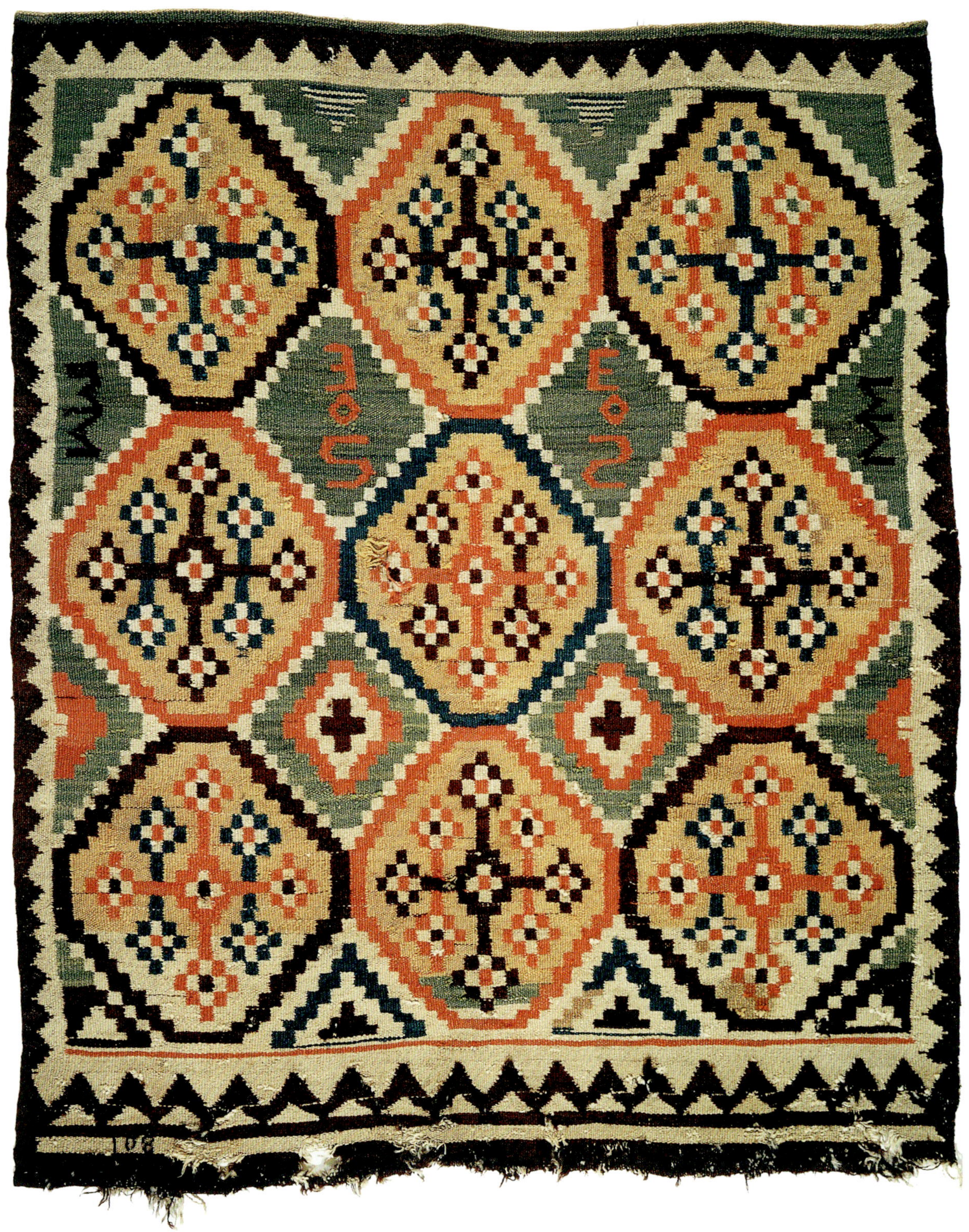

5.25 The nine cross. Note the initials
"EOS" in the center and "MM" on the sides.
Gudbrandsdal. *Historical Museum, University
of Bergen.*

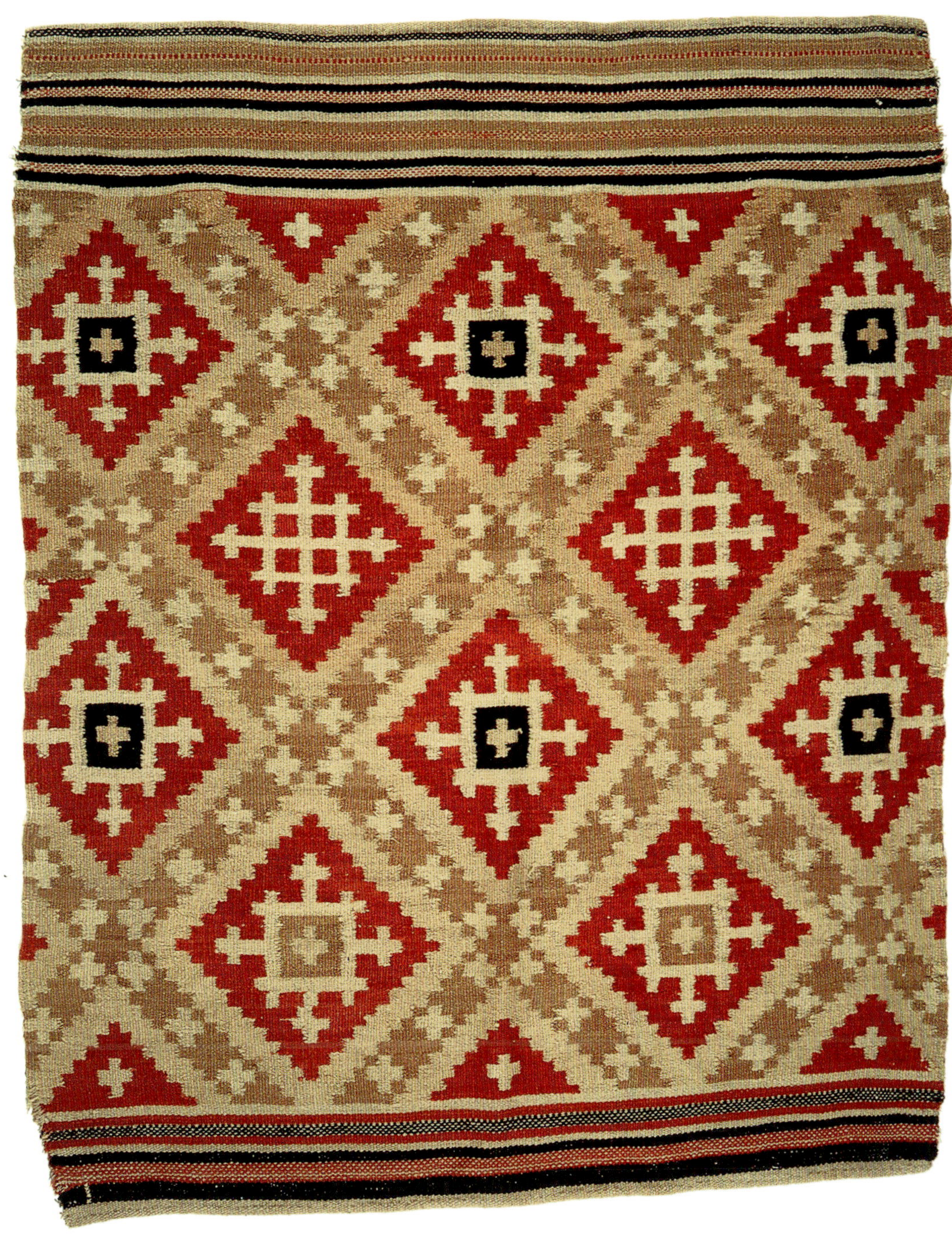

5.26 The cross with a central square
motif. Sogn and Fjordane. *Historical
Museum, University of Bergen.*

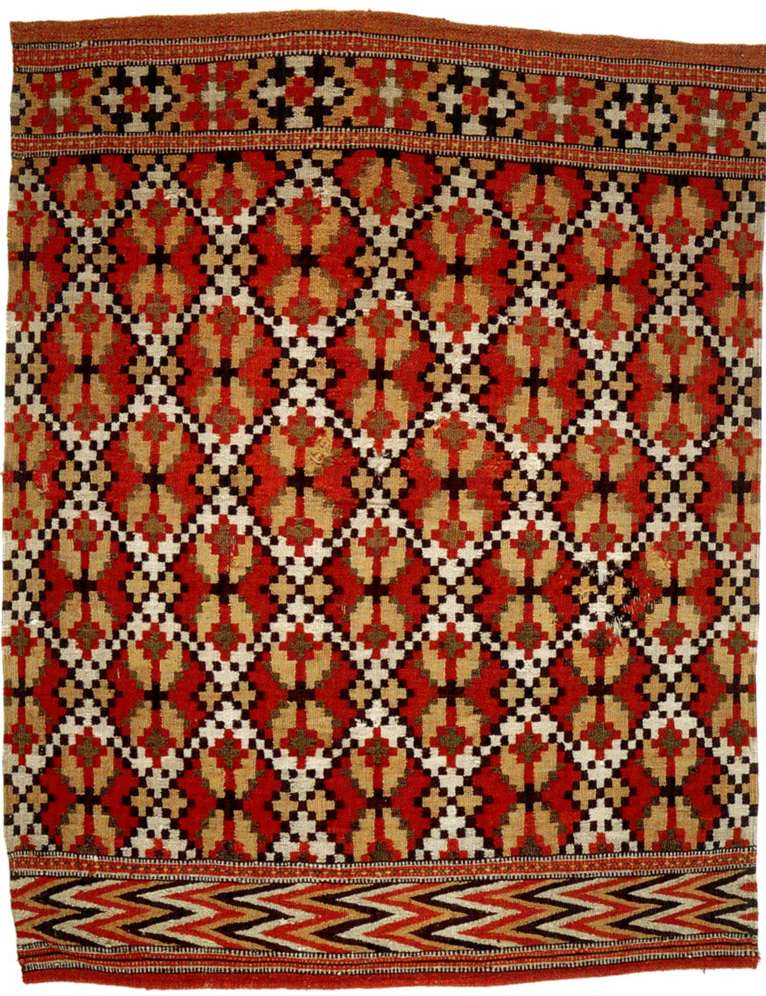

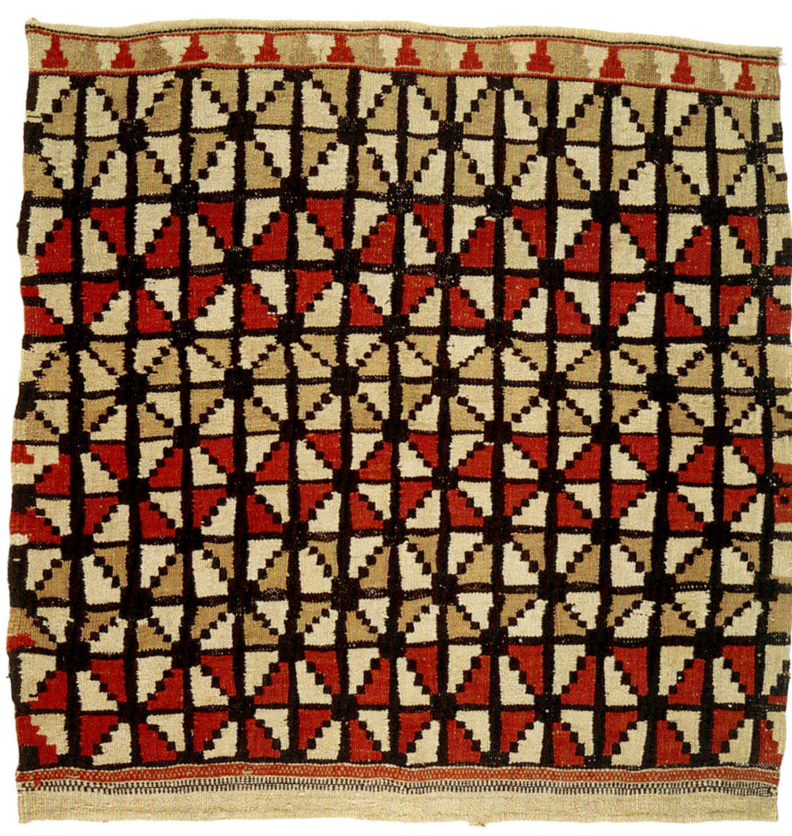

5.27 A pattern resembling the eight-petaled rose interspersed with small crosses. Sogn and Fjordane. *Historical Museum, University of Bergen.*

5.28 A design based on squares divided into triangles. *Historical Museum, University of Bergen.*

Materials and Looms

The square-weave coverlet was commonly woven of a two-ply woolen weft and a two-ply linen warp, sometimes used in a double thickness. Occasionally a warp of tightly spun wool was used, and in a few cases linen was used as a weft material in areas of light color. Warp threads could be as widely spaced as four ends per inch, requiring the use of thick weft yarn and resulting in a coarse, heavy coverlet, or they could be set as closely as eight ends per inch, using finer yarns to produce a much more supple, lightweight weaving. The average size of a square-weave coverlet was four by five feet, varying no doubt from family to family depending on the size of the particular box-shaped bed for which it was intended.

Most of the square-weave coverlets were woven in one piece, indicating the probable use of the warp-weighted loom with its single long top beam. In a few areas of western and southern Norway, square-weave coverlets were woven on a variation of the upright loom, with two beams between which the warp threads were tightly strung (figs. 5.29–5.30). Another loom, surviving in only one instance, used weights to tension the warp threads, which were attached to a lower beam and passed over the top beam to hang behind the loom (fig. 5.31). Both variations of the upright loom were probably patterned after the tapestry looms introduced into eastern Norway during the sixteenth century. A small percentage of square-weave coverlets were woven in two pieces that were sewn together with a middle seam. Coverlets of this type, mostly from the southern districts, were probably woven on the narrower horizontal loom.

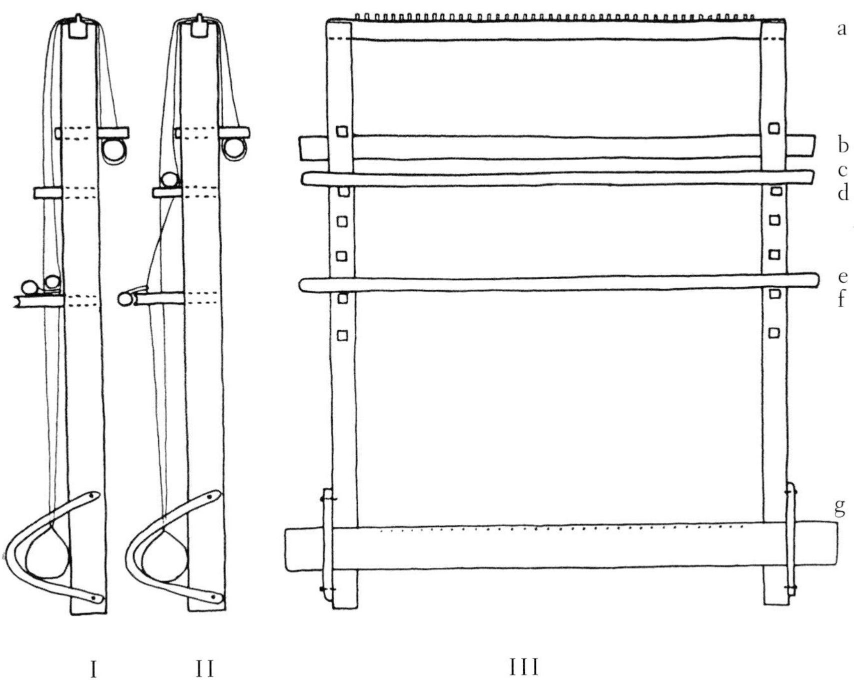

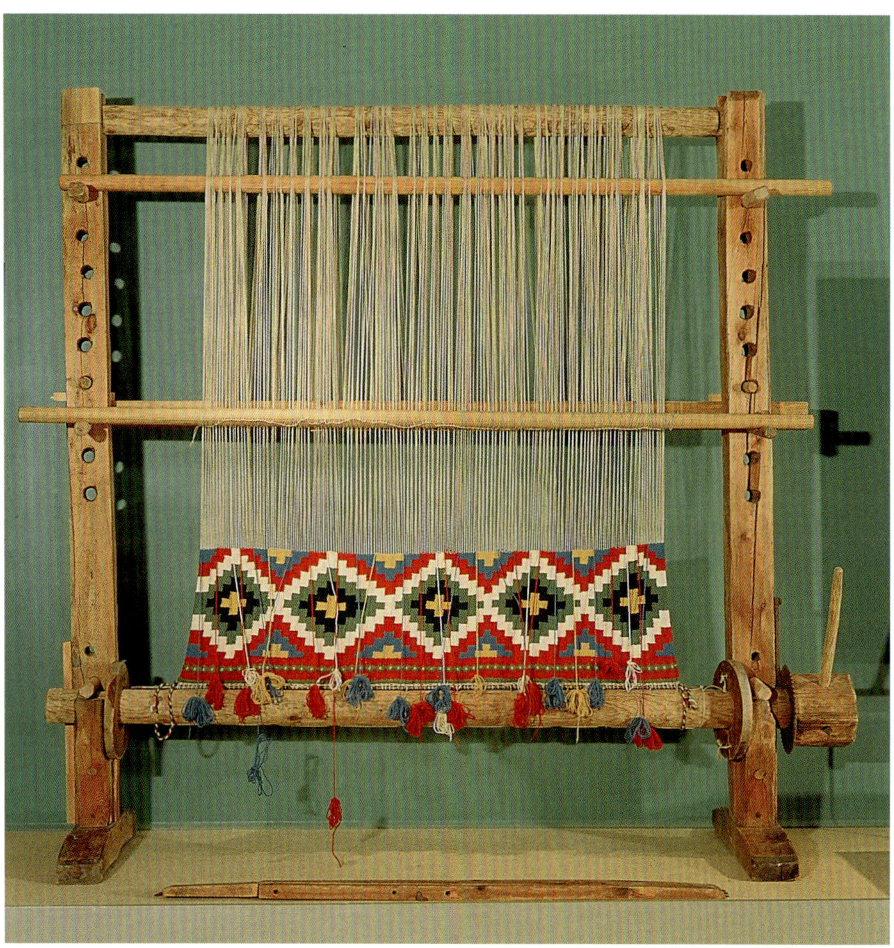

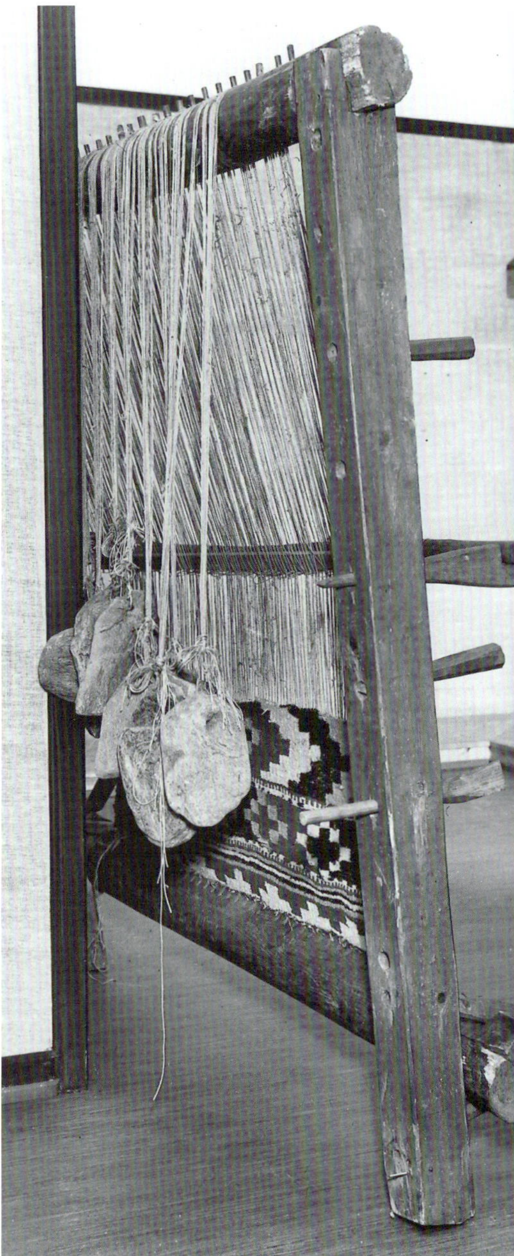

5.30 A two-beamed upright loom from Hordaland. The movable upper beam, just visible above the heddle rod, is held in place behind the loom by pegs in the uprights. As weaving progresses and the finished fabric is wound onto the lower beam, the upper beam will be advanced towards the top of the loom and eventually move to the front. *Norwegian Folk Museum.*

5.31 The cloth beam is at the bottom of this warp-weighted loom in reverse. Warp threads run from the cloth beam over the top beam and hang behind the loom, where they are weighted with stones. *Norwegian Folk Museum.*

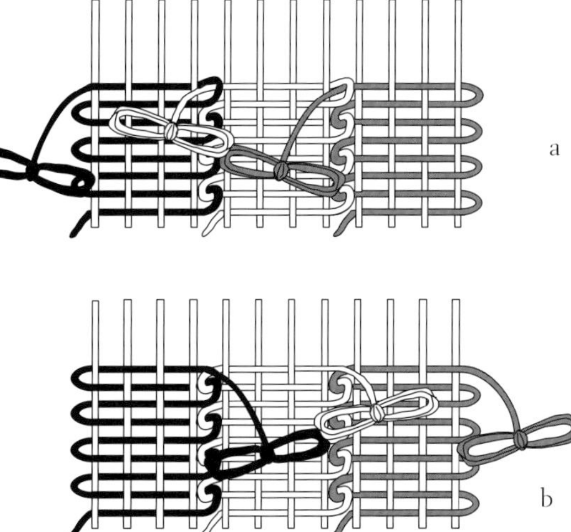

5.32 In square weave, the weft bobbins are woven in their own color area, one after another, across the entire width of the fabric. In this example of the single interlock technique: *(a)* beginning at the right, each bobbin is picked up in turn, interlocked with its neighboring bobbin, and then woven across its pattern area; *(b)* returning from the left, bobbins are woven across their own areas but are held out of the way of the next bobbin so that the two weft threads do not interlock.

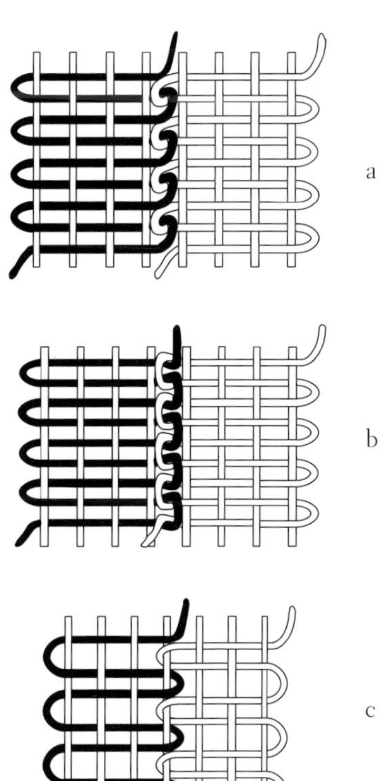

Weaving Techniques

Square-weave coverlets were woven in a weft-faced plain weave that, like tapestry, was worked with small bobbins of weft thread that traveled back and forth within their own area of the warp. However, the geometric nature of the pattern allowed a more methodical approach than was possible in tapestry. The pattern was built one row at a time as bobbins were picked up one after another and woven in turn across the entire width of the fabric (fig. 5.32). At the beginning of a new row of the design, the weft bobbins either expanded into a new area or contracted according to the pattern. When necessary, new color bobbins were introduced, or bobbins were discontinued.

At the vertical lines which separated squares of pattern, neighboring weft threads were joined by one of three interlocking methods: single interlock, double interlock, or single dovetailing. (In some areas of southern Norway, the single dovetailing and interlocking techniques were used in combination.[4]) The single interlock, so named because the weft threads interlocked only when traveling in one direction, joined neighboring weft threads invisibly between the warp threads at the border of the adjoining color areas, resulting in a completely reversible weaving. The double interlock was produced by interlocking the weft threads as they moved in both directions. This caused a ridge to be formed along the joined area on the side facing the weaver, which made the weaving nonreversible. The single dovetailing method required weft threads of neighboring areas to overlap, passing alternately around a common warp thread. A reversible weave resulted, but the join between the two areas of weft had a slightly sawtoothed appearance (fig. 5.33). At the University of Bergen's Historical Museum, which has one of the largest collections of square-weave coverlets in Norway, nearly half of the coverlets are woven in the single interlock technique. Slightly less are woven with the double interlock method, while single dovetailing accounts for only about ten percent of the coverlets.[5]

5.33 Interlocking techniques used in square weave: *(a)* the single interlock makes a smooth reversible fabric; *(b)* the double interlock forms a ridge along the vertical color border on the back of the weaving; *(c)* neighboring weft threads share the same warp thread in the reversible dovetailing technique.

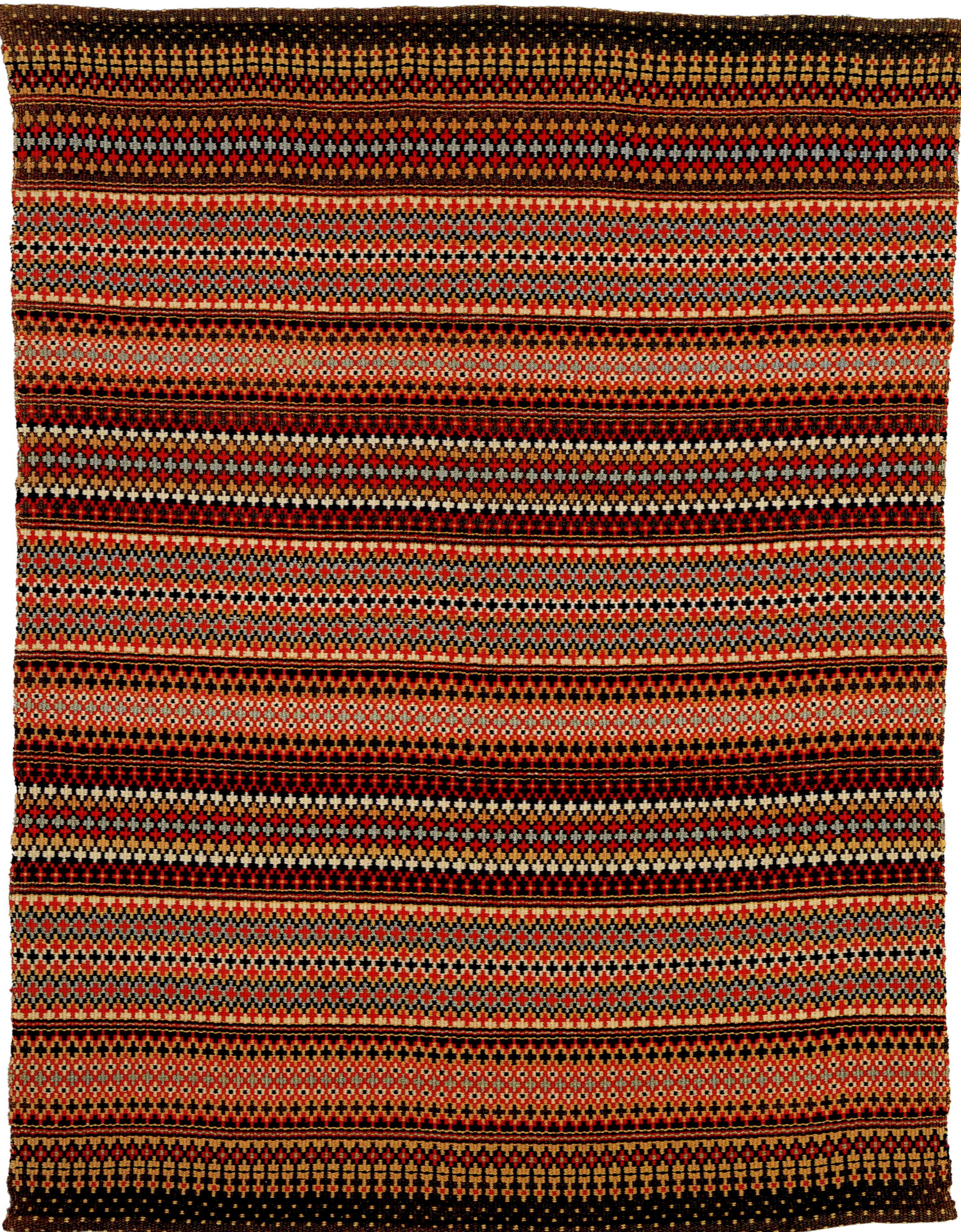

6 / Bound Rosepath Coverlets: Krokbragd

KROKBRAGD MEANS "CROOKED PATTERN," A reference to the jagged designs typical of these weavings, not the torturous movements of the tongue required to say the name. (All of the letters are voiced, quite a mouthful for most Americans.) In English, this weave is often referred to as boundweave or bound rosepath, but it is also known by its Norwegian name of krokbragd.

Although krokbragd coverlets were well known in most parts of Norway (except for the northern districts of Nordland, Troms, and Finnmark), the technique never commanded the respect given to coverlet weaves such as tapestry or square weave. Perhaps this was because the krokbragd technique presented the weaver with less artistic latitude. Yet a multitude of colorful patterns were possible on the smooth, tapestry-like surface of a krokbragd weaving, and the structure of floats on the reverse side made it extra thick and warm as a coverlet. Relatively quick and easy to weave, krokbragd coverlets were a popular choice for everyday use in many Norwegian homes (fig. 6.1).

Origins

It is difficult to say how old the krokbragd weaving tradition is in Norway. Although the earliest pieces preserved in Scandinavia date from the eighteenth century, some authorities believe this type of weaving was known in the Nordic countries at least as early as the Middle Ages.[1] Krokbragd was well known in Finland and the Baltic countries, and was found in weavings from the Middle East as well. In fact, it has been suggested that the earliest experiments in weaving with more than two harnesses (outside of the Far East) began more than two thousand years ago in Syria with a three-harness, weft-faced twill such as krokbragd.[2]

Design and Color

The krokbragd coverlets were composed of rows of small patterns running from selvage to selvage. Crosses, diamonds, and Xs were all variations derived from the chevron, or point-twill, threading of the harnesses, but each of these basic designs could be elongated, shortened, or cut in half and recombined into something completely new (fig. 6.2). The seemingly profuse patterns seen in the krokbragd coverlets were mainly combinations of these few designs presented in a variety of colors. In many coverlets, the zigzag nature of the krokbragd patterns predominated, but coverlets with discrete bands of pattern separated by horizontal stripes were also common (figs. 6.3–6.6).

Traditional krokbragd coverlets had patterns based on a three-harness threading. Additional harnesses could be added to make the patterns more intricate, but this was seldom done. Some coverlets were woven in a variation known as double krokbragd, a slightly different threading that resulted in patterns with doubled points (figs. 6.7–6.10).

At least five colors and sometimes more were used in the krokbragd coverlets, the variety of color combinations adding interest to the ever-changing patterns. Natural sheep white, black, or brown were a part of most color schemes, with shades of red, gold, green, and blue added as the weaver's fancy and supplies of yarn allowed.

Materials and Looms

Krokbragd coverlets were made from a weft of two-ply wool and a warp of linen, hemp, or tightly spun wool, sometimes mixed with goat hair. Warp threads were spaced at five to ten ends per inch depending on the desired result. Widely spaced warp threads called for thicker weft yarns and produced a coarse, heavy weave. A tighter spacing of the warp threads required the use of thinner weft material and resulted in a more supple weave. The traditional single krokbragd was usually woven of thicker materials with warp threads at a setting of five to eight ends per inch. Double krokbragd had somewhat longer floats on the reverse side of the weaving created by the greater distance between pattern points. As a result, this variation was commonly woven with finer weft materials and a closer spacing of the warp threads, from eight to ten ends per inch, which reduced the length of the floats.

Coverlets in the krokbragd technique were generally four to five feet in width and five to six feet in length, and could be woven in one piece or in two pieces sewn together lengthwise. A coverlet made of two pieces indicates the use of the horizontal loom, which made up for its lack of weaving width by offering an easier system for producing the three-harness krokbragd weave. When woven on the two-shed, warp-weighted loom, two of krokbragd's three sheds had to be picked up by hand (fig. 6.11).

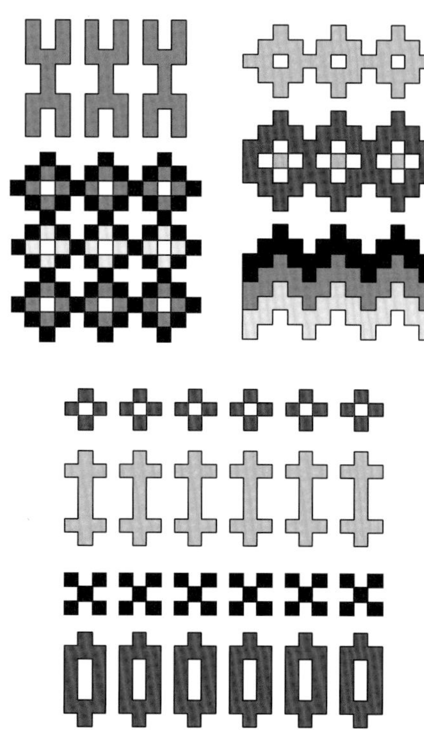

6.2 Krokbragd patterns are repeated across the width of the coverlet. Each pattern can be elongated, truncated, or mixed with another pattern to create variations.

6.3 A krokbragd coverlet brought to the United States from Hol, Hallingdal *(detail below). Photo: Mark Frey. Nordic Heritage Museum.*

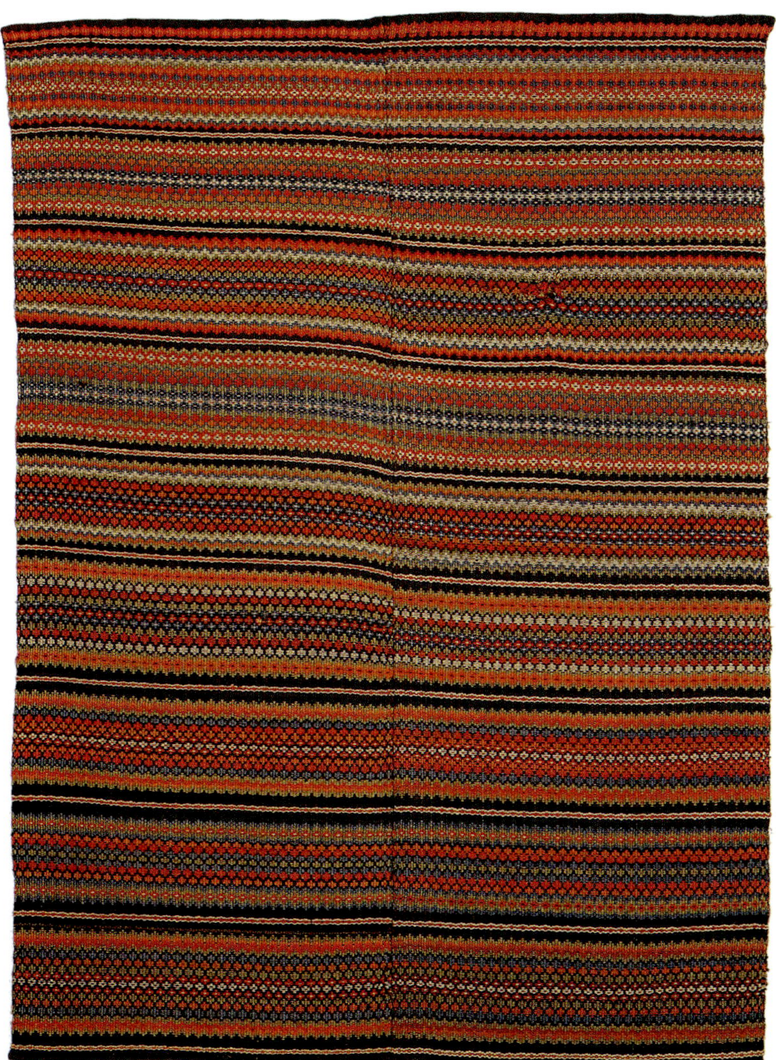

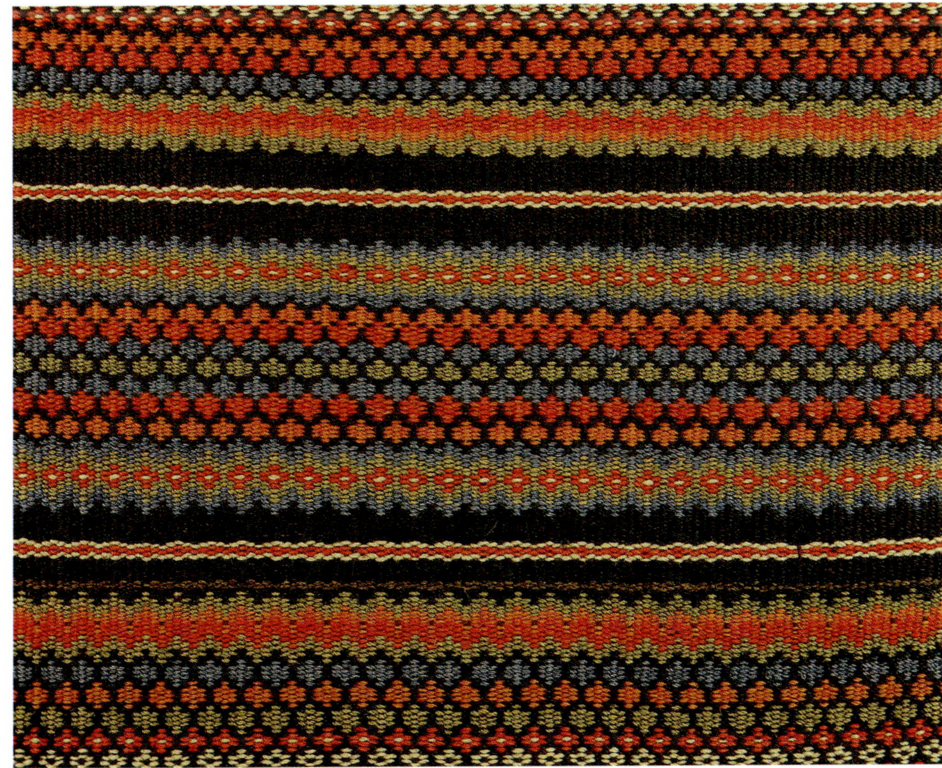

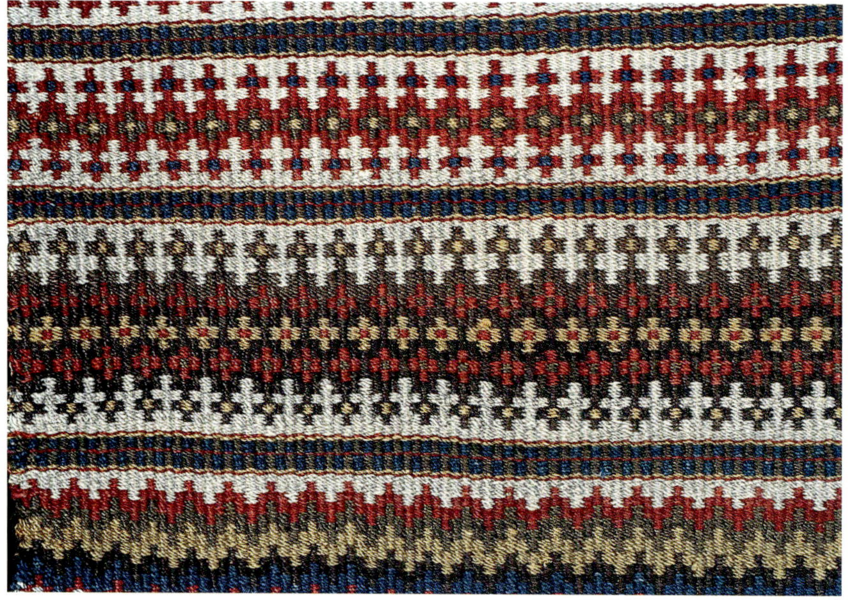

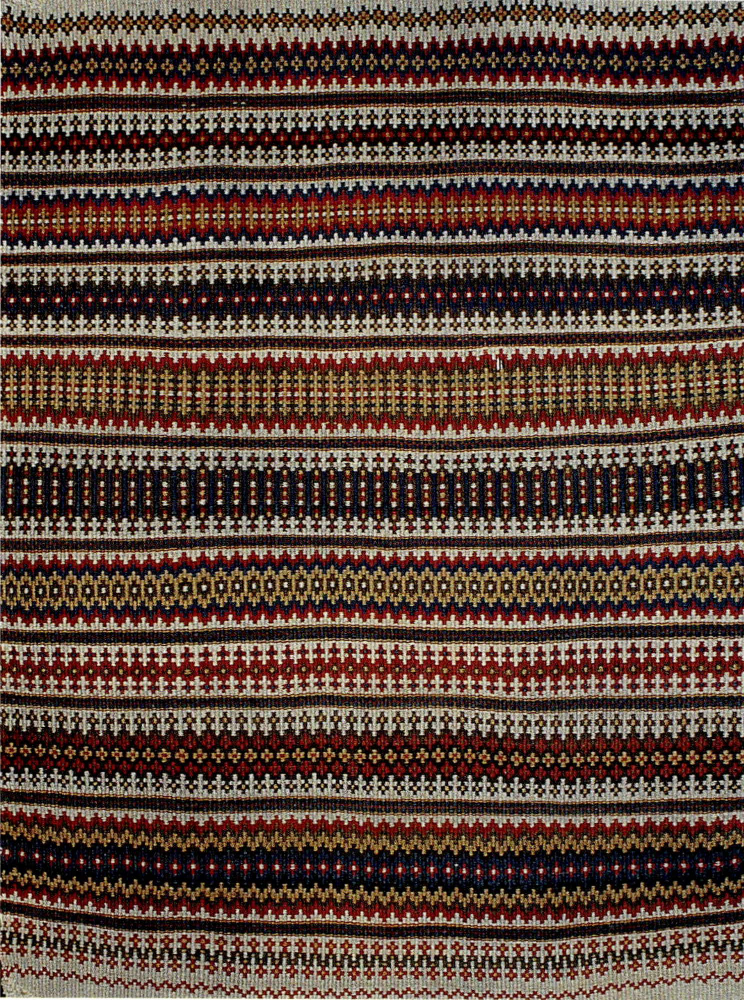

6.4 A krokbragd coverlet from Sunnhordland, brought to the United States in 1896. Detail *(left)* and full view *(below left). Luther College Collection, Vesterheim Norwegian-American Museum.*

6.5 Detail of a krokbragd coverlet from Vest-Agder. *Norwegian Folk Museum.*

6.6 This krokbragd coverlet from Voss was brought to the United States by immigrants in 1868. *Vesterheim Norwegian-American Museum.*

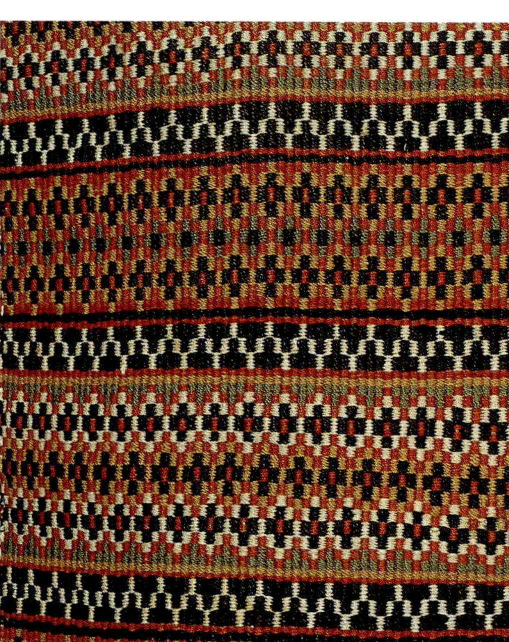

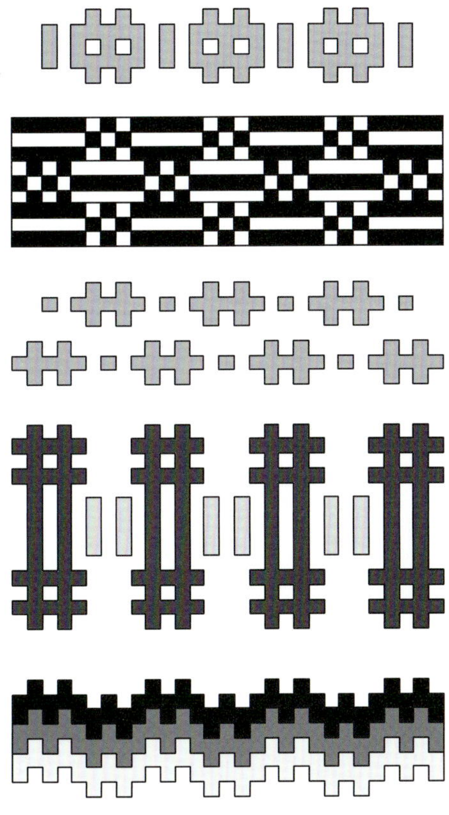

6.7 Double-krokbragd patterns are similar to single krokbragd but with doubled points.

6.8 *(Right)* double-krokbragd coverlet from Sogn and Fjordane *(detail below)*. *Photo: Mark Frey. Nordic Heritage Museum.*

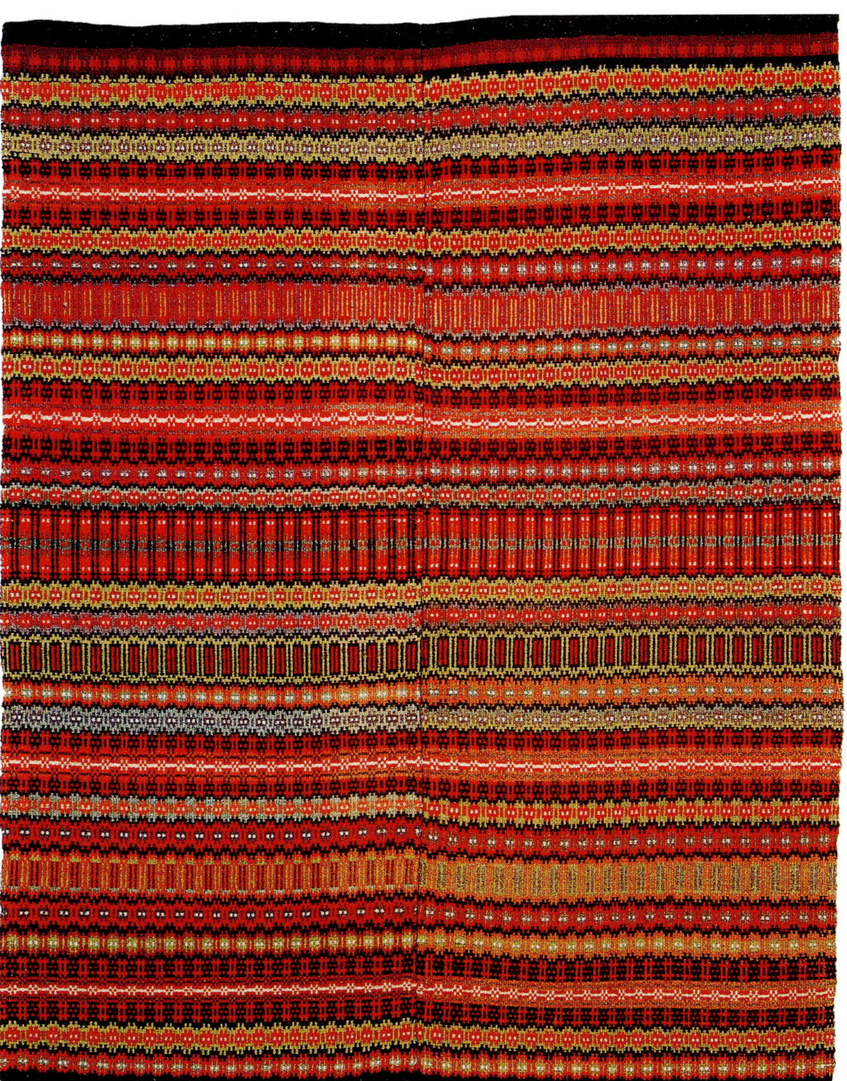

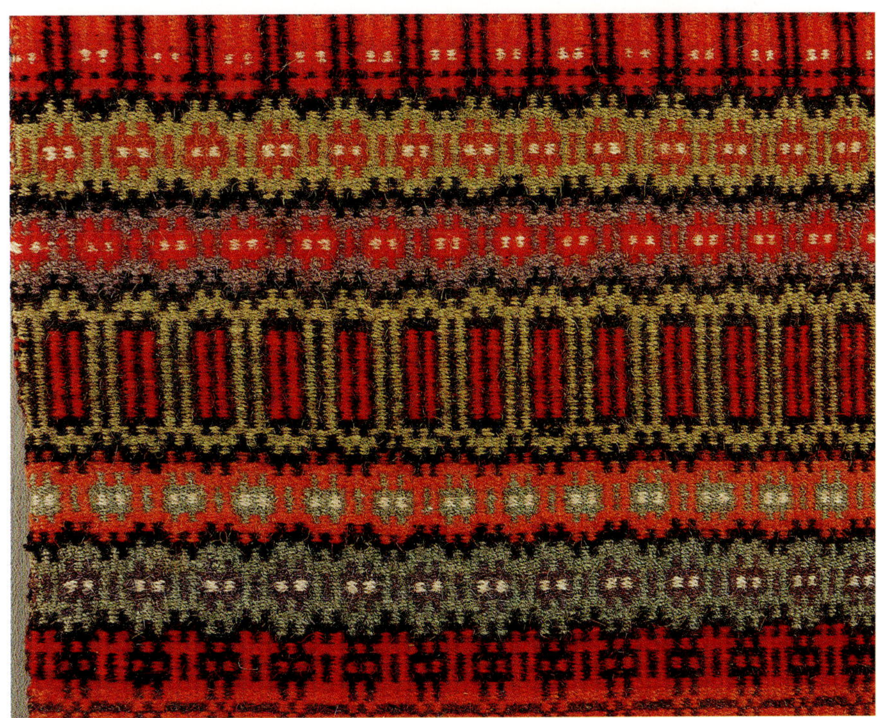

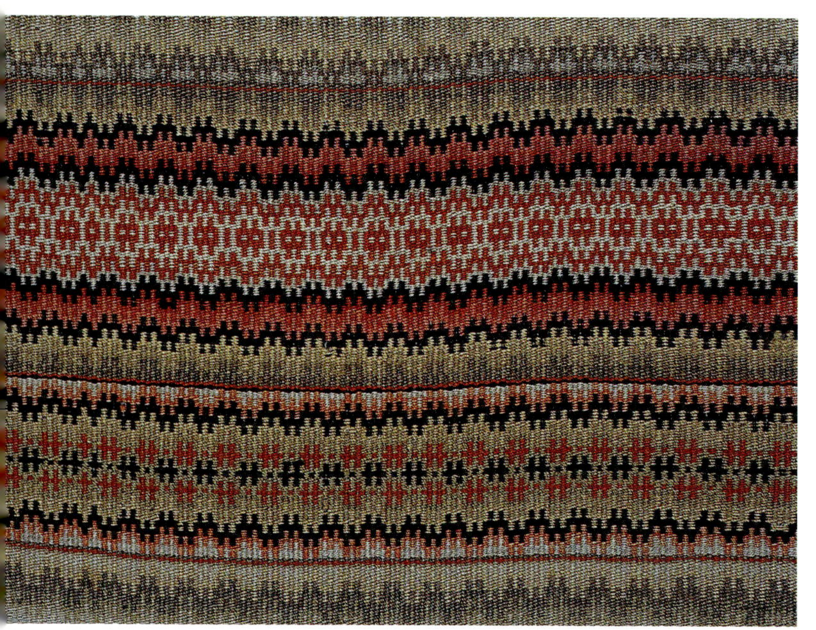

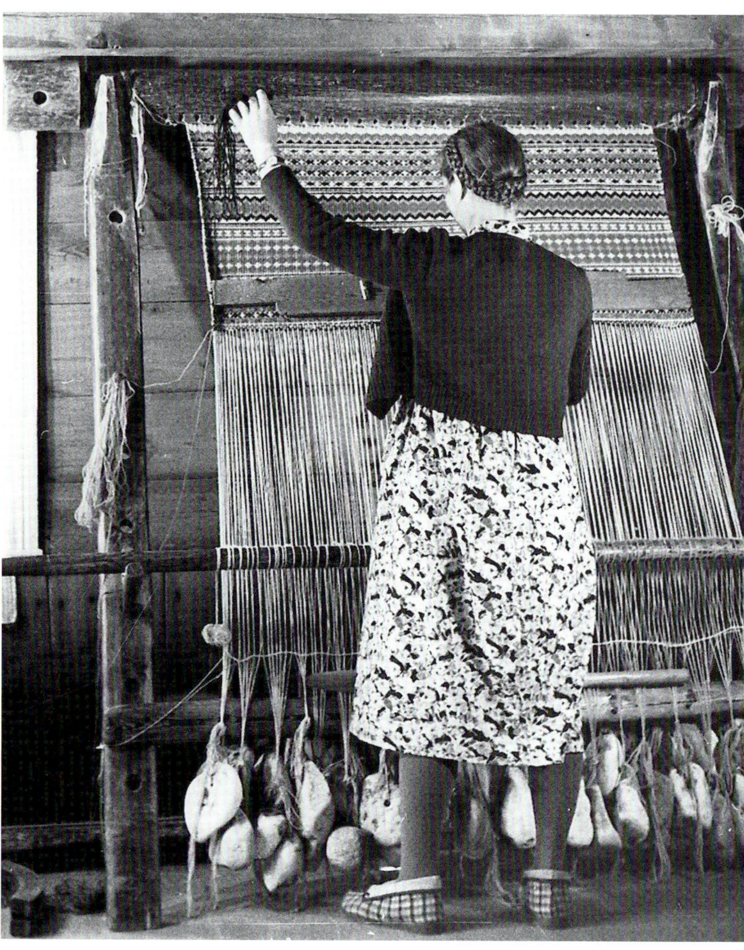

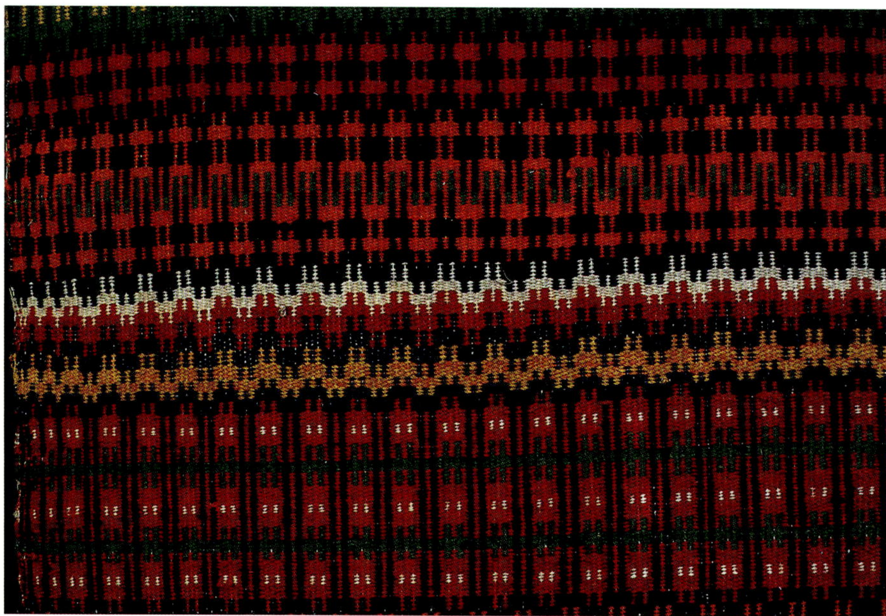

6.9 Detail of a double-krokbragd coverlet from Gudbrandsdal. *Vesterheim Norwegian-American Museum.*

6.10 *(Left)* Detail of a double-krokbragd coverlet from Sogn and Fjordane. Note the area of single krokbragd (at left) that strengthens the selvedge. *Vesterheim Norwegian-American Museum.*

6.11 *(Above)* A krokbragd coverlet is being woven on the warp-weighted loom. The weaver has just woven a shot of dark yarn and is setting the weft bobbin aside. A temple (an adjustable flat wooden stick with teeth at each end) has been placed on the weaving to maintain the proper width of the coverlet. Hordaland. *Norwegian Folk Museum.*

Weaving Techniques

The *krokbragd* coverlets were created from a weft-faced point-twill structure not far removed from the regular over and under of plain weave. The two harnesses of plain weave, which control alternate, or even and odd, warp threads, were supplemented by a third harness that split the work of one of the plain weave harnesses. Where two shots of weft thread covered all the even and odd warps in a plain weave, three shots were needed in krokbragd to cover the even warps and the two sets of odd warps (fig. 6.12). Floats were formed on the back of the weaving whenever the weft threads skipped behind the odd-numbered warp threads, while on the right side of the weaving the possibilities for pattern were expanded tremendously from that available in a plain weave (fig. 6.13). Krokbragd was woven with a steady repetition of the three harnesses (1, 2, 3, 1, 2, 3 . . .), with one shot of weft thrown through the shed opened by each harness. Patterns were determined by the color of yarn selected for each pass of the weft thread.

6.12 Cross section of plain weave and krokbragd. *(a)* The weft in a plain weave travels alternately over and under the warp threads in step 1, and over and under the opposite warp threads in step 2. After two shots of weft, every warp thread is covered. *(b)* In krokbragd, the odd-numbered warp threads are split between two harnesses, and a plain-weave harness controls the even-numbered warp threads. Three shots of weft are now required to cover all of the warp threads. Half the odd-numbered warps are covered in step 1, the second half in step 2, and all the even-numbered warp threads are covered in step 3 (the plain-weave harness).

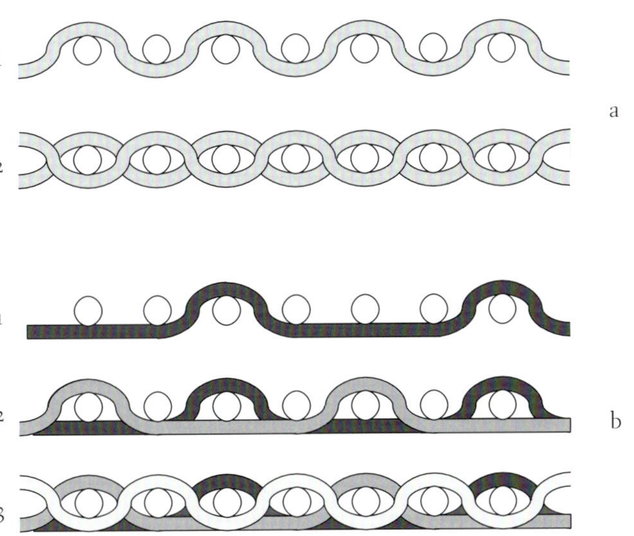

6.13 Krokbragd coverlet folded to show both sides (detail of fig. 6.1). The distinctive patterns created on the front *(right)* are made possible by a layer of floats underneath *(left)*. *Photo: Mark Frey. Nordic Heritage Museum.*

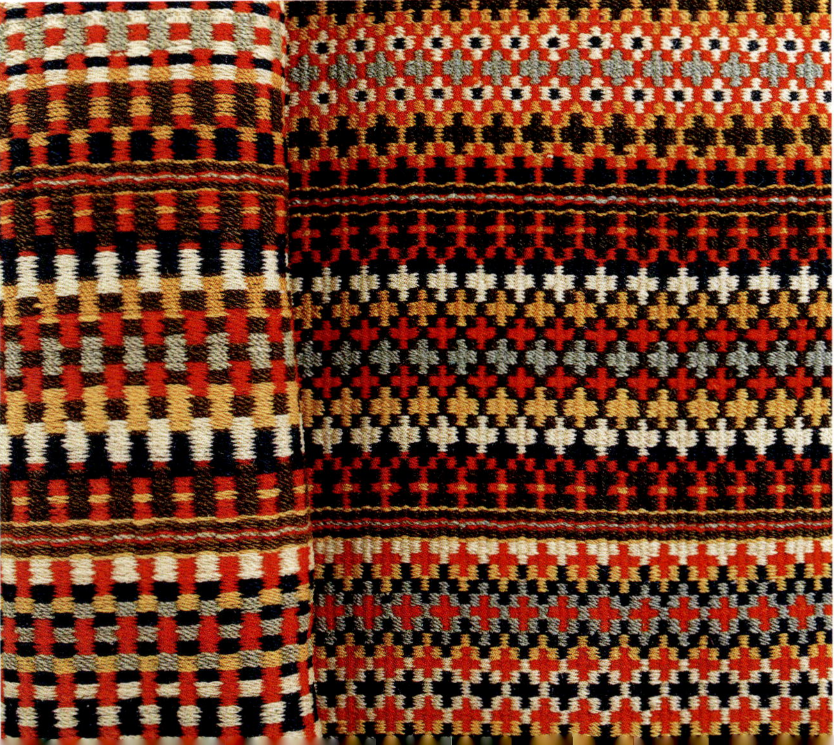

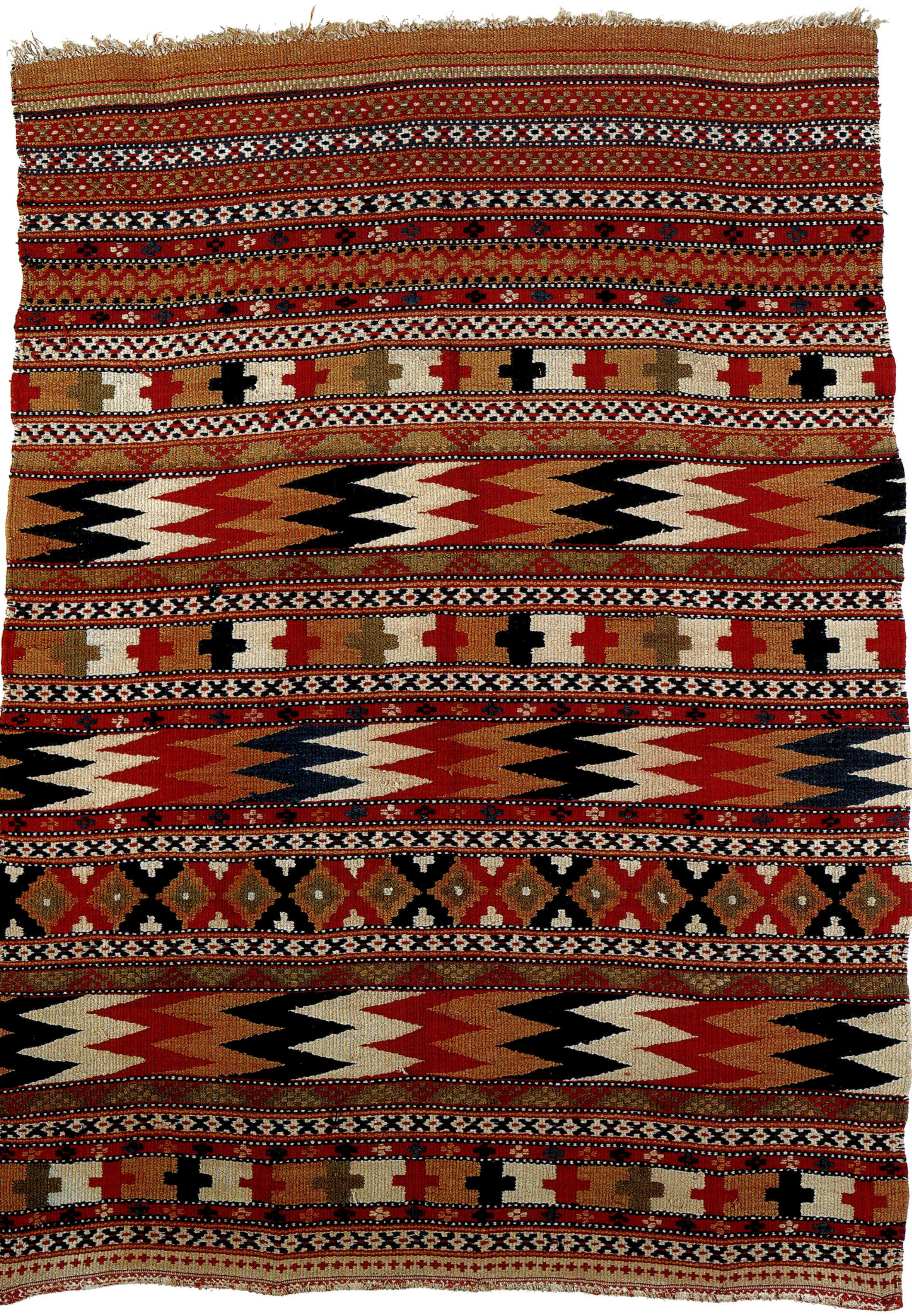

7 / *Other Weft-Faced Coverlets: Kjerringtenner, Grene, Lynildvev, Vestfoldsmett, Dansk brogd*

A NUMBER OF COVERLETS WOVEN IN THE BASIC weft-faced structure form their own distinct groups, often localized to one district of the country. Included in this category are coverlets in the pick-and-pick technique (used throughout Norway but most notably by the Sea Sami), lightning weave, brocading, Danish weave, and a group that combines many of the weft-faced techniques within one coverlet (fig. 7.1).

Pick-and-Pick Coverlets: Kjerringtenner

The most basic of the weft-faced weaves found in the Norwegian coverlets is the vertical and horizontal striping known as *kjerringtenner*, or old woman's teeth, a reference to the gap-toothed smiles that were once the hallmark of old age. This weft-faced plain-weave technique, referred to as pick-and-pick in English, was often used to produce simple coverlets. By alternating the color of weft yarn, a variety of patterns derived from variations of vertical and horizontal stripes was possible (fig. 7.2). Colorful, serviceable coverlets with pattern throughout, or coverlets with regular bands of pattern, could be produced in a fraction of the time required for one of the tapestry weaves (figs. 7.3–7.5).

Although this quick and easy technique was probably common for some everyday uses, such weavings were not of heirloom quality, and relatively few examples are represented in today's museum collections. The pick-and-pick technique was frequently used, however, in the borders of the square-weave coverlets, where it often comprised the entire pattern or served as a divider between other types of weaving.

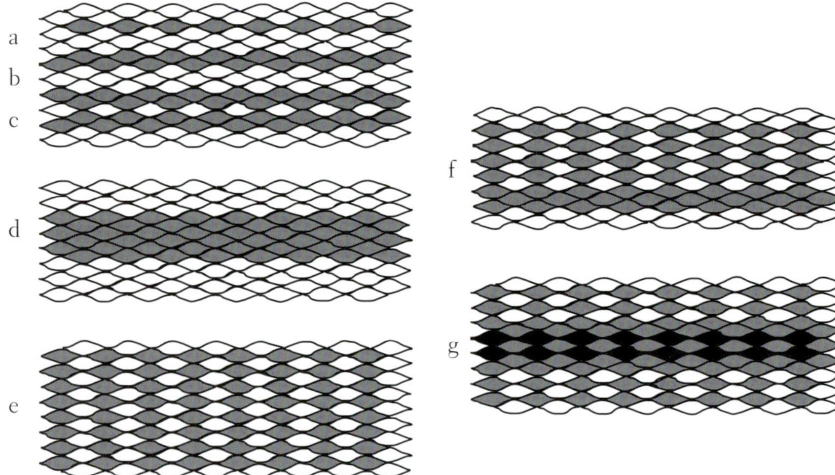

7.2 Patterns in the pick-and-pick technique are created by varying the color of the weft yarn in weft-faced plain weave: (*a*) one shot of weft in a contrasting color creates a row of dots; (*b*) two shots of weft in a contrasting color gives a thin line; (*c*) a combination of (*a*) and (*b*) creates a chain-like pattern; (*d*) several shots of a contrasting color results in a horizontal stripe; (*e*) alternating shots of two contrasting colors create vertical stripes; (*f*) a combination of horizontal and vertical stripes produces a comb-like pattern; (*g*) combinations of the above steps result in patterns such as a row of "crosses."

7.3 Coverlet of simple horizontal stripes. In the detailed view (*below*), note that each smaller stripe consists of four shots of a contrasting color. Jølster, Sogn and Fjordane. *Vesterheim Norwegian-American Museum, private collection.*

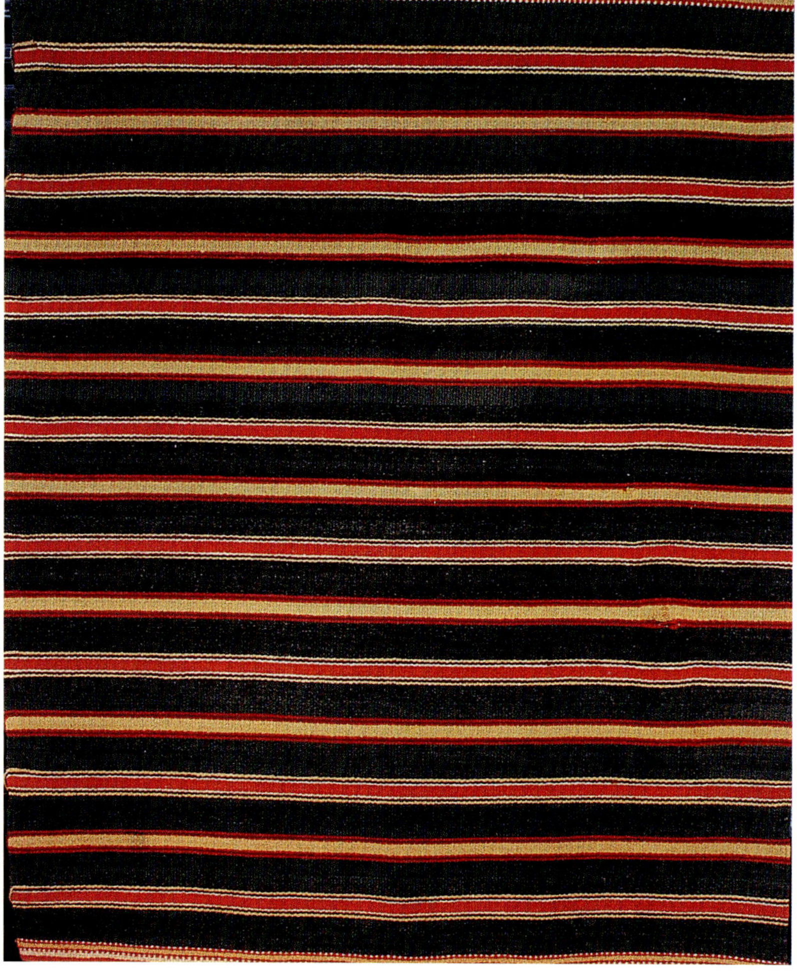

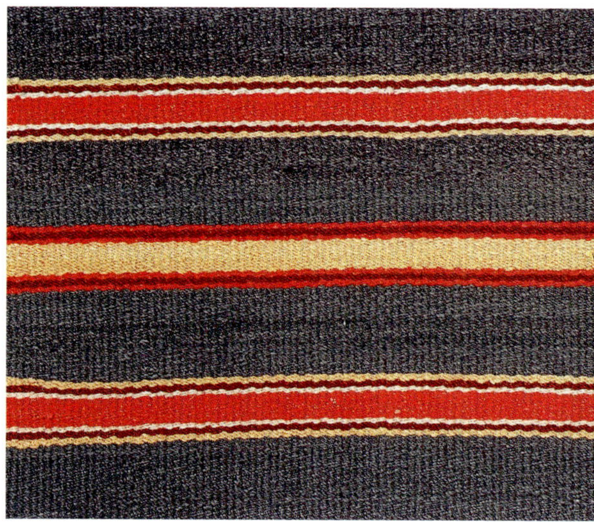

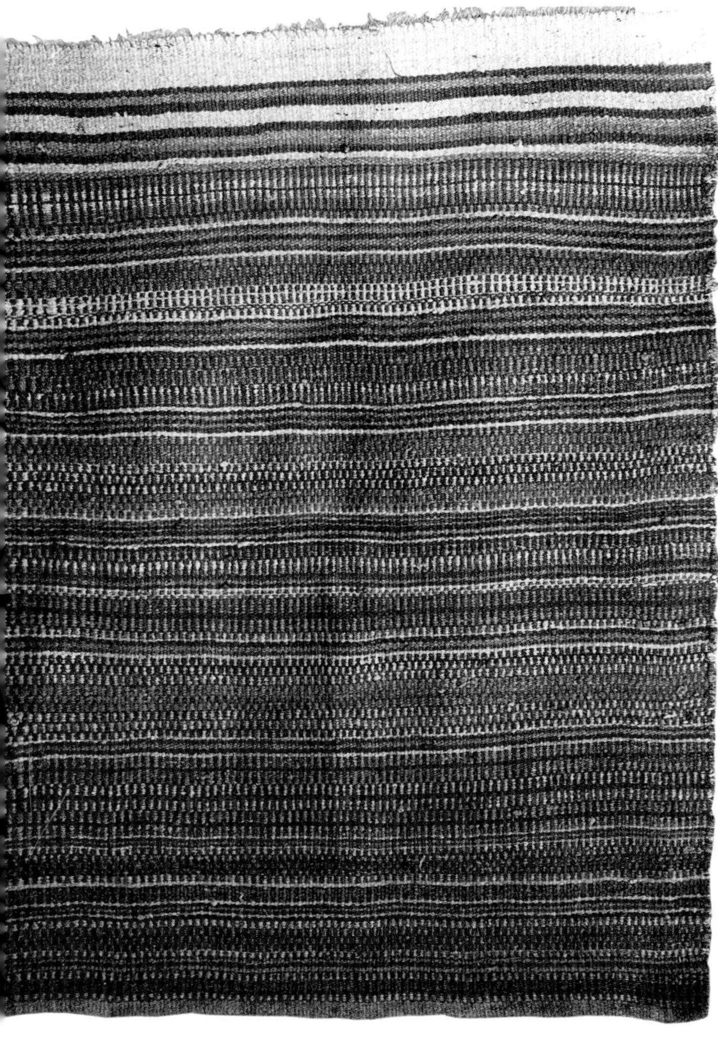

7.4 Pick-and-pick coverlet with pattern
throughout. Hordaland. *Historical Museum,
University of Bergen.*

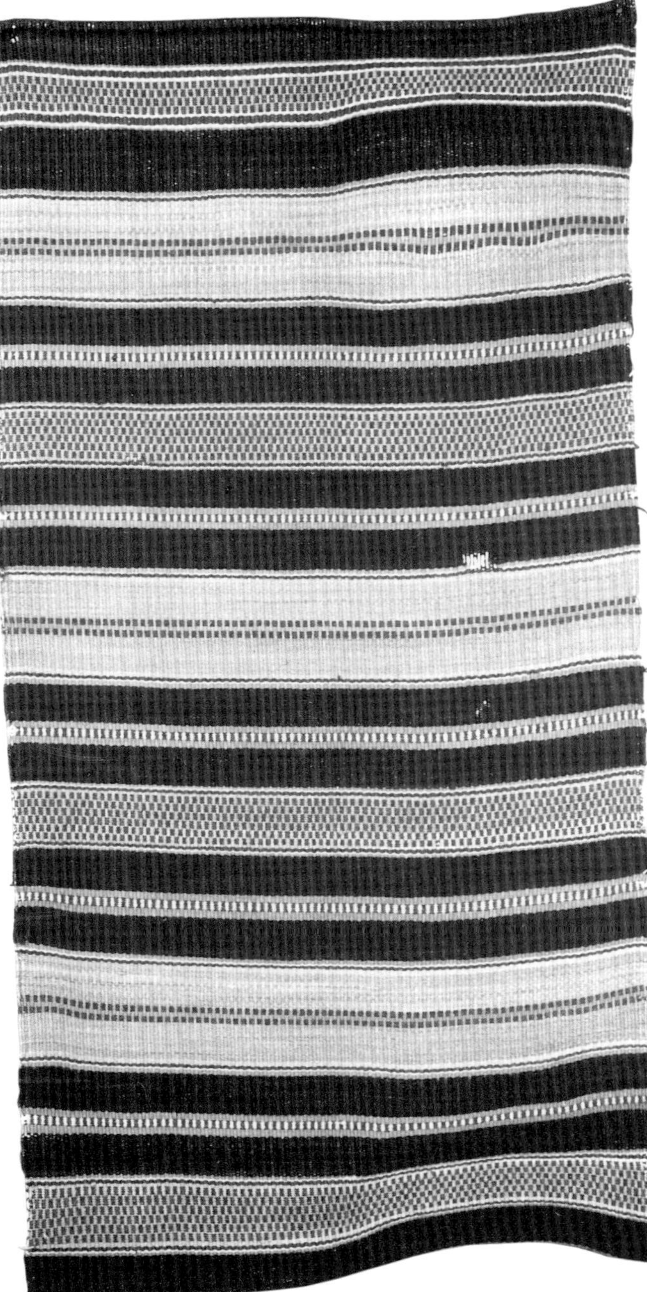

7.5 Bands of pick-and-pick pattern alternating with plain areas woven in contrasting
colors. Sør-Trøndelag. *National Museum
of Decorative Arts, Trondheim.*

Sea Sami Coverlets: Grene

In the Arctic region of northern Norway, a distinctive type of coverlet known as a *grene* was woven by the Sami. Although the grene was woven from the simple pick-and-pick technique (see above), the use of thick woolen yarn and the characteristic horizontal striping in natural wool colors made these coverlets unique (fig. 7.6).

The Sami are an indigenous people that live in the Norwegian districts of Troms and Finnmark and in the northern reaches of Sweden, Finland, and Russia. The Sea Sami of coastal Norway, whose settled lifestyle allowed them to raise sheep, wove *grener* (pl. of grene) for their own use and as trade goods for traveling merchants from other parts of Norway. They also traded grener to the nomadic Sami, although sometimes these wandering reindeer herders wove their own coverlets using wool from sheep raised for them by their coastal relatives.

In the harsh conditions of the Arctic, a thick warm coverlet had many uses. Primarily a bed cover in either hut or tent, the grene was also used as a lap robe by those riding in a sled or a boat, and as a tarp for covering a load lashed onto a sled. Worn grener were used as tent canvas during the winter (fig. 7.7). Such everyday uses for the grene were common in northern Norway until the Second World War.

The materials of a traditional grene were a single-strand wool that was tightly twisted to the right (Z twist) in the warp and loosely twisted to the left (S twist) in the weft. Warp threads that were doubled in the warping process and set at about four ends per inch, combined with the thick fleecy weft, produced a heavy, tightly packed weave. Grener were traditionally woven with a background of white interspersed at regular intervals with rows of horizontal stripes and dots in brown or black, although in more recent times the color scheme has been reversed in some grener (fig. 7.8). Occasionally vegetable dyes were used to contribute rows of color to the otherwise stark appearance of the grene.

A distinctive characteristic of the grene was the starting border, a narrow band of weaving that was perpendicular to the rest of the coverlet and ended with tassels that hung down on either side. This border, which gave the grene a third selvage, was the result of the warping method used for the warp-weighted loom on which the grene was traditionally woven (see "Warping the Warp-Weighted Loom," page 100). The warp ends at the bottom of the grene were tied in simple overhand knots, leaving a long fringe.

7.6 The traditional Sami coverlet known as a *grene* in Norwegian (*rátnu* in Sami). *Vesterheim Norwegian-American Museum.*

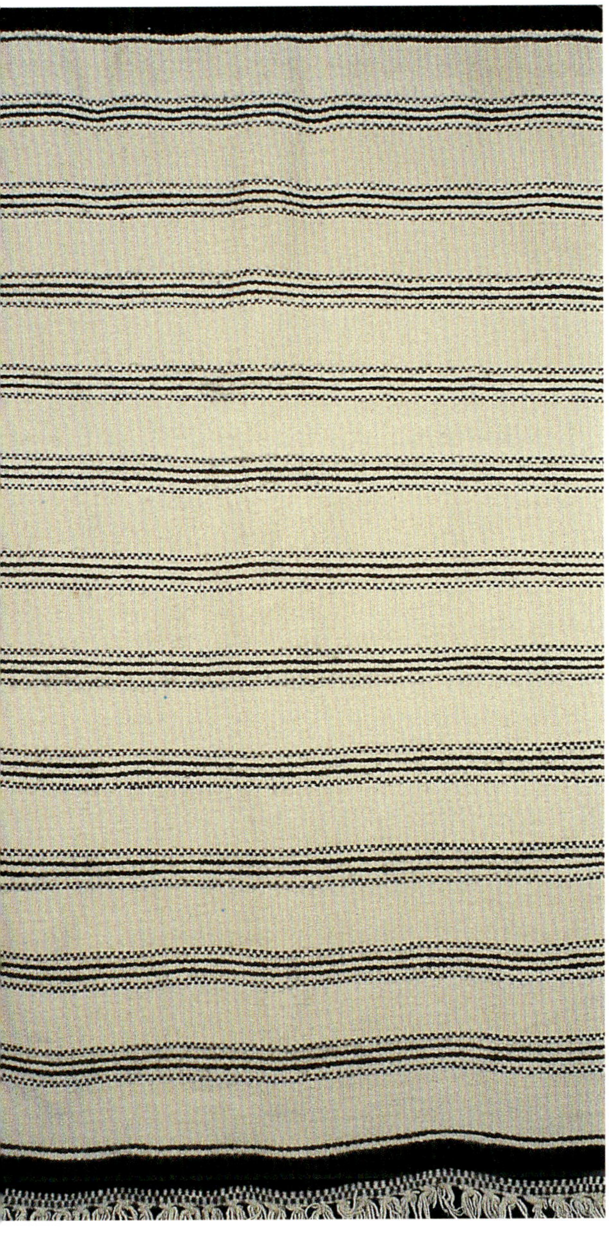

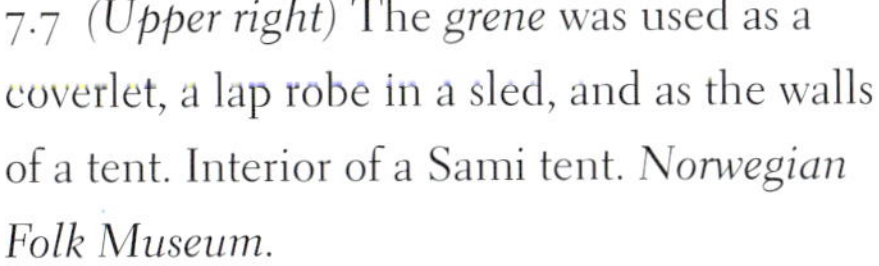

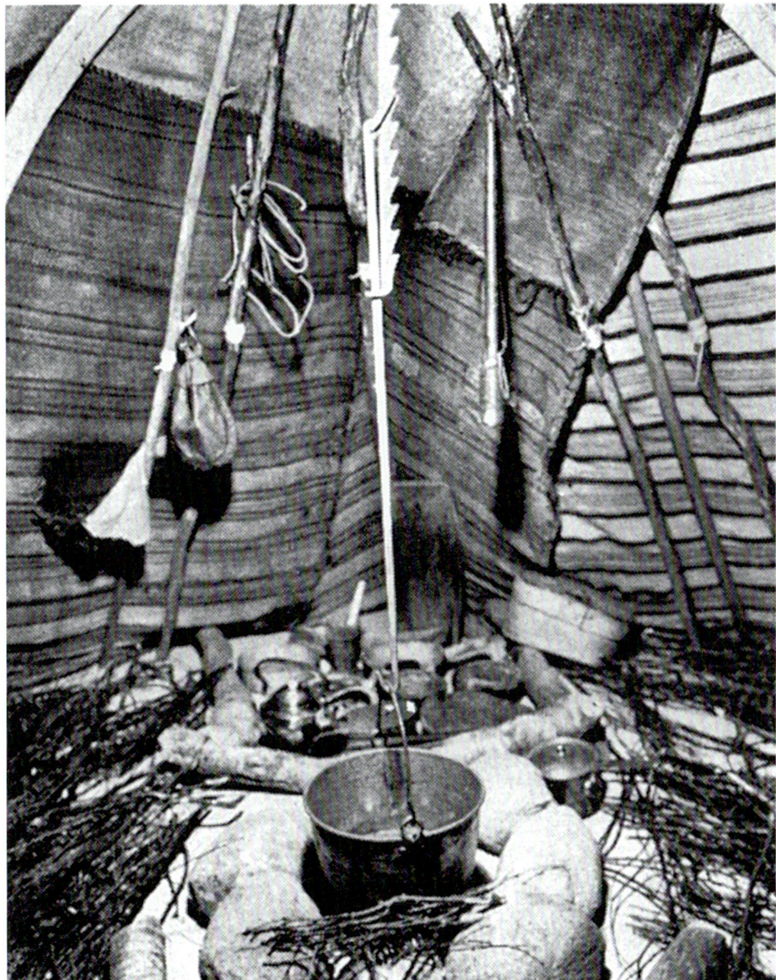

7.7 *(Upper right)* The *grene* was used as a coverlet, a lap robe in a sled, and as the walls of a tent. Interior of a Sami tent. *Norwegian Folk Museum.*

7.8 A distinctive starting border with tassels at the ends is characteristic of the *grene*. Two types of *grene* are seen here, the traditional white with black stripes, and the more recent black with white stripes. *Norwegian Folk Museum.*

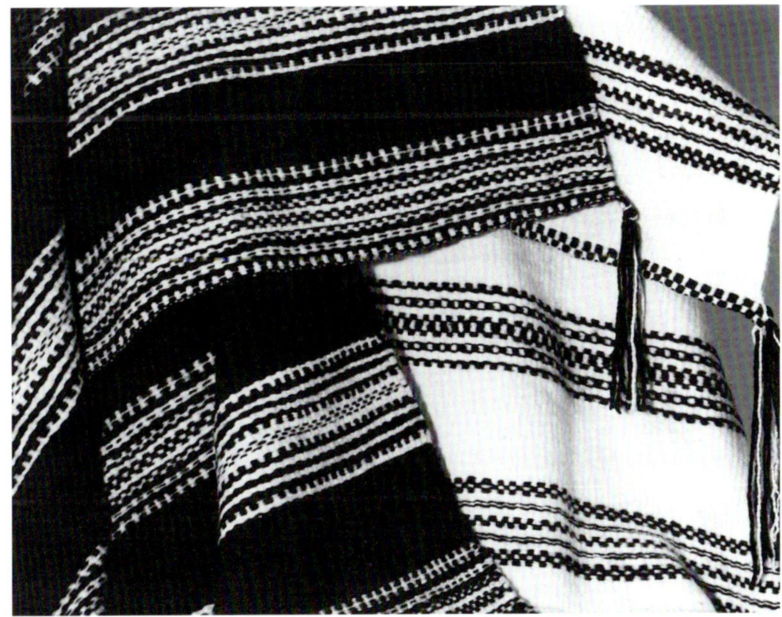

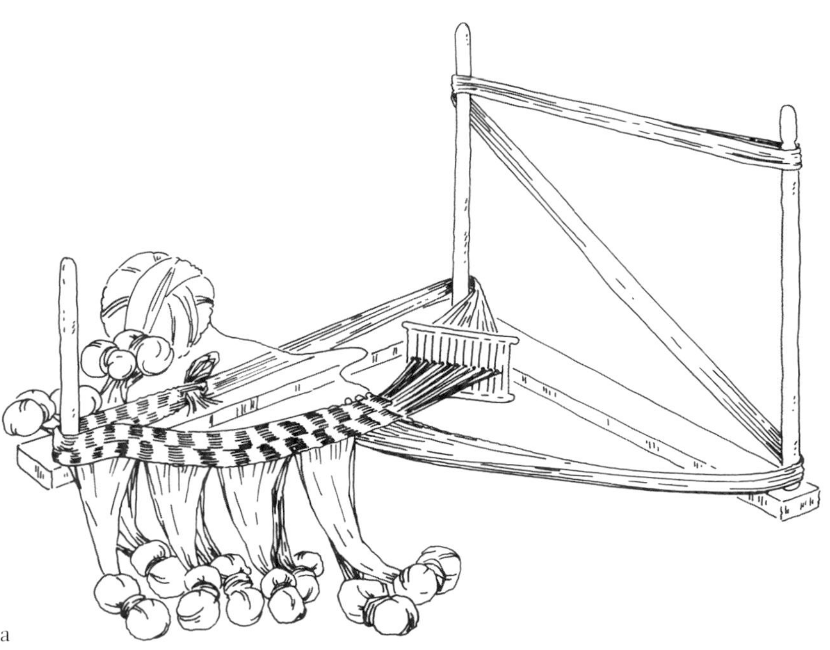

a

7.9 The Sami method of warping: *(a)* A band of black and white stripes is woven
with a rigid heddle (the small fence-like loom often used for bandweaving, *center*).
Large loops of weft thread extend from one side of the band to wrap around the
warping frame. Completed bundles of weft loops lie in groups on the floor. *(b)* A
loop of weft is passed through each shed of the band and will be passed around the
warping frame. Two weft threads are in each shed of the band. The ball of weft
material remains to one side of the band during weaving. *Drawings by Kate Holmsen
Sevëg in Haugen, Samisk husflid i Finnmark (Landbruksforlaget 1987).*
Facing page: (c) A Sami weaver sits on the floor beside her warping frame, preparing
the warp for a grene. (d) When the band is attached to the top beam of the loom, the
loops of weft hanging from the side of the band become the doubled warp threads
of a grene. (e) The warping band is visible at the top of this partially woven grene.
Norwegian Folk Museum.

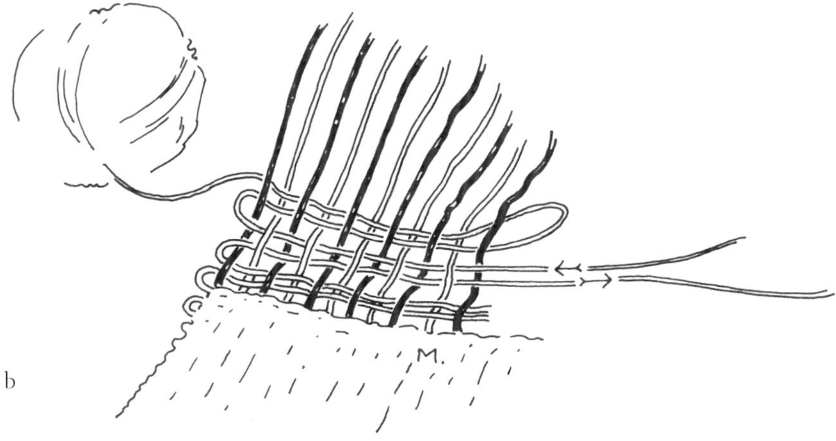

b

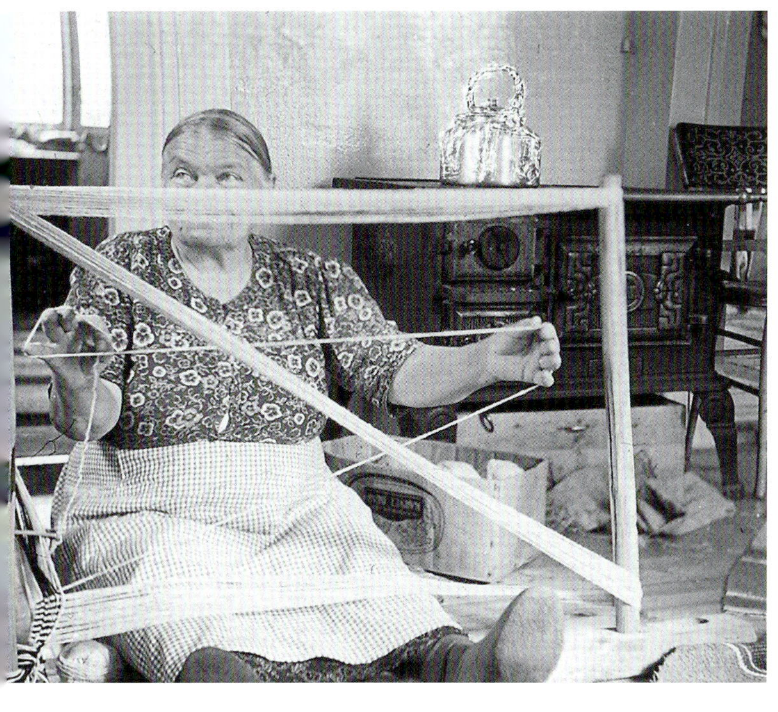

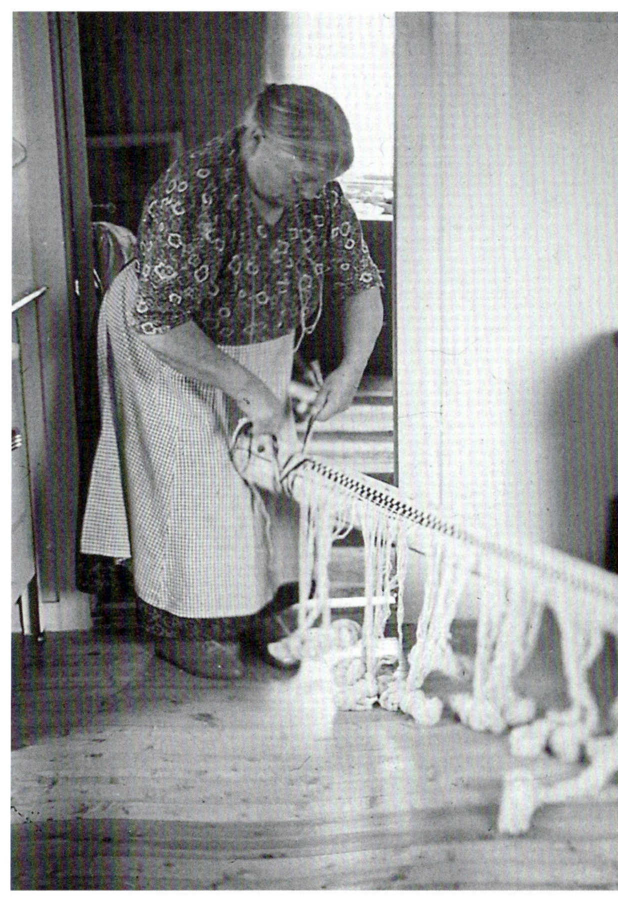

d

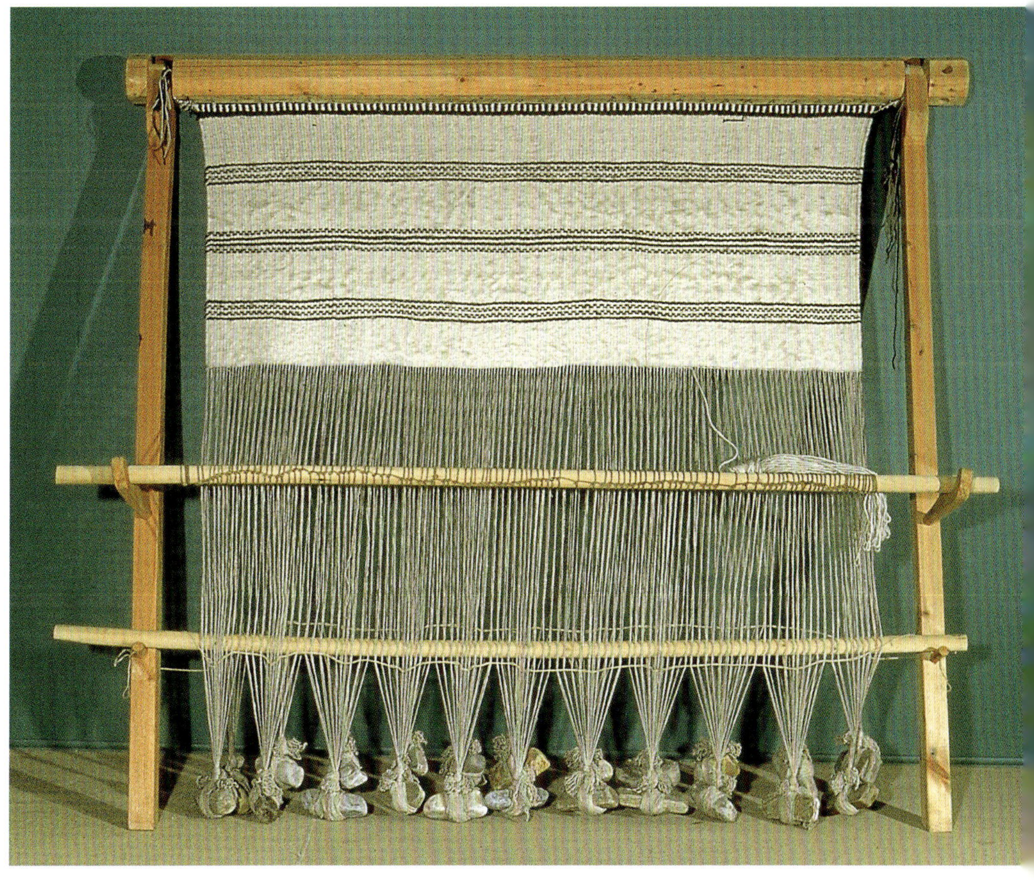

e

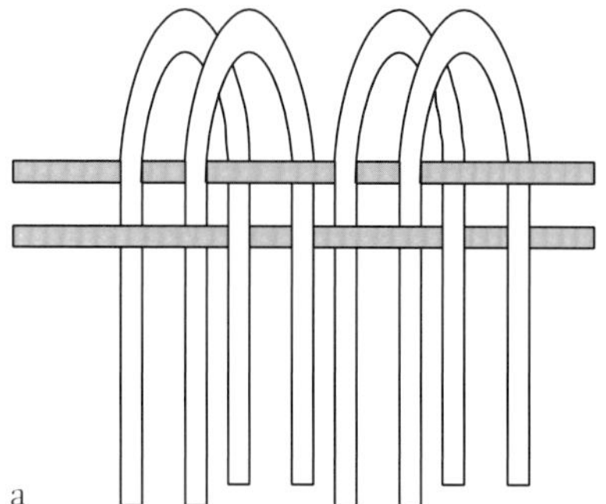

a

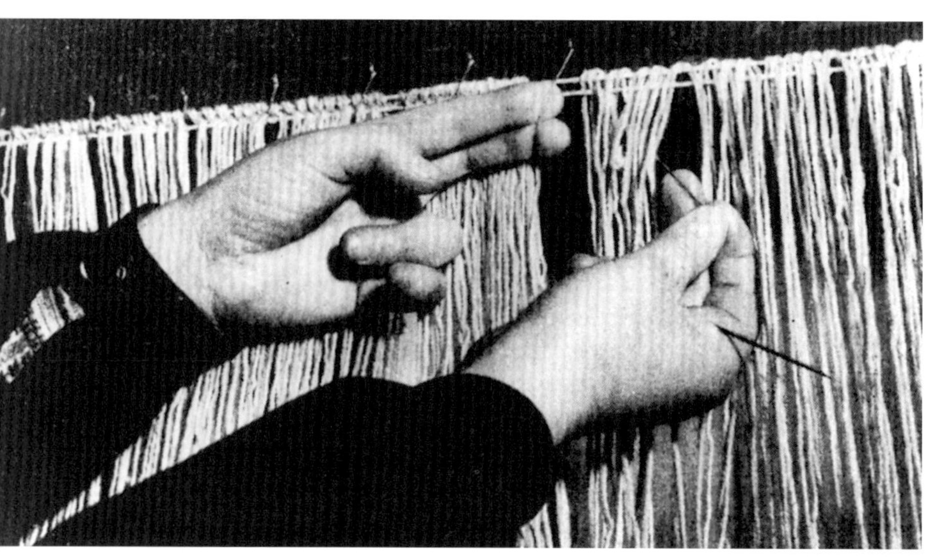

b

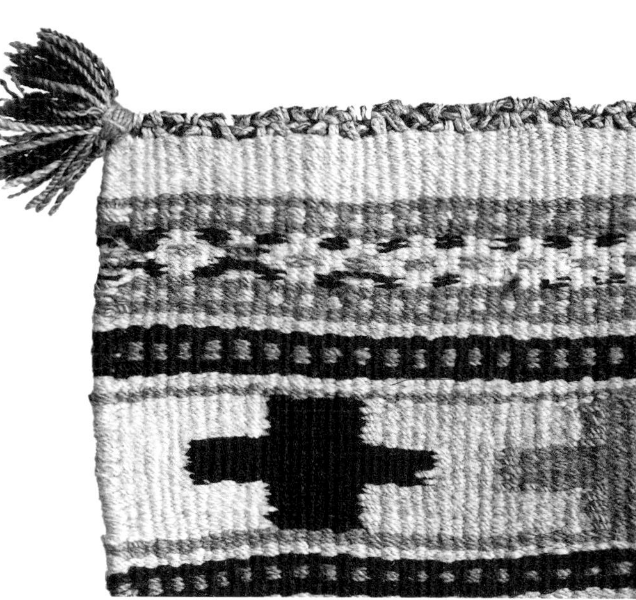

c

7.10 An alternate method for warping the warp-weighted loom: *(a)* A heading cord is threaded through loops of warp material. *After Engelstad 1958. (b)* The heading cord is sewn to the top beam of the loom. *Norwegian Folk Museum. (c)* The heading cord becomes a part of the finished weaving, as seen in this square weave coverlet. *Historical Museum, University of Bergen.*

Lightning-Weave Coverlets: Lynildvev

In the western and southern districts, the pattern of zigzags known as lightning weave that commonly appeared as a border in square-weave coverlets was occasionally transformed into the central theme (figs. 7.11–7.12). The lightning weave is a tapestry technique composed of vertical stripes that slant back and forth over one another in a variety of ways. Regularly stacked columns of zigzags, wildly vibrating sequences of zigzags, and zigzags with feathered points all bring to mind the spectacular flashes of light for which this weave is named (figs. 7.13–7.14).

In other respects, the lightning-weave coverlets were similar to those woven in square weave. The zigzag motif filled the central pattern area, borders at the top and bottom were composed of a variety of techniques, and the materials were a warp of linen or wool and a weft of wool. In many cases the lightning-weave coverlets display the red, white, black, and gold color scheme favored in the square weaves of the western districts.

7.11 Lightning-weave coverlet with borders of
pick-and-pick above and supplementary weft
patterning below. *Historical Museum,
University of Bergen.*

7.12 *(Below right)* Lightning-weave coverlet.
Sogn and Fjordane. *Norwegian Folk Museum.*

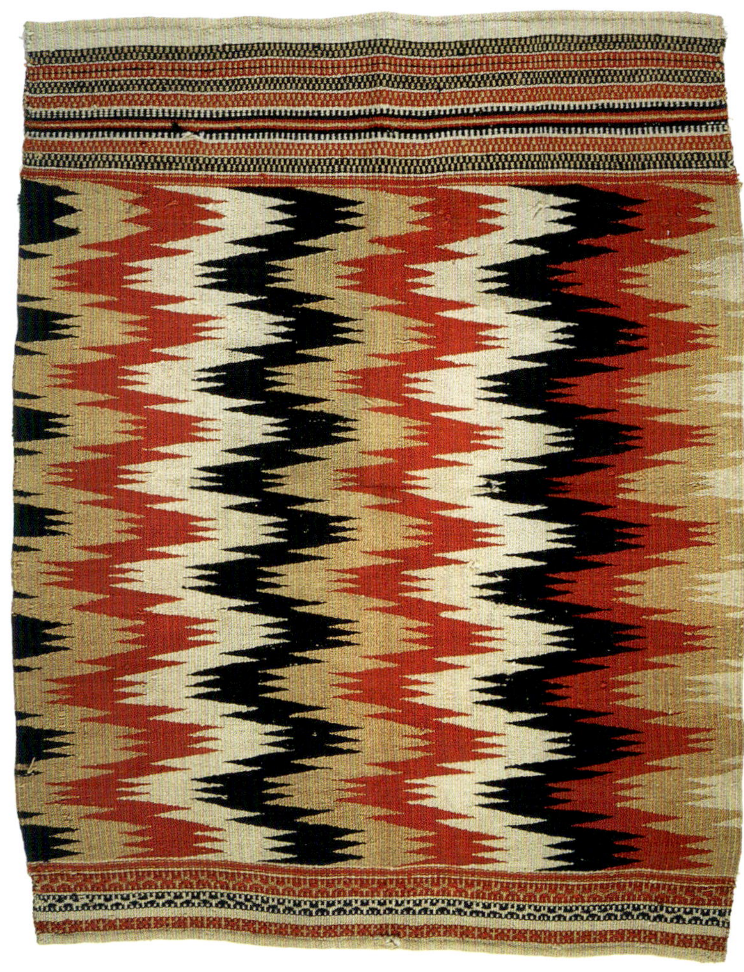

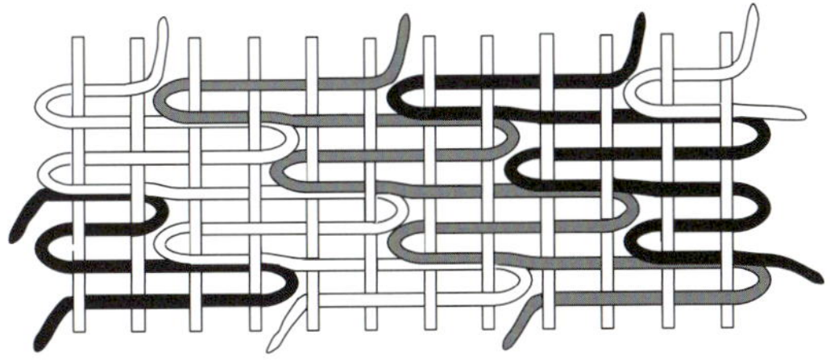

7.13 Vertical stripes zigzag back and forth
in lightning weave, a version of the tapestry
technique. Stripes generally covered more
warp threads in width than depicted here.

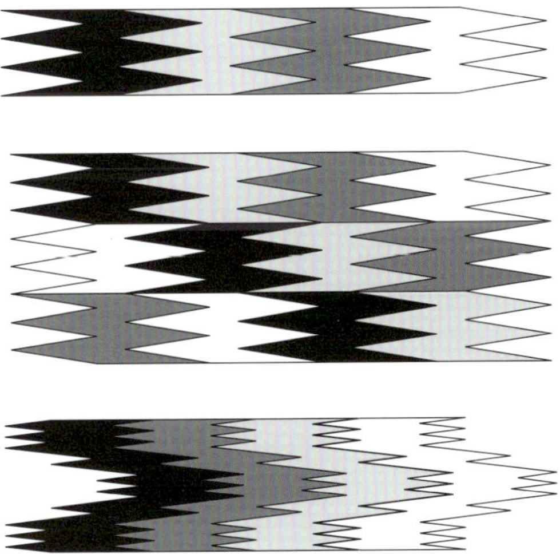

7.14 Variations of pattern in the lightning-
weave coverlets.

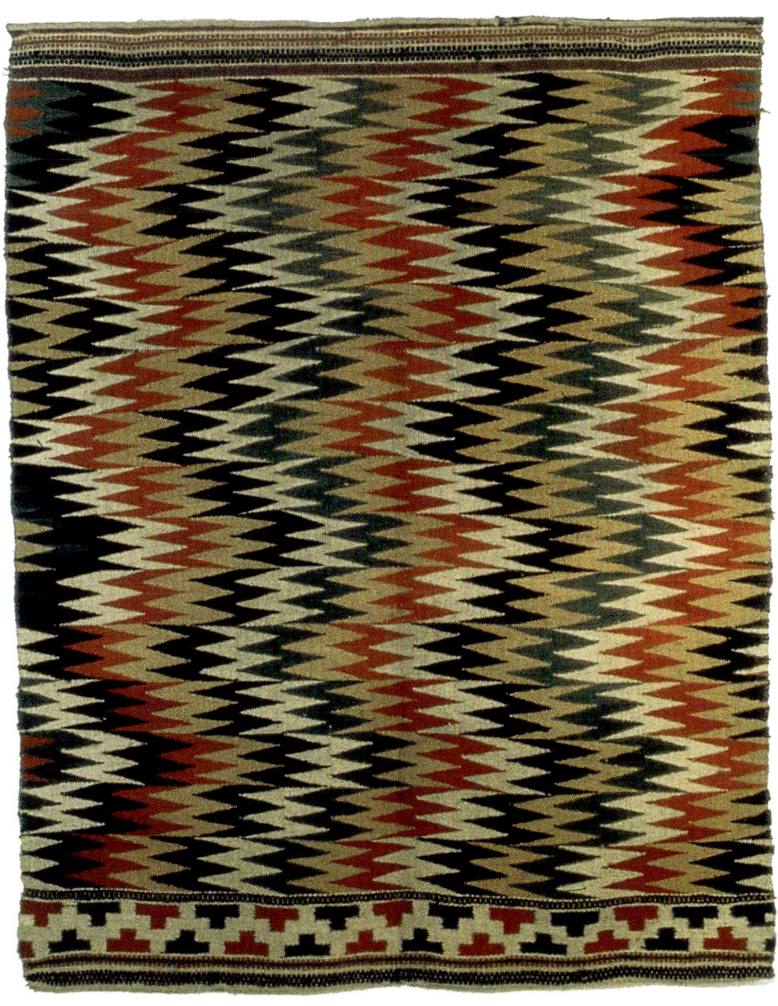

Brocaded Coverlets: Vestfoldsmett

A form of brocading that appeared in the borders of some square-weave coverlets was the primary technique in a small group of coverlets from the district of Vestfold (fig. 7.15). In brocading, patterns are created by a supplementary weft thread that floats over and under a ground weave, a simple idea that was interpreted in a variety of ways throughout the world. A similarity in pattern and technique can be seen, however, between the Vestfold coverlets and brocaded textiles from Russia and some Eastern European and Mediterranean countries. In Norway, evidence of brocaded weaving was discovered in the Oseberg Viking ship, excavated from a ninth-century burial mound which, interestingly, was located in the district of Vestfold. Whether the brocaded coverlets of Vestfold were the result of a long standing tradition or whether they indicate later influences from abroad is unknown.

The Vestfold coverlets, woven on a ground weave of weft-faced plain weave, contained brocading in two variations plus a supplementary weft patterning that traveled from selvage to selvage. Individual bobbins were used to create brocaded patterns in discrete portions of the weaving. In the first variation of this technique, often referred to in English by its Swedish name, *krabbasnår*, patterns were built of constantly shifting horizontal lines. In the second variation, known as *halvkrabba*, the pattern was composed of blocklike shapes (figs. 7.16–7.17). The selvage-to-selvage patterning technique echoed the brocaded effect, with a supplementary pattern weft floating over and under a set number of warp threads across the width of the weaving. This fairly simple technique was sometimes combined with vertical stripes of pick-and-pick to create more detailed patterns (figs. 7.18–7.19).

Coverlets in the Vestfold brocading techniques were usually composed of horizontal bands of pattern. Larger bands of brocaded patterns—diamonds, zigzags, representations of plants and flowers, and other intricate designs—were interspersed with smaller bands of the selvage-to-selvage technique, pick-and-pick, or a combination of the two. The ground weave was woven in colors that varied from one band of pattern to the next, and the brocaded and selvage-to-selvage designs were accentuated by the use of contrasting colors.

The Vestfold coverlets were all woven in two pieces of approximately five feet in length and two feet in width that were sewn together. The warp material was linen, set from six to ten ends per inch, and the weft material was a two-ply wool.

In other districts, simple brocading appears in coverlets composed of a combination of techniques (see "Combined-Technique Coverlets," below). The selvage-to-selvage/pick-and-pick technique was also used in the borders of square-weave coverlets from many areas, and occasionally served as the basis for patterning throughout an entire coverlet (fig. 7.20). The brocaded effect in these coverlets was quite simple, however, differing markedly from the ornate coverlets of Vestfold.

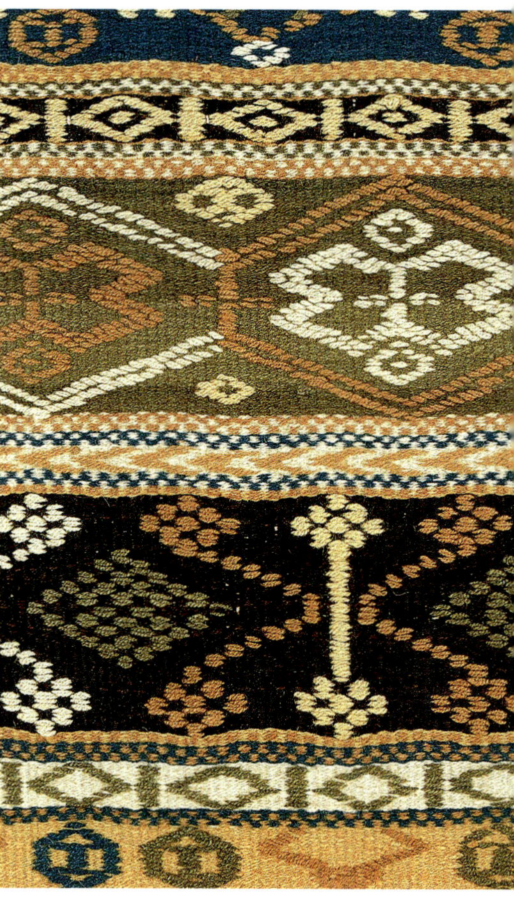

7.15 A coverlet woven in the Vestfold brocading technique. In the detailed view (*above*), supplementary weft patterning is seen in the small panels at top, center, and bottom. Brocaded patterns with blocklike designs (black background) and diagonal designs composed of shifting horizontal lines (green background) are seen in the larger panels. Andebu, Vestfold. *Vestfold County Museum.*

7.16 A bobbin of weft yarn travels back and forth in a small pattern area to create brocaded patterns (*far right*).

7.17 Brocaded patterns were composed of: (*a*) blocklike shapes; (*b*) shifting lines; (*c*) a combination of blocks and shifting lines. Diagrams of these and additional brocaded patterns from Vestfold coverlets can be found in Thorrud 1992.

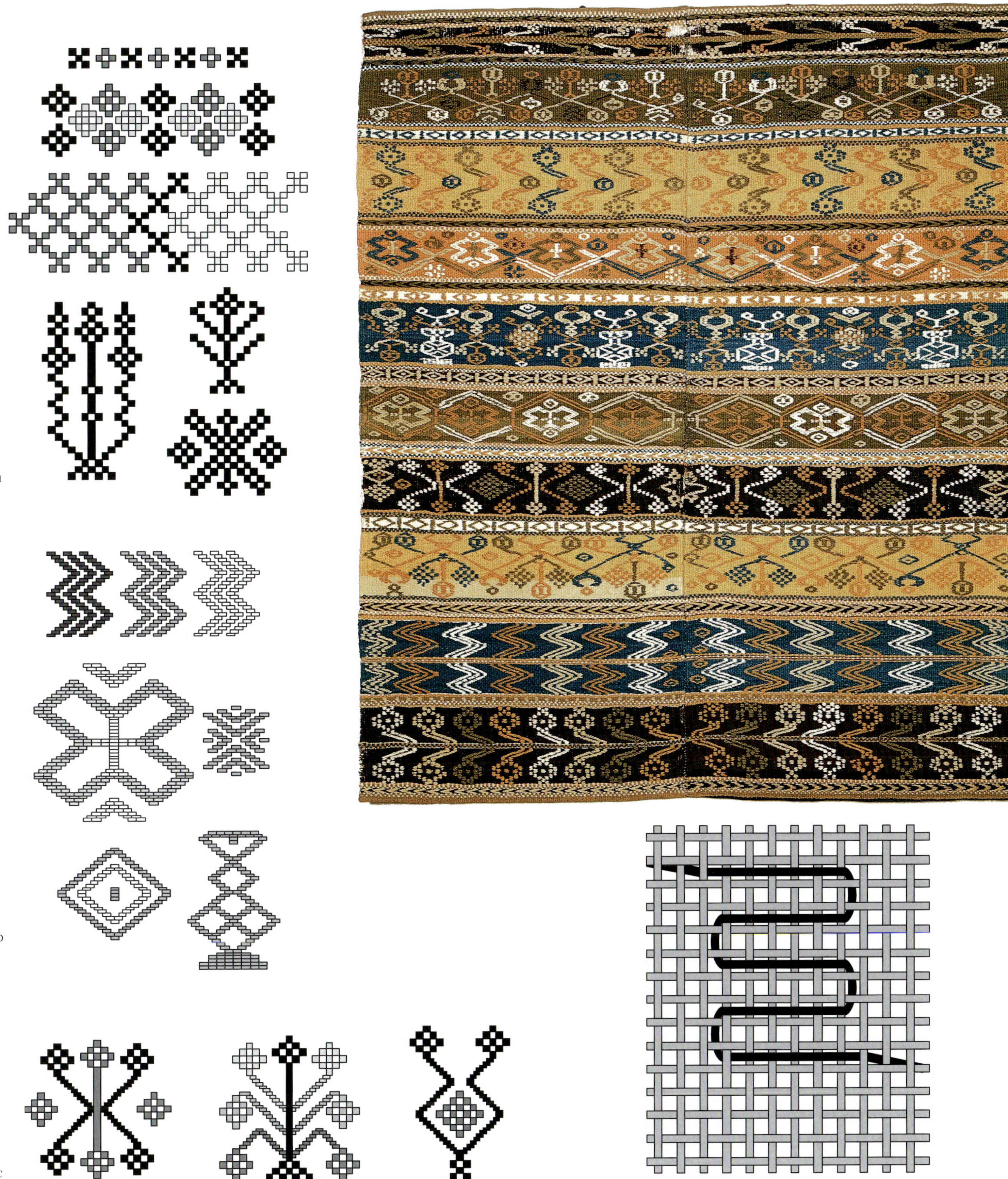

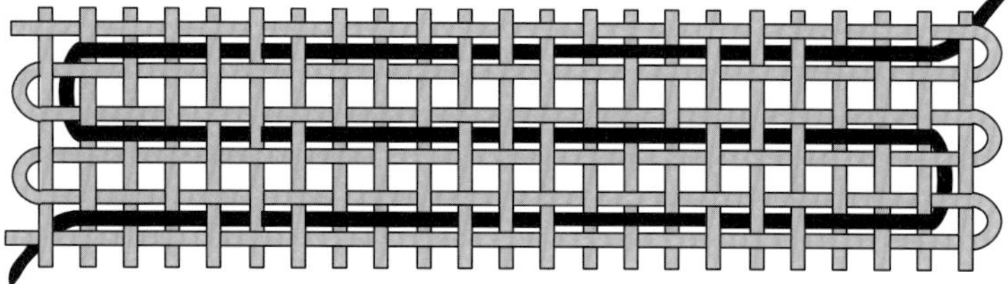

7.18 Pattern weft in the supplementary weft-patterning technique travels over and under a selected number of warp threads from selvage to selvage.

7.19 Supplementary weft patterning: *(a)* Pattern weft inserted over and under varying numbers of warp threads created diamonds, chevrons, and Xs. *(b)* When combined with the small vertical stripes of pick-and-pick to form larger patterns, supplementary weft patterning commonly traveled over and under three warp threads.

a
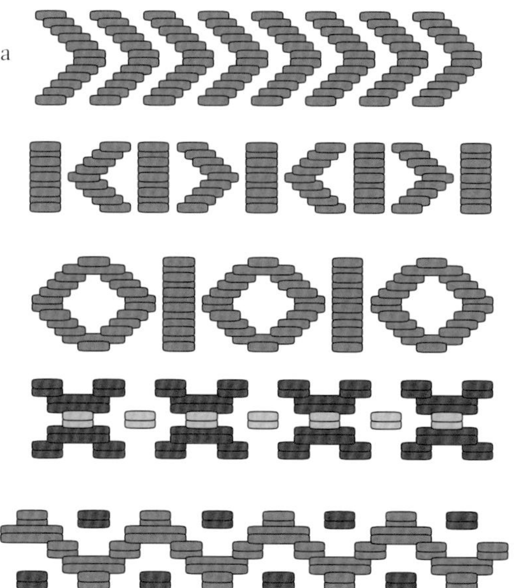

b
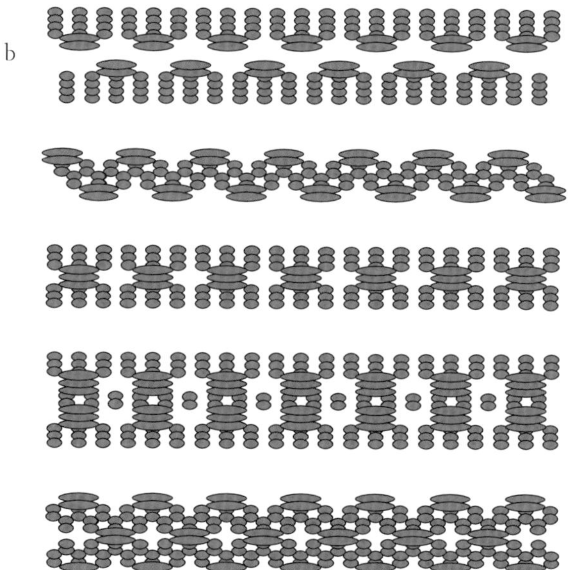

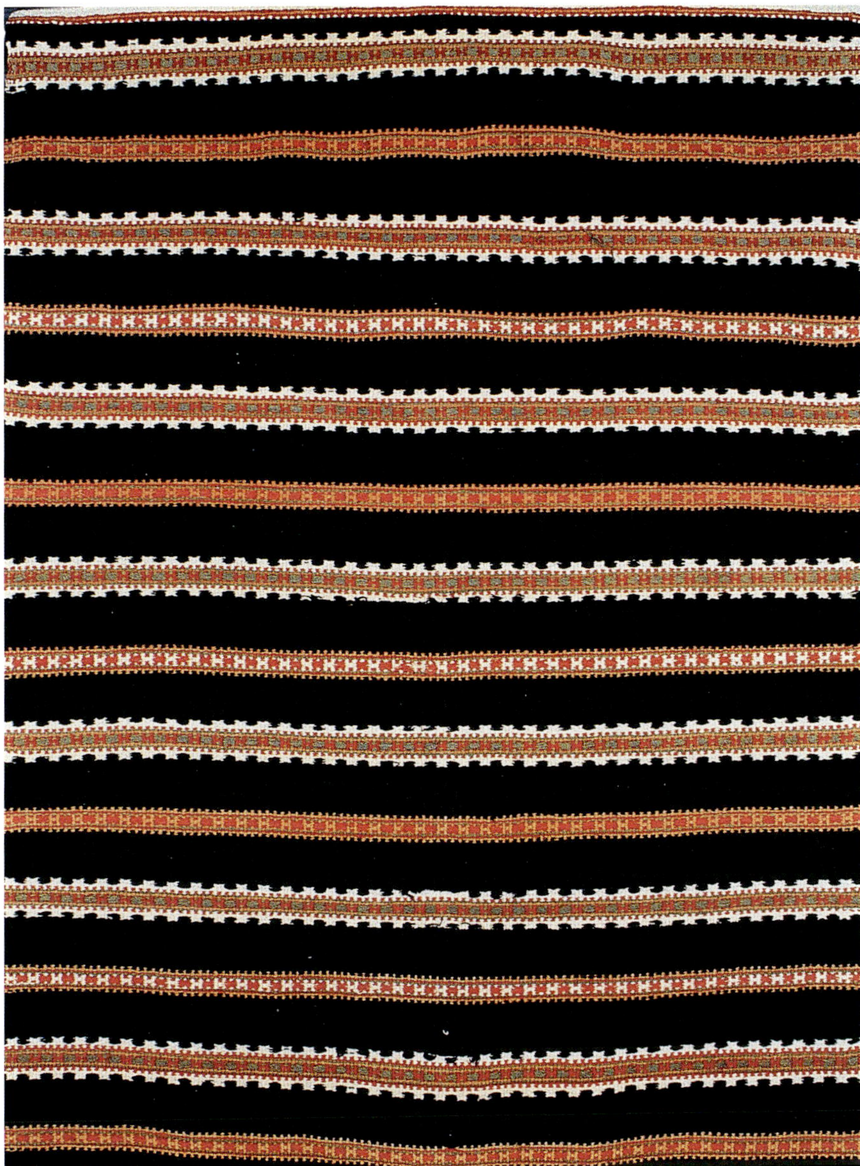

7.20 Bands of supplementary weft patterning and pick-and-pick alternate with plain horizontal stripes. In the detailed view, note the simple float sequence of three over and three under. In the center band of pattern this is seen with both a plain background (black on a white ground), and combined with pick-and-pick (green on red and green pick-and-pick). Jølster, Sogn and Fjordane. *Vesterheim Norwegian-American Museum. Private collection.*

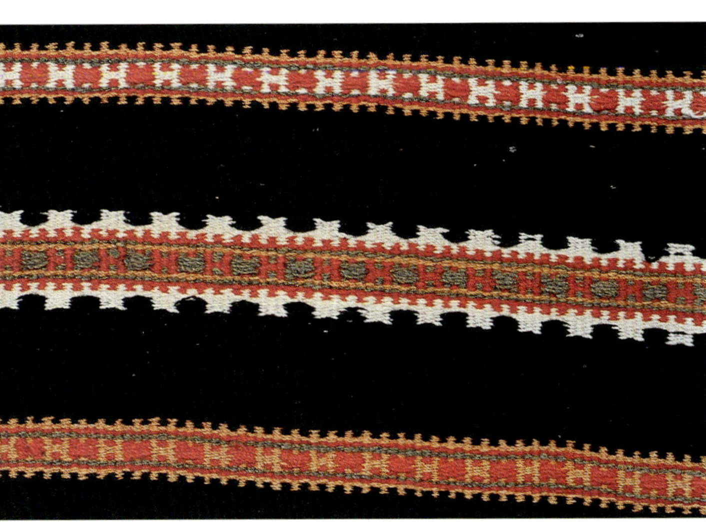

Danish-Weave Coverlets: Dansk Brogd

In the southern district of Vest-Agder, a type of weft-faced coverlet known
as *dansk brogd*, or Danish weave, was woven (7.21–7.22). Danish weave is
similar to the technique referred to in English as skip plain-weave (or plain
weave with weft substitution), variations of which were known in the
Middle East and also pre-Columbian Peru.[1] A coverlet in Danish weave is
noted in mid-eighteenth-century estate documents from Vest-Agder,[2] but
an earlier tradition is possible. Although the history of these coverlets in
Norway is unclear, the name would seem to point to Denmark as a possible
avenue of introduction.

Danish-weave coverlets were noted for broad rows of pattern in stippled
Xs, diamonds, and chevrons (fig. 7.23). Background colors alternated in
horizontal stripes, often accompanied by changing colors in the patterns
themselves. Separating the areas of Danish weave were bands of pattern
in krokbragd and/or pick-and-pick.

When woven with the two-harness threading of pick-and-pick, patterns
were created by splitting one of the two plain-weave sheds so that two wefts,
pattern and background, did the job of one. Where the pattern weft came to
the surface, the background weft floated underneath, and vice versa. In the
open pattern-shed, a pick-up stick was used to select threads from the bottom
half of the shed, allowing a shot of pattern weft to be woven. The opposite
threads in the still-open shed were then selected, and a shot of background
weft was woven, covering the remaining warp threads in that shed. In the
second shed, only a single shot of the background weft was woven (fig. 7.24).
As the design progressed, the pattern and background sheds alternated to
accommodate the shifting lines of Xs and diamonds. The same procedure
was followed when weaving in three-harness krokbragd, except that occasionally one of the krokbragd sheds matched the pattern exactly, requiring no
pattern pick-up.

Dimensions and materials in the Danish-weave coverlets were similar to
those of other weft-faced coverlets.

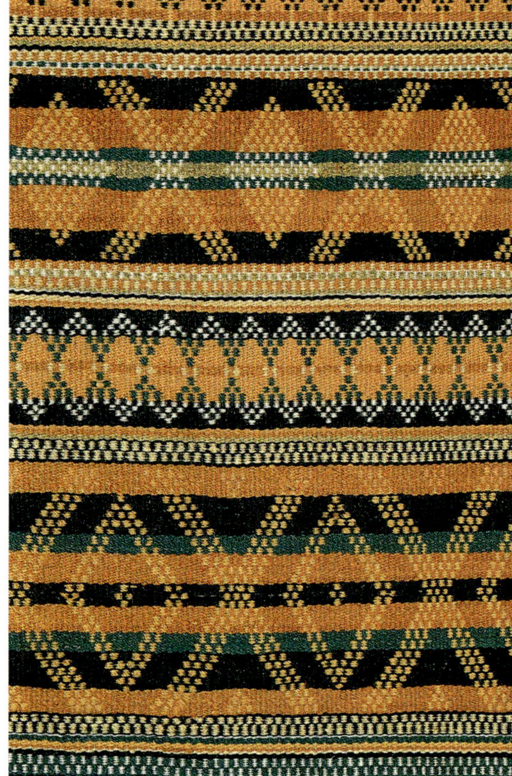

7.21 The Danish weave and pick-and-pick
techniques are combined in this coverlet
from Øyslebø, Vest-Agder. *Photo: K. B.
Holmegërd. Private collection.*

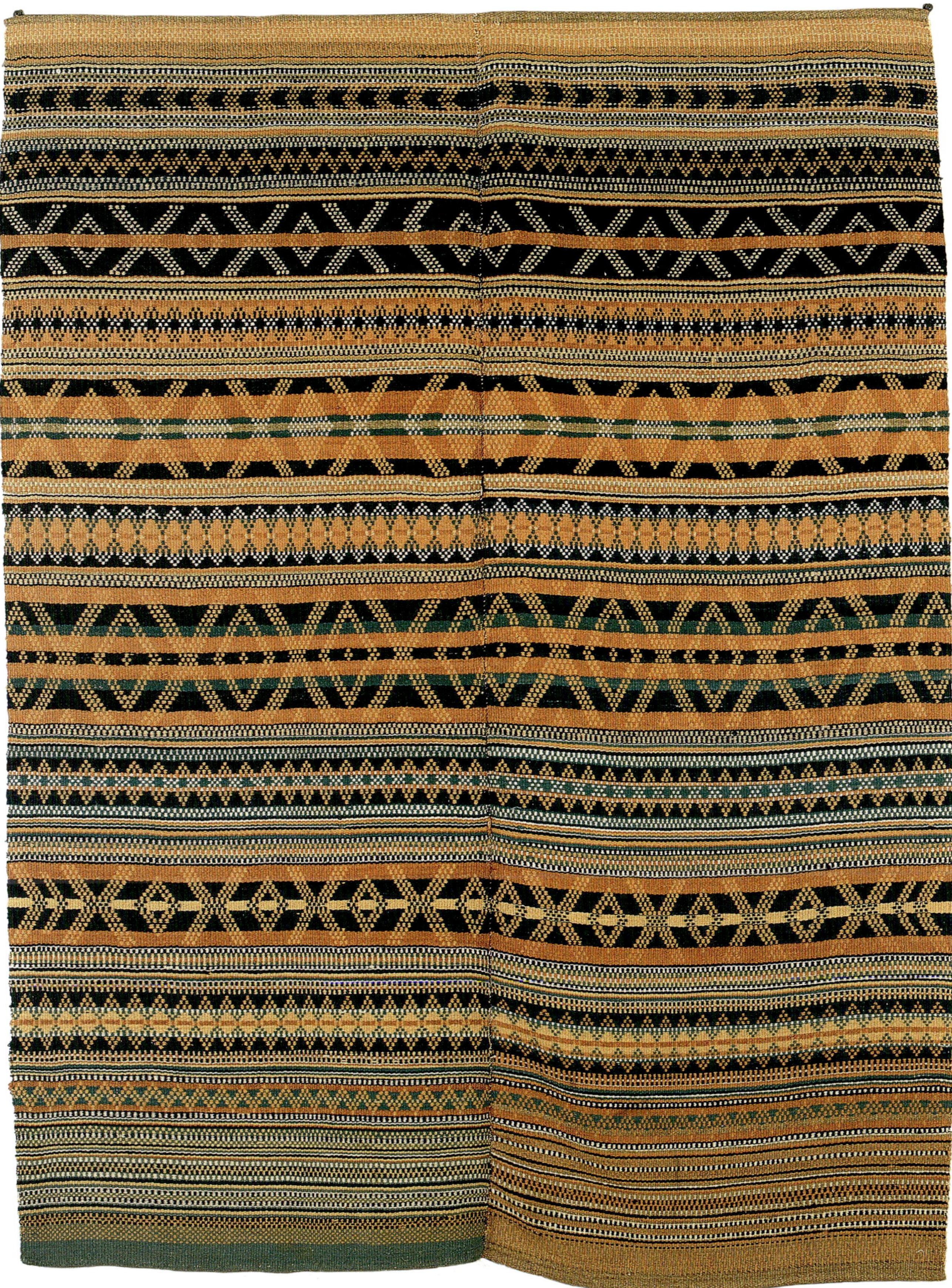

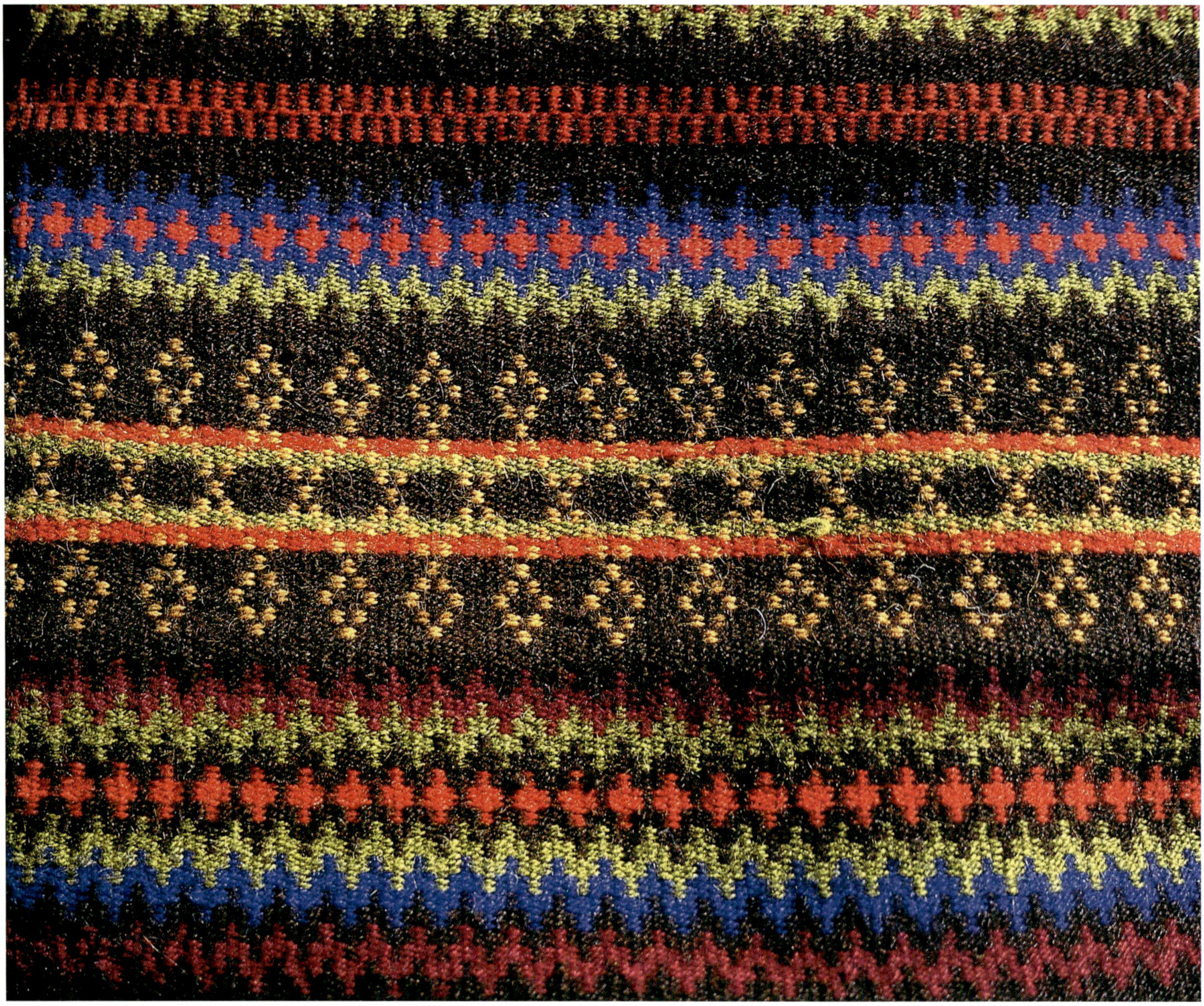

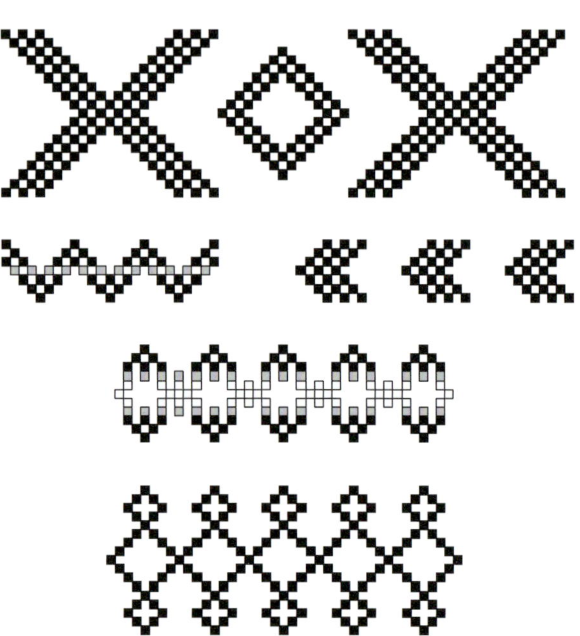

7.22 Reproduction by Kathrine H. Bringsdal of a coverlet from Øyslebø, Vest-Agder, combining the Danish weave, *krokbragd,* and pick-and-pick techniques. *Photo: K. B. Holmegård. Private collection.*

7.23 Diamonds, Xs, and chevrons were common patterns used in Danish weave coverlets.

7.24 In Danish weave, pattern warp-threads
are selected with a pick-up stick from the
back warp-threads of the open shed before
a pattern weft is inserted. Remaining warp
threads in that shed and all warps in the
alternate shed are woven with a background-
colored weft. In this illustration the warp
threads in the back position are indicated by
gray shading and warps selected by the pick-
up stick are indicated by arrows.

(a) The shed in which the pattern will be
selected is opened. After the pattern warps
are selected from the back warp threads with
a pick-up stick, a shot of dark pattern-weft is
inserted. (b) In the same shed, the non-pattern
warps are selected from the back warp threads
and covered with a shot of background weft.
(c) The shed is changed and a shot of background weft is inserted. (d) As a pattern segment is complete, the next shed receives a
shot of background weft. (e) The new pattern
segment, shifting by one warp thread towards
the center, begins in the following shed.

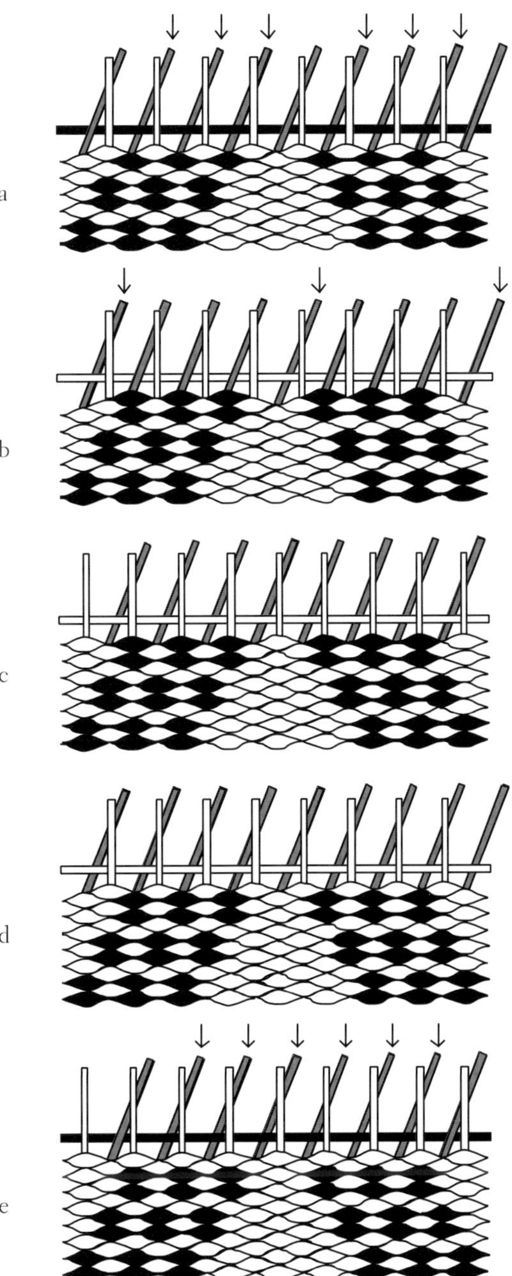

In some coverlets, a variety of techniques were combined in horizontal bands of pattern (figs. 7.25 and 7.1). Square weave, pick-and-pick, lightning weave, brocading, supplementary weft- patterning, and krokbragd often appeared together in these lively and pleasantly confused samplers. This type of coverlet was particularly common in the district of Hordaland. The materials, size, patterns, and colors of these coverlets were generally the same as those woven in the individual techniques.

7.25 A variety of weft-faced techniques are combined in this coverlet: square weave, lightning weave, brocading, pick-and-pick, and *krokbragd*. Nordhordland. *Historical Museum, University of Bergen.*

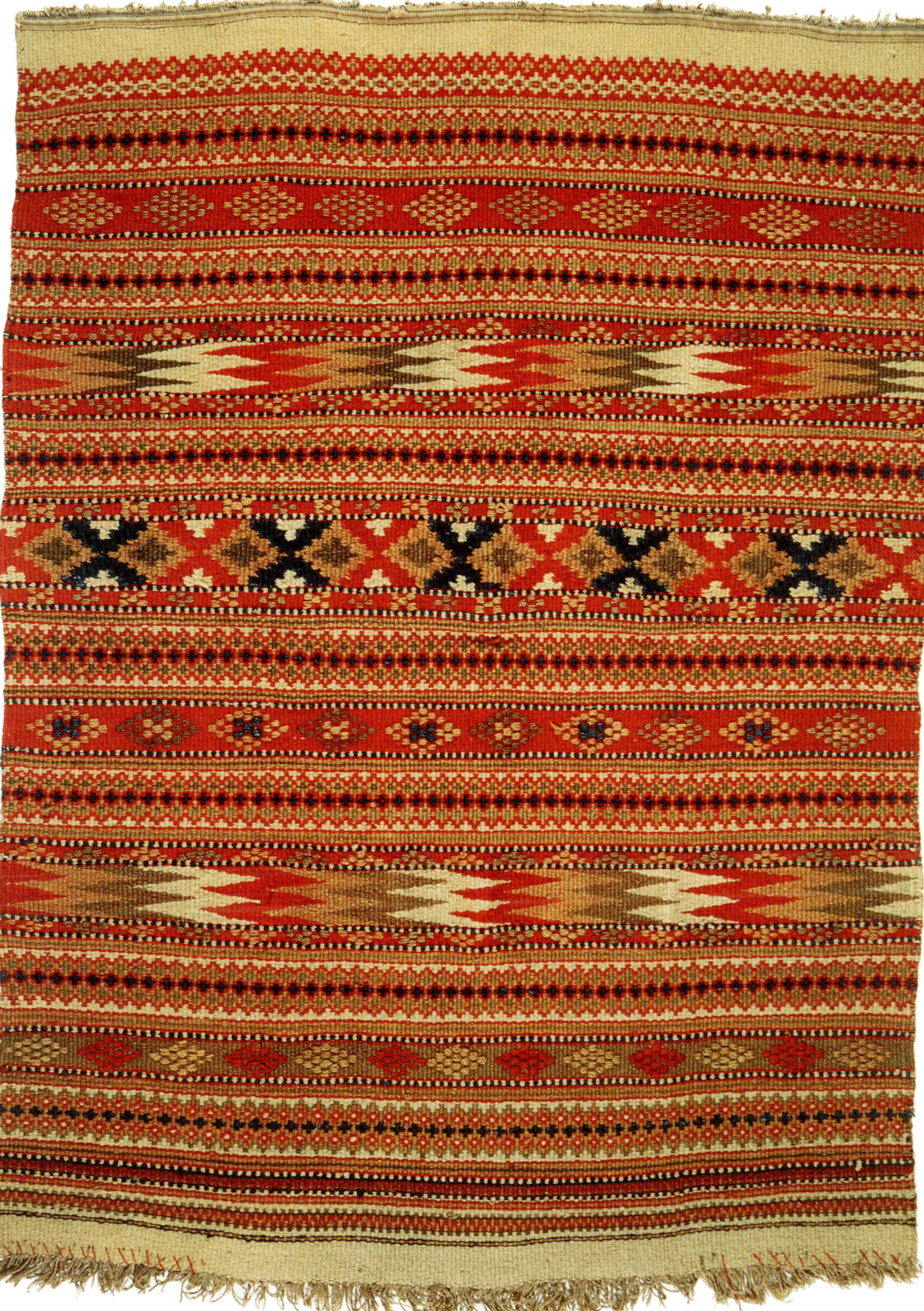

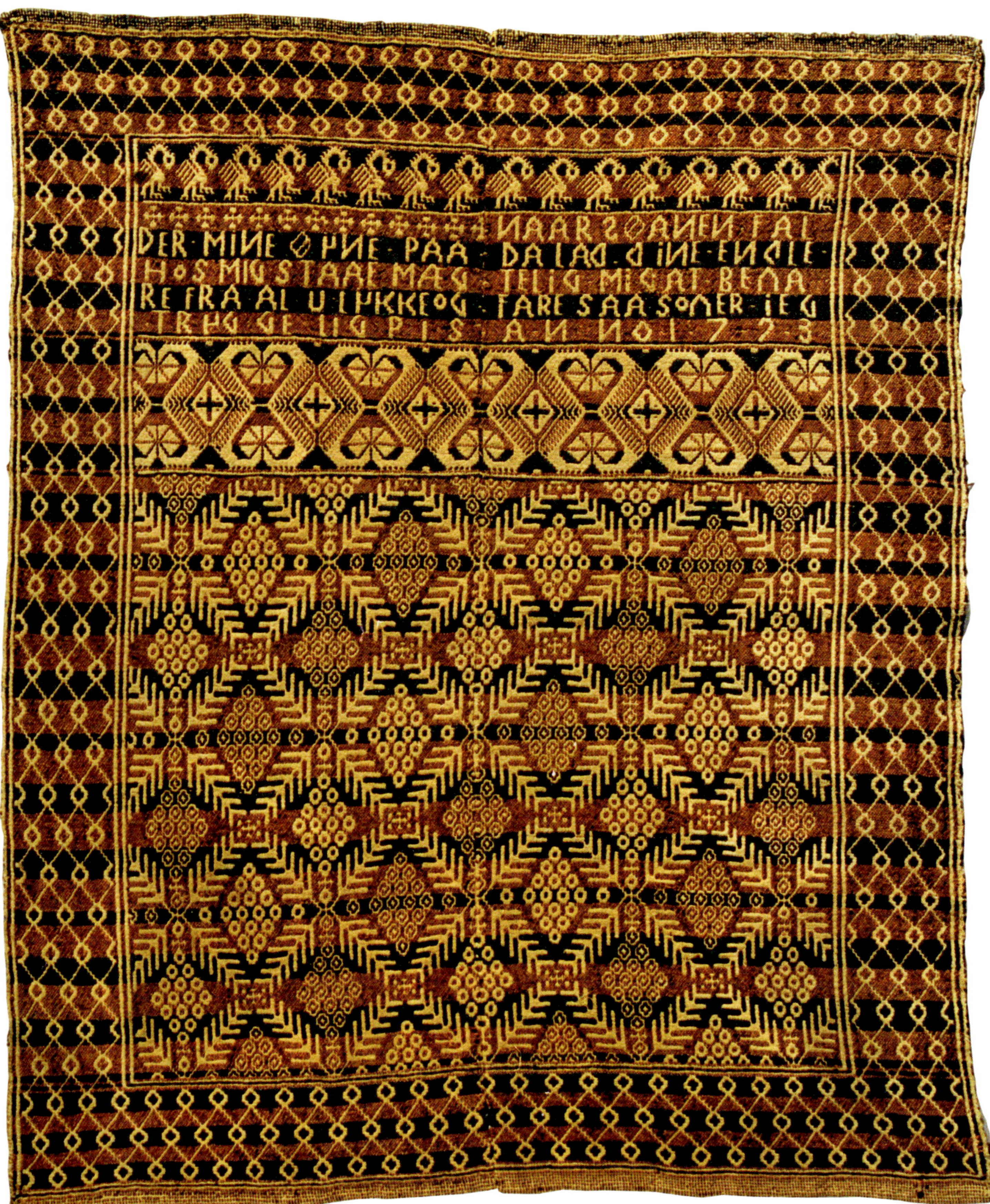

114

8 / *Double-Weave Coverlets*: Dobbeltvev

8.1 *"When sleep falls upon my eyes . . ."*
A double weave coverlet woven in 1793.
Probably Sør-Trøndelag. *Nordic Museum,
Stockholm.*

NAAR SØVNEN FALDER MINE ØYNE PAA
DA LAD DINE ENGLE HOS MIG STAAE
MÆGTELIG MIG AT BEVARE
FRA AL ULYKKE OG FARE
SAA SOVER IEG TRYGGELIG

When sleep falls upon my eyes
Then let Your angels stand with me
To protect me with their might
From all misfortune and danger
So that I sleep securely

—*Inscription from a double-weave coverlet woven in* 1793 *(fig. 8.1)*

TUCKED INTO BED UNDER A COVERLET THAT offered not only warmth but a prayer for protection, one couldn't help but sleep securcly (fig. 8.1). Double-weave coverlets were woven from two layers of fabric that interchanged in pattern areas. Inscriptions such as the one above were occasionally a part of the design, as were a myriad of other patterns. At home in the silks of the East, the double-weave technique took root in Norway long ago and was displayed with pride on the bedsteads of families living in northern Gudbrandsdal and Sør-Trøndelag.

Origins

The double-weave technique may have developed independently in areas
as diverse as Asia and pre-Columbian Peru, but it appears likely that the
technique was introduced into the Nordic countries from outside. The
technique possibly spread from China, where a type of double weave
was known as early as 200 B.C., to India and Persia, and thence into the
Mediterranean countries and Russia. Following trade routes up the rivers
of Russia and Eastern Europe, the double-weave technique probably arrived
in Scandinavia by at least the eleventh or twelfth century, if not earlier.[1]
In medieval Sweden it was referred to as either Finnish weave or Russian
weave, pointing to its probable path of entry into the north. This connection is underscored by the many similarities to be seen in the Scandinavian
double weaves and those of Finland, the Baltic countries, and Poland.

Aside from the inevitable trade in textiles, the church provided another
possible avenue for the introduction of the double-weave technique into
Scandinavia. With the coming of Christianity in the eleventh century,
Norway was brought into contact with a social structure that stretched as
far as the Mediterranean Sea. Clerical textiles imported by functionaries of
the church were often sumptuous fabrics woven in silk by the professional
weavers of Byzantium. Upon arrival in the northern countries, such finery
was copied in the local wool and linen. This translation to a coarser material required considerable simplification of pattern, but even so, many of the
motifs found in Norwegian double-weave textiles can be traced to the East.
An interesting example is seen in fig. 8.2, where the Persian representation
of four ducks enclosed in a circle has been faithfully reproduced in spirit
but with remarkably different results in the pattern from a Norwegian
coverlet.

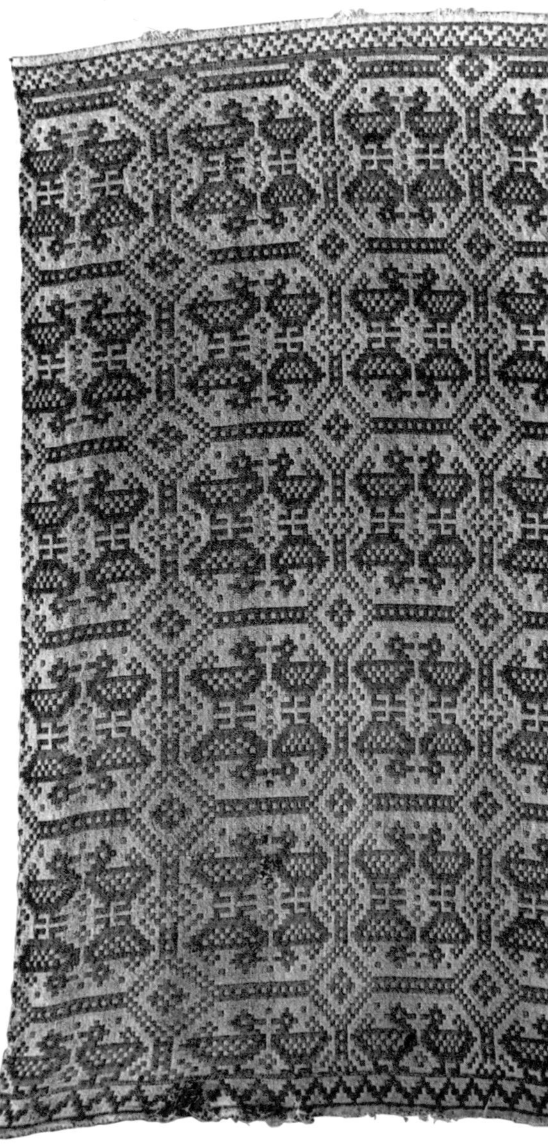

8.2 Similarities can be seen between the
pattern of ducks woven into a Norwegian
double-weave coverlet *(below)*, and a twelfth-
century Persian silk fabric*(below left)*. *Oslo
Museum of Applied Art; Textile Museum,
Washington, D.C.*

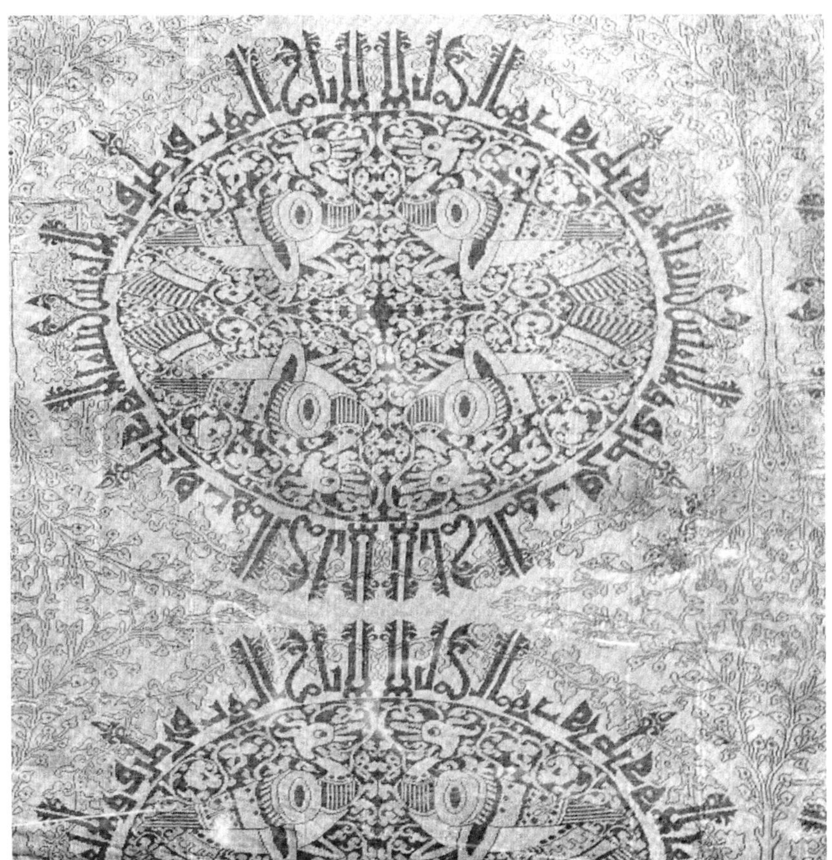

8.3 A double-weave coverlet from the early
Middle Ages, possibly a burial drape. Note
the small knots within a larger knotwork
design in the upper (damaged) panel. Similar
knot patterns are seen in the 9th-century
Oseberg tapestry (see fig. 4.2) and in later coverlets in the square-weave technique (see fig.
5.16). The gridwork design in the lower panel
is also found in other textile fragments from
the Oseberg find and later double-weave coverlets (fig. 8.33). Lom Stave Church,
Gudbrandsdal. *Norwegian Folk Museum.*

The oldest surviving examples of double weave in Norway are church
textiles from the Middle Ages. Of particular interest in these weavings is the
use of several small motifs that show a continuity with textiles from both
earlier and later periods (figs. 8.3–8.4). A number of double-weave textiles
from a slightly later period, still arranged in the frieze format common in
medieval wall hangings, depicts the wedding procession. The bride and
groom on horseback, surrounded by fertility signs and magical symbols, are
accompanied by rows of men and women performing the traditional chain
dance. The style of clothing seen in these weavings indicates that they most
likely were products of the early seventeenth century (fig. 8.5). The point
at which the double-weave technique was adopted for use as a coverlet is
uncertain. The majority of coverlets that have been preserved date from
the eighteenth and nineteenth centuries, but there is little doubt that these
weavings are the result of a much older tradition.

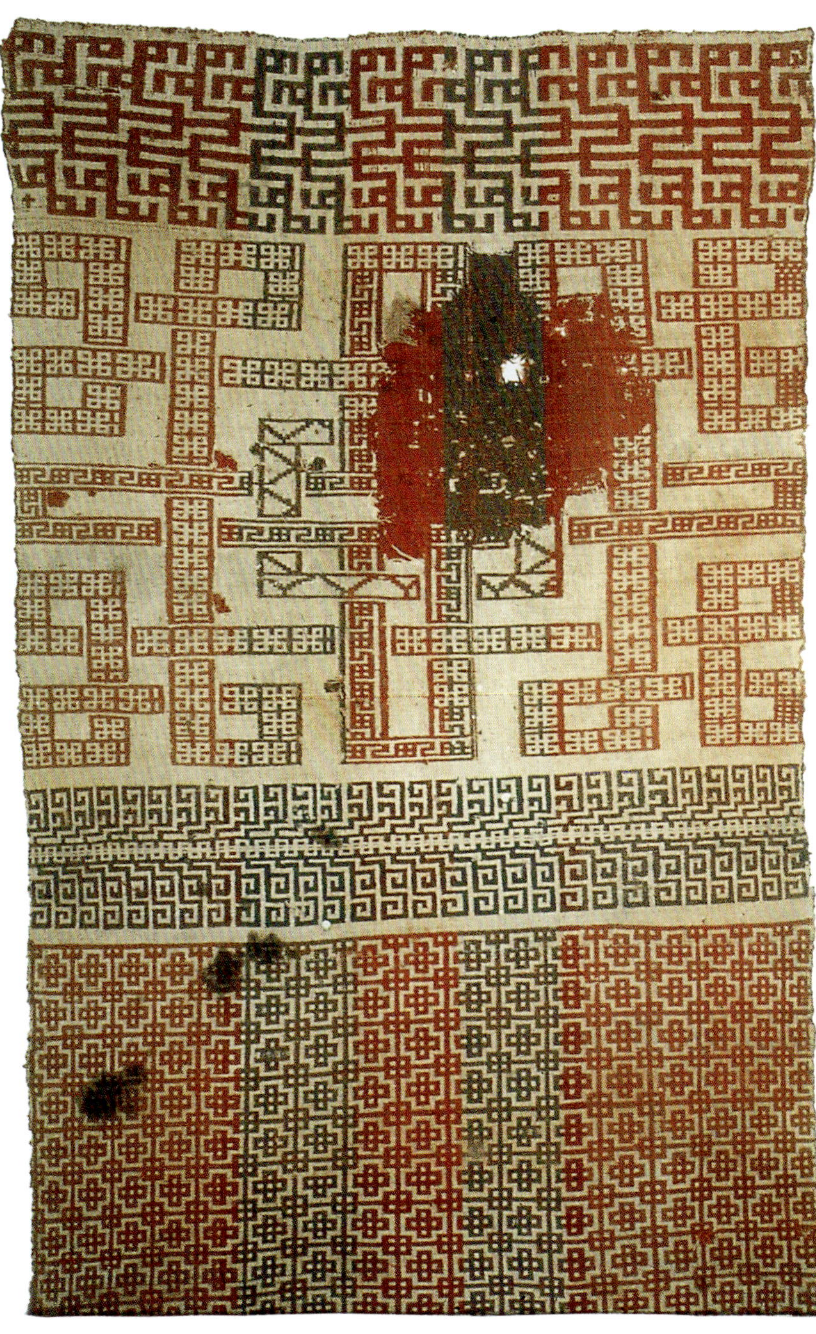

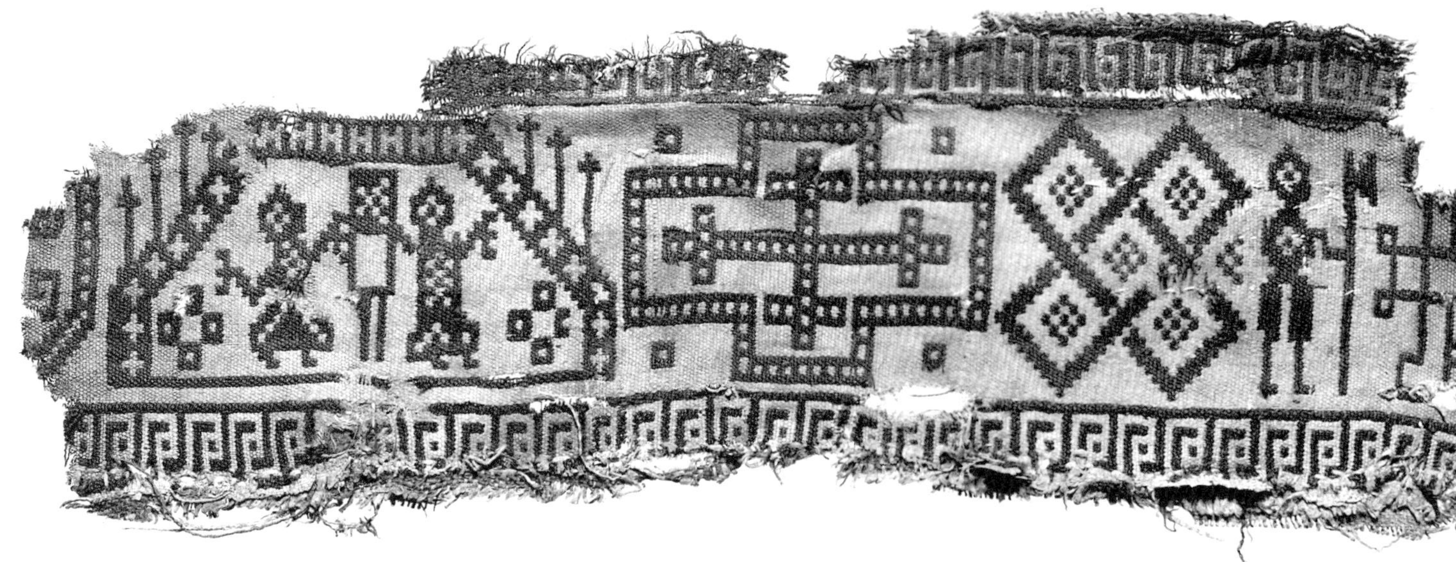

8.4 A medieval double-weave fragment from Rennebu church in Trøndelag. Note the figures of women, possibly working at a loom, and the man with an axe. The large cross motif in the middle is seen in later double-weave and square-weave coverlets (see figs. 5.24 and 8.18). *University Museum of National Antiquities, Oslo.*

8.5 A double-weave fragment from the seventeenth century showing a wedding procession. The wedding party rides on horseback, surrounded by magical symbols (knots and squares) and fertility signs (trees). The ram, symbolizing virility, and the deer, symbolizing virginity, are seen under the male and female riders; above them, men and women hold hands in the traditional chain dance. *Oslo Museum of Applied Art.*

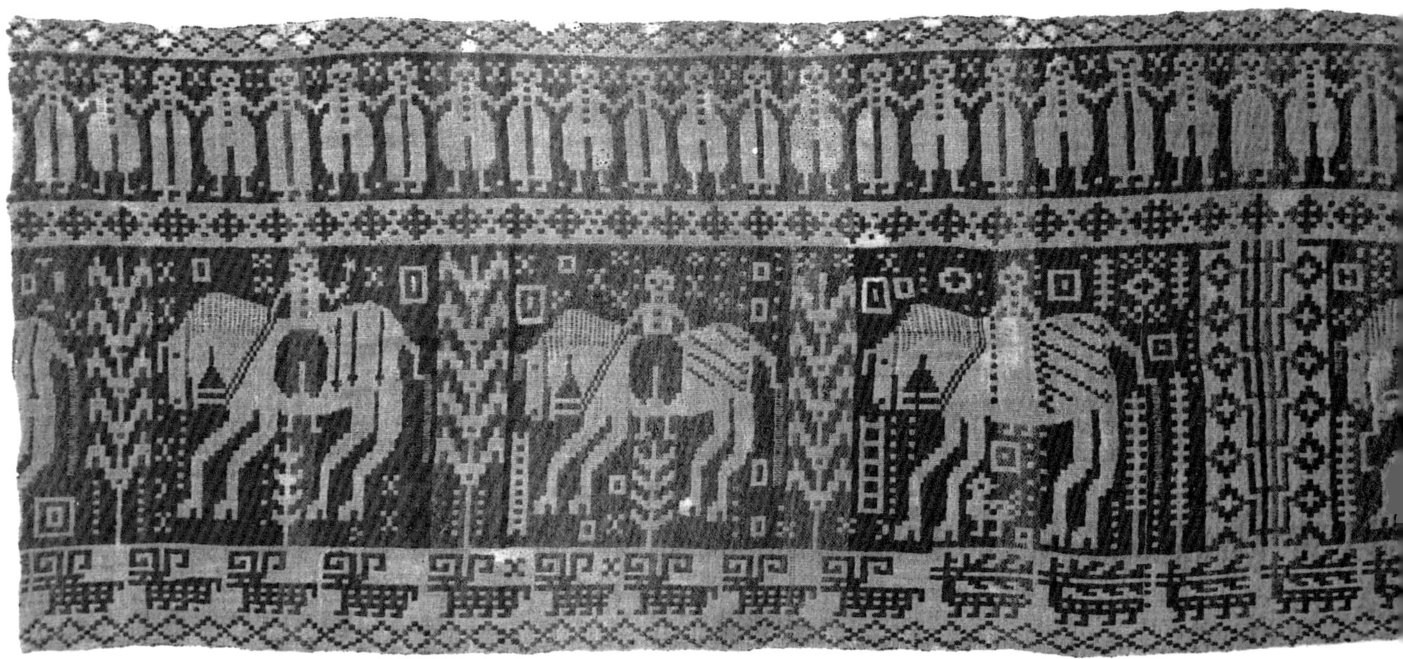

In northern Gudbrandsdal and Sør-Trøndelag, a double-weave coverlet was found on the beds in many homes. Taking the time to make such a coverlet, however, was not something that every housewife could afford. Weaving a twenty-two-inch length of cloth in one day was considered good progress when working in this painstaking technique.* Such a commitment of time, not to mention the commitment of a loom that was needed to make yardage for other purposes, was often impractical. As was the case with tapestry, a few local weavers began to specialize in the double-weave technique, weaving for relatives and friends to supplement their own family income. Often a widow trying to make ends meet would turn to such specialized work, as did the well-known Berit Hilmo of Tydal in Sør-Trøndelag. Widowed early in life, she wove over 450 double-weave coverlets in the course of her ninety-five years. The coverlets of "åkle-Berit" can be identified by numbers that she began to weave into each coverlet several years into her career (fig. 8.6), but there were more than twenty other weavers in the Trøndelag area who specialized in making double-weave coverlets for the people in their community.

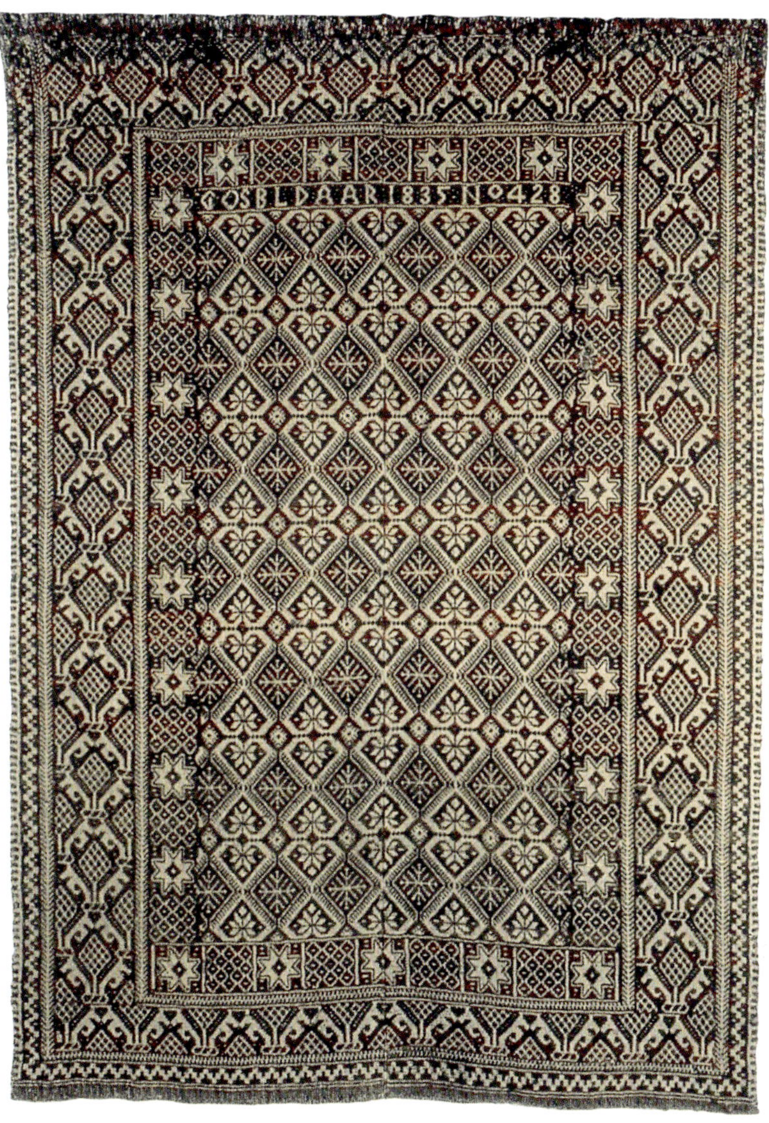

8.6 One of the many numbered double-weave coverlets woven by Berit Hilmo, "åkle Berit." The initials "GOS" and "BLD", the year "1835", and the number "428" appear at the top of the inner panel. Stugudal, Sør-Trøndelag. *Norwegian Folk Museum.*

Design and Color

Two variations of the double-weave technique were used in Norwegian coverlets. The *likesidig* (like-sided), or reversible double-weave coverlets, had patterns that were identical on the front and the back, although in opposite colors (fig. 8.7). The *ulikesidig* (unlike-sided), or nonreversible double-weave coverlets, had a definite right and wrong side, the result of a slight difference in the pattern weaving technique (fig. 8.8). In some parts of Scandinavia, particularly in neighboring Sweden, the older, less sophisticated, reversible double-weave technique was replaced completely by the more complex nonreversible technique. Of the two areas in Norway where double weave was common, Gudbrandsdal retained the older reversible form of the weave, and Sør-Trøndelag, which maintained close contacts with Sweden, adopted the new nonreversible refinement.

The reversible and nonreversible double-weave coverlets had their own distinctive patterns due in part to their separate histories. The reversible double weave, introduced into Norway during the Middle Ages, retained many motifs from this early period. The conservative nature typical of most folk arts was evident in the uniform, rigidly repeated style in which these coverlets were woven, a style that allowed patterns to exist unchanged for generations. The nonreversible technique, a product of later influences from abroad, drew many of its patterns from contemporary Renaissance motifs. Soon after their adoption into the conservative folk culture, however, the "newer" Renaissance patterns became as rigidly repetitive as those found in the reversible technique.

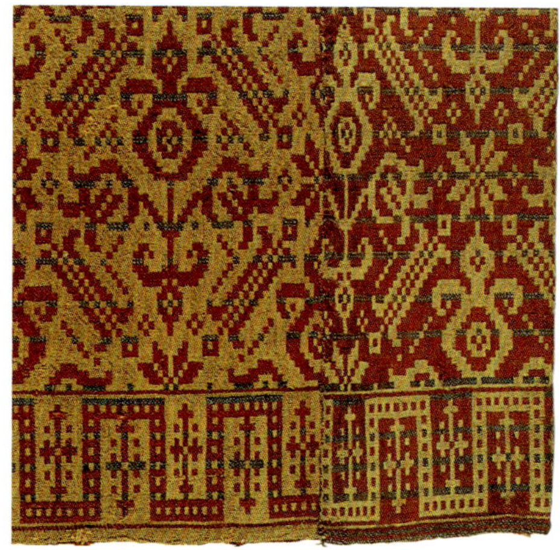

8.7 Reversible double-weave coverlet, folded to show both sides. The tulip motif in the main design and the cross motif in the lower border are equally clear on the back (*left*, yellow background) and the front (*right*, brown background). Gudbrandsdal. *Historical Museum, University of Bergen.*

8.8 Patterns are slightly different on the front (*left*) and back of nonreversible double-weave coverlets. Note differences in the border zigzag pattern, and in the outline and central cross of the eight-petaled rose. *Norwegian Folk Museum.*

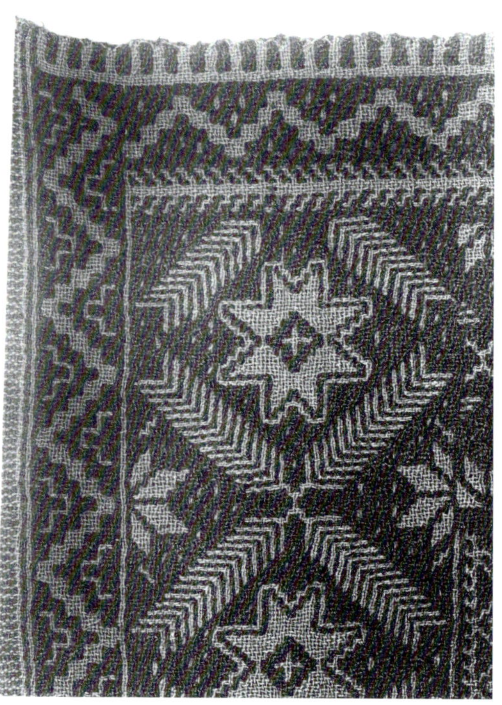

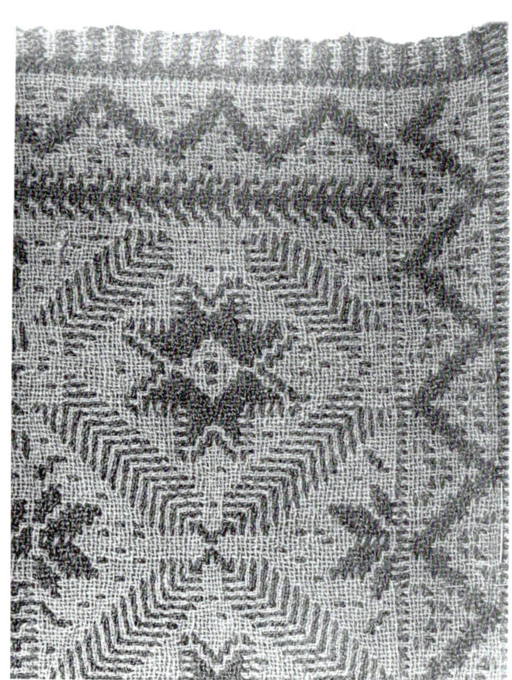

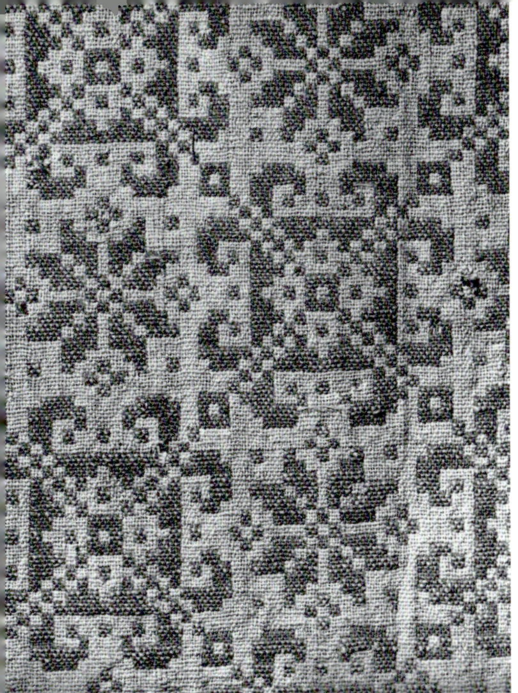

8.9 Detail of a coverlet from Lom, Gudbrandsdal, woven in the reversible double-weave technique. Patterns are large and clearly defined, and slanted lines are woven in right-angle stair steps. *Oslo Museum of Applied Art.*

8.10 The nonreversible double weave technique makes possible the delicate pattern lines seen here in the Tydal rose, eight-petaled rose, opposing hearts, and cross motifs. Detail of figure 8.6. Stugudal, Sør-Trøndelag. *Norwegian Folk Museum.*

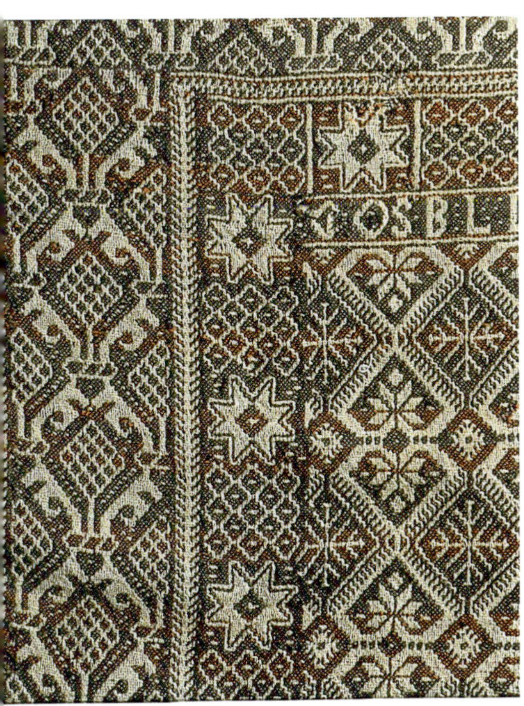

Differences in the weaving technique associated with the two types of double weave also affected the possibilities for pattern development. Patterns in reversible double weave were usually composed of blocky shapes with clear, clean lines. Slanted lines, which reacted differently when traveling to the right versus the left, were replaced with large right-angled "stair steps," individual pattern squares were commonly three- or four-warp-threads wide, and fine details were avoided. These measures insured that the slight blurring at the edges of pattern elements would be unnoticeable. In contrast, nonreversible double weave was free of the limitations of the reversible technique. Pattern edges were always clear, making possible the use of fine details and slanting lines, and pattern elements could be reduced to two warp threads in width (compare figs. 8.9 and 8.10). Although some of the same motifs appeared in both types of double-weave coverlets, the blocky interpretations of the reversible technique were transformed into the distinctive, delicate patterns characteristic of the nonreversible technique.

Coverlets in the two double-weave techniques differed to some extent in their overall design. The reversible coverlets generally presented one or two major motifs repeated in a regular array of octagons, rows, or diagonal grids, with fairly minor borders at the top and bottom of the coverlet (fig. 8.11). In contrast, coverlets in the nonreversible technique were often composed of several broad borders, each displaying a particular motif, with a somewhat larger panel presenting the main pattern (see fig. 8.31). In the nineteenth century, coverlets with frame-like borders surrounding a central pattern area became common in the nonreversible technique. Inscriptions, initials, or dates could appear at the top of the central pattern areas in these coverlets, or an inner panel with an alternate motif might highlight the center (figs. 8.12 and 8.34).

Four colors predominated in both styles of the double-weave coverlets: gold, brown, red, and blue. Generally the warp and weft threads of the lighter bottom layer were gold. This provided good contrast with the darker top layer, usually composed of brown warp threads and a weft of brown, red, and blue stripes. The overall effect was of pattern areas in gold on a brown background highlighted by subdued stripes of red and blue. This color scheme was common in both Gudbrandsdal and Sør-Trøndelag until the nineteenth century, when many coverlets in the Trøndelag area were woven in just two colors: a dark layer of sheep brown or black and a light layer of red (figs. 8.12–8.13).

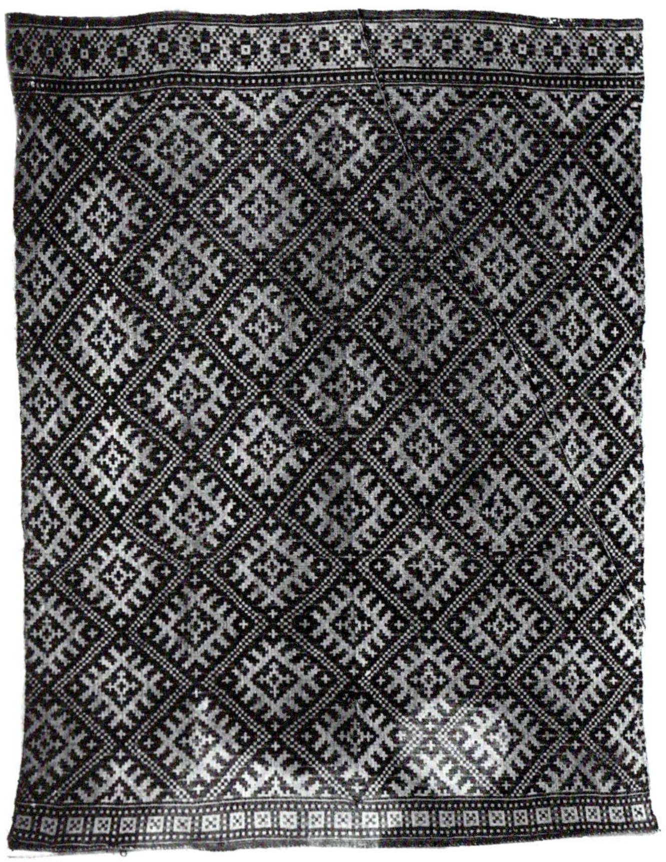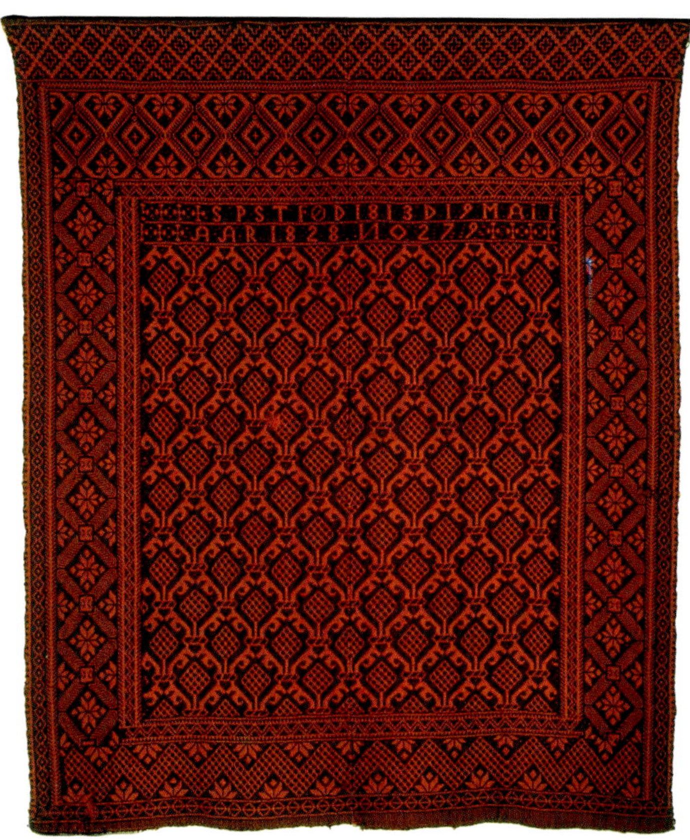
SPST OD 1813 D 9 MAI
AR 1828 N 27 9
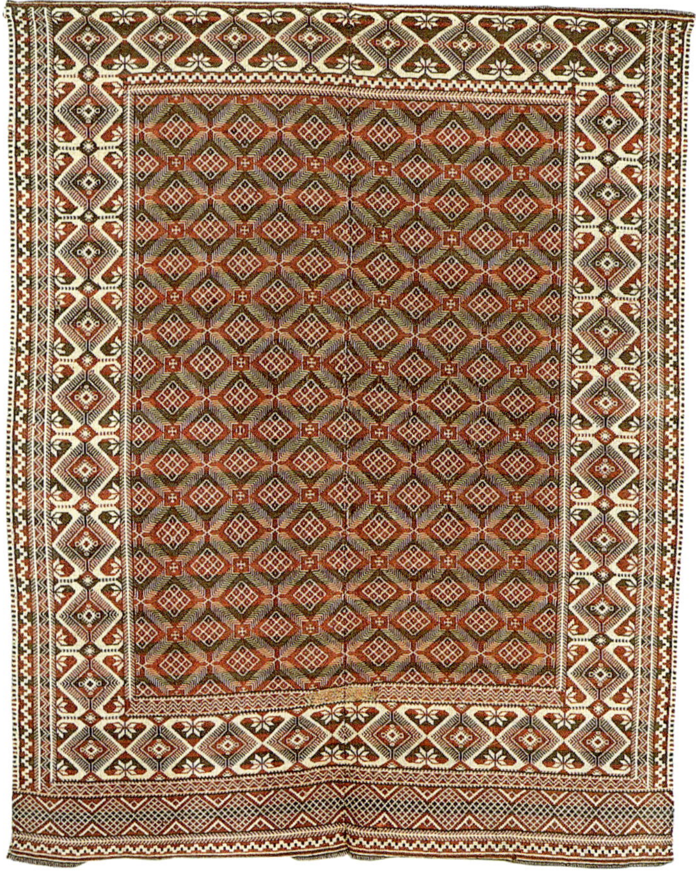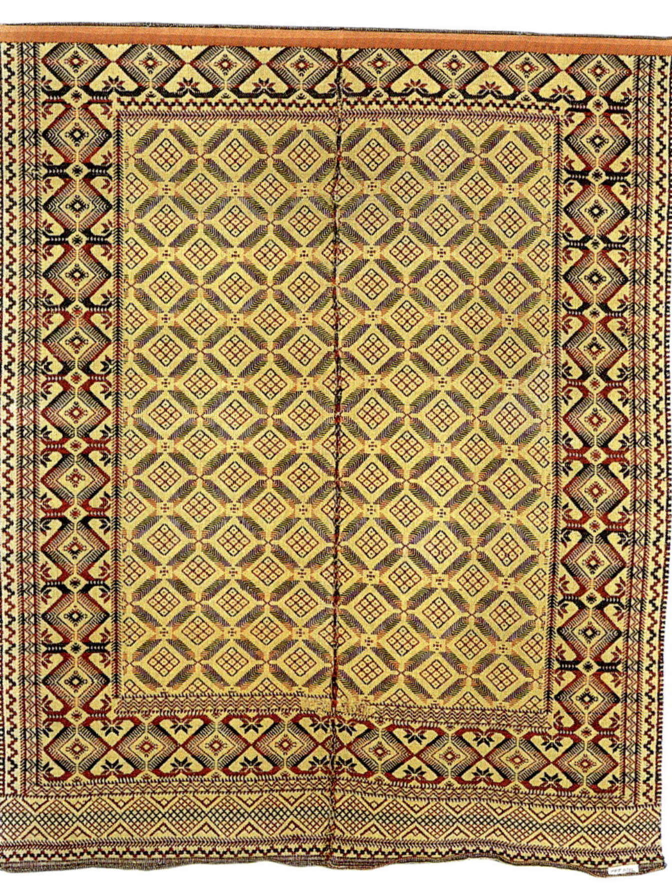

8.11 (*Upper left*) Crossed hatch-marks in reversible double weave. Small borders above and below the main design are typical of the reversible double-weave coverlets. Gudbrandsdal. *Museum of Applied Art.*

8.12 (*Upper right*) Nonreversible double-weave coverlet composed of the Tydal rose motif surrounded by a frame-like border. The weaver, Berit Hilmo, included an inscription that indicates this was her 279th coverlet, woven in 1828. The initials and birthdate, "SPST May 19, 1813," were probably those of the person for whom the coverlet was made. The red and black colors were typical of coverlets from Trøndelag in the 19th century. See also detailed view, figure 8.32. Tydal, Sør-Trøndelag. *Norwegian Folk Museum.*

8.13 (*Bottom*) Nonreversible double-weave coverlet with the grapes-in-leaves motif. The color scheme of a brown warp with red and blue weft stripes in the dark layer and a gold warp and weft in the light layer was common in the double-weave coverlets: front (*left*) and back. *Trøndelag Folk Museum.*

8.14 Reversible double-weave motifs: (*a*) figures; (*b*) cross; (*c*) lily cross and lily square; (*d*) eight-petaled rose; (*e*) palmette heart and heart rosette; (*f*) crossed hatch-marks; (*g*) tulip.

Reversible Double-Weave Motifs (*fig. 8.14*)

Figures Groupings of ducks and alternating rows of lions and roosters were used as motifs in the reversible double-weave coverlets (figs. 8.15–8.16). Similar themes were common in double weaves from Sweden and Finland. The figures of riders on horseback, dancers, rams, and deer that were seen in early frieze-format double weaves do not appear as subjects in surviving double-weave coverlets.

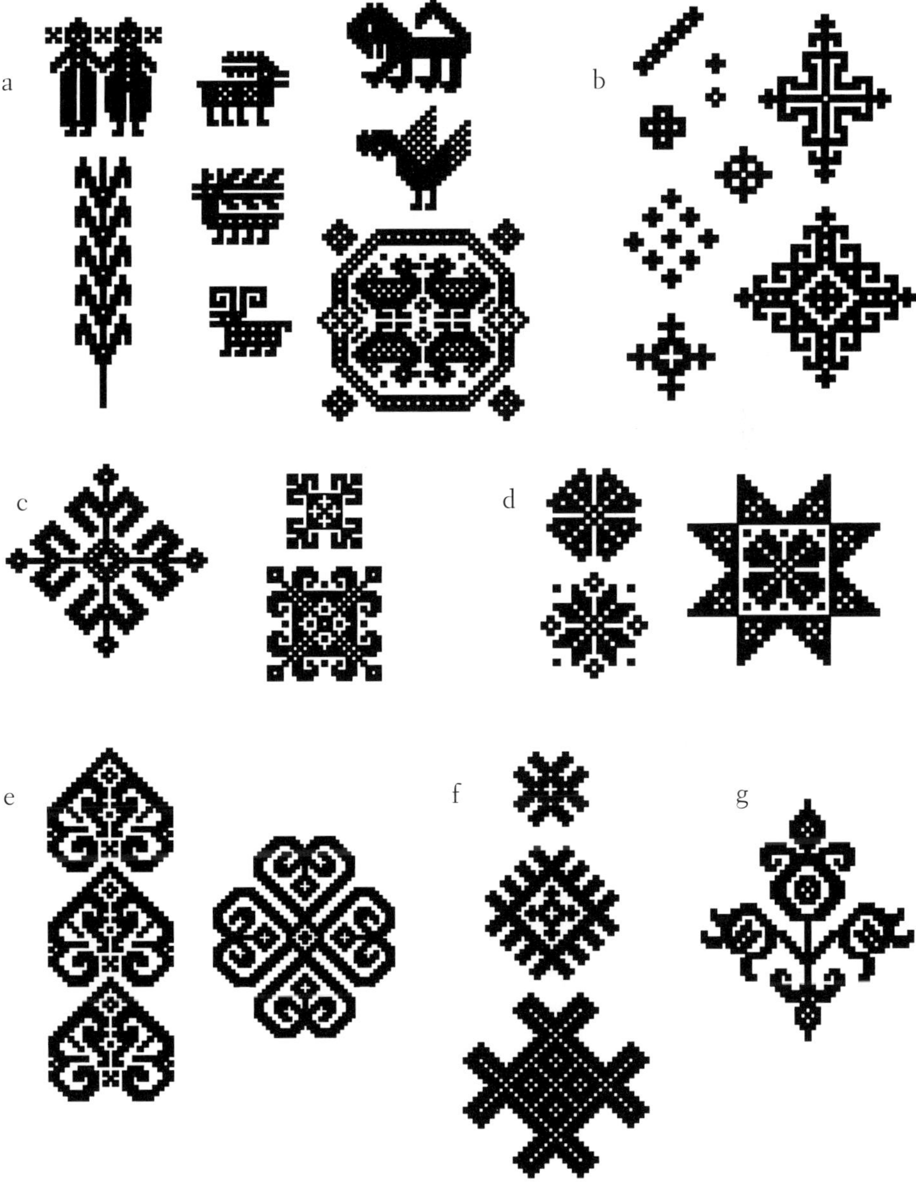

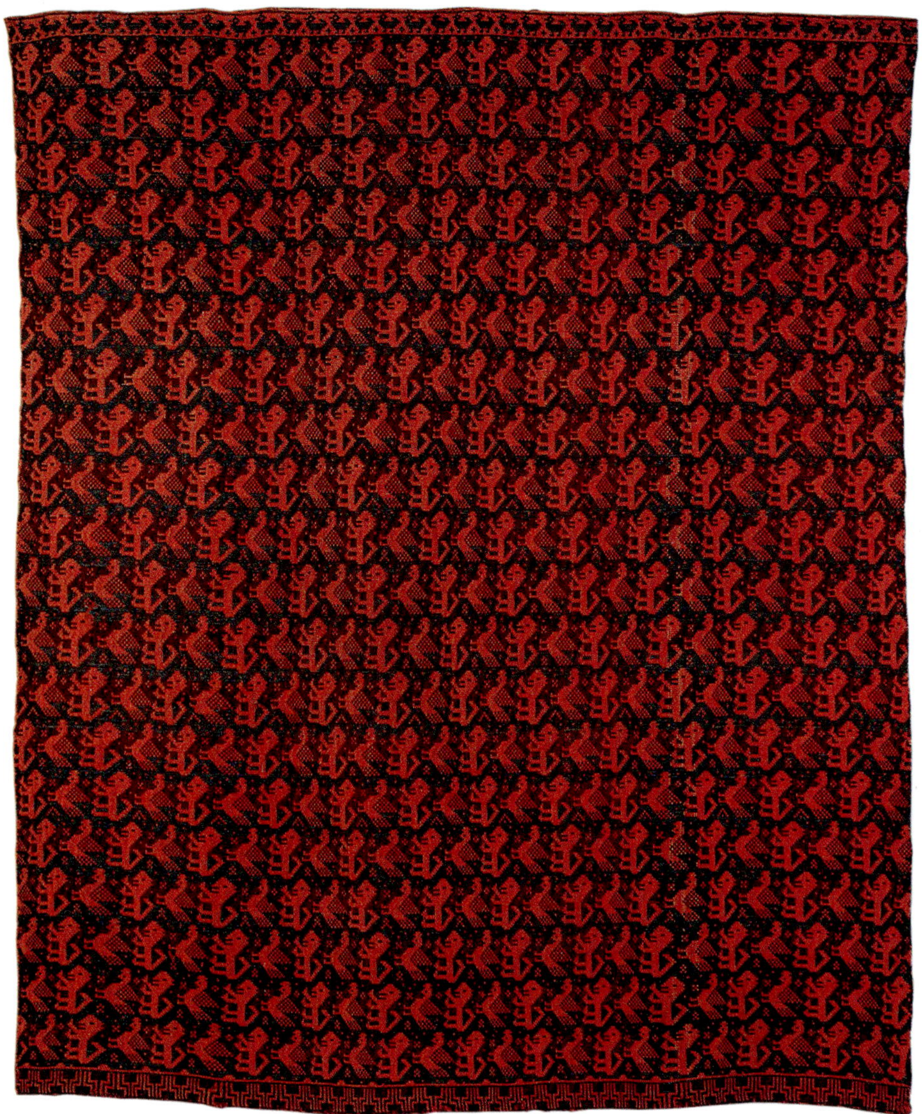

8.15 An array of lions and roosters. The under layer is red in both warp and weft, producing a red pattern on the front. The over layer has a warp of sheep-brown (natural brown wool) and a weft of brown and blue stripes. Note the top border of ducks. Vågå, Gudbrandsdal. *Norwegian Folk Museum.*

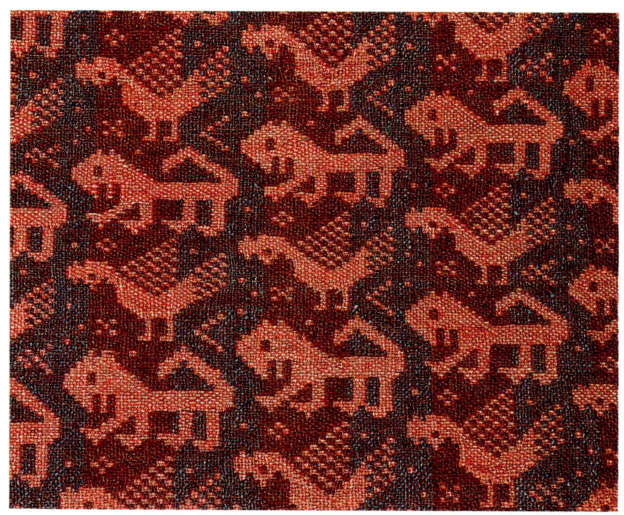

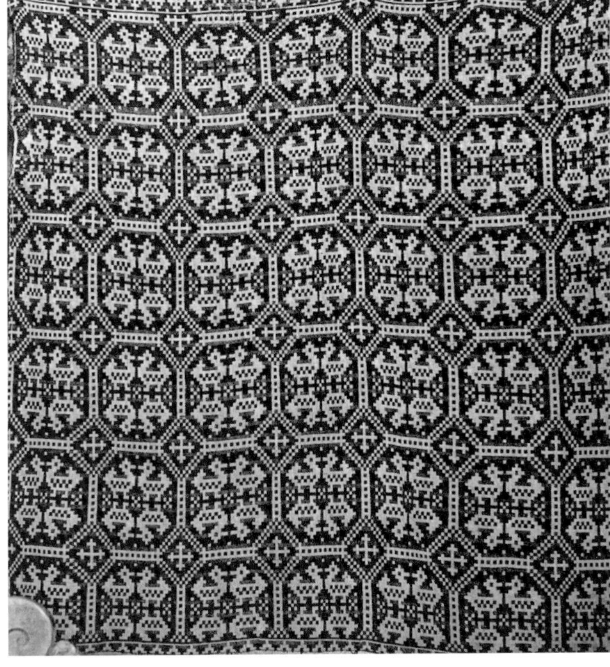

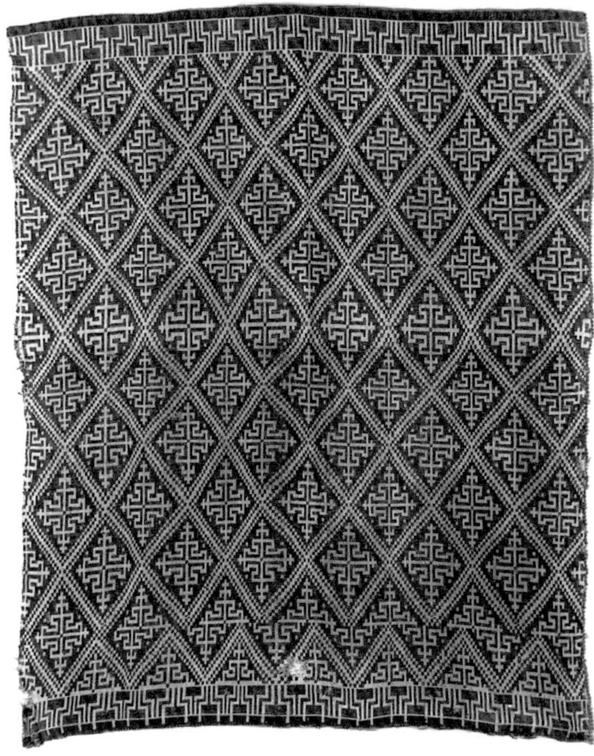

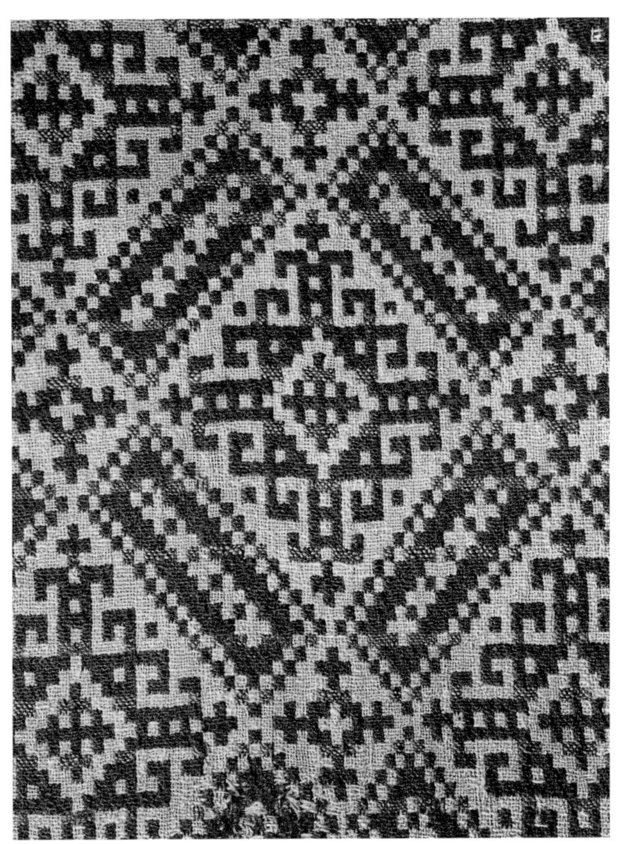

8.16 Groups of four ducks arranged in octagons. Vågå, Gud-brandsdal. *Maihaugen, The Sandvig Collection.*

8.17 An enlarged, outlined version of the cross motif. Note that the weaver adjusted the width of her pattern halfway through the first row, bottom. Vågå, Gudbrandsdal. *Oslo Museum of Applied Art.*

8.18 Three versions of the cross motif: a combination of the large cross and the lily square forms the main design, the five cross appears at top and bottom and to either side, and groupings of the simple cross appear in the middle and in the slanted borders. Vågå, Gudbrandsdal. *Oslo Museum of Applied Art.*

Cross The cross motif, seen in the oldest examples of Norwegian double weaves, was used in several variations. Aside from simple small crosses that served as fillers in and between other motifs, the five-cross and a larger out-lined version appeared. A further variation was formed by the combination of this larger cross with the lily square (figs. 8.17–8.18).

Lily Cross and *Lily Square* Using the medieval lily motif as a basis, the lily cross was composed of an arrangement of four stylized lilies radiating from a central point. The lily cross was fairly widespread in the Mediterranean countries and in Europe, appearing as early as the seventh century in Coptic textiles.[2] A popular motif in tapestry and voided-pile pillows (see figs. 4.18d and 9.10), the lily cross was used as the main motif in some double-weave coverlets. The lily square, resembling a square with horns at the corners, was a variation of the lily cross. The center of the lily cross was enlarged to form a square and realigned along a horizontal and vertical axis. The lily square often appeared in combination with the eight-petaled rose (figs. 8.19–8.20 and fig. 8.9).

Eight-Petaled Rose A favorite motif in many Norwegian textiles, the eight-petaled rose was interpreted in its three basic forms in the reversible coverlets, the standard rose with petals separated, the rose with petals joined, and the smooth-sided rosette variation. The eight-petaled rose was sometimes used in combination with the lily square. It was also placed in a slanted gridwork, either by itself or alternating with another motif, and several coverlets show a combination of two versions of the eight-petaled rose, one placed inside the other (figs. 8.21–8.23).

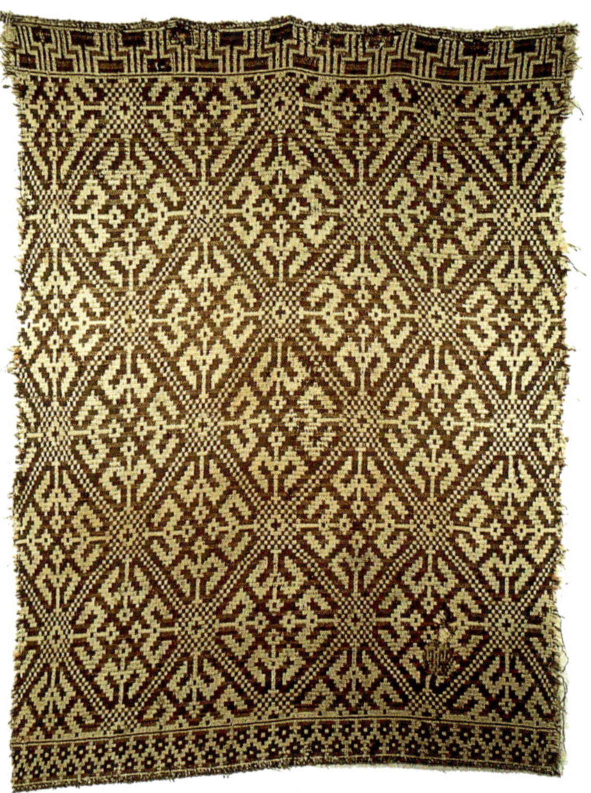

8.19 (*Left*) The lily cross. The pile of a *rya* is knotted to the reverse side of this double-weave coverlet (see fig. 9.24). Heidal, Gudbrandsdal. *Maihaugen, The Sandvig Collection.*

8.20 (*Above*) The lily-square motif alternating with a version of the eight-petaled rose. Vågå, Gudbrandsdal. *Oslo Museum of Applied Art.*

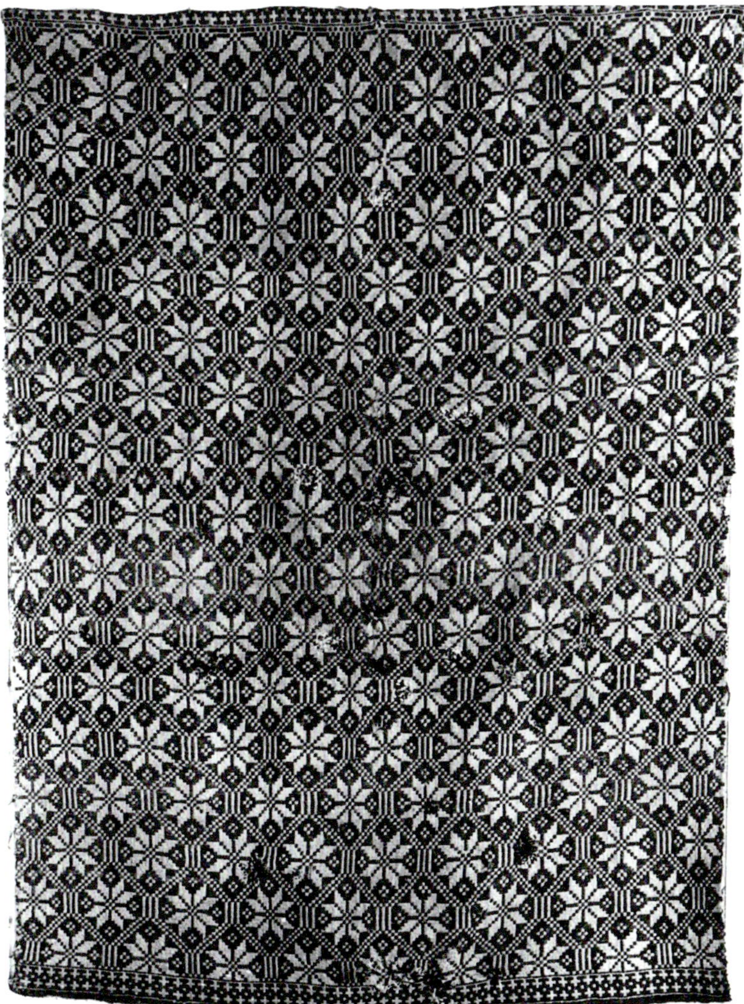

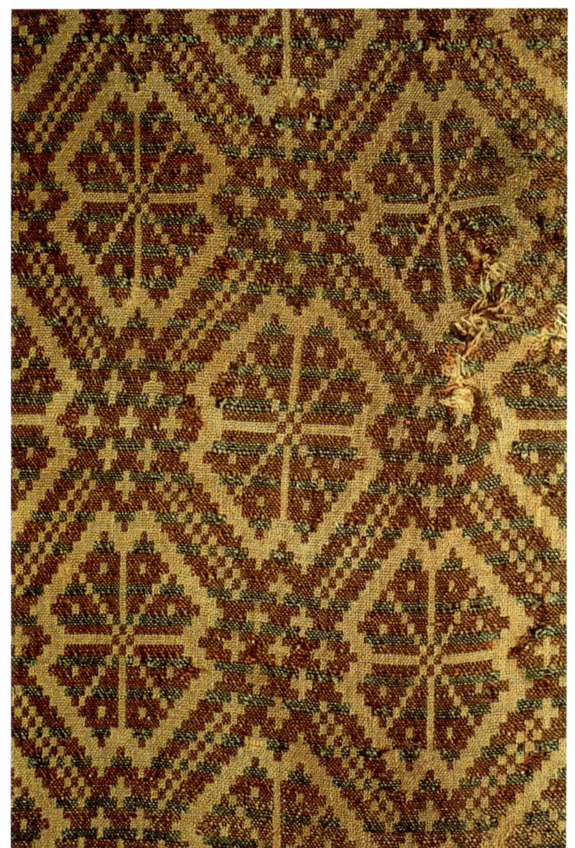

8.21 The eight-petaled rose in a hexagonal grid. Vågå, Gudbrandsdal. *Maihaugen, The Sandvig Collection.*

8.22 The smooth-sided eight-petaled rose alternates with a simple diamond-and-cross motif. Vågå, Gudbrandsdal. *Maihaugen, The Sandvig Collection.*

8.23 (*Right*) The eight-petaled rose with the smooth-sided rosette version in the center. Vågå, Gudbrandsdal. *Oslo Museum of Applied Art.*

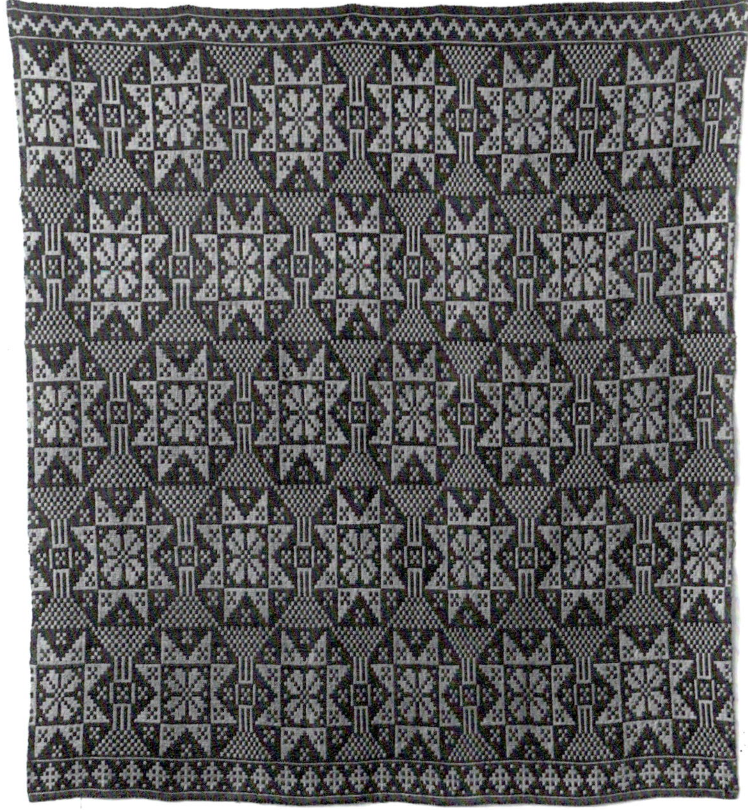

Palmette Hearts and ***Heart Rosettes*** The palmette heart was composed of a stylized palm leaf placed within the shape of a heart. Usually such hearts were stacked one on top of another, the point of one resting between the lobes of the next. Examples of this motif are found in other Scandinavian textiles from the Middle Ages and in Byzantine silks from the tenth century.[3] The heart rosette, also known in medieval Byzantine textiles, was composed of four hearts arranged with their points at the center, their lobes becoming the petals of a large flower. Within each heart was the shape of a lily instead of a palmette (figs. 8.24–8.25).

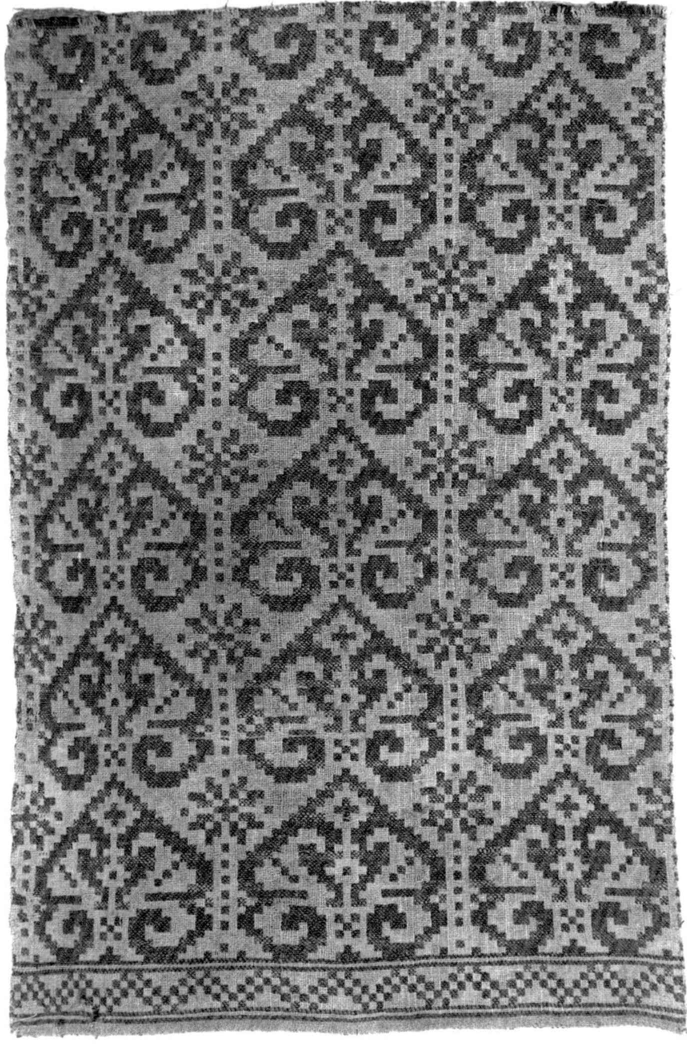

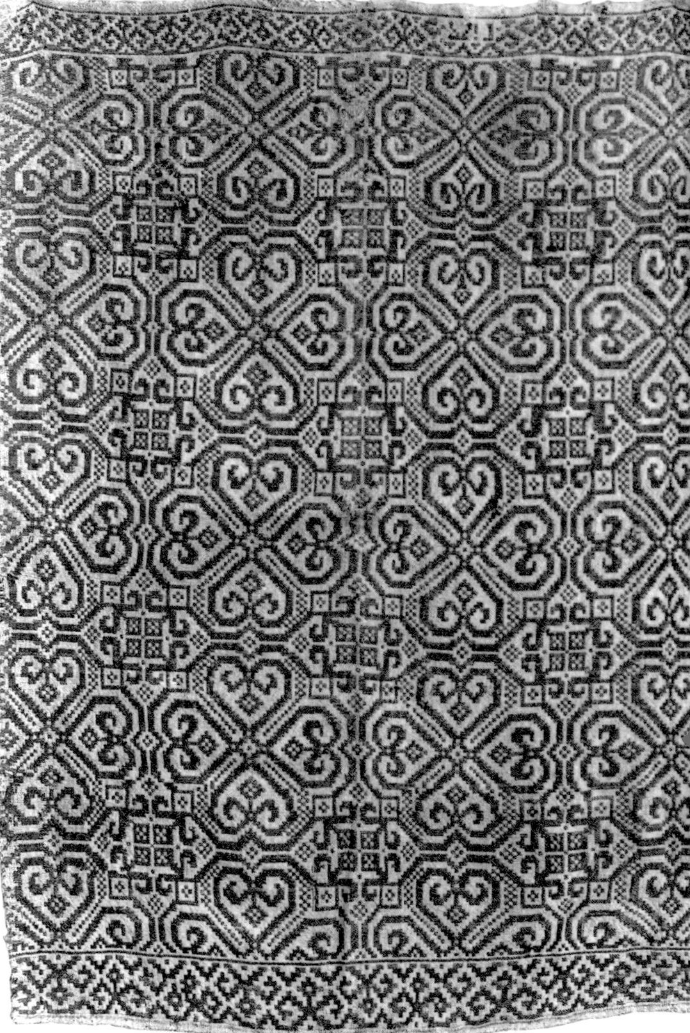

8.24 The palmette heart, composed of a stylized palm leaf enclosed by a heart shape, appears in columns in the double-weave coverlets. Vågå, Gudbrandsdal. *Oslo Museum of Applied Art.*

8.25 The heart rosette is formed by four hearts arranged in the shape of a rosette. The lily motif appears within each heart. Vågå, Gudbrandsdal. *Oslo Museum of Applied Art.*

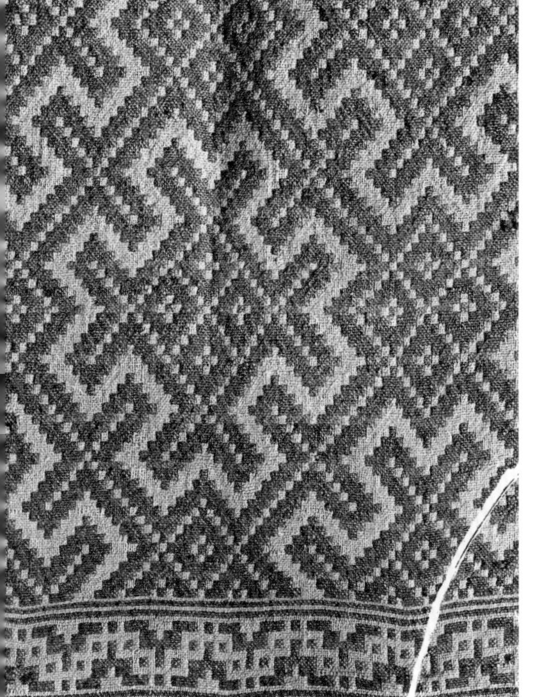

Crossed Hatch-Marks The crossed hatch-marks motif, consisting of two sets of parallel crisscrossing lines, is an ancient pattern identified in Russian textiles as a motif from "remote antiquity."[4] It also appeared in Venetian pattern books and Dutch linen work of the sixteenth century, and is still to be found in textiles from the Middle East. The motif was used in a number of variations in the Norwegian coverlets, usually placed in a diagonal gridwork (figs. 8.26–8.27 and fig. 8.11).

Tulip The tulip plant, introduced into Europe from the Middle East in the sixteenth century, was so popular that for a period it became the subject of a craze known as "tulipomania." The tulip was used as a motif in the textiles of many countries, and it appeared to a limited extent in reversible double-weave coverlets (fig. 8.28).

8.26 Crossed hatch-mark motif complemented by a diamond-and-cross design. Probably Gudbrandsdal. *Norwegian Folk Museum.*

8.27 (*Below*) Crossed hatch-mark motif set in a regular array. Gudbrandsdal. *Oslo Museum of Applied Arts.*

8.28 (*Right*) The tulip motif. Note the border of ducks, bottom. Vågå, Gudbrandsdal. *Oslo Museum of Applied Art.*

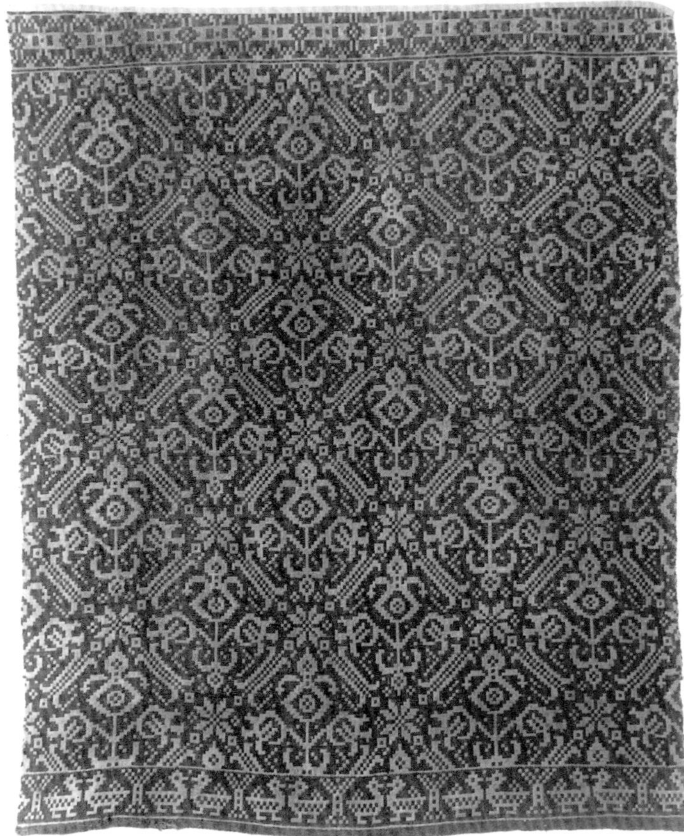

Nonreversible Double-Weave Motifs (fig. 8.29)

Inscriptions The amount of detail made possible by the nonreversible technique led to the extensive use of lettering. Initials and date appeared in many coverlets, and lines of verse from popular psalm books became a large part of the design in some cases. Such verses usually dealt with the subject of sleep and the protection of the Lord.

Inscription from a coverlet woven by Berit Hilmo of Tydal, Sør-Trøndelag, in 1819:

DAGEN ER SKABT TIL ARBEYD OG UMAG

DET KAND ENHVER HOS SIG MERKE

MEN NATTEN ER SKABT TIL ROE OG MAG

DE TRÆTTE LEMMER AT STÆRKE

GLÆDE OS GUD I HIMMERIG

The day is made for work and strife

As everyone can tell

But night is made for peace and rest

The tired limbs to strengthen

Give us joy God in heaven

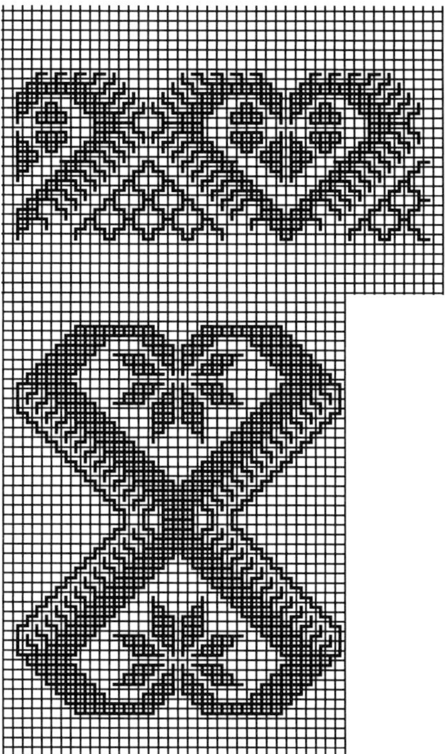

e

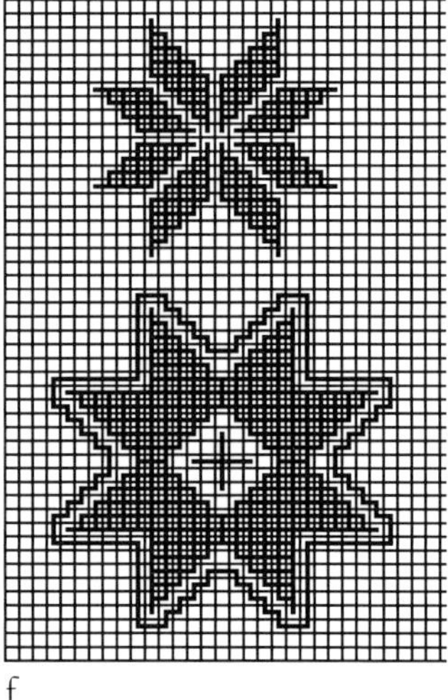

f

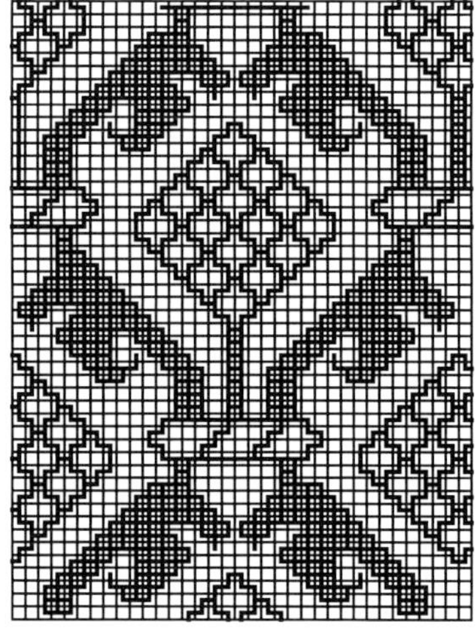

g

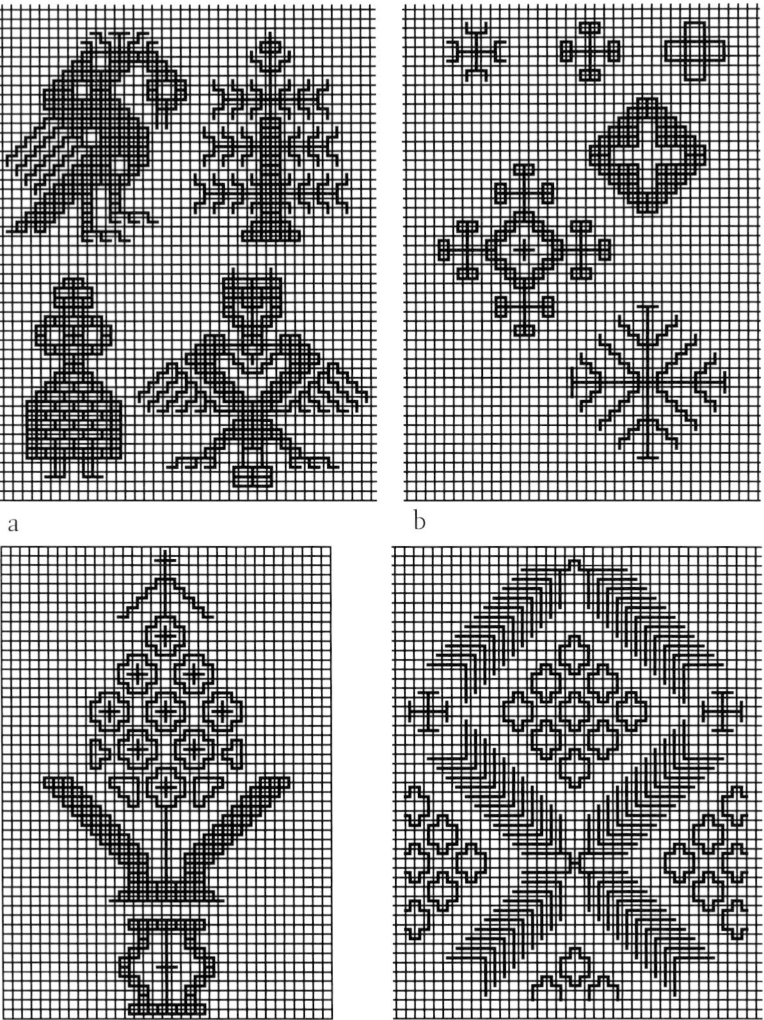

a

b

c

d

8.29 Nonreversible double-weave motifs: *(a)* figures; *(b)* cross; *(c)* vase of flowers; *(d)* grapes in leaves; *(e)* opposing hearts; *(f)* eight-petaled rose; *(g)* Tydal rose. In drawing nonreversible double-weave patterns, both the top and bottom layers are shown. The top layer is represented by the lines of the graph, one vertical line equaling one pair of warp threads and one horizontal line equaling one pair of weft threads. The bold lines represent the bottom layer, but only where it comes to the surface as pattern, one vertical stroke equaling one pair of pattern warp threads and one horizontal stroke equaling one pair of pattern weft threads. Looking at the tree in diagram *(a)*, the main portion of the trunk is composed of three sets of pattern warp threads (three vertical strokes), and the layer underneath, represented by the graphed lines, is composed of only two pairs of warp threads. In the same way, the number of weft pairs in the pattern area always encloses a lesser number of weft pairs (graph lines) in the underlayer. Although the graphed drawings do not look exactly like the pattern to be woven, they do provide an accurate representation of the two layers in nonreversible double weave.

8.30 Opposing hearts motif with double inscription (translation, *above right*). Note the row of pelicans, top. Tydal, Sør-Trøndelag. *National Museum of Decorative Arts, Trondheim.*

Two inscriptions woven into a coverlet from Tydal, Sør-Trøndelag, dated 1799 (fig. 8.30):

NU EN DAG IEG ÆLDRE BLEV
DET ER SOM MIT TANKE BREV
TA IEG MED MIN VANDRINGS STAF
NÆRMER HÆLDER TIL MIN GRAV

Now one day older I've become
It is like my reminder (mental note)
That I with my wandering staff
Draw ever nearer to my grave

IEG VIL TIL SOVE STÆDEN GAA
TI HVILE MIG BEHAGER
AT IEG DES BEDRE SOVE
MAA MIN KLÆDNING IEG AFDRAGER

I go to my sleeping place
Because rest gives me comfort
That I may sleep the better
I must remove my clothes

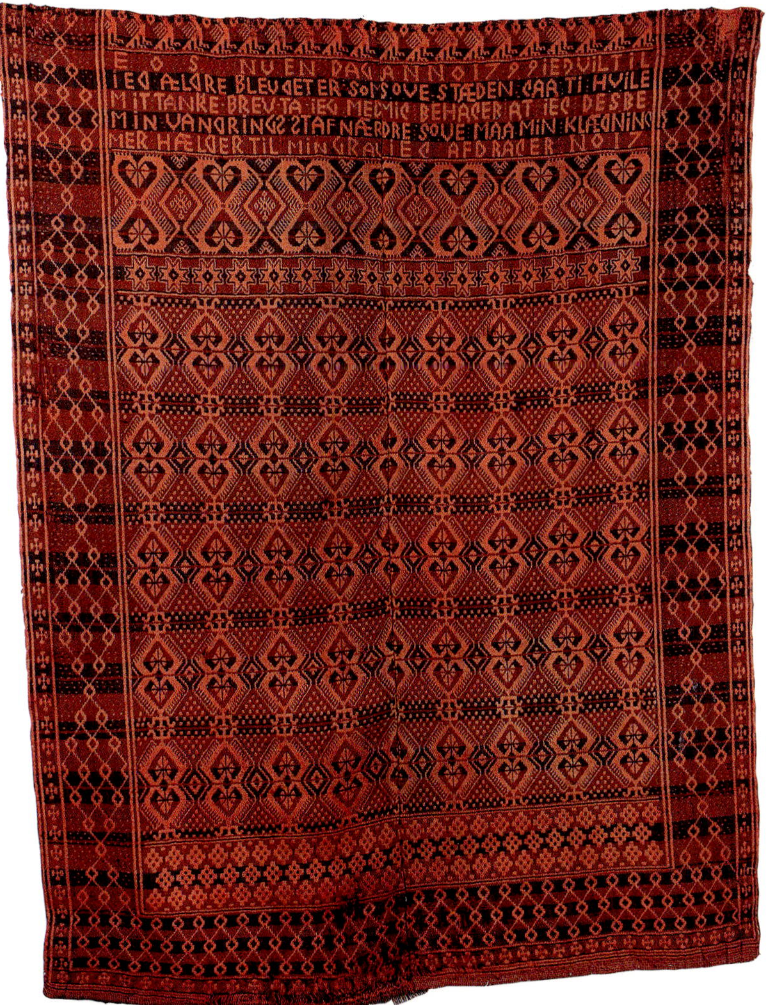

Coverlets were often used as a covering for the coffin during funeral services or on the way to the churchyard for burial. For this reason, some double-weave coverlets were woven in a long, narrow shape specifically designed for use as a coffin drape, and included inscriptions designed to provide comfort and inspiration for the bereaved.

Inscription from a number of double-weave burial coverlets:

FARVEL IEG AFSKED TAGER

DEN SORG SOM I NU SMAGER

VIL ANDRE FLERE SKEE

GUD EDER SELV LEDSAGE

SAA SKAL VI UDEN KLAGE

HVERANDRE SNART FOR THRONEN SEE

Farewell, I take my leave
The sorrow that you now feel
Many others will experience
God Himself will lead you
So shall we without complaint
Soon meet before the throne

Figures Figures of people, trees, and birds were used in nonreversible double weave but with greater detail than in the reversible technique. The shapes of women were clearly defined, trees were given delicate branches, and more complex bird forms such as the eagle and the pelican could be attempted. Individual figures were commonly grouped in rows and placed within a larger design (figs. 8.30–8.31 and fig. 8.37).

Cross Several forms of the cross motif appeared in the nonreversible coverlets. A simple cross could be shown in outline, as a bold design on an otherwise solid background, or with bars added to the arms. A larger cross tipped with small diamonds was set in a diagonal gridwork as the major motif of some coverlets, and a variation with lines radiating from both the center and the arms of a large cross sometimes alternated with the opposing hearts motif (figs. 8.31–8.32).

Vase of Flowers and ***Grapes in Leaves*** The vase of flowers was a well-known motif in Renaissance textiles. In Norwegian double weave the motif was barely recognizable as clusters of flowers enclosed in a diagonal gridwork that connected the vases. The flowers were represented by ovals that were either filled with pattern or shown in outline, a variation that usually alternated between clusters, and the shape of the vase varied from coverlet to coverlet. Over time, the vase-of-flowers motif became simplified until the vase disappeared entirely and the flowers began to resemble a cluster of grapes surrounded by a diagonal grid of leaves (figs. 8.33–8.34 and 8.13).

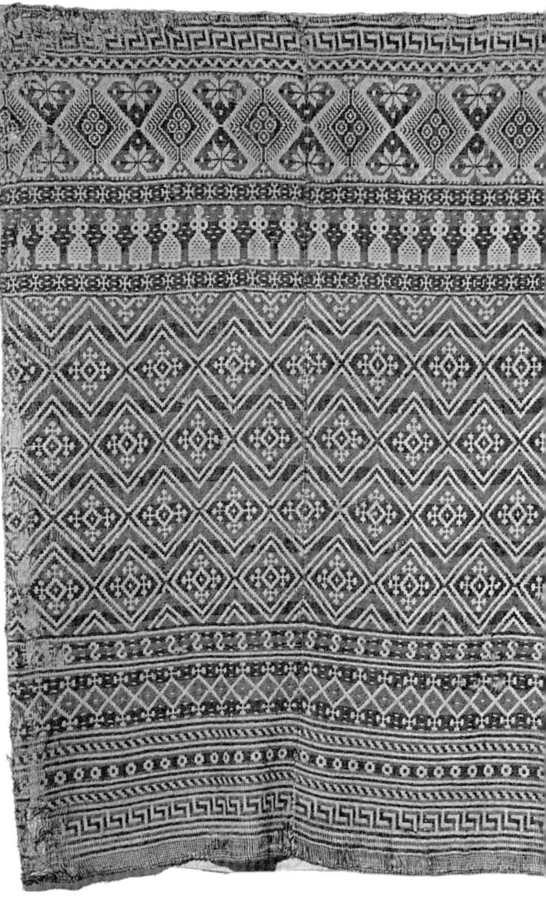

8.31 Broad bands of pattern bordering a fairly small, main design area were typical of early coverlets woven in the nonreversible technique. Here the cross motif is bordered at top and bottom by rows of various patterns, including opposing hearts and a row of ladies. Trøndelag. *National Museum of Decorative Arts, Trondheim.*

Facing page:
8.32 (*Upper left*) Small variations of the cross motif were frequently used to enhance other patterns. In this detail of figure 8.12, three variations of the cross are seen: in the top border, between the opposing hearts motif, and following the inscription. Tydal, Sør-Trøndelag. *Norwegian Folk Museum.*

8.33 (*Upper right*) Stylized vases and flowers are still discernable in this early version of the vase-of-flowers motif. Bands of various patterns, including a row of pelicans, appear above and below. Note the similarity between the lower border of crosses and those found in the early medieval coverlet from Lom, figure 8.3. *Maihaugen, The Sandvig Collection.*

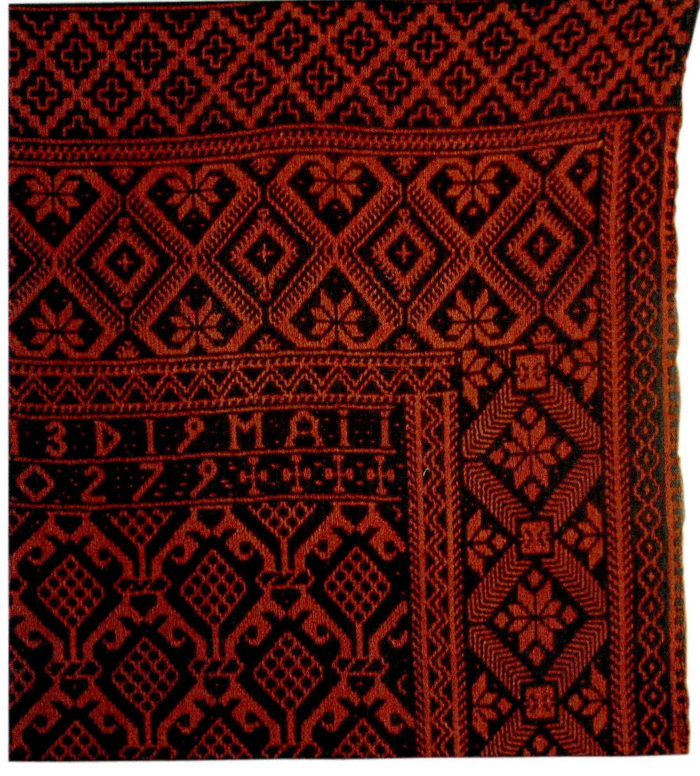

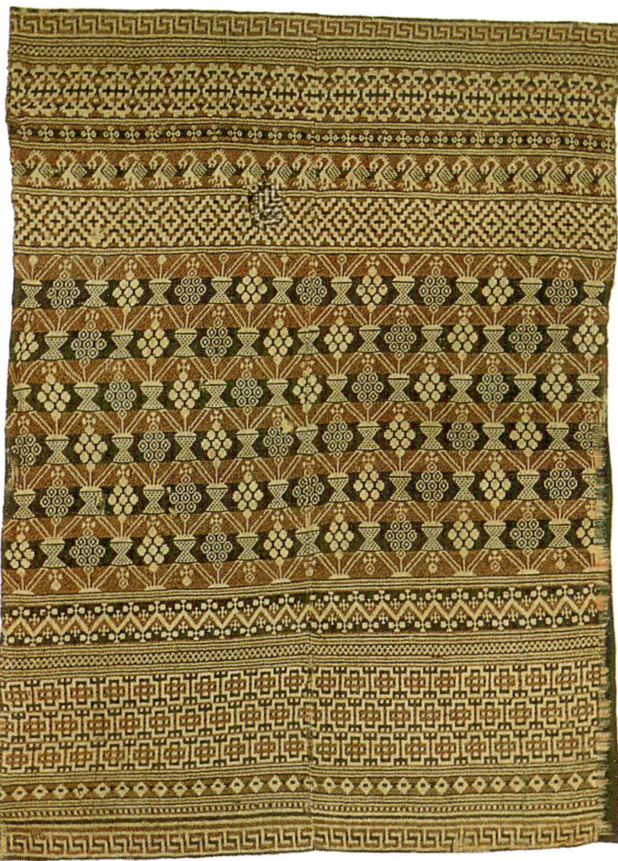

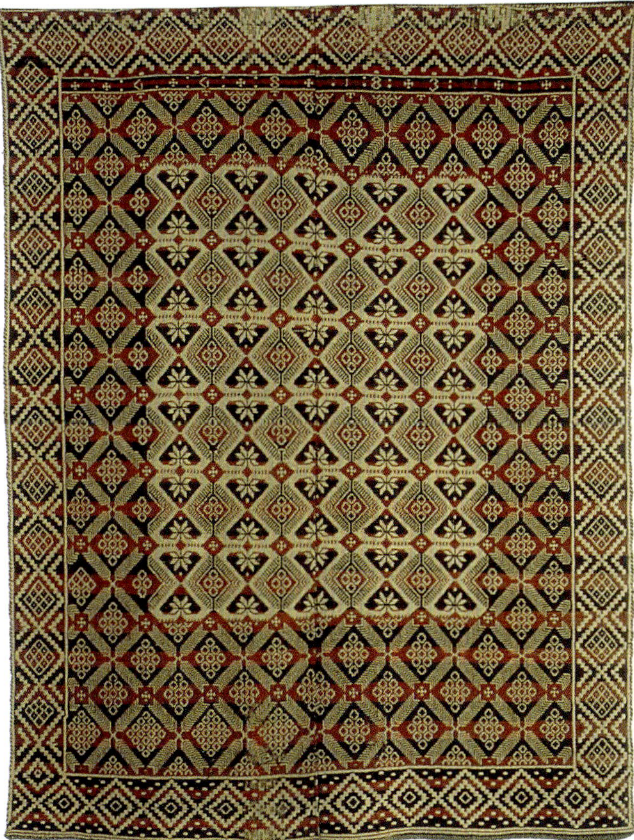

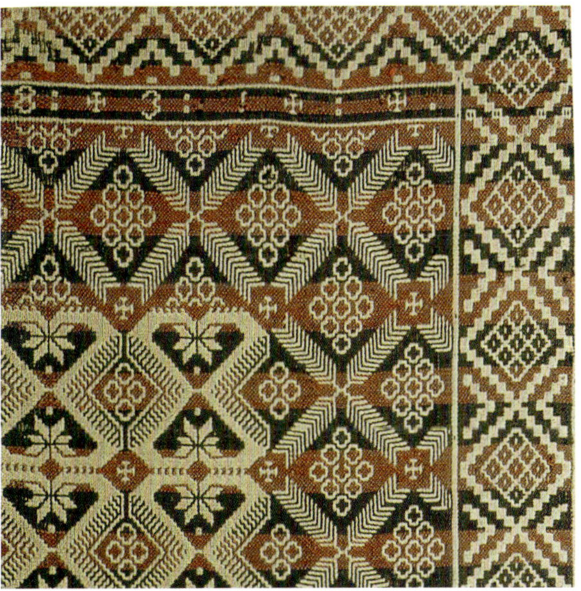

8.34 A coverlet with a central panel inside the main design was
known as a *speilåkle*, or mirror coverlet. Initials "GGS" and "1831"
appear in the top border. The central panel of opposing hearts and
the grapes-in-leaves border are clearly seen in the detailed view
(*above*). Tydal, Sør-Trøndelag. *Norwegian Folk Museum.*

Hearts The heart motif appeared in the nonreversible double-weave coverlets as two opposing heart shapes touching each other point to point, or sometimes as a row of single hearts placed side by side. A comb-like border outlined each heart, and a portion of the eight-petaled rose or smooth-sided rosette appeared within (figs. 8.34 and 8.6).

Eight-Petaled Rose The ever-popular eight-petaled rose appeared in more delicate form in the nonreversible coverlets. Petals were separated in some versions, and in others they were joined and complemented by an outline surrounding the entire flower. The eight-petaled rose often formed the center of other motifs, such as the opposed hearts and the Tydal rose. It also appeared in a gridwork of stylized leaves, and was frequently used as a border motif (figs. 8.35–8.36).

Tydal Rose The Tydal rose is a form of the pomegranate, a popular motif in Italy and Spain during the Renaissance. It was usually placed in offset rows, completely filling the central pattern area of a coverlet. Although named for the valley of Tydal in Sør-Trøndelag where it was a common motif, in Tydal it was referred to as the *værhorn*, or ram's horn, due to the curlicues on either side of the pattern. The center of the Tydal rose was filled with a slanted gridwork or an eight-petaled rose (figs. 8.37–8.38).

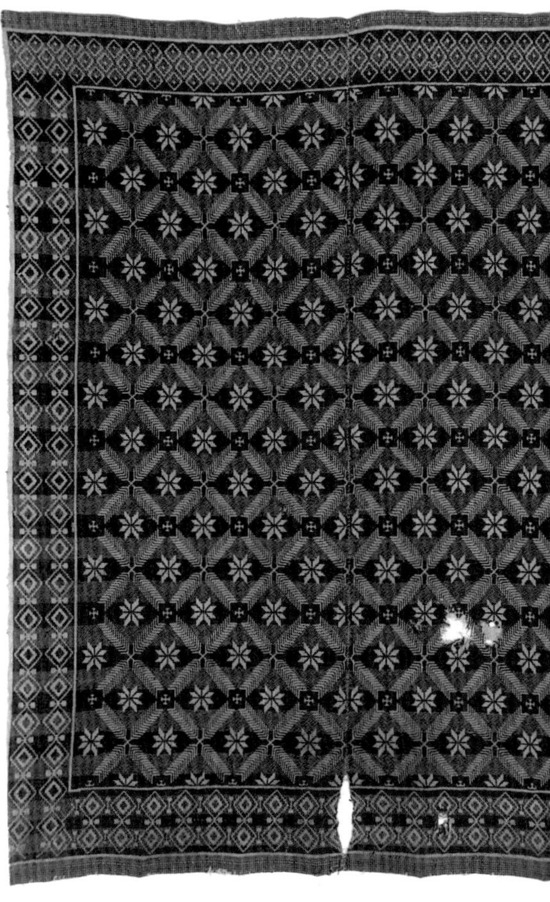

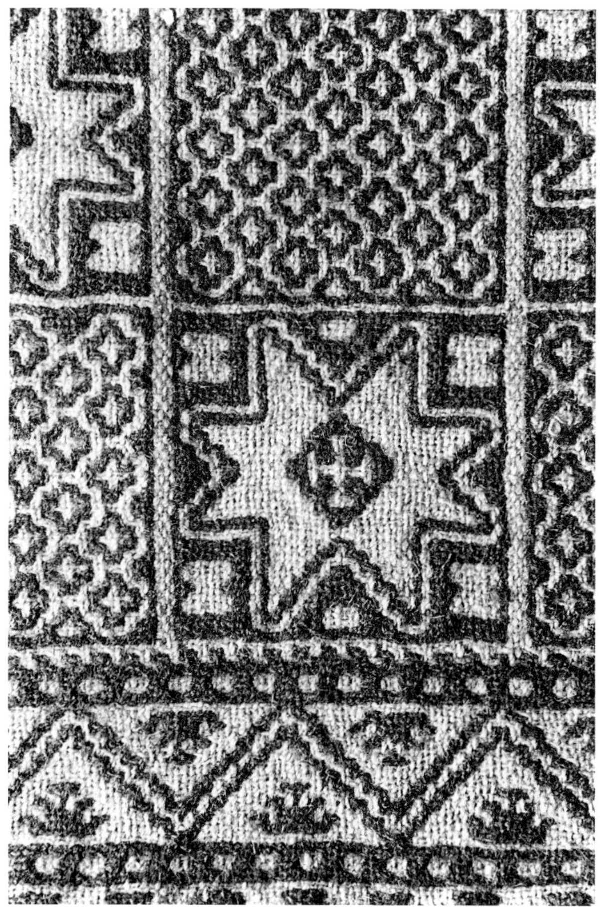

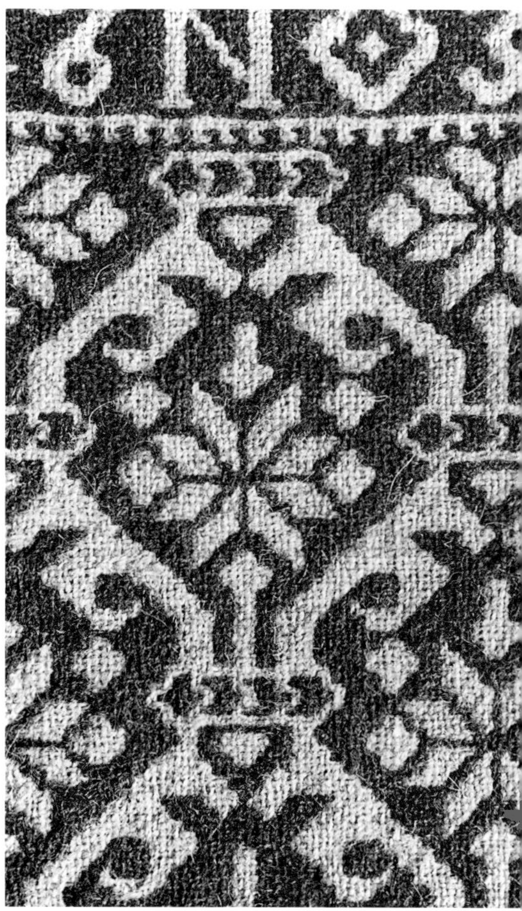

Facing page:
8.35 The eight-petaled rose in a gridwork of leaves. Nord-Trøndelag. *Oslo Museum of Applied Art.*

8.36 Variations of the eight-petaled rose: in outlined form (*bottom left*), and as the center of a Tydal rose (*bottom right*). Details from a coverlet woven in 1846. Tydal, Sør-Trøndelag. *Norwegian Folk Museum.*

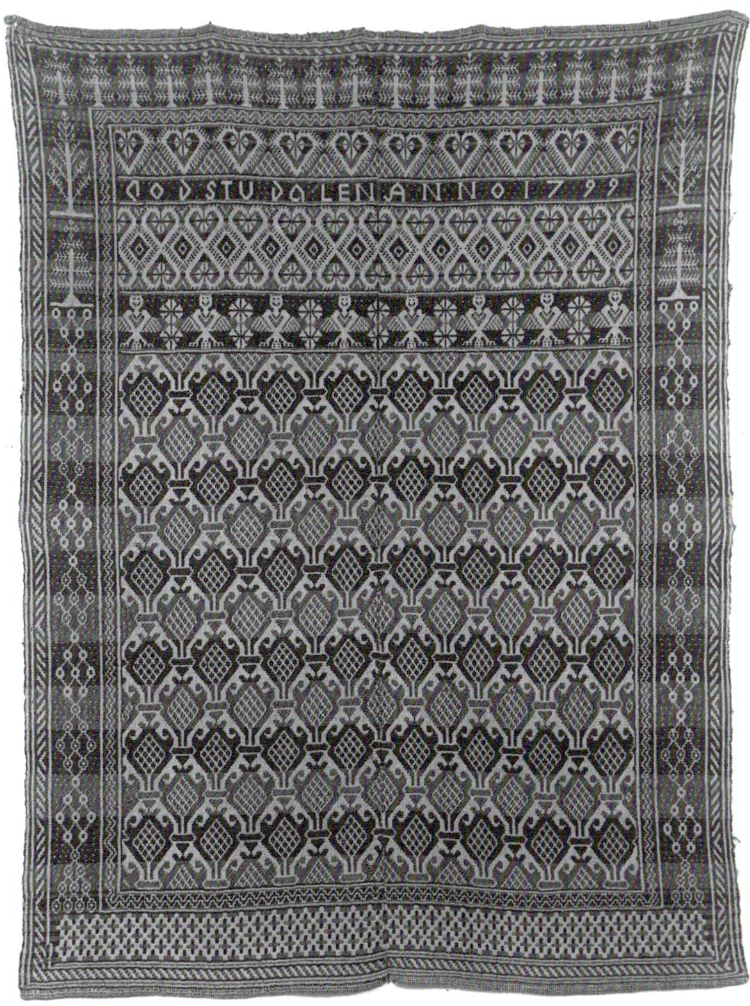

Right
8.37 The Tydal rose with central gridwork. The initials "GOD" and the location "STU-DALEN" appear with the year "1799" in the upper panel. Note the row of eagles directly above the central design, and the trees in the top and upper side borders. Tydal, Sør-Trøndelag. *Oslo Museum of Applied Art.*

8.38 The Tydal rose with central eight-petaled rose. The initials "RHD" and the year "1840" appear below the top border. *National Museum of Decorative Arts, Trondheim.*

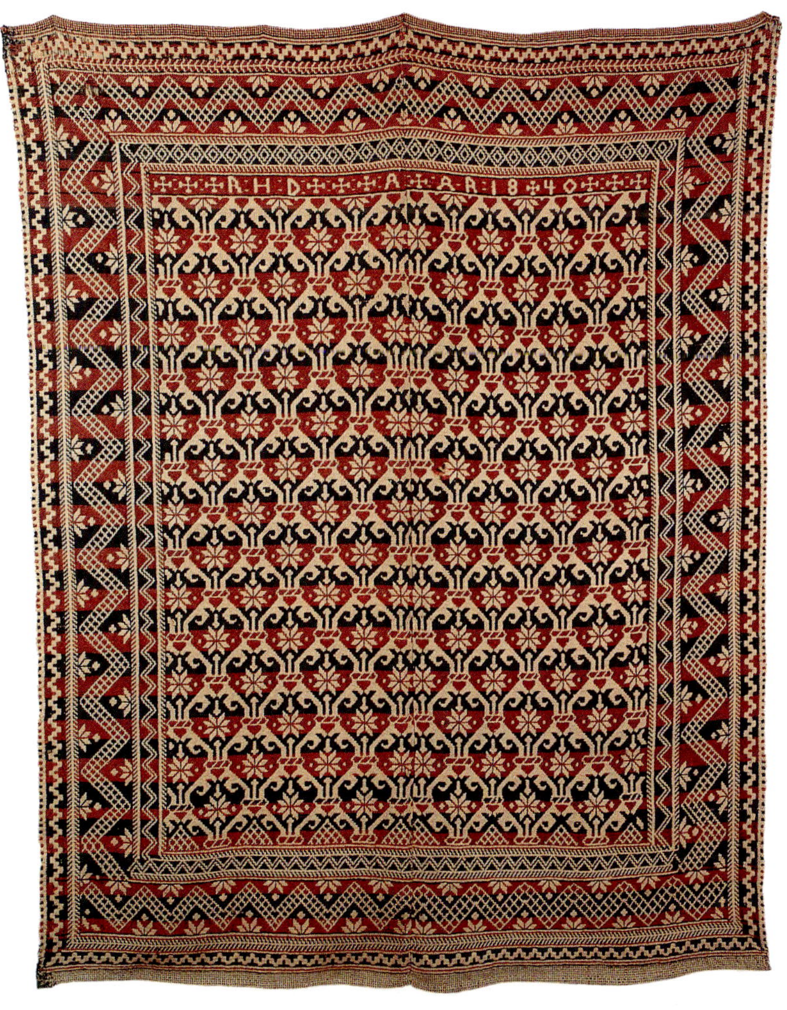

Materials and Looms

The medieval Norwegian double weaves were woven with one layer of linen and one of wool, but later wall hangings and coverlets were composed of two layers of wool. A thin, tightly spun two-strand yarn was used for both warp and weft, the guard hair of the Norwegian *spælsau* being particularly prized for this type of weaving due to its lustrous quality. Warp threads were set at approximately fourteen to sixteen ends per inch.

Reversible double-weave coverlets from Gudbrandsdal were usually woven in one piece, approximately five-and-one-half to six-and-one-half feet in length and four to five feet in width, a size indicating the probable use of the warp-weighted loom. Several of the Gudbrandsdal coverlets still retain the heading cord by which they were attached to the long top beam of this type of loom (see "Warping the Warp-Weighted Loom," page 100). The nonreversible coverlets from Trøndelag, on the other hand, were woven in two pieces approximately four to five feet in length and twenty-two to twenty-six inches in width, which were sewn together to make a complete coverlet. This extra step was made necessary by the constraints of the narrower horizontal loom, introduced into Norway at about the same time as nonreversible double weave and apparently readily adopted in Trøndelag for weaving the new technique.

Weaving Techniques

The double-weave coverlets were created from two layers of balanced plain-weave that were woven at the same time. In the nonreversible double weave coverlets, two layers of warp were wound together onto a four-harness loom, two harnesses for each layer. Two shots of weft in the top layer alternated with two shots of weft in the bottom layer. In areas that had no pattern, such as the one to two inches sometimes woven at the beginning or the end of a coverlet, the two layers were actually woven separately and had no interaction (fig. 8.39 [a]). (These areas were turned towards each other and sewn together as a hem during finishing.) When a design was to be woven, the two layers changed places in areas of pattern. This was accomplished with the use of two pick-up sticks that separated the pattern and background warps of the bottom layer while two shots of the top layer were woven, and then separated the pattern and background warps of the top layer while two shots of the bottom layer were woven. These two steps allowed the bottom layer to come to the surface in pattern areas while the top layer traveled underneath (fig. 8.39 [b]). In picking up the design, care was needed to count the warp threads according to the selected pattern, usually copied from an older coverlet. In nonreversible double weave, there were always two less warps and two less wefts in the bottom layer for each pattern element, giving the patterns in the top layer their crisp, smooth edge.

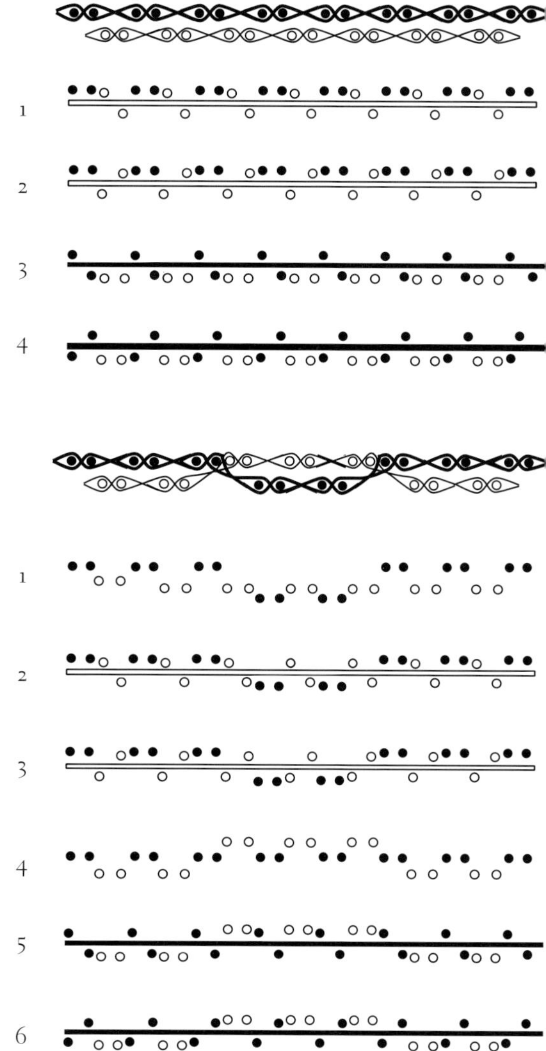

8.39 Nonreversible double weave in cross section. Wa[rps] are grouped in pairs that are offset between the two lay[ers] top layer in a pattern area always has one more pair of [weft] weft) threads than the layer beneath it. (*a*) When there [is no pat-] tern, the layers are woven separately: two shots of light [weft, steps 1] and 2, followed by two shots of dark weft, steps 3 and 4[. (*b*) When] a pattern is desired, the dark warp threads in the patter[n are] picked down and the non-pattern threads picked up (s[o that] two shots of light weft are woven (steps 2 and 3). The p[attern] threads in the light warp are then picked up and the n[on-pattern] threads picked down (step 4) before two shots of the da[rk weft are] woven (steps 5 and 6). *After Engelstad 1958.*

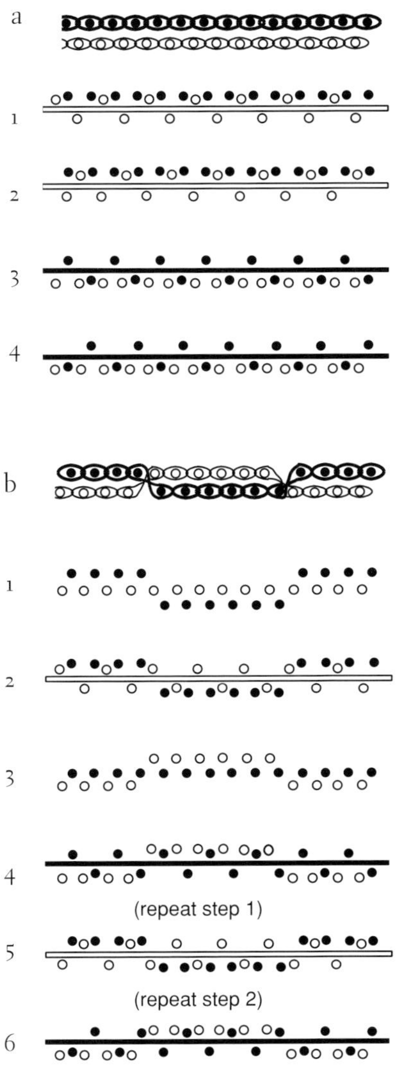

No examples of the older upright loom, probably warp-weighted but possibly a local variation (see figs. 5.29–5.31), have survived in Gudbrandsdal where the reversible double-weave coverlets were woven. As a result, the exact method for weaving double weave on these looms is not known, but weaving with four sheds was possible. In eighteenth-century Iceland, the warp-weighted loom was equipped with three harnesses for weaving wadmal (a woolen twill), the fourth shed arising naturally from the fall of the warp threads. The harness tie-up used in creating this twill structure, however, was inappropriate for double weave, and although the four sheds commonly used for double weave are technically possible on the warp-weighted loom, textile authority Marta Hoffmann speculates that double weave may have been woven with only two sheds, requiring the pattern to be picked up by hand.[5]

In other respects, the weaving technique for reversible double weave was the same as that for nonreversible with two exceptions. Patterns in reversible double weave were woven with the same number of warp and weft threads in the top and bottom layers. This gave the finished fabric identical designs in reverse colors on both sides, but it also created the second difference between the two techniques. If two shots of weft were woven after each row of pattern pick-up, as in the nonreversible technique, a jagged edge developed along the top or bottom and along one side of pattern elements. The problem could be overcome to a degree by weaving one shot of weft instead of two after each pick-up of pattern. Although this doubled the amount of pick-up work required, this was the technique used for many of the reversible coverlets (fig. 8.40).

8.40 Reversible double weave in cross section. Warp threads are offset between layers, but are treated individually instead of as pairs. In a pattern area, both layers have the same number of warp (and weft) threads. *(a)* When there is no pattern, the layers are woven separately: two shots of light weft, steps 1 and 2, followed by two shots of dark weft, steps 3 and 4. *(b)* When a pattern is desired, the dark warp threads in the pattern area are picked down and the non-pattern threads picked up (step 1) before one shot of light weft is woven (step 2). The pattern threads in the light warp are then picked up and the non-pattern threads picked down (step 3) before one shot of the dark weft is woven (step 4). The pattern pick-up in step 1 is repeated before the second shot of light weft is woven (step 5), and the pattern pick-up in step 3 is repeated before the second shot of dark weft is woven (step 6). *After Engelstad 1958.*

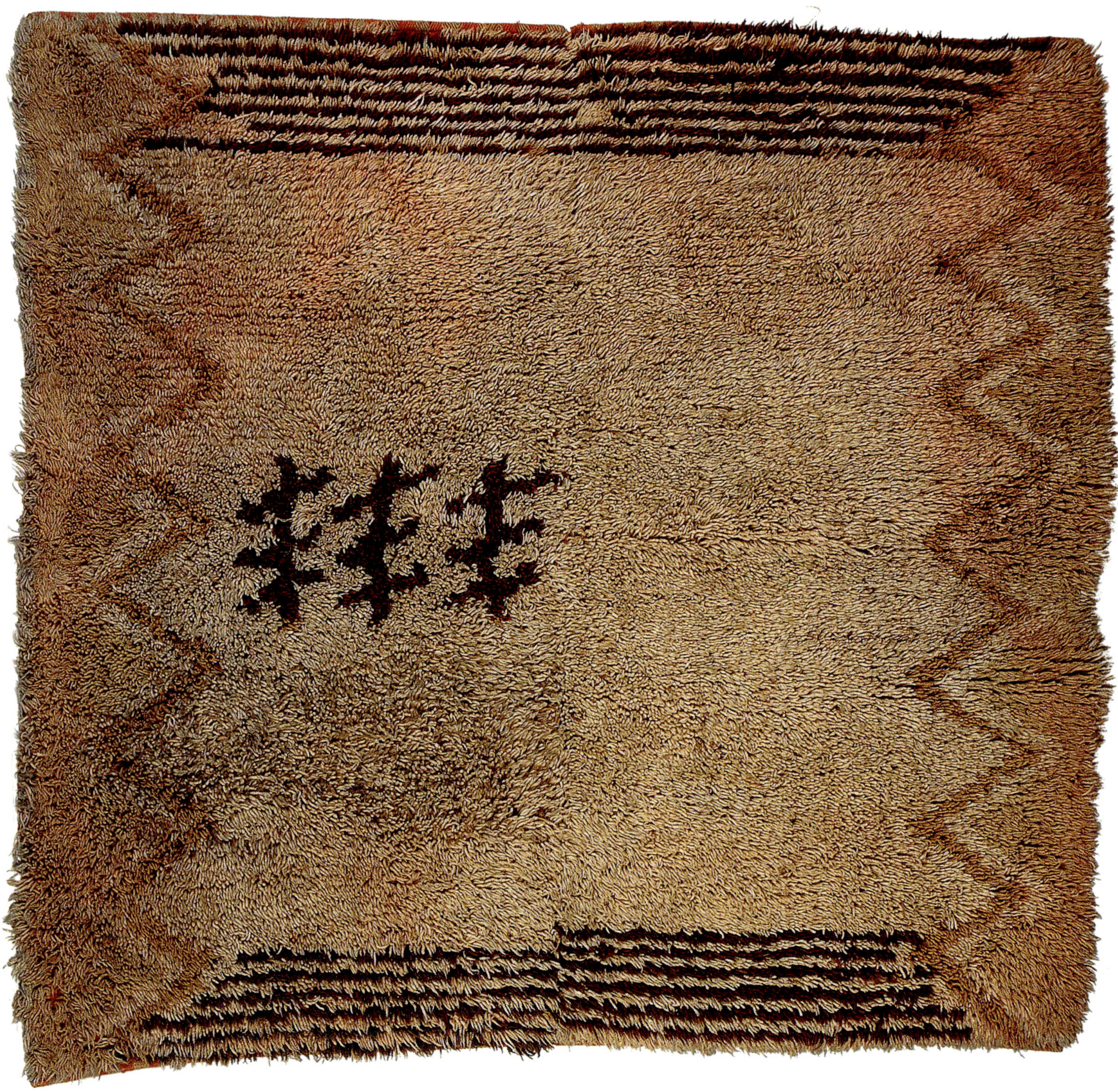

9.1 Zigzags and stripes form a frame for the simple pattern, probably an owner's mark, in the pile side of this rya. Orkedalen, Sør-Trøndelag, late nineteenth century. *National Museum of Decorative Arts, Trondheim.*

9 / Knotted-Pile Coverlets: Rye

They laid the sail as a roof over the bow, put a grene under and a rya and
sheepskin blanket over, and they slept nice and warm. But it was winter,
of course, and occasionally they had to shake the snow off themselves
when they got up in the morning.

—Overnighting in open boats on the way to the winter fishery in Lofoten[1]

THE SCANDINAVIAN KNOTTED-PILE TEXTILES
referred to in English by their Swedish name, *rya* (Norwegian:
rye), are well known for their vibrant colors and modernistic designs.
What is not as commonly known is that these shaggy textiles, now used primarily as rugs and wall hangings, were originally intended to serve as coverlets. With the all-important pile side turned towards the body, the rya made
a thick and welcome coverlet both on the bed at home and in open boats at
sea (figs. 9.1–9.2).

The long pile of the rya made these textiles so close an approximation
of a sheepskin that one might wonder why such a coverlet was woven at all
when the natural product was readily available (fig. 9.3). But the knotted pile
of a rya resisted daily wear and tear much better than the wool of a sheepskin, and, just as important to the seafaring Norwegians, a rya would tolerate
regular exposure to sea water if cared for properly. A sheepskin became stiff,
was difficult to dry and eventually rotted when exposed to such use.

Ryas were customary equipment in the small open fishing and trading
boats that plied the coastal waters and fjords of Norway. They were considered essential for the warmth and comfort of passengers, especially doctors

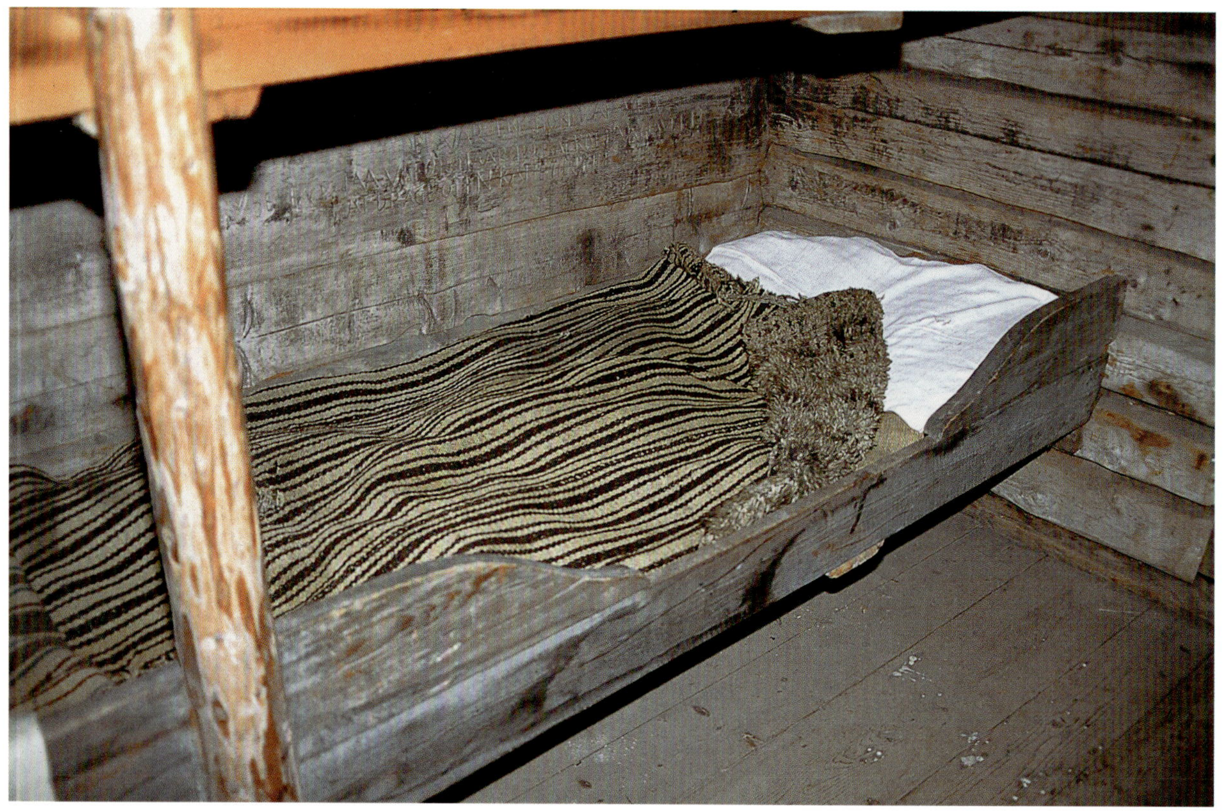

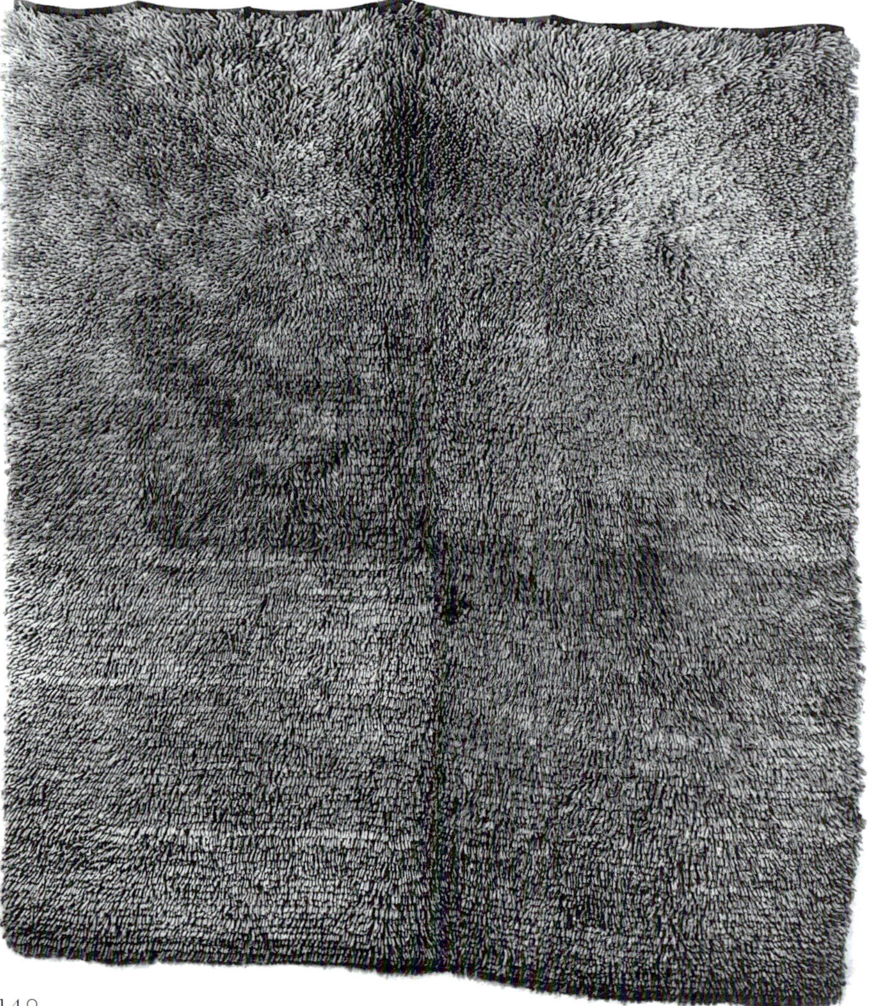

9.2 The *rya* was placed pile-side-down on the bed for maximum warmth, leaving the stripes or checks of the smooth side uppermost. A *rya* lies on the bunk of a fisherman's cabin from Halten, Trøndelag. Graffiti carved on the wall above begins: "In 1843 on March 25 there was a storm from the west so we could not take the boat out to sea. . . ." *Photo: Dino Makridis. Trøndelag Folk Museum.*

9.3 Many *ryas* looked remarkably like sheepskin blankets, but ryas were more durable, especially for use at sea. Sør-Trøndelag. *Norwegian Folk Museum.*

or priests who often needed transportation from one farm to the next, and they were an indispensable part of a fisherman's gear (fig. 9.4). The well-known story of the fisherman from northern Norway who, floating in the water near his capsized boat, instructed his rescuers to "save the rya first," illustrates the value placed on these warm, heavy textiles by those who dwelt in the country's coastal regions.[2]

At one time the rya was also used in the inland areas of Norway as a coverlet and as a lap robe for the sled. Estate records from farms in eighteenth-century Gudbrandsdal indicate that ryas even outnumbered other types of coverlets by a substantial margin at that time.[3] The rya gradually became less common in inland areas, but along the coast its value remained undiminished, and these large shaggy coverlets continued to be used well into the twentieth century.

Origins

The origin of pile weaving and its probable age in the Scandinavian countries is the subject of much speculation. Although Norway's oldest surviving ryas date from the seventeenth century, and positive references to the technique go back no further than the fifteenth century, the history of pile weave in the northern countries is probably much older. Fragmentary remains of an unidentified type of pile weave from the eighth century have been found in Sweden, and evidence of a pile weave using the same type of knot as that found in Norway comes from third- or fourth-century Poland.

9.4 A *rya* hangs on the side of a boat in Frosta, Nord-Trøndelag. *Ryas* were standard equipment on coastal fishing and trading boats. *Norwegian Folk Museum.*

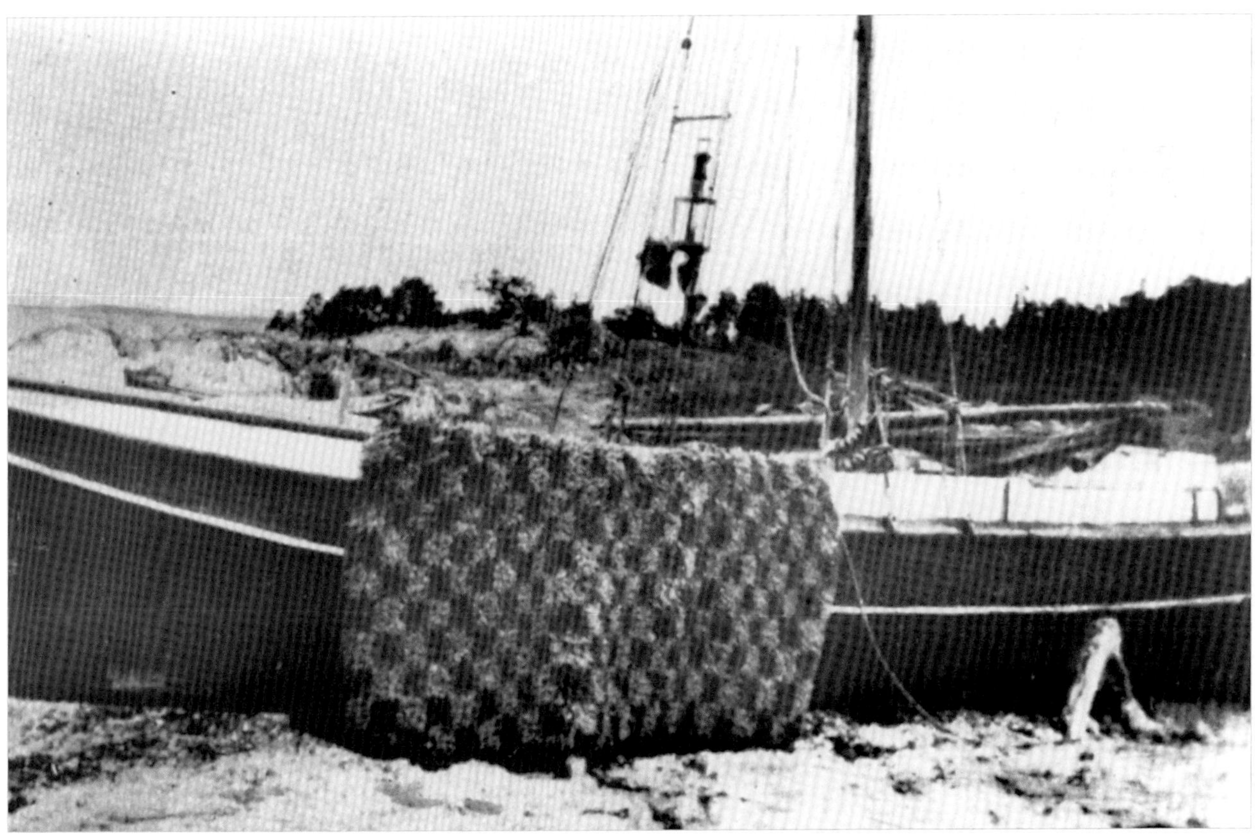

It is commonly believed that knotted-pile weaving developed in the
Middle East at least a thousand years before the birth of Christ and possibly
much earlier.[4] Of the two knots most commonly used in Middle Eastern textiles, the Ghiordes knot, also known as the Turkish knot, was the type found
in the Norwegian rya (fig. 9.5), and thus it is possible that the development
of the pile-weaving tradition in Scandinavia owes its origin to impulses from
the East. But there is a world of difference between the Middle Eastern car-
pet, a densely packed and finely patterned weave used with the pile side up
and intended for sitting or walking upon, and the Norwegian rya, a coarse,
shaggy coverlet designed for warmth and used with the pile side down. One
authority has theorized that the knotted pile technique may indeed have
spread from the East but at a very early point in history, as was the case with
other ancient types of weaving, such as *sprang* (a warp twisting technique)
and tablet weaving (a warp twining technique). Such an early divergence
would allow subsequent differences to arise according to the needs and materials of various cultures.[5] Another authority raises the possibility that since no
examples of Scandinavian ryas older than the seventeenth century remain,
the Ghiordes knot may actually represent a recent adaptation. She points to
the old Norse term *ryja*, which referred to locks of wool gathered from the
old breed of sheep that shed its fleece each year, and suggests that this may
have been the original material used to create the pile of a rya—but not nec-
essarily a knotted pile. A variety of inlaid pile weaves were known in Europe
during the Viking Age and earlier. An interesting example of these is seen
in a type of shaggy cloak known in Iceland during the tenth or eleventh
centuries in which loose locks of wool were laid into the open shed (fig. 9.6).
According to this authority, the possibility exists that the Scandinavian ryas
were woven with such an inlaid pile and that the knotting technique was
adopted later through contacts with other cultures.[6]

   Whatever the origins of the traditional rya, influences from the Middle
East and continental Europe can be seen in the development of a different
type of rya in the late seventeenth and eighteenth centuries. In these textiles,
emphasis was placed on the decorative impact of the pile side of the weave,
and practical considerations of warmth and wear were largely discarded.
Replacing the traditional rya almost completely in Sweden and Finland,
the decorative rya appeared to a limited extent in Norway and only with
relatively simple patterns (figs. 9.7–9.8). Decorative pile weaving was found,
however, in the voided-pile pillow work known as *halvfloss*, or half pile. This
weave, composed of tapestry with pattern areas highlighted by knotted pile,
was a popular technique in the eastern valleys of Norway (figs. 9.9–9.10).

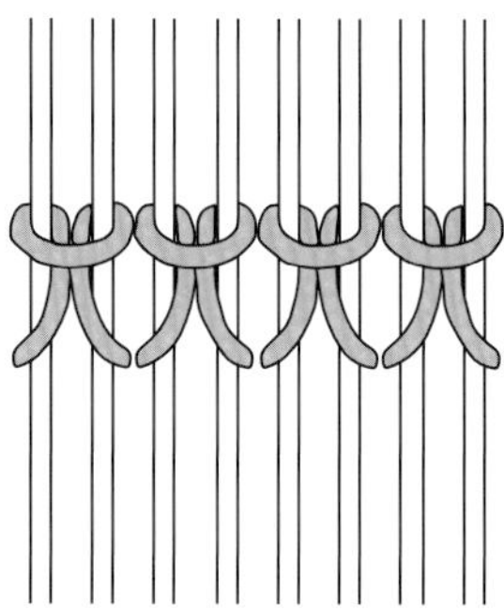

9.5 The pile of Norwegian *ryas* was tied using
the Ghiordes knot.

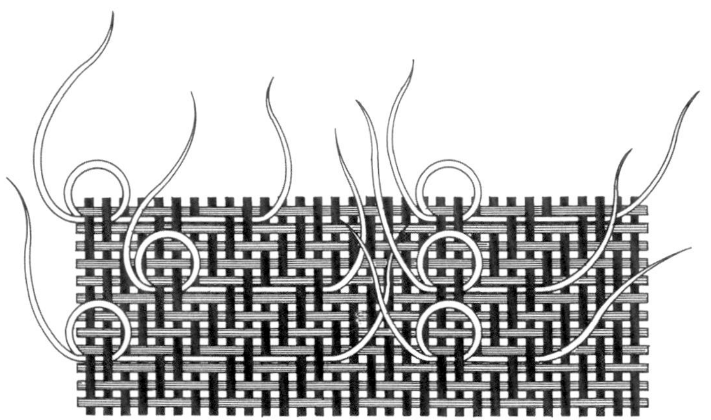

9.6 A pile-weaving technique from tenth- or
eleventh-century Iceland, from a fragment
of cloth excavated at Heynes, Iceland, in 1959.
*Drawing: S. Olafsson, figure 4 in Gudjonsson
1980.*

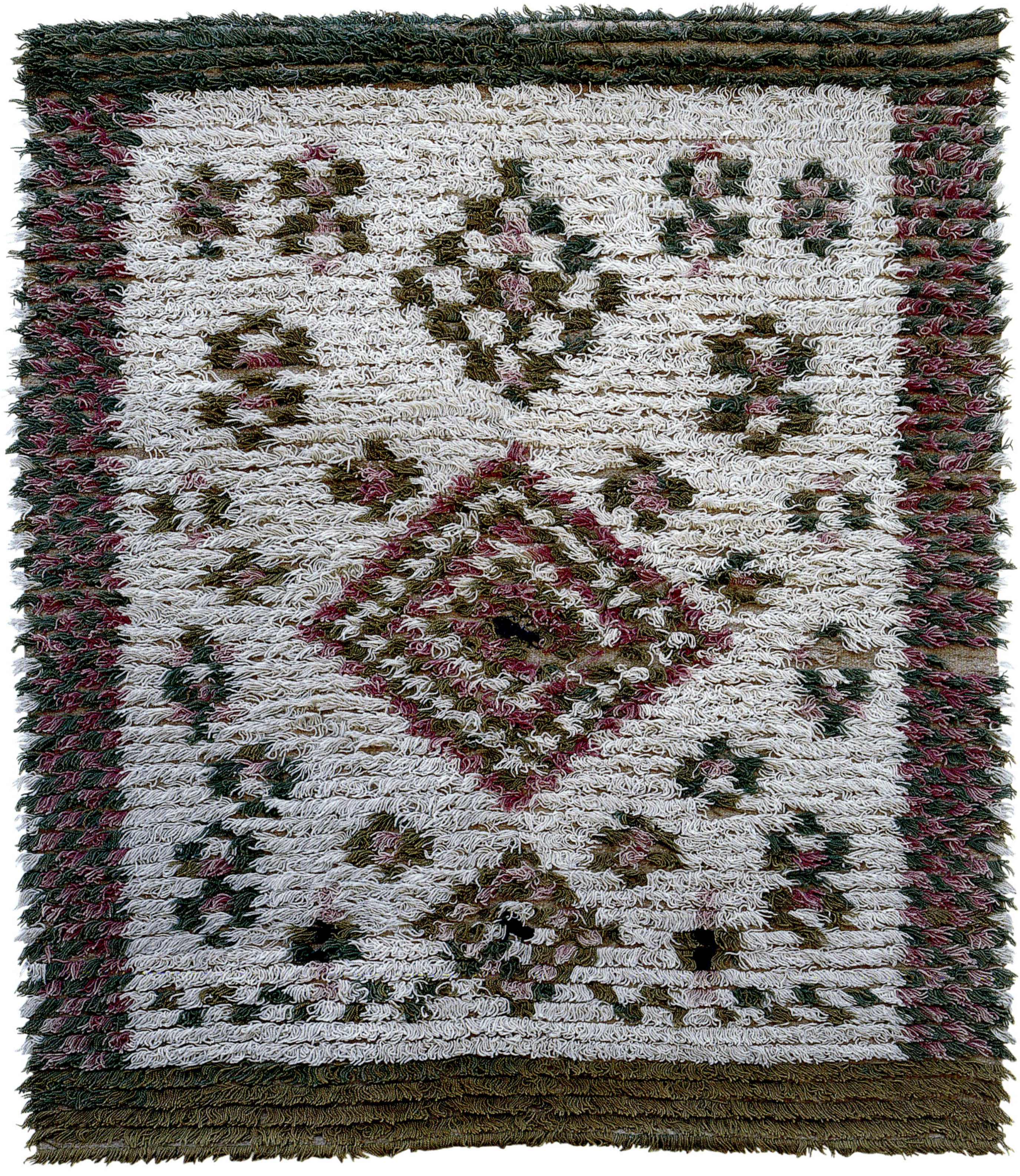

9.7 A decorative *rya* from Andebu, Vestfold, with simple patterns knotted
into the pile side. *Vestfold County Museum.*

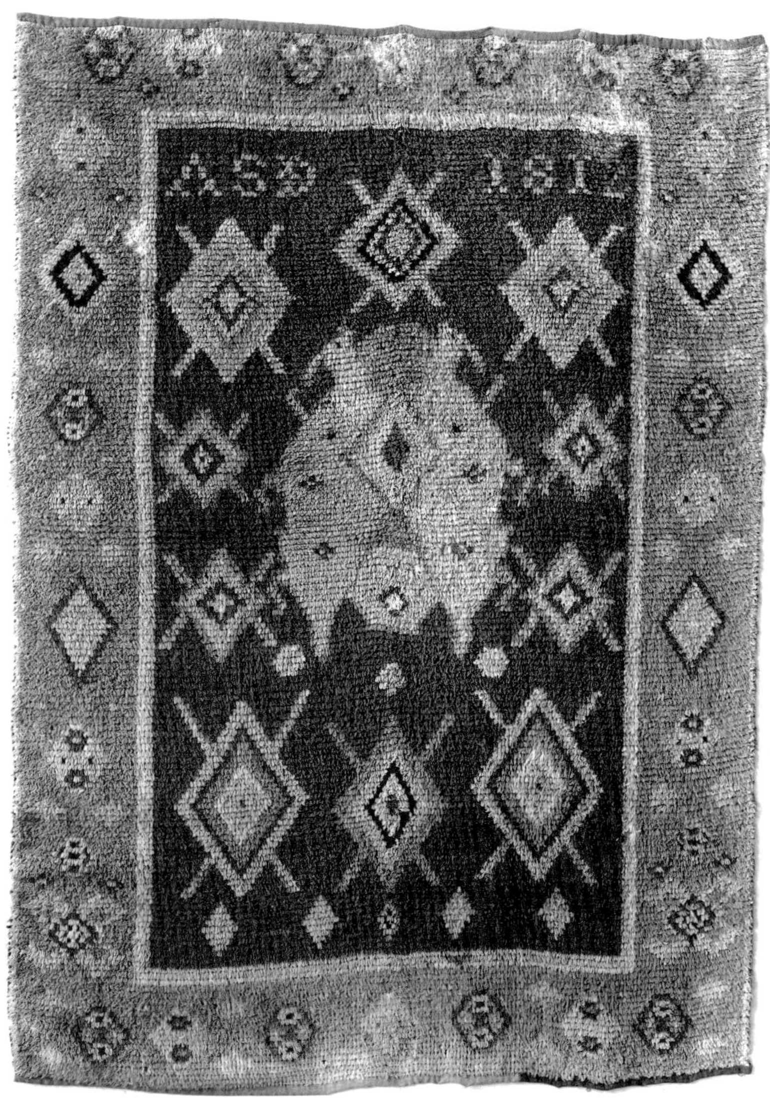

9.8 A decorative *rya* from Bohuslän, Sweden. Decorative *rya*s were more common, and their designs more elaborate, in Sweden and Finland (compare with fig. 9.7). *Nordic Museum, Stockholm.*

9.9 (*Below right*) The voided-pile technique is a combination of both *rya* and tapestry techniques.

9.10 (*Below left*) A pillow in the voided-pile technique showing the lily cross-motif. Probably Gudbrandsdal, late seventeenth century. *Oslo Museum of Applied Art.*

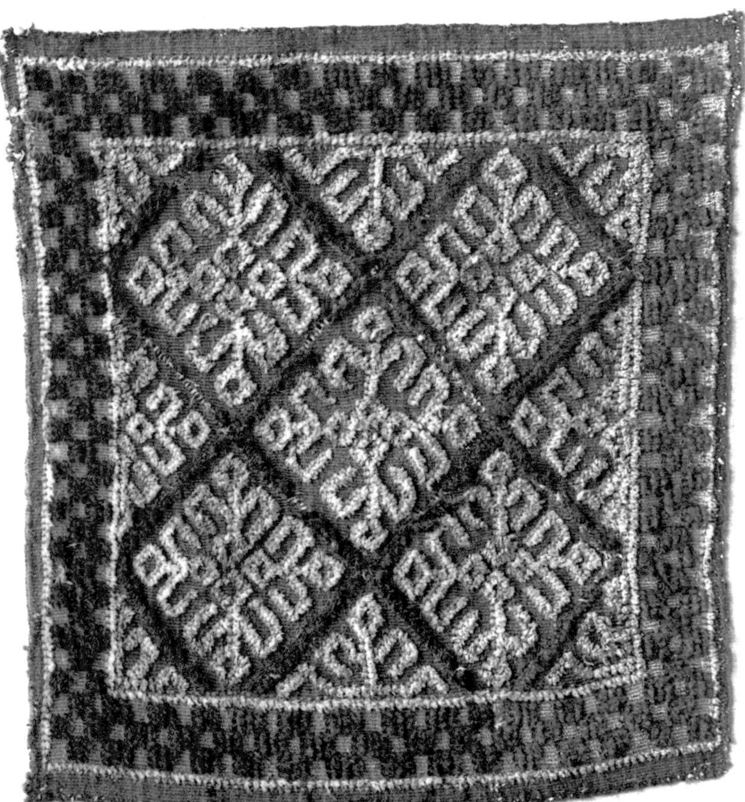

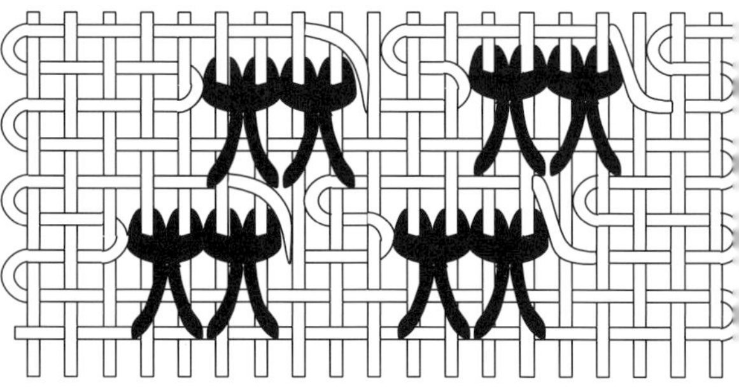

Design and Color

Although the pile side of the rya was not normally seen, some patterns were usually included in the knot work. Such designs had to be fairly large in scale since the shaggy pile blurred the lines between pattern areas. Simple stripes, squares, diamonds, or zigzag lines, and bold crosses and Xs were common patterns (figs. 9.11–9.14). Sometimes a border of a special color framed the entire piece so that it would appear as a fringe around the smooth side of the rya, and occasionally figures of people or animals and identifying marks, dates, or large monograms were woven into the pile (figs. 9.14–9.17 and 9.1).

Patterns on the smooth side of the rya were chiefly plaids, checks, or warp-wise stripes in a variety of twills. Diamond twill accentuated by the contrasting colors of warp and weft, and a point twill with distinctive warp-wise diamond stripes were also common (figs. 9.18–9.23). Occasionally double weave was used as a rya ground weave, as preserved in one instance. In this coverlet the pile was knotted into one layer, with a row of knots tied for each row of the double-weave design. The backs of the knots were completely hidden between the two layers of fabric (fig. 9.24).

Many ryas that survive today exhibit a surprisingly muted range of colors, considering the lively hues normally associated with folk arts. The most common colors—white, brown, black, and mixtures of gray and tan—are those of natural sheep's wool and probably reflect the purposes for which these last ryas were used. In the coastal regions, where ryas were valued as much for warmth in a boat as for a coverlet on the bed, the selection of colors was usually determined by practical considerations, for although the ryas themselves could survive continual exposure to sun and salt water, the colors of dyed yarns faded from such use. For this reason, natural wool colors predominated (particularly on the less visible pile-side of the rya) in districts where sea use was common. This was not the case with ryas in the inland areas of the country. Estate documents from the seventeenth century make it clear that distinctions were made between "gray" ryas that used only natural colors and "colored" ryas.[7] The colored ryas, more prevalent in inland areas, were considered to be twice as valuable as the natural gray ryas. The relatively few colored ryas represented in museum collections show the full range of colors, and occasionally the colors found on the pile side of the rya matched the design of stripes, checks, or plaids on the smooth side.

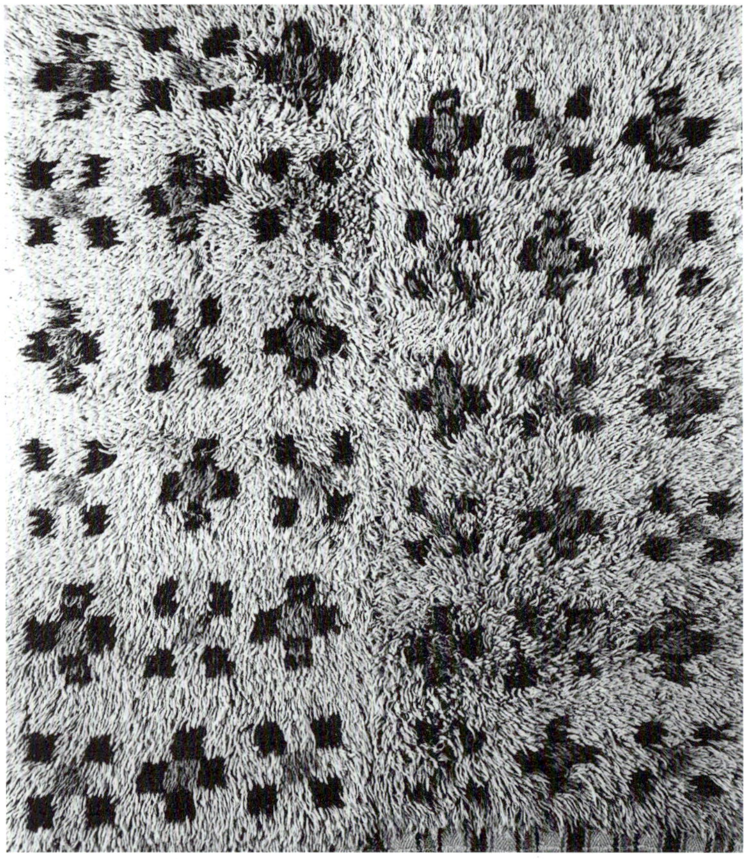

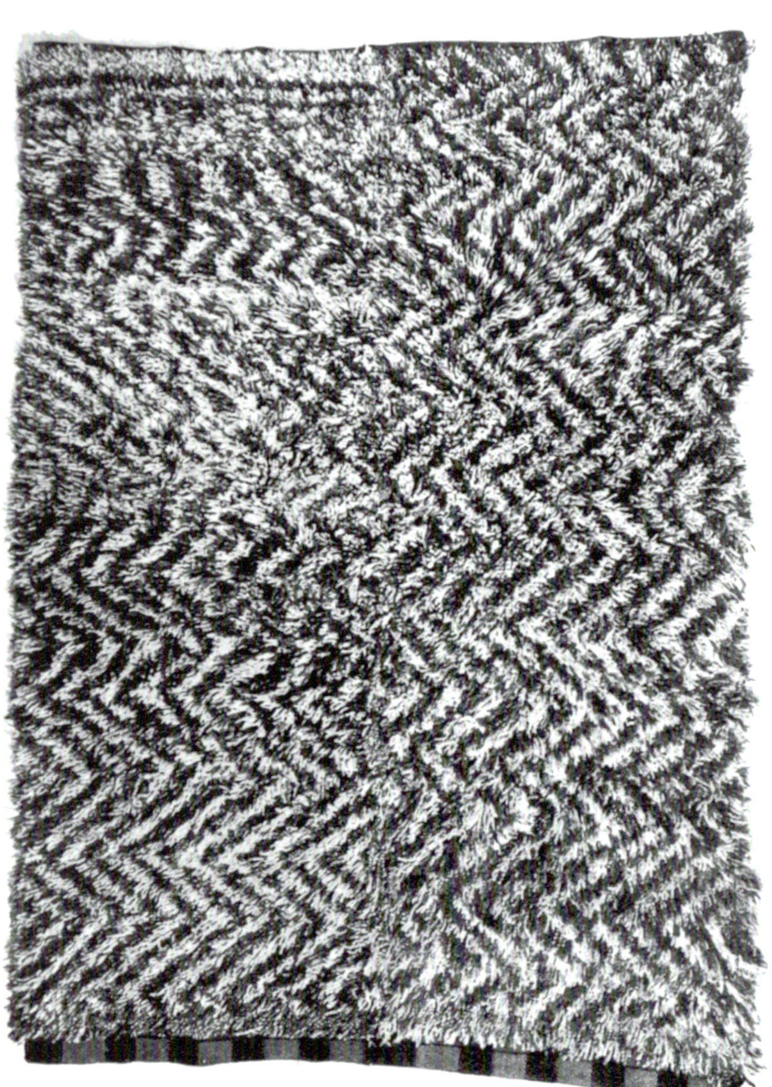

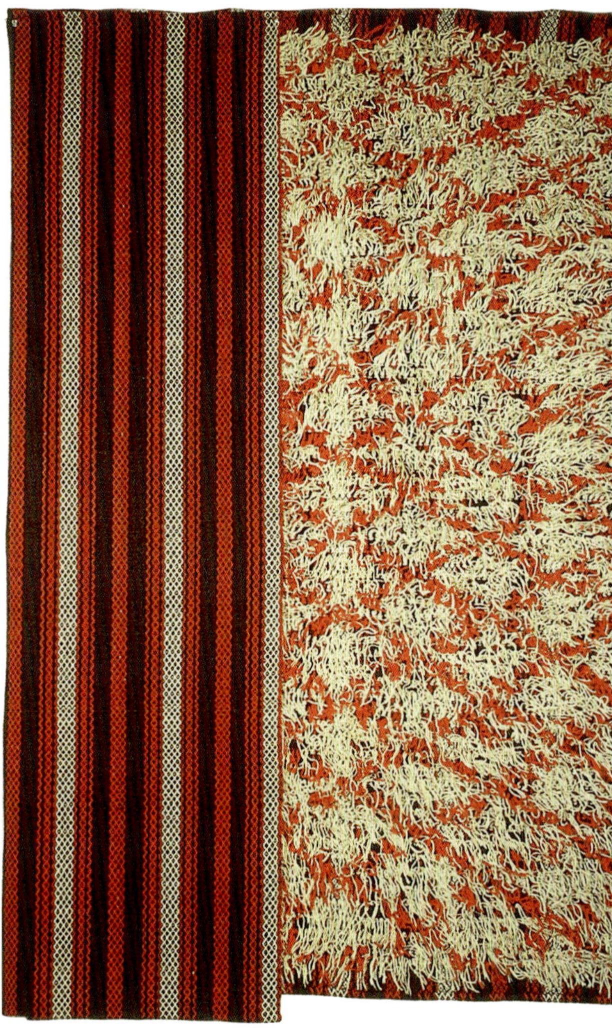

9.11 A simple pile design of crosses and Xs. *Historical Museum, University of Bergen.*

9.12 *(Left)* Pile design of zigzags. Lofoten, late nineteenth century. *Photo: Engelstad 1942. Private collection.*

9.13 *(Above)* A pile design of diamonds, with warp-wise stripes of small diamonds on the smooth side. Kvæfjord, Troms, mid-nineteenth century. *Norwegian Folk Museum.*

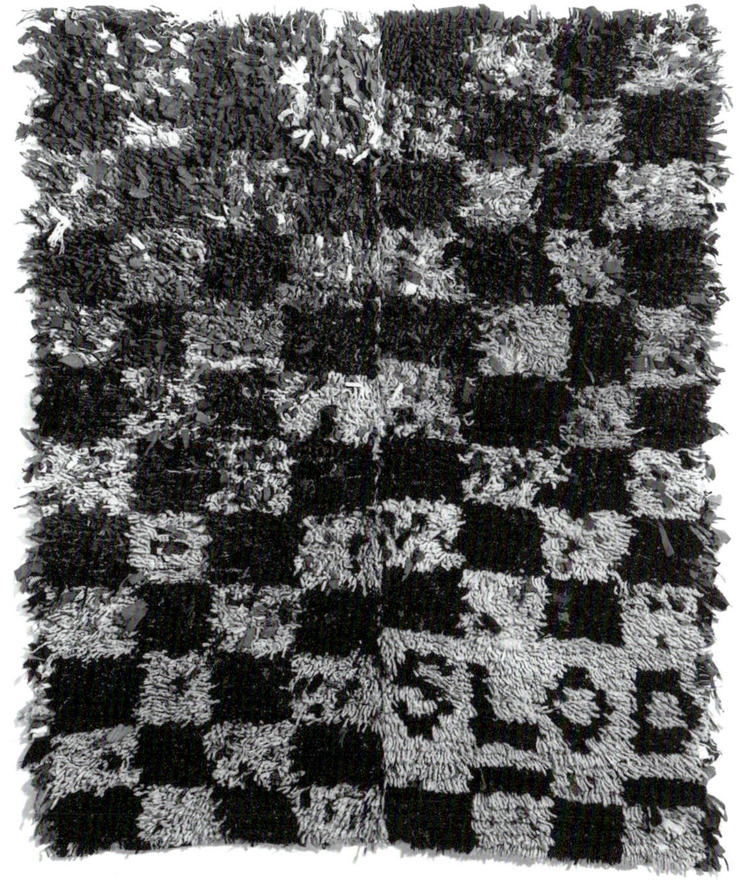

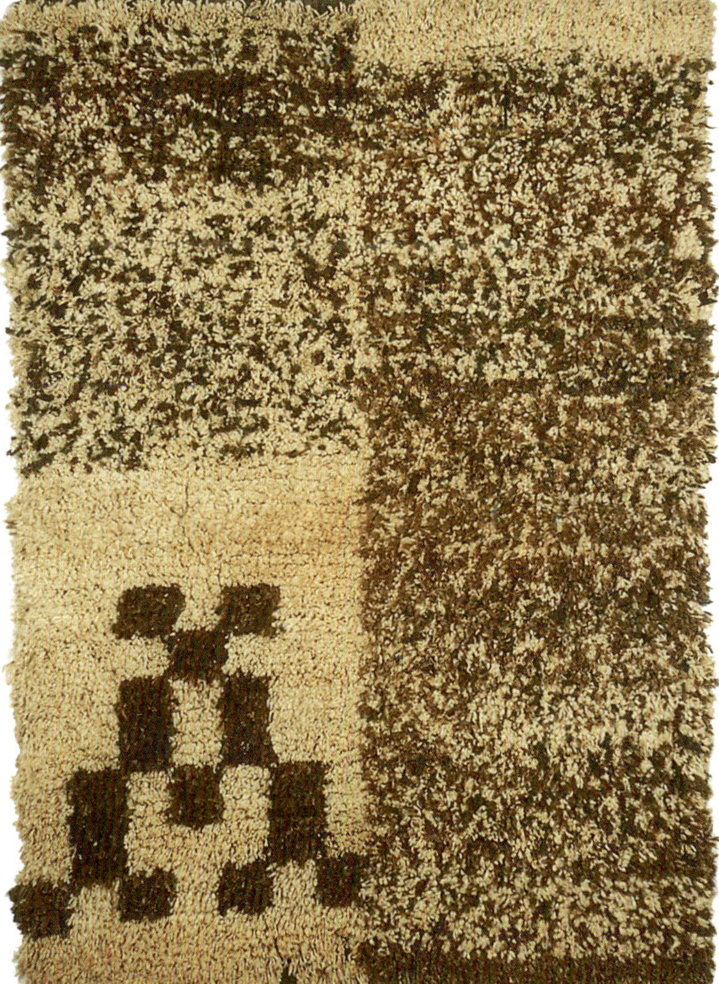

9.14 Checkered pile design with initials "SLOD." The pile is supplemented with strips of rags. Stordal, Sunnmøre, early nineteenth century. *Oslo Museum of Applied Art.*

9.15 A monogram letter "A" decorates the pile side of this *rya*. Strips of rags have been used to supplement the pile in much of the *rya*. Kjerringøy. *Photo: Norwegian Folk Museum. Nordland Museum.*

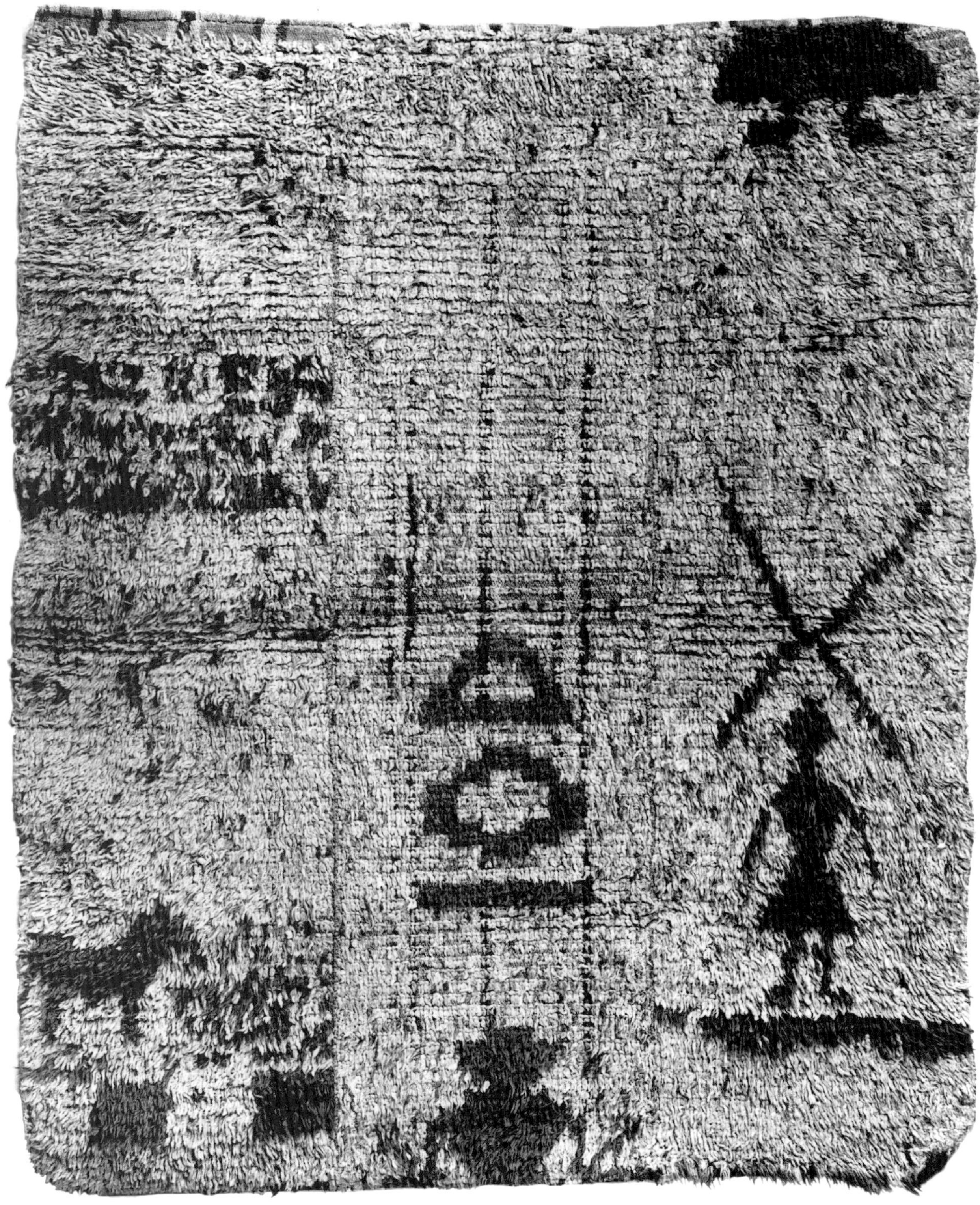

9.16 *Rya* made up of three panels sewn together. The pile is decorated with figures of a man, woman, and dog, although apparently the weaver miscalculated and had to cut the figure of the woman in half. An "X" and the initials "IOD" are also a part of the pile design. Rennebu, Sør-Trøndelag. *Norwegian Folk Museum.*

9.17 Pile design of initials and the year "ASP
1816" above a row of checkers. The *rya* is composed of three panels sewn together.
Orkedalen, Sør-Trøndelag. *National Museum
of Decorative Arts, Trondheim.*

9.18 *(Below left)* Ground weave of simple
warp-wise stripes in a three-harness twill.
Kjerringøy. *Photo: Norwegian Folk Museum.
Nordland Museum.*

9.19 *(Below right)* Ground weave of warp-wise
stripes in a three-harness point twill (reverse
side of figure 9.14). Stordalen, Sunnmøre,
early nineteenth century. *Oslo Museum of
Applied Art.*

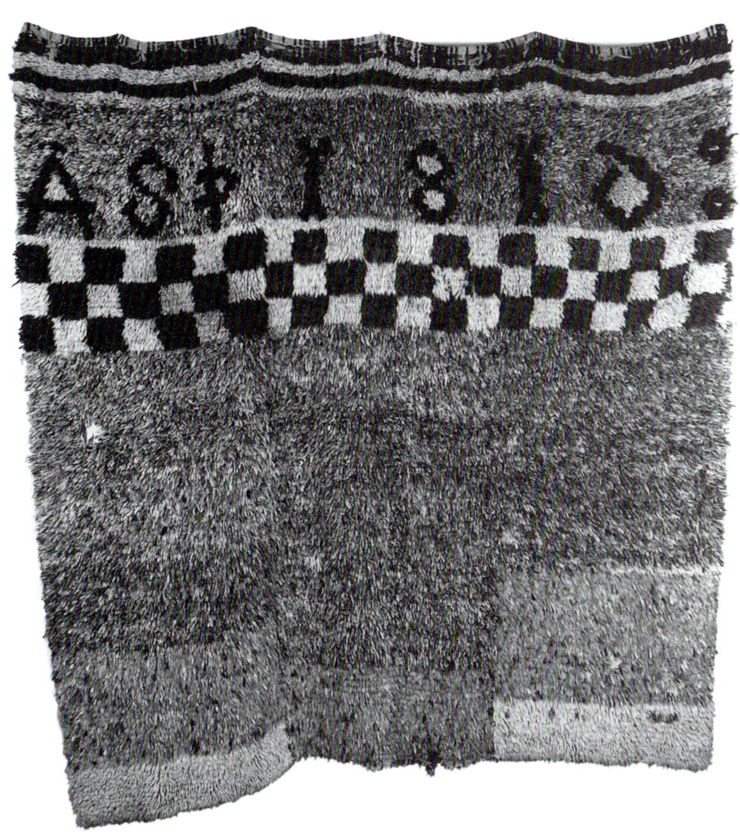

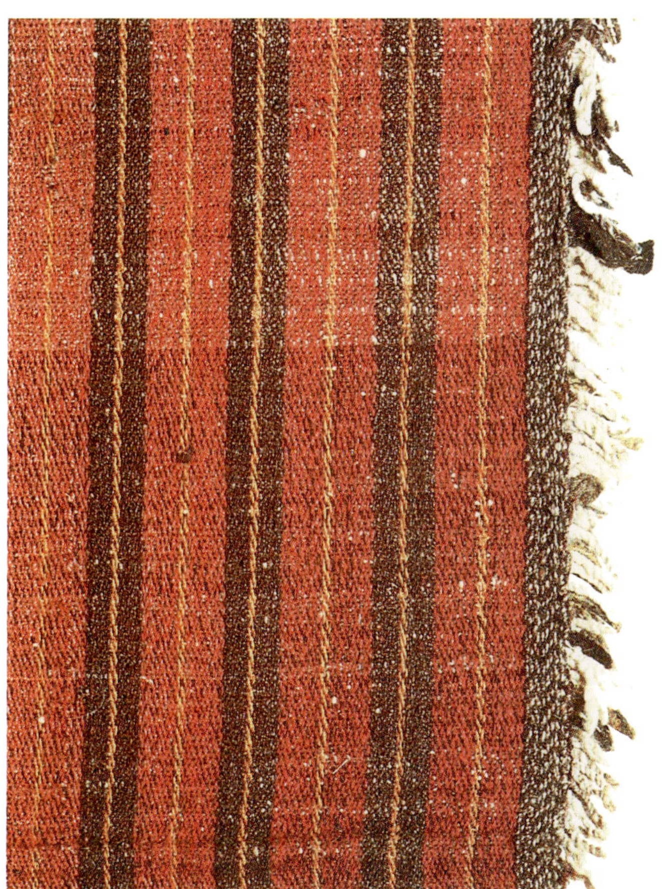

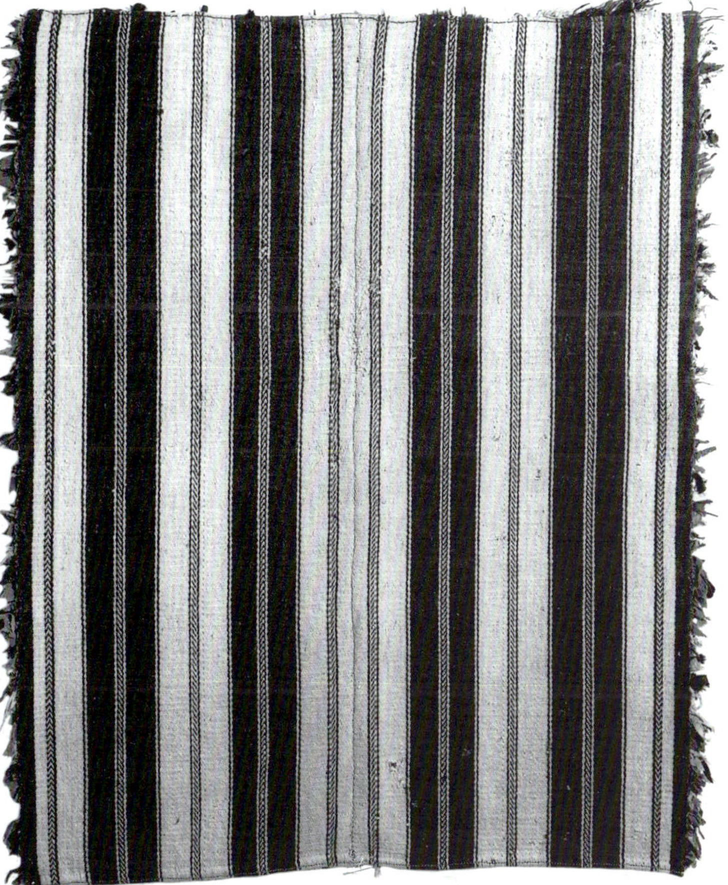

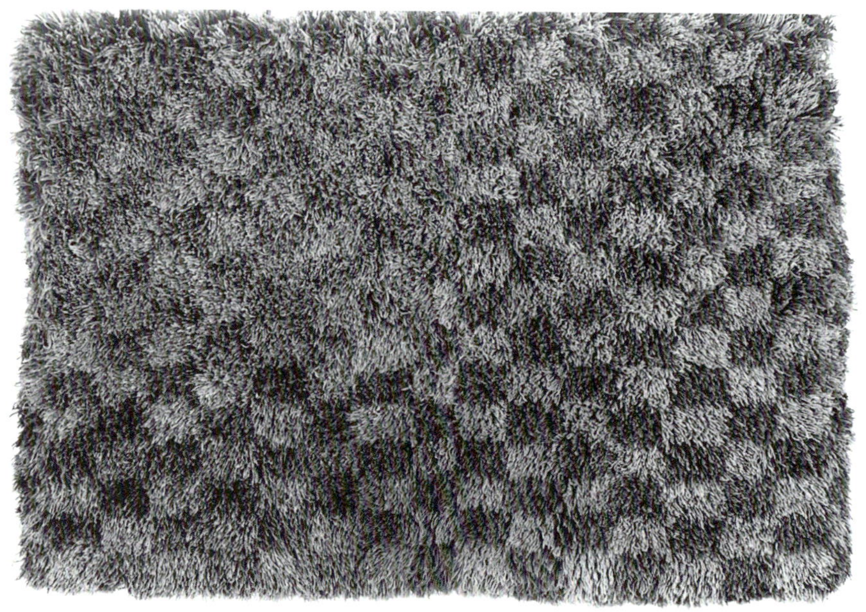

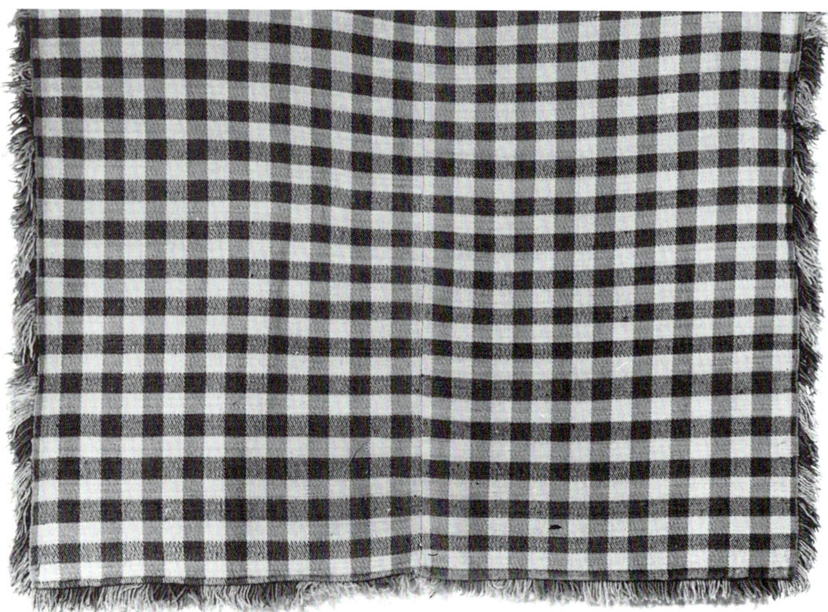

9.20 A checkered pattern decorates both the pile side *(top)* and the smooth side *(middle)* of this *rya*. Frosta, Nord-Trøndelag. *Norwegian Folk Museum.*

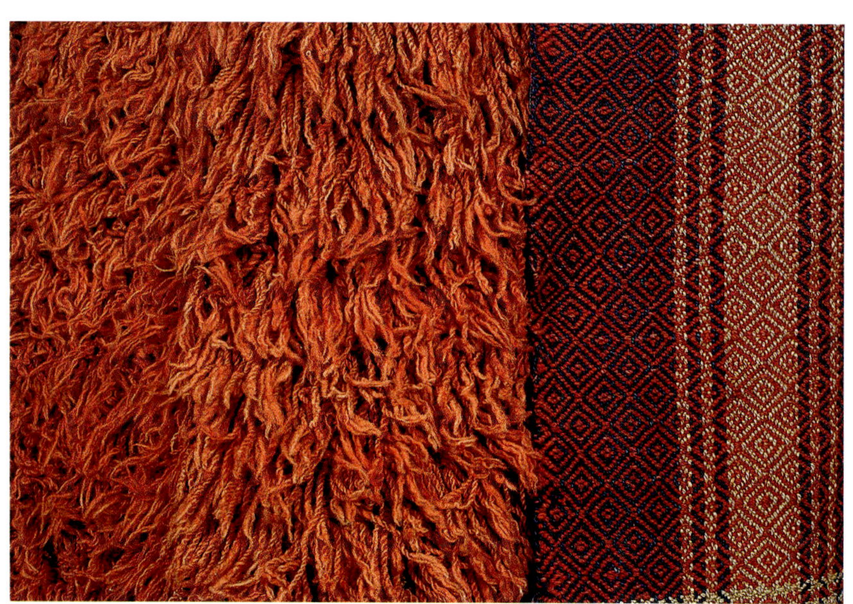

9.21 A ground weave of diamond twill *(bottom)* in contrasting warp and weft colors is accented by a border of lighter-colored warp stripes. *Vesterheim Norwegian-American Museum.*

9.22 Ground weave in a plaid diamond twill. *Luther College Collection, Vesterheim Norwegian-American Museum.*

9.23 *(Below left)* Small, warp-wise diamond stripes accent an otherwise dark twill ground-weave. *Vesterheim Norwegian-American Museum.*

9.24 *(Below right)* A ground weave in the double-weave technique is evident through the worn pile of this coverlet. A patch from another double-weave coverlet can be seen in the upper right. Reverse side of figure 8.19. Heidal, Gudbrandsdal. *Maihaugen, The Sandvig Collection.*

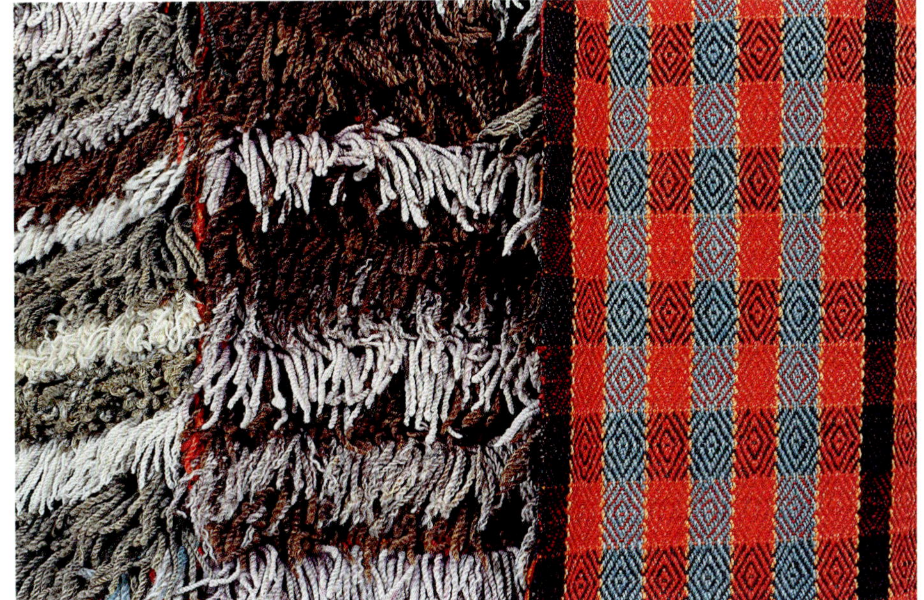

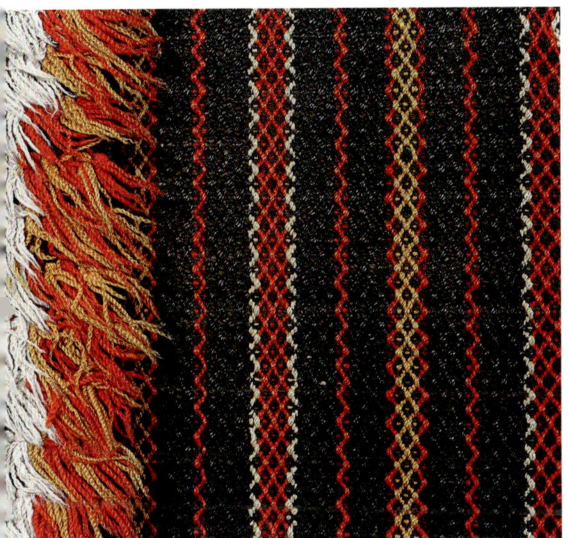

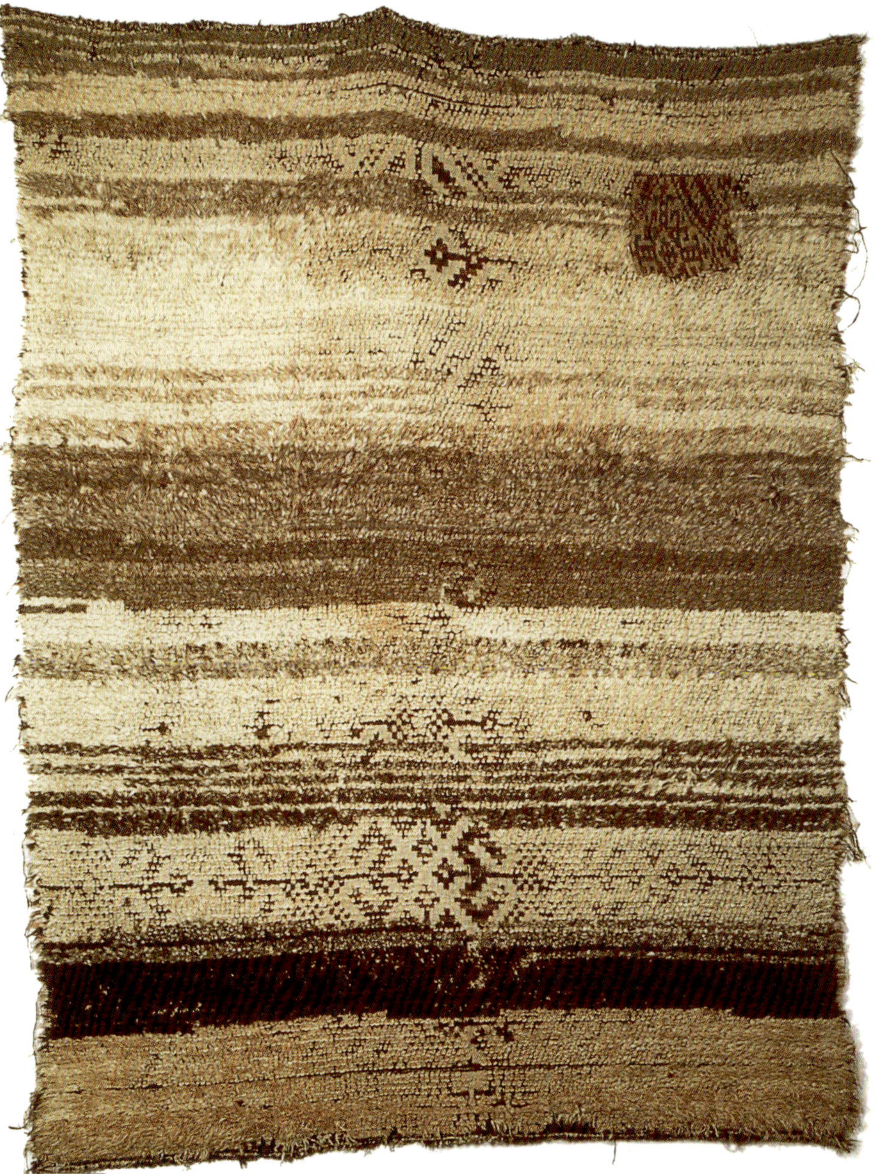

A two-ply wool yarn was generally used in the warp of most ryas, spaced from twenty to twenty-seven ends per inch. A one- or two-ply wool yarn was commonly used as weft. When hidden from view by a warp-faced twill, an inferior grade of wool was frequently used, sometimes mixed with cow's hair. For the warp, however, the strong and resilient guard hair of the *spælsau* was considered best.*

The pile of a rya was generally made of two- or three-ply wool yarn, although occasionally loose lengths of unspun or lightly spun wool were used. Either the guard hair or the softer underlayer of wool could be used for the pile with slightly different results. The softer wool held its twist more successfully and was sometimes even felted. In contrast, pile made of the guard hair often lost its twist, making the rya more closely resemble the look of a real sheepskin. For economical reasons, the pile of a rya was sometimes supplemented with strips of woolen rags. This detracted somewhat from the warmth and appearance of the coverlet but served the dual purpose of reducing the huge amount of yarn required by a rya and using up worn-out scraps of old clothing (see figs. 9.14 and 9.15).

The materials used in a decorative rya were slightly different than those in one designed for warmth. The smooth side of these ryas was clearly intended as the back of the weaving and not to be seen. Accordingly, the ground weave was a simple warp of doubled linen thread and a weft of wool thread often mixed with cow hair. The knotted designs on the front, or pile side of the rya, were composed of two-ply wool yarn.

Most ryas were woven in two pieces approximately five to six feet in length and twenty-eight to thirty-two inches in width. The two halves were sewn together lengthwise, sometimes arranged so that the knots lay in opposite directions. This may have been to insure that the reinforced selvage, threaded into the warp on one side of the loom, and any selvage pattern, would be identical on each side of the finished rya when the two lengths were sewn together. Since the smooth side of the rya was primarily the one to be seen, the fact that the knots were lying in different directions would be of little importance.[8] Few examples remain of a rya woven in one large piece, an indication that the technique adapted well to the narrow width of the horizontal loom. However, a rya sewn from narrower widths may actually have had a practical advantage. One authority[9] cites evidence that in some cases the two halves of a rya were clipped apart and re-sewn to facilitate handling the heavy, wet textiles during washing.† Ryas that were intended for use by coastal fishermen could be quite large, sometimes composed of three panels instead of two, with a total width of about seven feet. Such "boat ryas" were thick and heavy, weighing as much as twenty pounds, a sharp contrast with the smaller, lighter-weight ryas of inland areas (see figs. 9.16–9.17).

**For ryas used by coastal fishermen, the fleece of the primitive sheep (see "Fibers," p. 6) was highly desirable. With a much higher lanolin content (a result of the animals' overwintering outdoors), and without shorn ends that absorb water, the naturally shed fibers of this sheep are virtually water repellant (Lightfoot 1997:13–14).*

†Washing a rya was not an easy task, as is evident from the following description: "First the rya was placed in a large tub of soapy water. Then the housewife climbed into the tub and tromped on it good and long. Afterwards it was taken down to the pier in a wheelbarrow and made fast so that it was rinsed clean by the incoming tide. Following washing and rinsing, the rya was hung in the boathouse until the next season" (Kjellmo 1996:90).

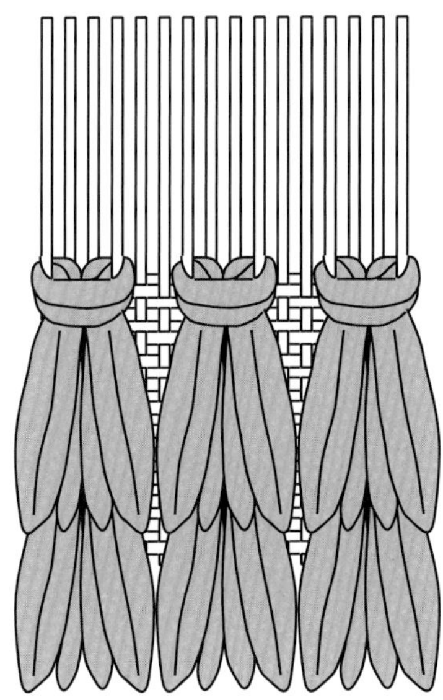

9.25 Rows of knots were separated by a number of shots of ground weave. The pile from one row of knots generally covered the knots of the preceding row.

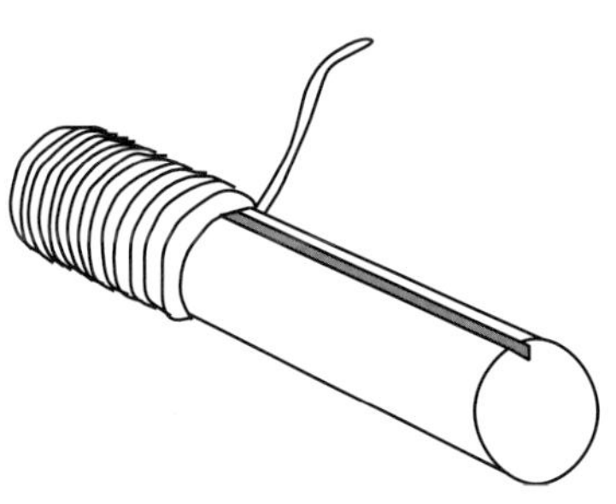

9.26 Yarn for the pile of a *rya* was wound around a grooved stick of the appropriate size and then cut into lengths for knotting.

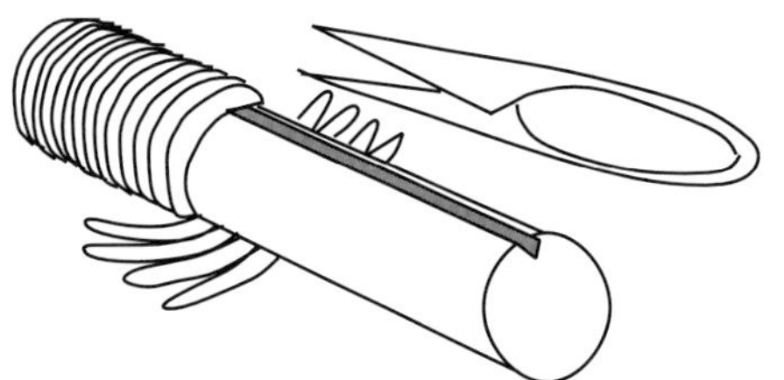

Weaving Technique

The rya coverlet consisted of an underlying structure of warp and weft threads supplemented by rows of knotted pile. The ground weave was built up of several shots of weft that alternated with a row of knots tied to the warp threads (fig. 9.25). The density of the pile was determined by the amount of ground weave interspersed between the rows of knots. A thick and therefore more valuable rya resulted when rows of knots were separated by only three or four shots of weft yarn. Sparser ryas had as many as twelve to fifteen shots of weft separating the rows. Usually the pile was slightly longer than the distance between the rows of knots so that as the pile lay down, the knots of one row were covered by the pile of the next. Material for tying the knots was cut into lengths by winding yarn around a stick of the appropriate thickness. The resulting rounds of thread were then clipped down a groove in the stick (fig. 9.26).

Three- and four-harness twills formed the ground weave of the majority of rya coverlets, and the structure of the selected twill determined the spacing of the knots. Knots were usually tied to two, and sometimes four, warp threads as they rose to the surface on the pile side of the weaving (fig. 9.27). Close warp spacing, the twill structure, and a slight tug given to each knot as it was tied combined to leave the back of the knots completely hidden on the smooth side of most ryas. In some cases, however, the knots were tied such that they would not only be seen, but become a part of the design on the smooth side of the rya (figs. 9.28–9.29).

Ryas woven for decoration instead of warmth not only used different materials but had a slightly different structure as well. The warp threads no longer needed to hide the knots, as the pile side was the only one intended for viewing. A simple weft-faced, plain-weave structure replaced the twill and allowed the weaver to line up knots evenly at every row, with one knot tied around every pair of warp threads. This regular framework made pattern work much easier than in the variable structure created by a twill (fig. 9.30). The combination of a linen warp and a tightly packed weft resulted in ryas that were slightly less pliable than those intended for warmth.

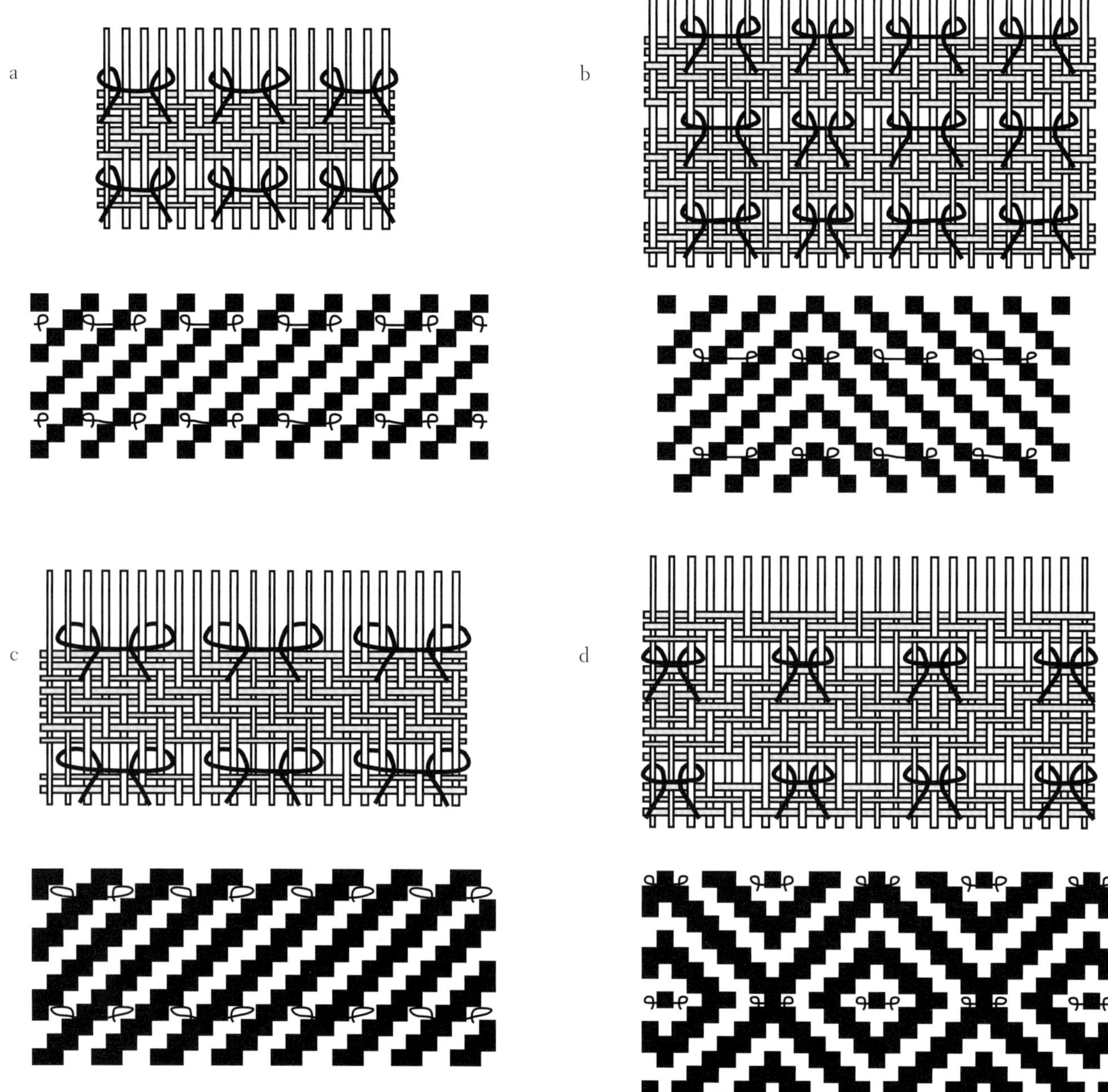

9.27   The sequence for tying knots in a *rya* was determined by the type of twill selected and the desired thickness of the pile. Knots were usually tied where the warp threads came to the surface so that the backs of the knots would be invisible on the smooth side of the *rya*. These illustrations show common methods for tying *rya* knots in three- and four-harness twills (after Engelstad 1942). Each illustration is accompanied by a geometric diagram known as a draw-down. A draw-down showing the warp and weft threads as they appear on the surface (white squares = warp threads, black squares = weft threads) clearly presents the pattern created by each twill threading, and provides an easy system for judging the placement of the knots. Knot symbols indicate the sequence for tying the pile: *(a)* 1/2 diagonal twill; *(b)* three-harness point twill; *(c)* 2/2 diagonal twill; *(d)* diamond twill.

9.28 A ground weave of diamond twill is seen on the smooth side of this *rya*. The pattern is enhanced by a special method of tying the pile, which allows the back of some knots to be visible. In this coverlet the knots show as light dots at the center of the diamond patterns. *Voss Folk Museum.*

9.29 (*Below right*) Knots tied so that they were visible on the smooth side of the *rya*: (*a*) tying knots sideways was one method for making the backs visible; (*b*) knots tied sideways in the center of diamond patterns alternate with regularly tied knots that are invisible on the smooth side. *After Arnøy 1975, and Nygaard.*

9.30 (*Below left*) A weft-faced, plain-weave structure formed the ground weave of decorative *rya*s. The weft completely covers the warp when packed down during weaving, and the backs of the knots are visible on the smooth side of the *rya*. *After Engelstad 1942.*

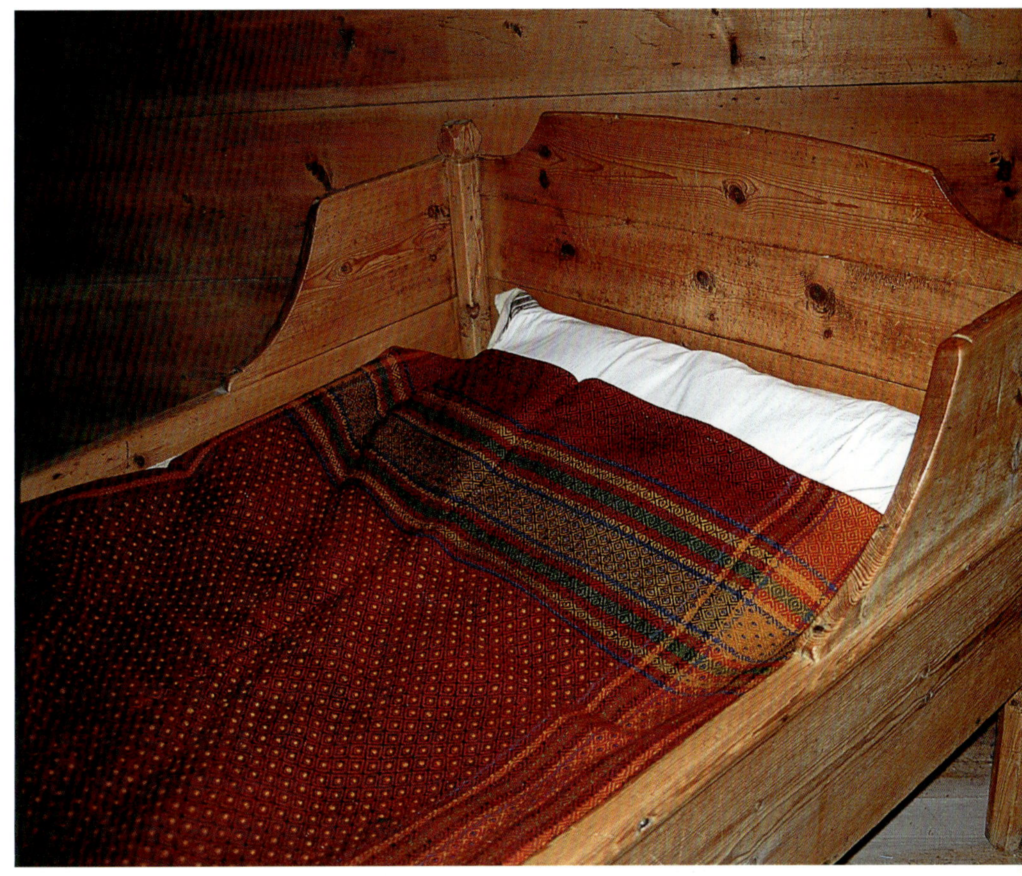

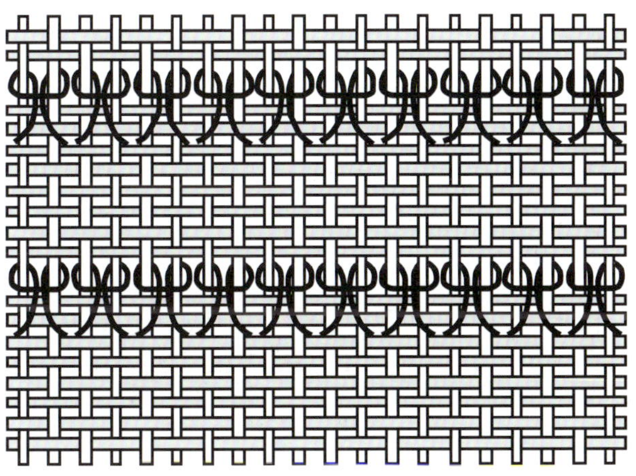

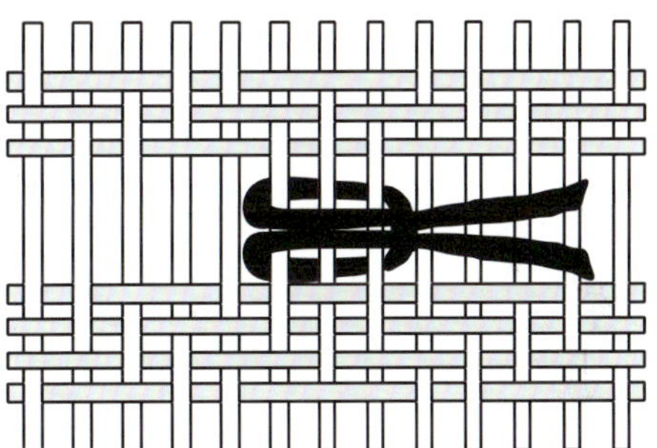

a

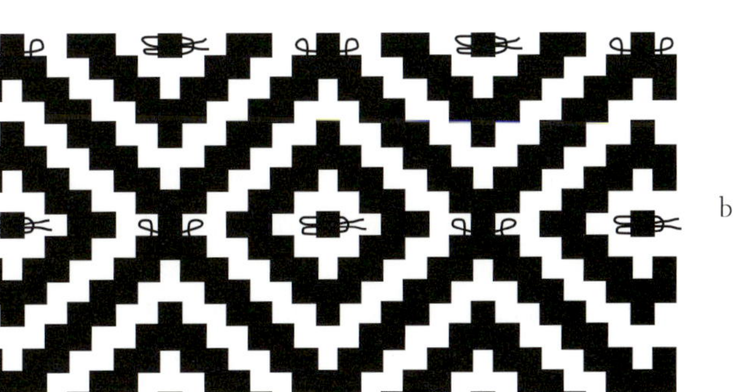

b

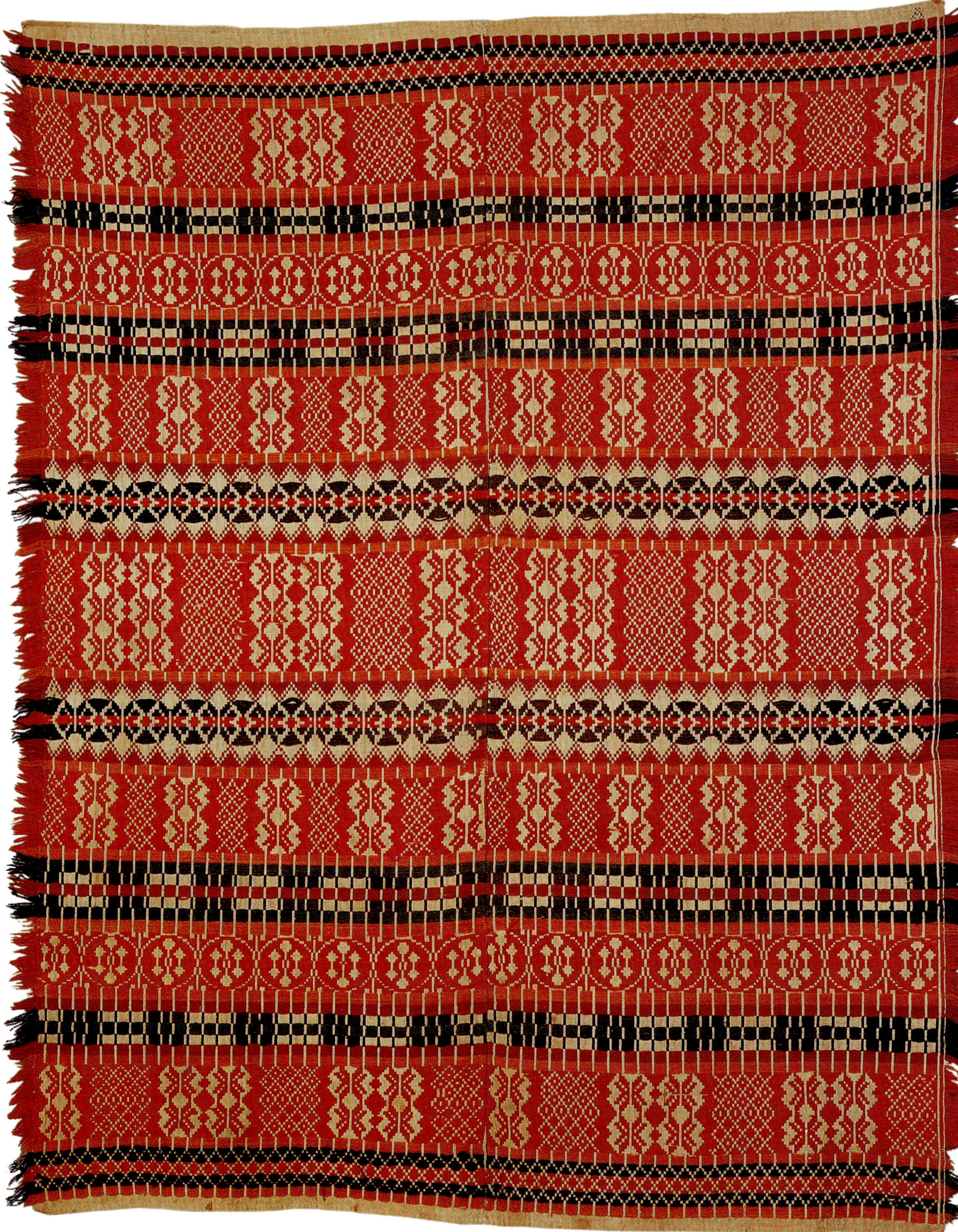

10 / Overshot Coverlets: *Tavlebragd, Skillbragd*

I N   M A N Y   P A R T S   O F   N O R W A Y ,   T H E   T E R M   *K R I S T N A Å K L E ,* or christening coverlet, referred to the lightweight coverlets that were especially preferred for this important ceremony. Woven in two overshot techniques typical of Scandinavia, these coverlets were characterized by colorful patterns in wool that floated over and under a fine white ground-weave of linen or, later, cotton. To improve their effectiveness as a bed cover, the relatively thin overshot weavings were often sewn to the back of a sheep-skin blanket. Outside the home these coverlets were sometimes used as shawls by women in the southern district of Setesdal, but they found use throughout Norway as christening blankets. And as one authority describes, if several infants were brought to church on the same day, then "folk used their eyes" to judge which baby was wrapped in the most colorful coverlet[1] (figs. 10.1–10.2).

The Norwegian overshot coverlets were woven in two different techniques. The block-patterned *tavlebragd*, which derives its name from the checks of a game board (*tavle*), is known in English as monk's belt. The more elaborate *skillbragd* (pronounced "shill-bragd"), named for the opening in the threads, or *skill*, by which the patterns were made, is sometimes referred to in English by its Swedish name, *opphämta*. Both techniques were found throughout most of Norway, although monk's-belt coverlets were more well known in the northern districts. In some parts of Norway these weavings were also referred to as Swedish coverlets, a reference to the many overshot textiles exported from western Sweden, particularly the district of Västergötland, during the seventeenth and eighteenth centuries. Both of the overshot techniques were practiced throughout Scandinavia, however, and what might be referred to as a Swedish coverlet in, for example, the Norwegian district of Rana, was called a Rana coverlet in the neighboring district in Sweden.[2]

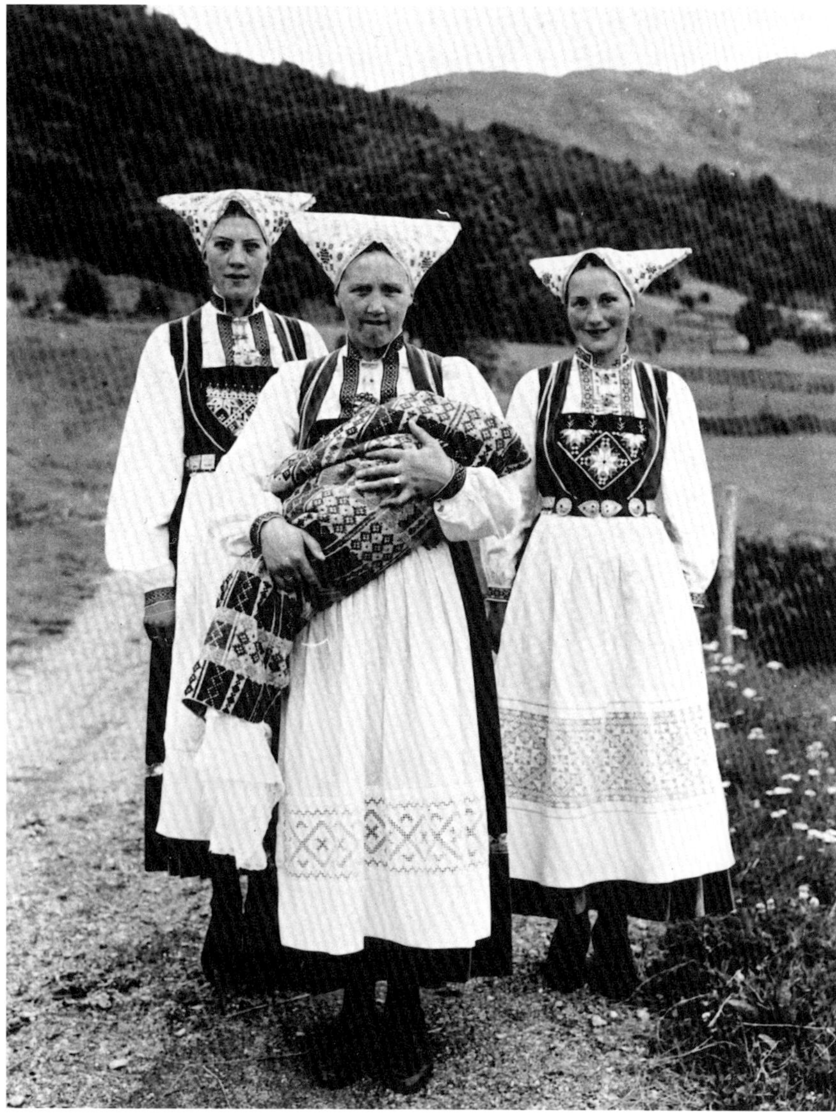

10.2 Three women from Voss bring a baby, wrapped in a skillbragd coverlet, to church for christening. *Skillbragd* coverlets were often selected for this important ceremony. *National Archive, Oslo.*

Origins

Overshot coverlets were mentioned in estate documents from most parts of Norway as early as the seventeenth century. The discovery of cloth fragments in a find from twelfth-century Tønsberg in Vestfold, however, indicates that the technique is much older in Norway. Fabrics with supplementary weft threads that float over and under a ground weave are known from European Neolithic and Bronze Age finds,[3] although not specifically of the Scandinavian overshot type. Some of the earliest examples of pattern and technique similar to the Scandinavian overshot weaves come from Coptic Egypt in the first centuries A.D.[4]

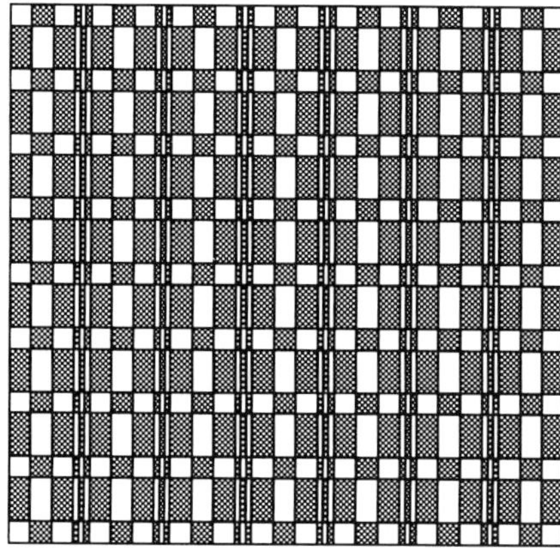

a

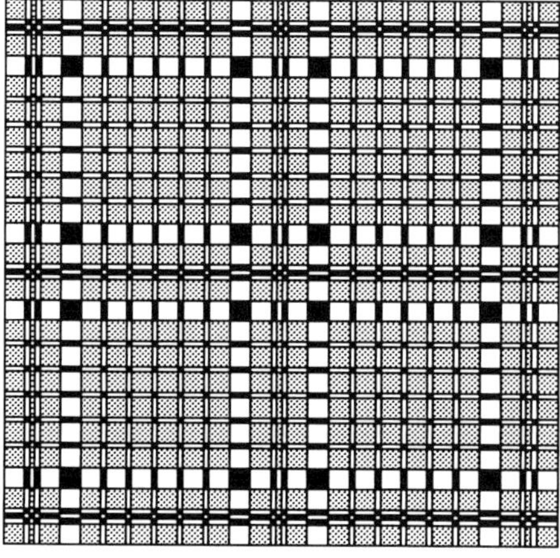

b

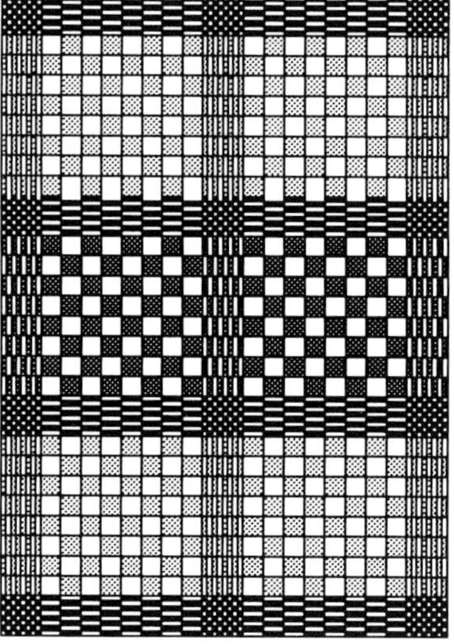

c

10.3 Patterns based on small and large rectangles and squares characterize the monk's-belt coverlets. Patterns using *(a)* one color; *(b)* two colors; *(c)* three colors. Diagrams of these and additional monk's-belt patterns can be found in Erlandsen and Petersen 1987.

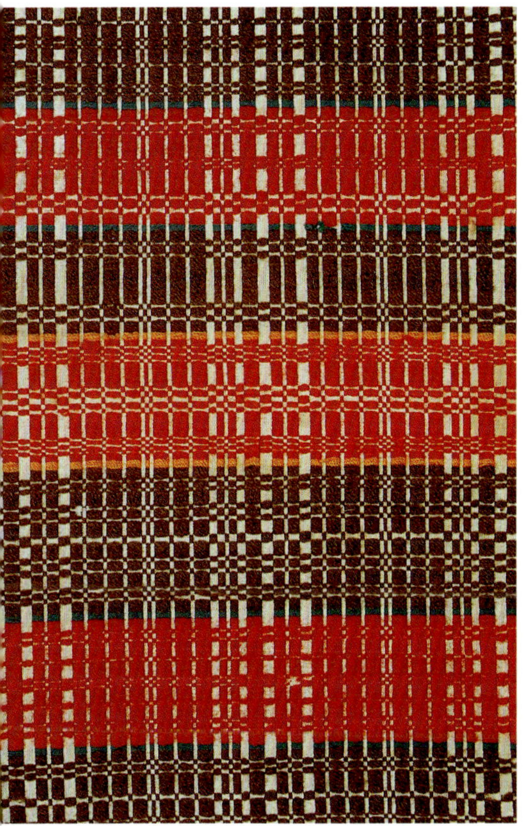

10.4 A monk's-belt coverlet in which warp-wise stripes are complemented by horizontal stripes of red and green. *Photo: Mark Frey. Nordic Heritage Museum.*

Design and Color

Designs in the monk's-belt coverlets were composed of small and large squares formed by the supplementary weft thread, or pattern thread, that ran from selvage to selvage. The arrangement of these squares of pattern depended not only on the system of threading the harnesses, but on the treadling sequence used by the weaver. A surprising number of designs could arise from such simple beginnings: rows of checks, eye-dazzling blends of small and large squares, and large blocks of squares separated by vertical and horizontal bars of smaller squares. When more than one color was used, designs were further defined by the interplay of colors. Red or a combination of red and black were the most common color schemes, but three and four colors were sometimes used to lend additional interest to the patterns (figs. 10.3–10.6).

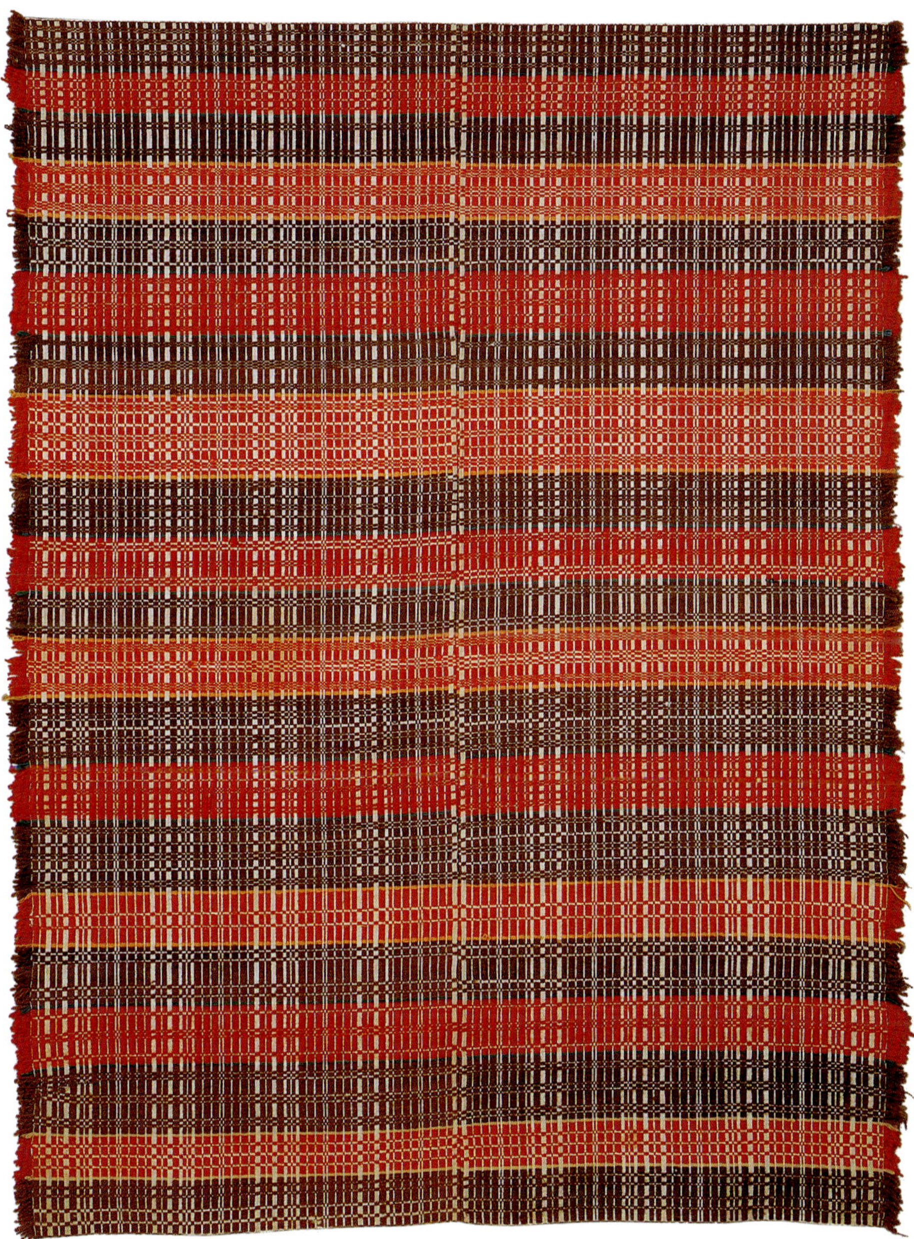

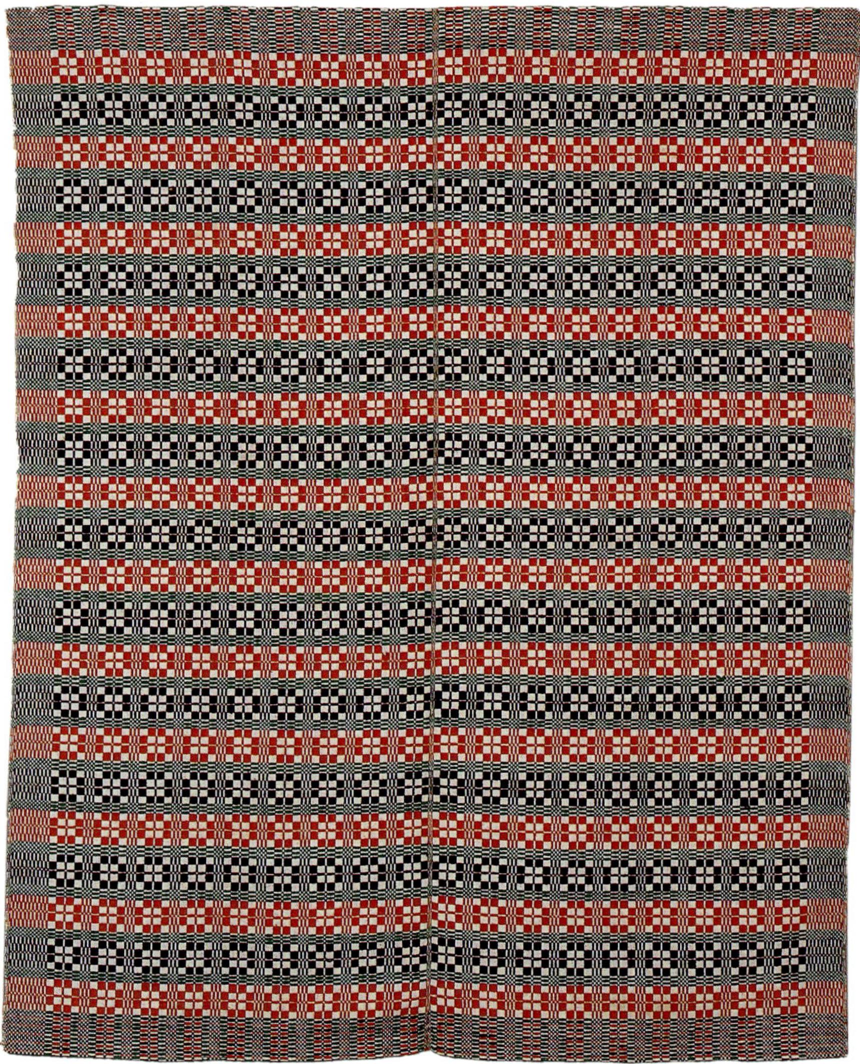

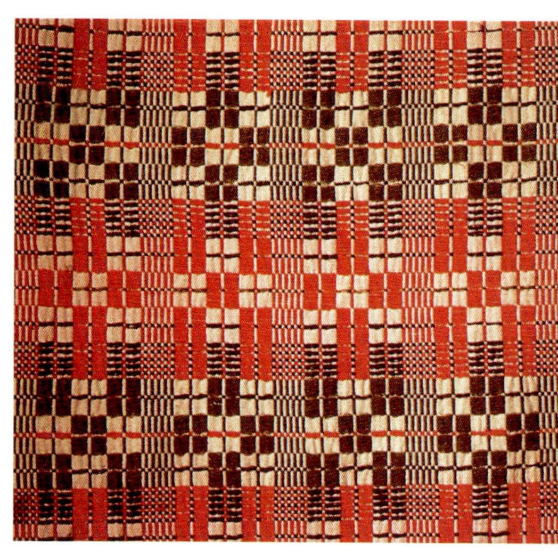

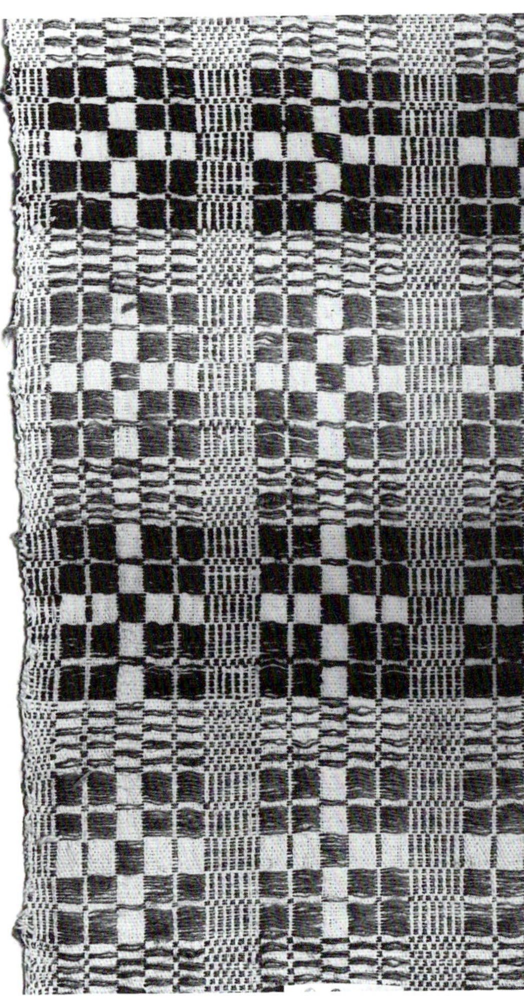

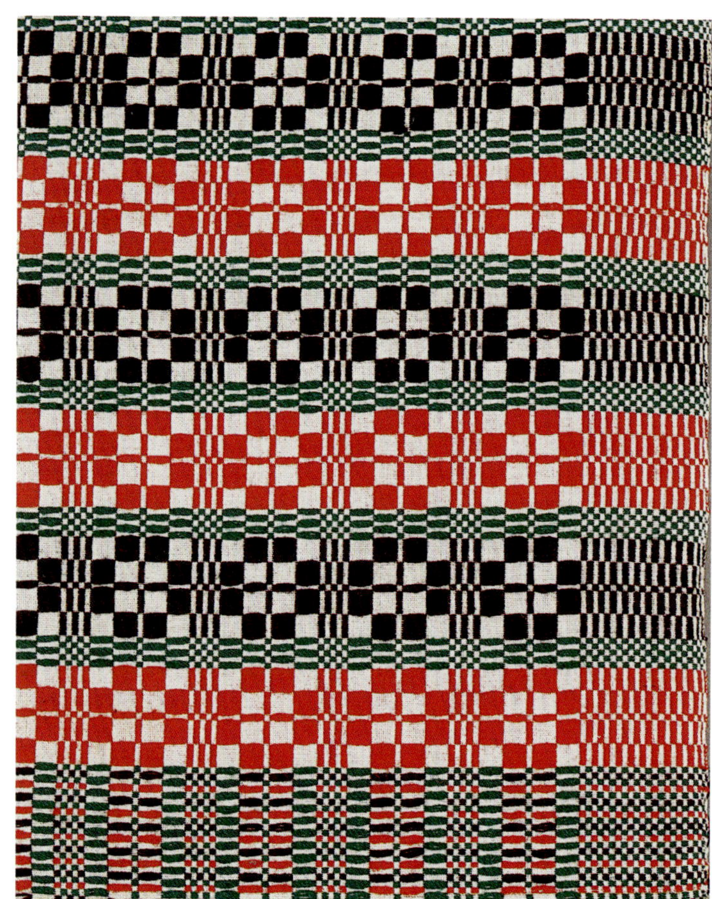

10.5 Monk's-belt coverlets with variations of a cross pattern: *(left)* Gudbrandsdal. *Photo: Mark Frey. Nordic Heritage Museum; (top right)* Nordland; *(bottom right)* Sør-Trøndelag. *Norwegian Folk Museum.*

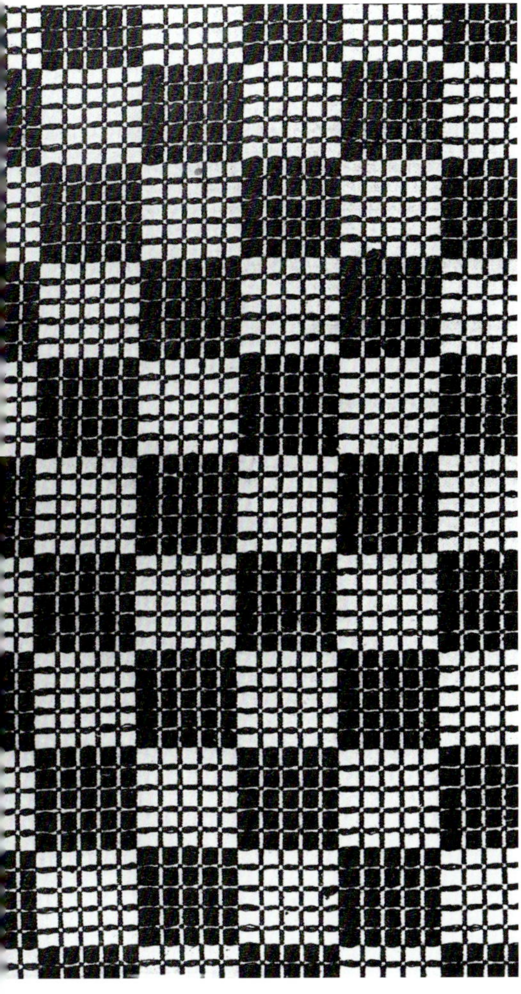

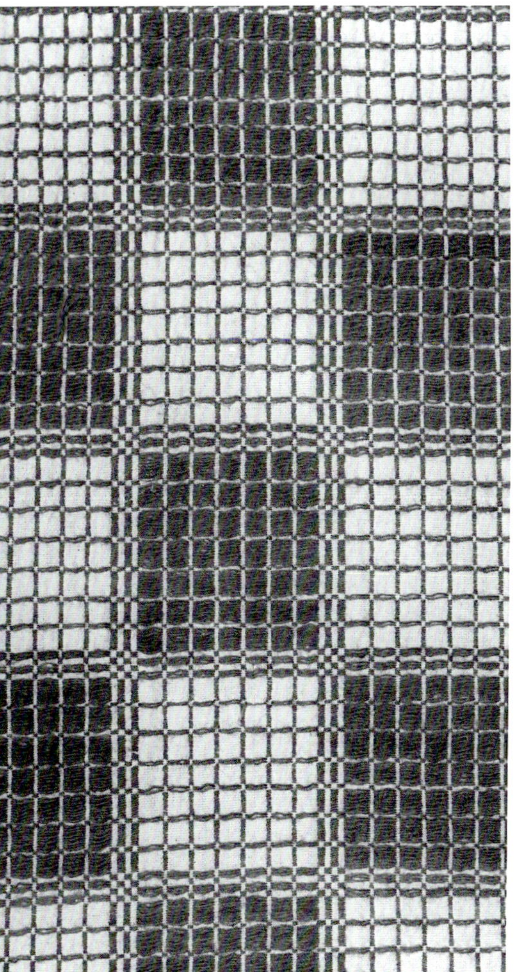

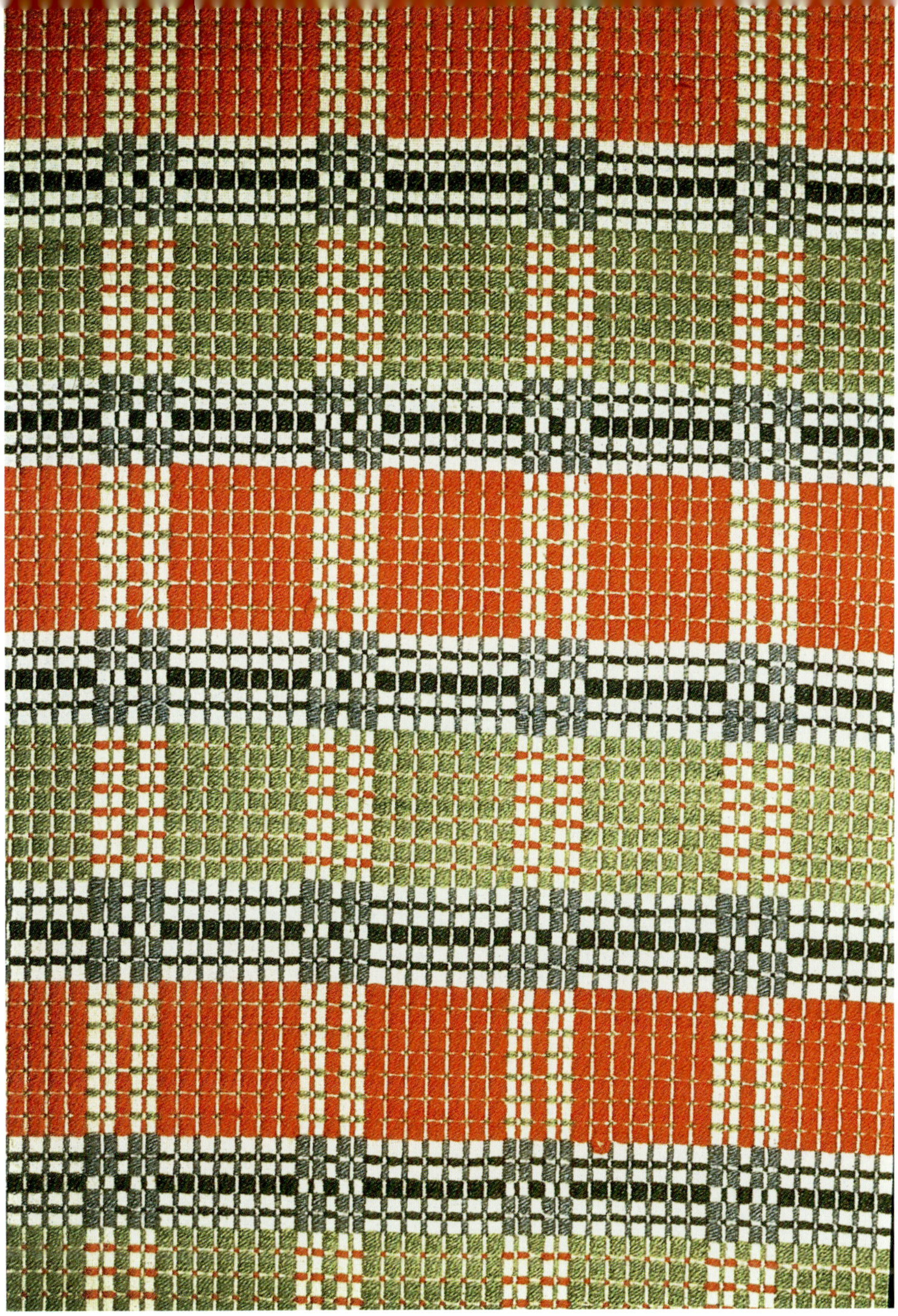

10.6 Monk's-belt patterns composed of large squares divided into a grid of smaller squares: *(top left)* Akershus; *(top right)* Troms; *(bottom)* Sør-Trøndelag. *Norwegian Folk Museum.*

The designs of the skillbragd coverlets depended on whether the patterns were picked up with a weaving sword or controlled by the threading of the loom. When a weaving sword (sometimes referred as a pattern board; see Appendix, page 179) was used, the design usually consisted of horizontal bands of eight-petaled roses and diamonds. Colors often alternated between bands of pattern or within the patterns themselves to highlight portions of the design (figs. 10.1 and 10.7–10.10).

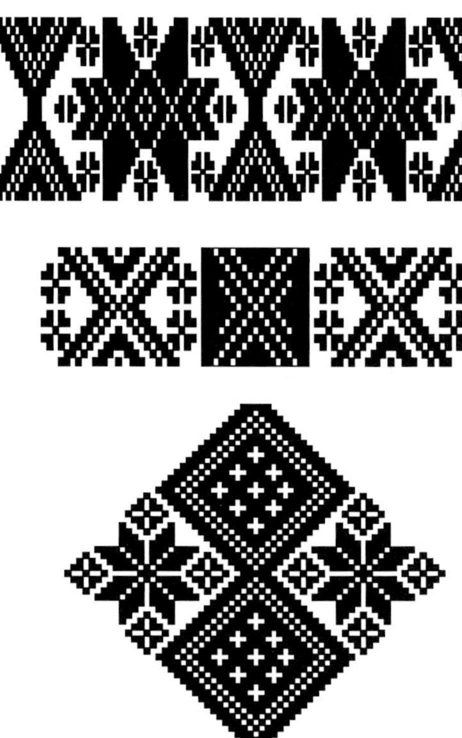

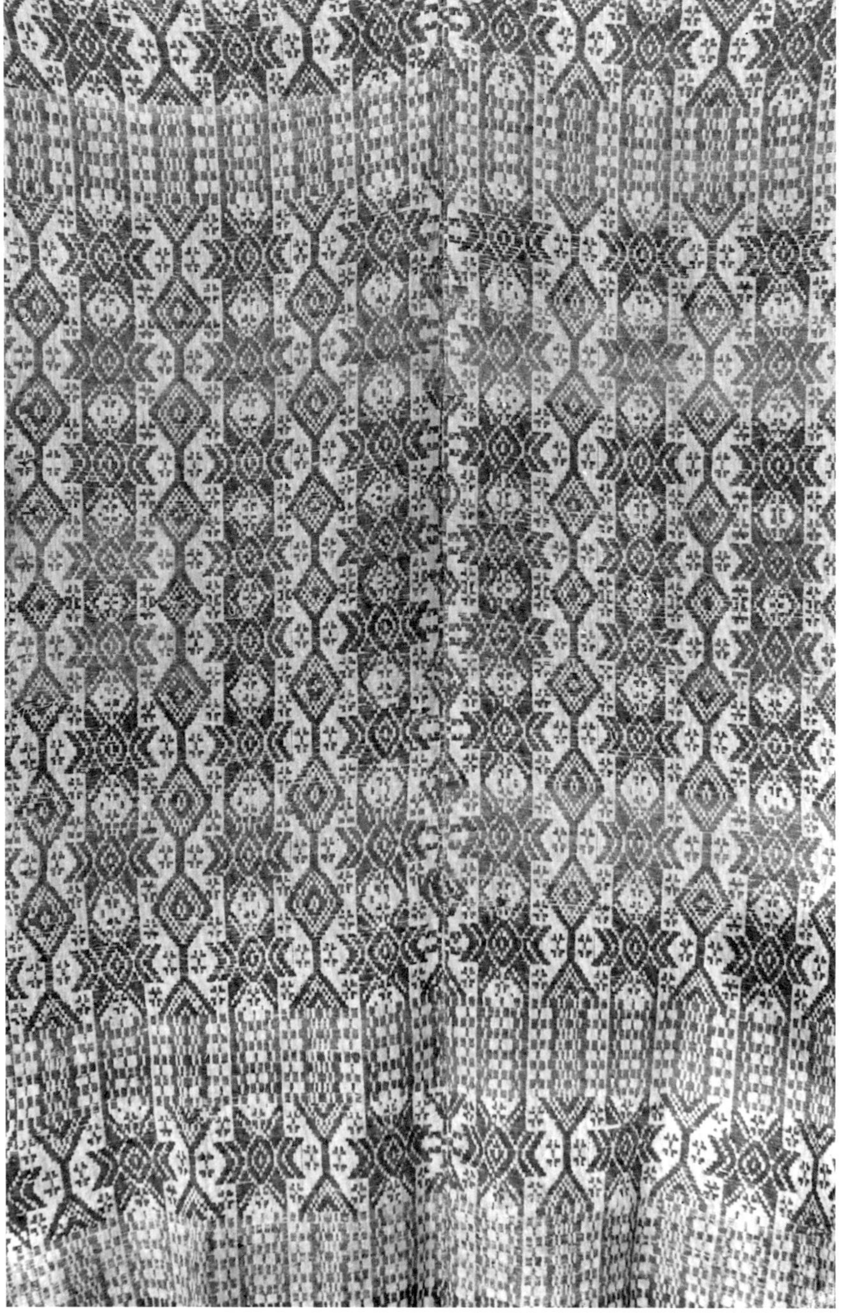

10.7 Eight-petaled roses, diamonds, and large Xs were common motifs in the skillbragd coverlets woven with a weaving sword.

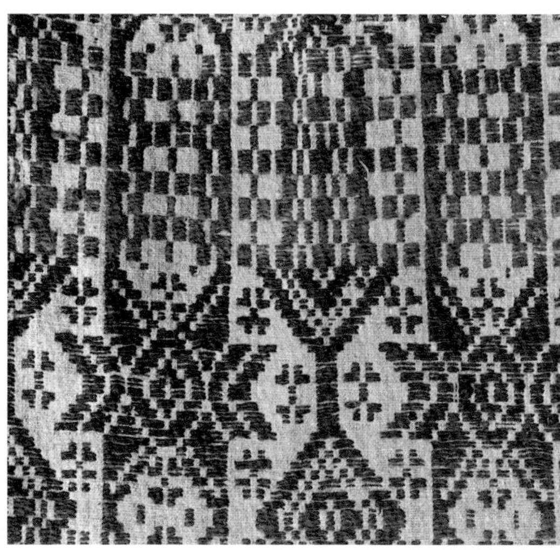

10.8 The eight-petaled roses in this *skillbragd* coverlet are repeated regularly except in three bands. These bands consist of two rows of pattern selected out of sequence and woven alternately before the regular pattern is resumed. Valle, Setesdal. *Norwegian Folk Museum.*

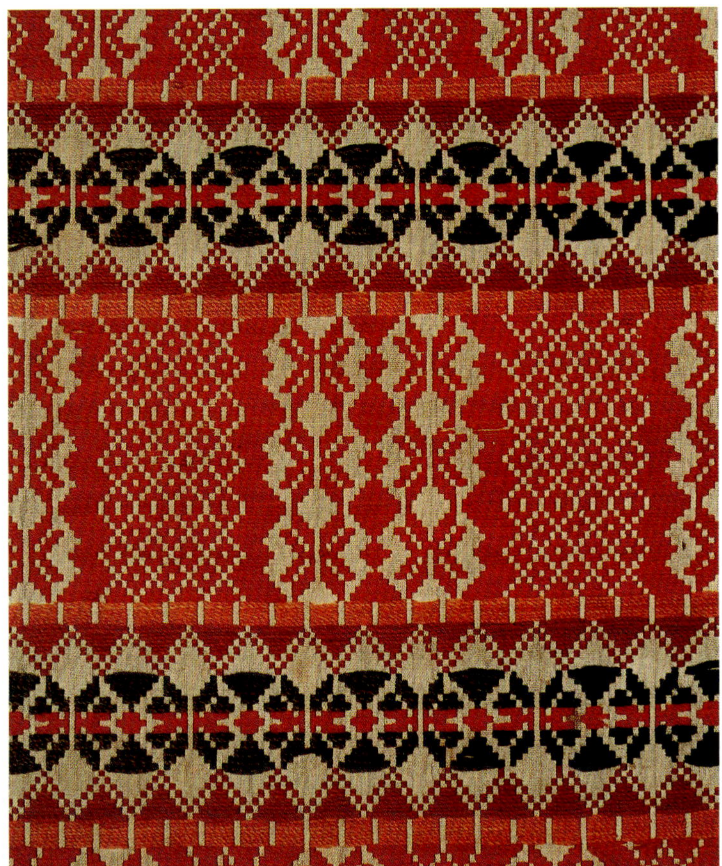

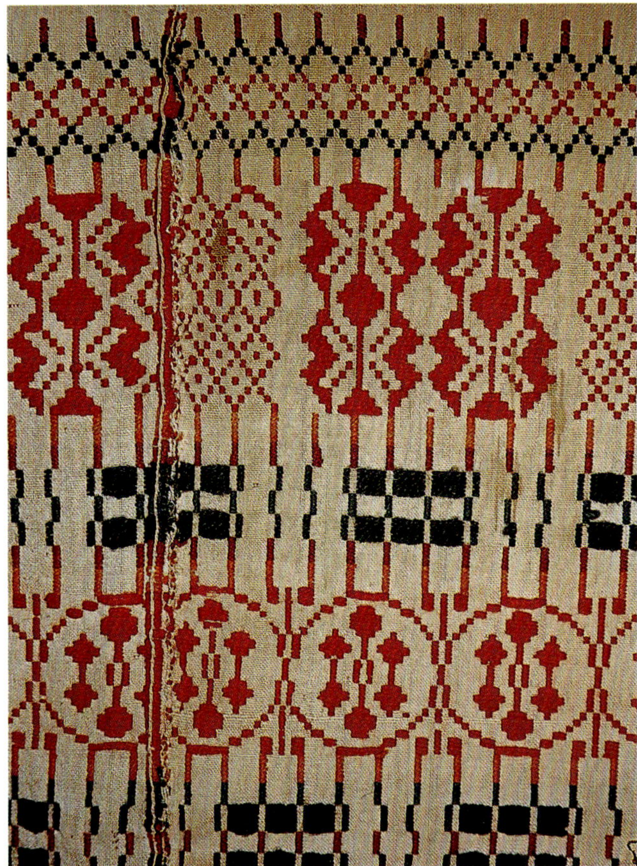

10.9 *Skillbragd* coverlet, detail of fig. 10.1. In the back view (*top right*), the center seam is visible on the left. Note the slight error in the diamond pattern (near the center seam, second pattern panel from top), corrected in the rest of the pattern. When using a weaving sword, such mistakes were usually corrected in the pattern pick-up of the next row. Mistakes in Nordland's and Telemark's weaves, however, resulted from threading errors, and thus were usually repeated throughout the coverlet. Nordfjord. *Nordic Heritage Museum.*

10.10 *Skillbragd* coverlet, probably woven with a weaving sword, with a regular array of eight-petaled roses and diamonds. Nordfjord, Sogn and Fjordane. *Norwegian Folk Museum.*

Skillbragd coverlets that were woven with a loom-controlled pattern
fell into two general categories. The first, usually referred to today as
Nordlandsvev, or Nordland's weave, were characterized by patterns oriented
in a warp-wise direction. Small diamonds, crosses, zigzags, and elongated or
truncated versions of these basic patterns were arranged in vertical columns.
Horizontal bands of color further accented the pattern of these coverlets.
A color combination of red and green was very common, as was red, green,
and black, but others colors were sometimes added (figs. 10.11–10.14). The
second type of loom-controlled skillbragd, generally referred to now as
Telemarksvev, or Telemark's weave, was distinguished by horizontal bands
of small ovoid patterns, truncated or elongated and repeated in a number
of ways. A variety of colors were used in these weavings, although red, black,
and green usually figured prominently in the color scheme. The alternating
use of color further accentuated the different bands of pattern created by the
weavers treadling sequence (figs. 10.15–10.17).

In many skillbragd coverlets, additional pattern wefts were inlaid in small
areas, following the overall design but in a different color. Such additions
served to accentuate a part of a particular pattern, but they could also give
the impression of an entirely separate design. Many coverlets displayed a
central panel highlighted in this manner by a contrasting color (figs. 10.16,
10.18, 10.19). In some districts such coverlets were used as burial drapes, with
the central square serving as a place to rest a candle or an ale bowl from
which to drink a farewell toast to the departed.[5]

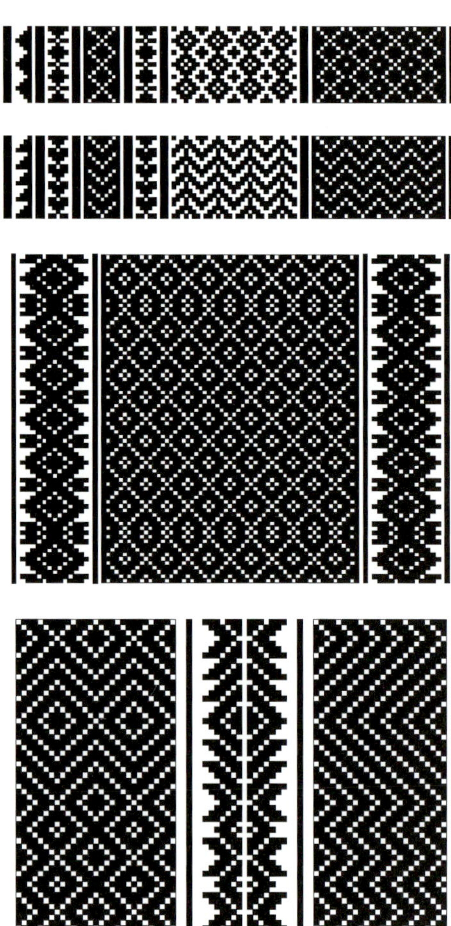

10.11 Patterns in the Nordland's-weave coverlets, typically threaded on four pattern harnesses, are characterized by vertical stripes.
A change in the treadling sequence reverses,
elongates, or truncates the basic pattern
threaded on the loom. (*a*) The treadling
sequence can be reversed after every fourth
row of pattern (1, 2, 3, 4, 3, 2, 1 . . .) to create
diamonds, above; or it can be repeated (1, 2, 3,
4, 1, 2, 3, 4 . . .) to produce chevrons, below.
(*b*) A slight variation can be introduced into
an otherwise regular treadling sequence. (c)
The treadling sequence can be reversed at
selected points to enhance the pattern.

10.12 The combination of red and green pattern-weft on a ground weave of white was
common in the Nordland's-weave coverlets.
*Luther College Collection, Vesterheim
Norwegian-American Museum.*

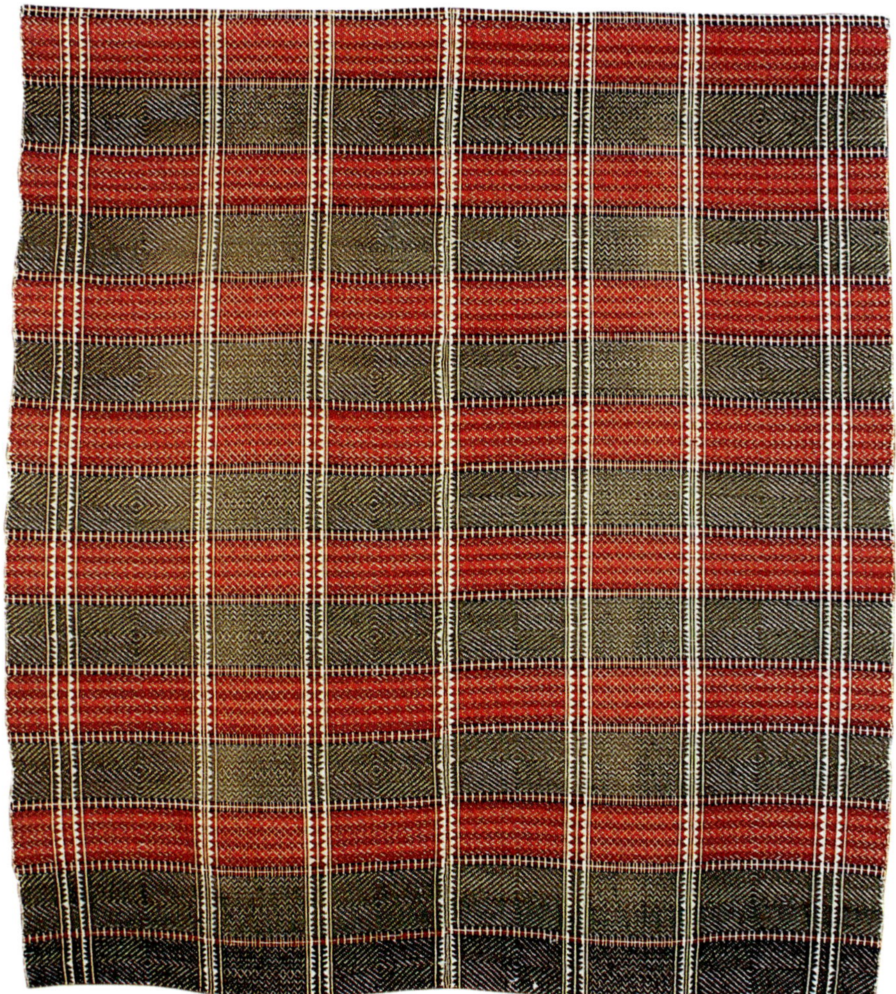

10.13 Warp-wise columns of diamonds were typical of the Nordland's-weave coverlets. Gudbrandsdal. *Luther College Collection, Vesterheim Norwegian-American Museum.*

10.14 Regular repetition of the diamond pattern is interrupted (olive bands) as the weaver repeats two pattern rows several times before progressing with the design. Sør-Trøndelag. *Vesterheim Norwegian-American Museum.*

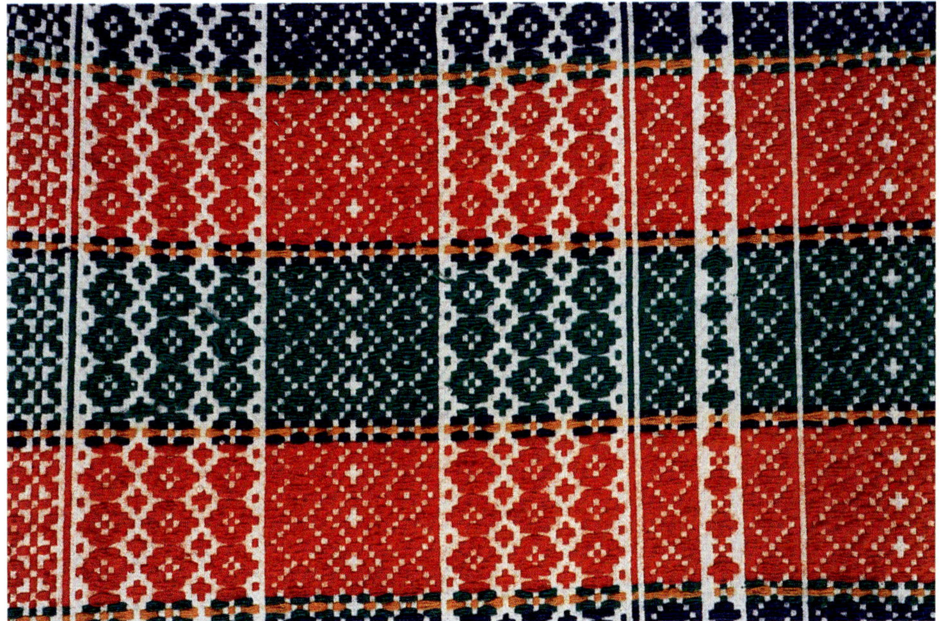

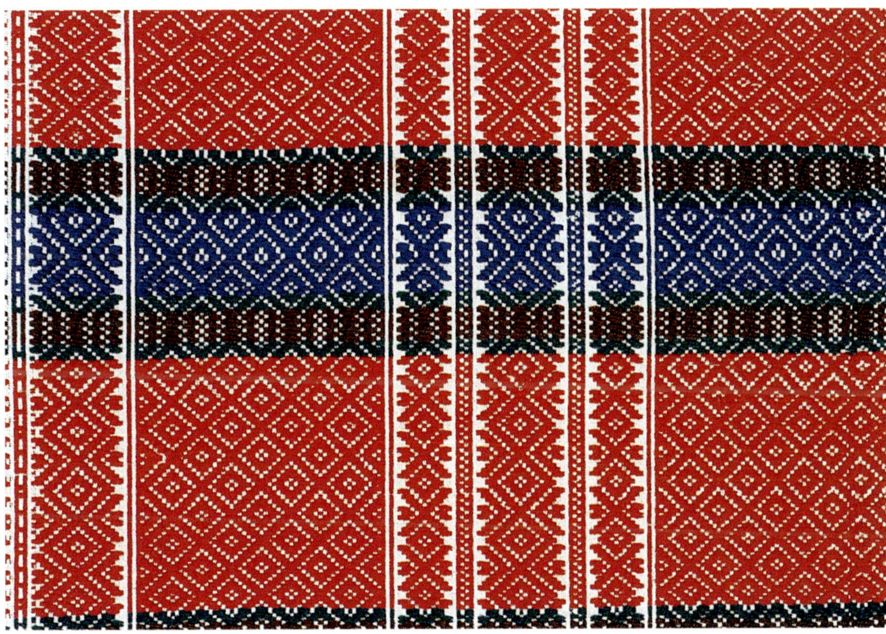

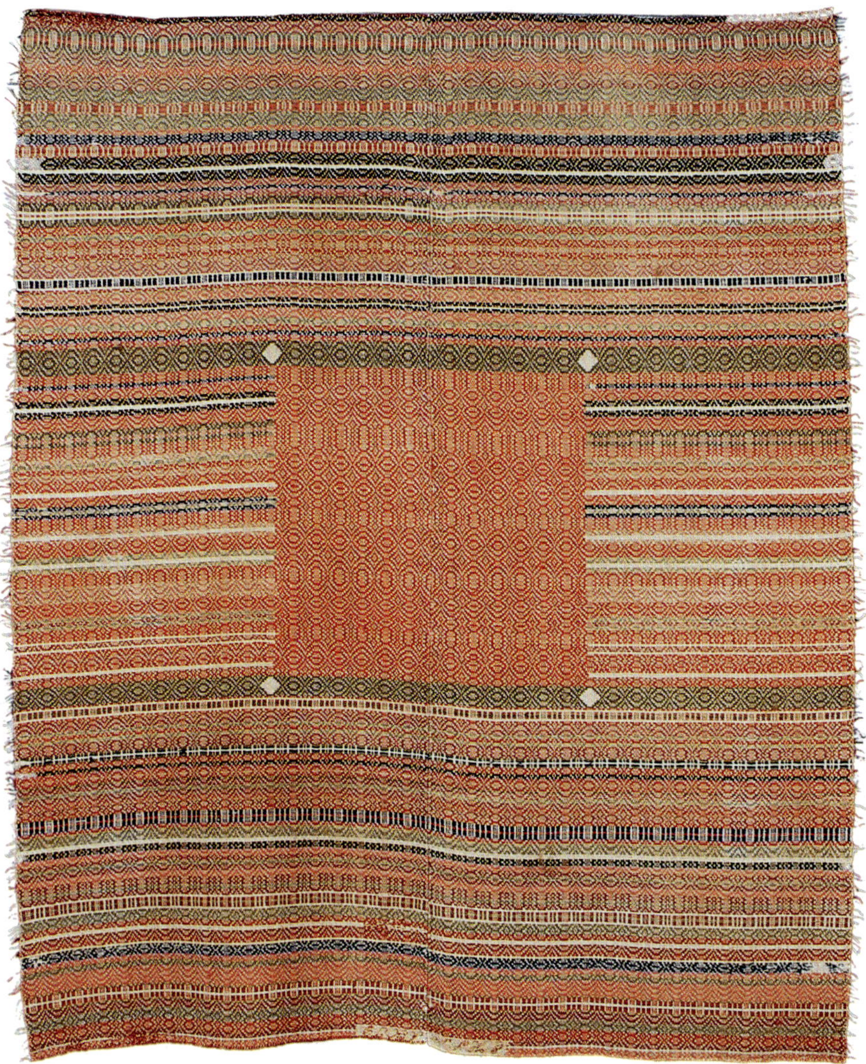

10.16 Telemark's-weave coverlet with central square. In the detailed view below, note the contrasting stripes of weft yarn laid into selected portions of pattern shed to create the large red square. Small white diamonds inlaid at each corner further highlight the central pattern. *Luther College Collection, Vesterheim Norwegian-American Museum.*

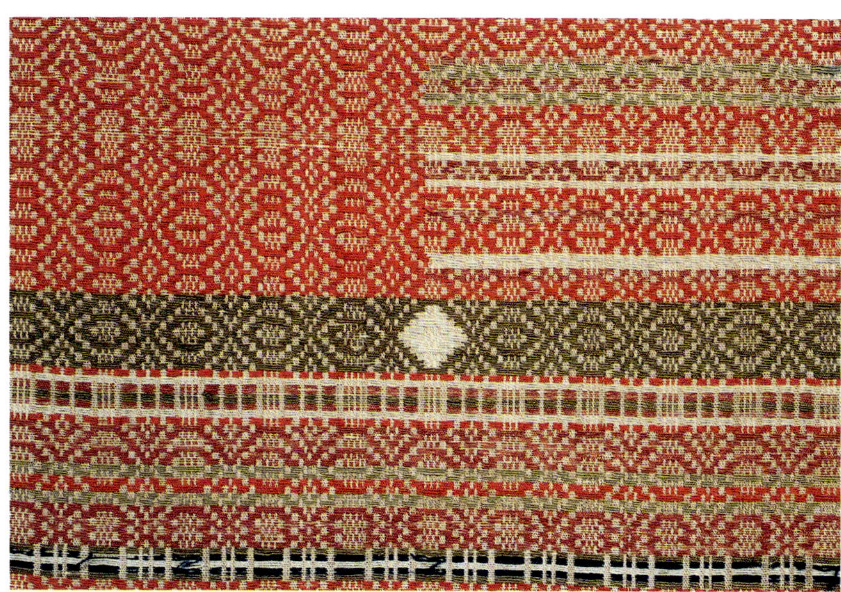

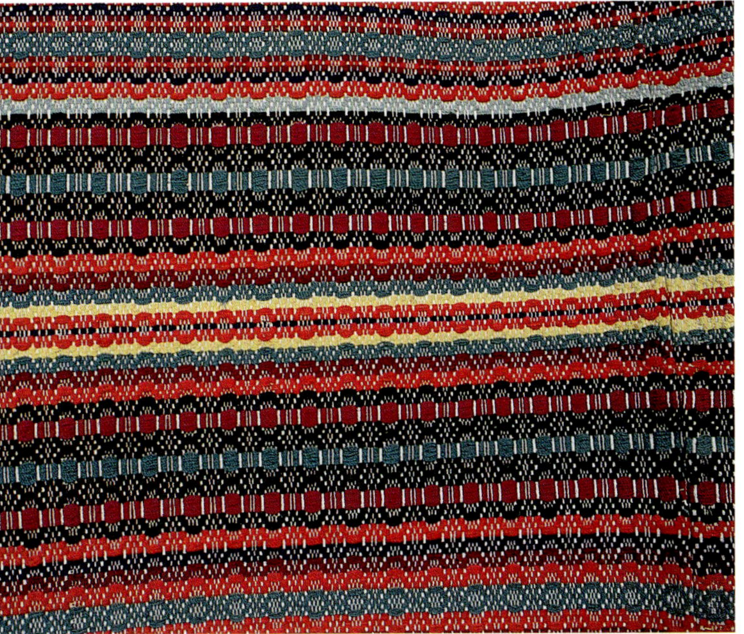

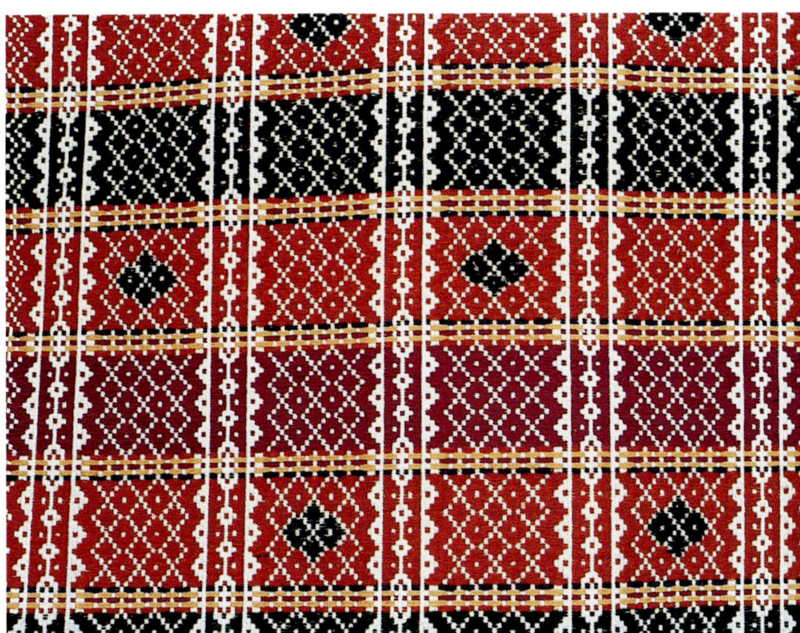

10.17 Ovoid patterns highlighted by bands of alternating color were typical of the Telemark's-weave coverlets. Probably Telemark. *Vesterheim Norwegian-American Museum.*

10.18 *(Upper right)* A contrasting color laid in during weaving serves to highlight the diamond design in this Nordland's-weave coverlet. Probably Valdres. *Vesterheim Norwegian-American Museum.*

10.19 Nordland's-weave coverlet with inlaid central design in the shape of a cross. Nesna, Nordland. *Norwegian Folk Museum.*

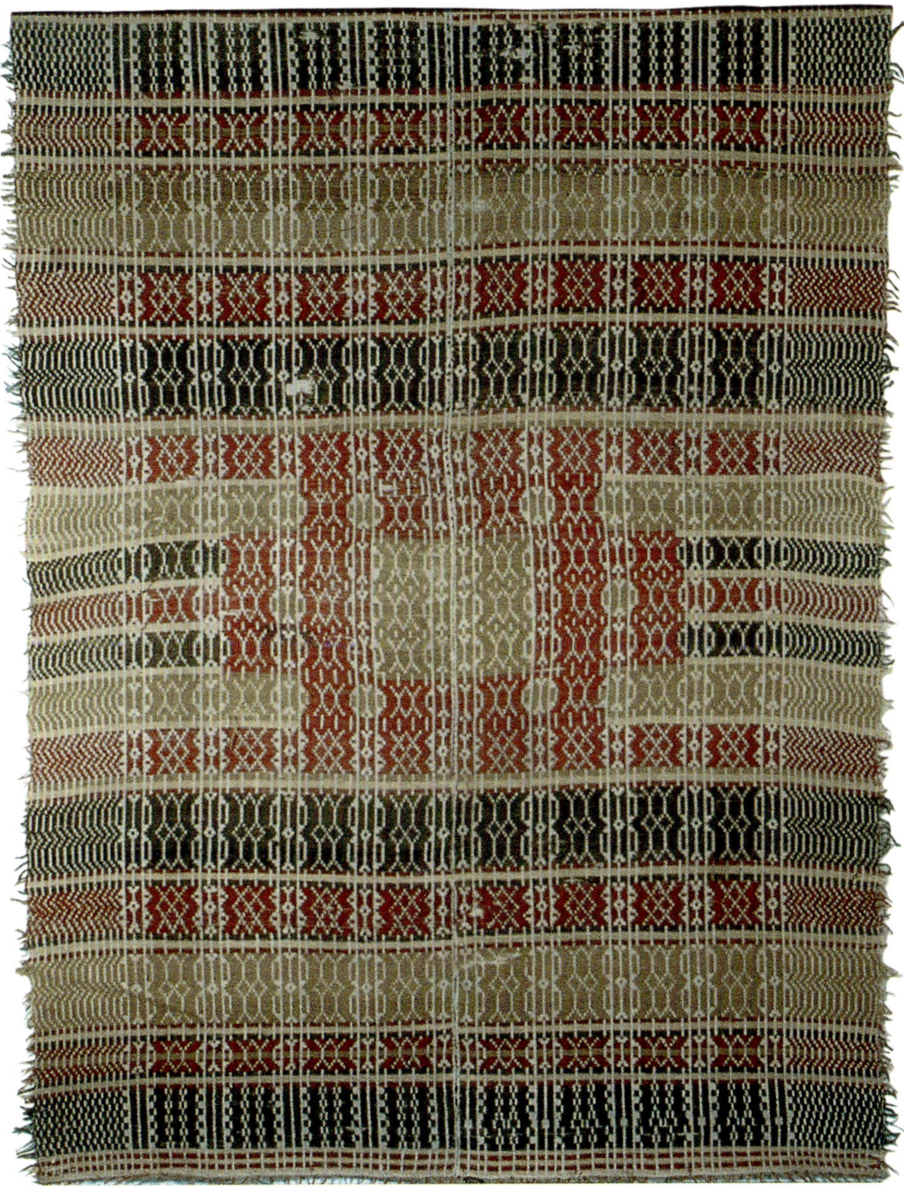

Materials and Looms

The ground weave in the overshot coverlets was traditionally a fine, single-ply linen in both warp and weft. The warp threads could be set as closely as forty ends per inch, although many coverlets were not this fine. When cotton became readily available in the nineteenth century, many weavers switched from the inelastic linen to this easier-to-manage material. The pattern weft was usually a fine, single-ply wool, homespun even when commercially produced cotton was used for the ground weave.

Overshot coverlets were woven in two pieces approximately twenty-four to twenty-eight inches wide by five to six feet long that were sewn together lengthwise. The midseam is nearly invisible on many of the coverlets that are now contained in museum collections, a tribute to the skill of the weavers who were able to match such fine patterns with near perfection over the entire length of a coverlet.

Typically a four-harness horizontal loom was used to weave the overshot coverlets, although six and sometimes eight or ten harnesses were used for more complex patterns (fig. 10.20). At the beginning of the twentieth century, a simple version of the draw loom, on which skillbragd coverlets were frequently woven in Sweden, was introduced into Norway. A draw loom allowed the weaver to access pattern harnesses at the back of the loom by pulling the cords of a draw system. Classes in this new technology were offered in parts of Norway, but few weavers had such a loom at home, and the draw loom never became an important factor in weaving Norwegian overshot coverlets.

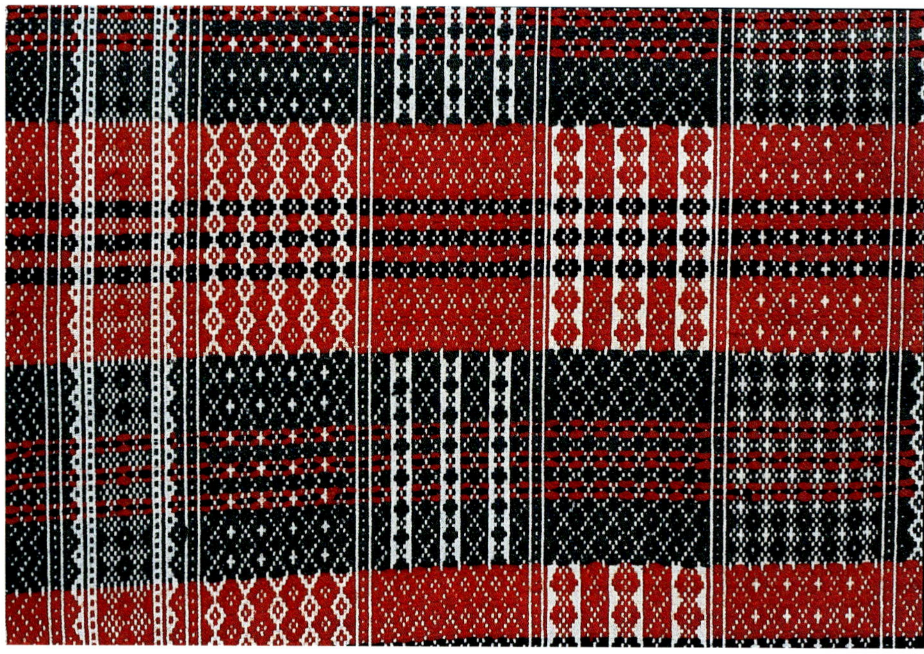

10.20 Nordland's-weave coverlet woven with eight pattern-harnesses. Two designs, each requiring four harnesses, are emphasized by stripes of red and green as they alternate throughout the coverlet. Sør-Trøndelag. *Vesterheim Norwegian-American Museum.*

10.21 Nordland's-weave coverlet, folded to show front *(right)* and back *(left)*. The supplementary pattern weft floats over and under the ground weave, appearing primarily on the front of the fabric. Detail of figure 10.12. *Luther College Collection, Vesterheim Norwegian-American Museum.*

10.22 The pattern weft passes over and under selected warp threads of the ground weave in skillbragd and monk's-belt coverlets: *(a)* plain-weave ground; *(b)* basket-weave ground (doubled warps and wefts).

Weaving Techniques

The overshot coverlets consisted of a supplementary pattern weft that appeared primarily on the "right" side of the fabric as it floated over and under a ground weave (fig. 10.21). Some weavers preferred to work with the reverse side up in order to check the weft turns on the back of the weaving, and others wove with the right side up. The ground weave was usually a balanced plain weave, although sometimes the doubled warp and weft threads of a basket weave were used. After every one, or in some cases two, shots of ground weft, a pattern weft was inserted according to the intended design (fig. 10.22). The ground weave was controlled by the regular system of harnesses on the loom, but the pattern shed was created in several ways in the different types of overshot coverlets.

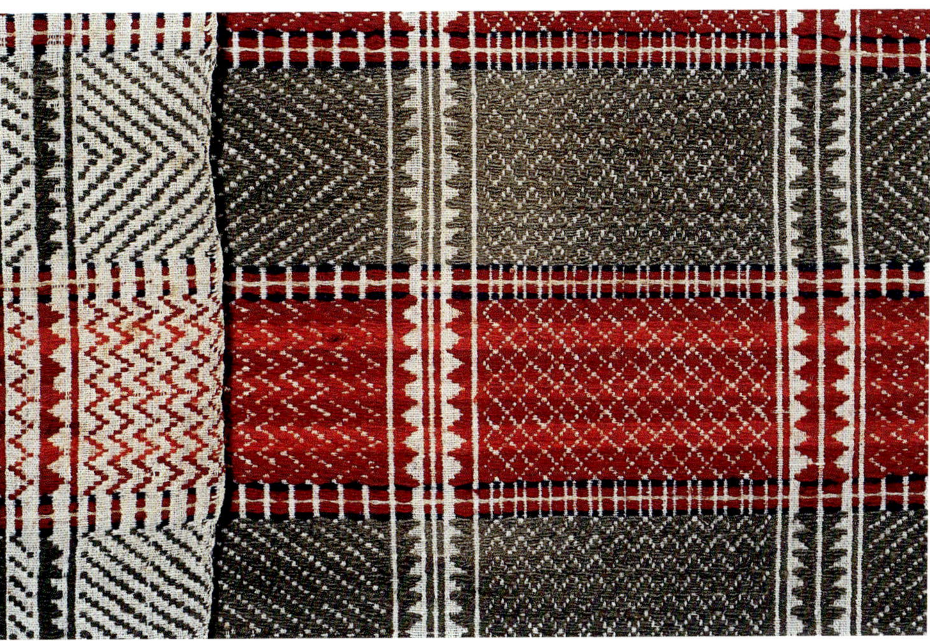

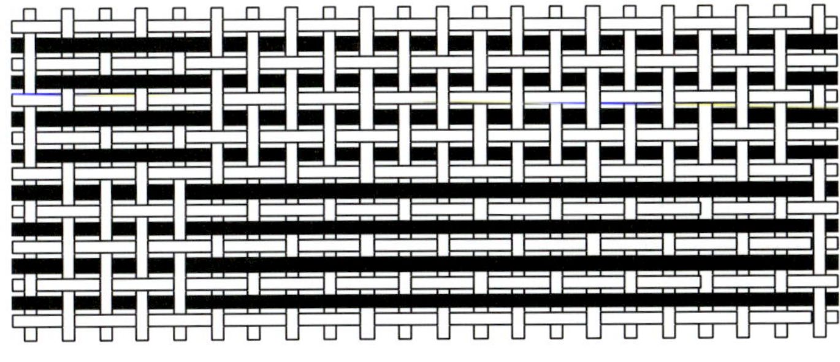

a

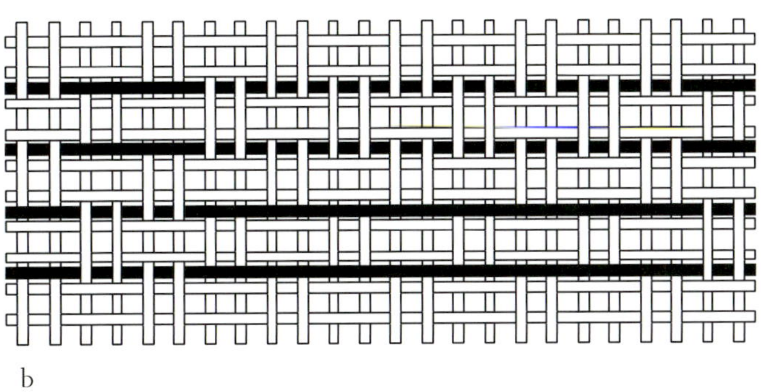

b

The monk's-belt technique had the simplest system. Originally monk's belt may have been an early skillbragd pattern, woven with the help of a weaving sword.[6] It was easily adaptable to a four-harness loom, however, through the combination of a plain-weave threading and a pattern threading that alternated between two groups of harnesses. These two blocks, or threading units, were the basis of the monk's-belt patterns. The ground weave and the pattern weave were both controlled by the same set of harnesses, and the weaver merely alternated her treadling sequence to create a plain-weave shed or a pattern shed as required (fig. 10.23). The small and large squares on which the technique is built were usually four- and sixteen-warp-threads wide, respectively, and the order in which they appeared across the width of the fabric was determined by the threading of the harnesses. But the weaver was free to choose which pattern block to use and how long to use it provided that she continued to maintain the steady progression of one or two shots of ground weave between each shot of pattern weft. Usually the design was woven so that the overall pattern was "squared," that is, the weaver continued one pattern block until the main pattern elements set forth in the threading were as high as they were wide.

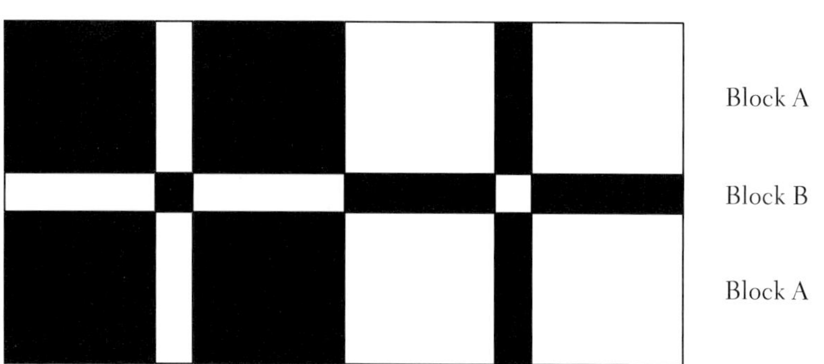

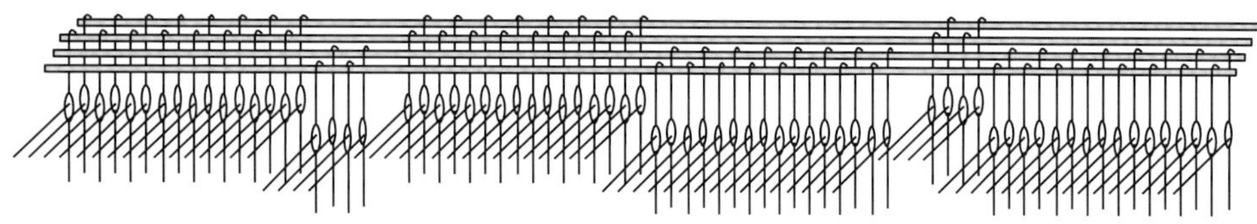

10.23 The warp threads are threaded through four harnesses for the monk's-belt technique. The two plain-weave sheds are created by using harnesses 1 and 3 together, alternating with 2 and 4 together. The two pattern sheds are created by using harnesses 1 and 2 together (pattern Block A) and 3 and 4 together (pattern Block B). The threading of the harnesses seen in the bottom of this illustration will produce the pattern seen at the top: Block A is woven until the pattern is squared, then Block B until the smaller pattern is squared, then Block A again. A shot of ground weft is inserted between each shot of pattern.

The skillbragd coverlets were woven in two ways. The oldest method required the use of a weaving sword, a long flat stick about three inches wide. Patterns were first picked up across the entire width of the warp with a thinner pick-up stick. The small shed created by the pick-up stick was then transferred to the weaving sword further back in the loom, behind the ground-weave heddles. For this procedure to work, the eyes of the heddles through which the regular ground-weave was threaded had to be extra long, or approximately three inches. When the weaving sword was turned on its side, the shed created passed through the heddles to the front of the loom. Each row of picked-up design was usually woven several times, depending on the height desired for the overall pattern, and between each of these shots of pattern weft a shot of ground weave was required. At these times, the weaving sword was laid flat and pushed further back in the loom to allow the ground-weave heddles to open fully (fig. 10.24).

10.24 Using a weaving sword: (*a*) A pick-up stick is inserted into the warp, picking up the desired pattern threads. (*b*) The weaving sword is inserted behind the heddles into the small shed formed when the pick-up stick is turned on edge. (*c*) When turned on its side, the weaving sword creates a shed through which the pattern weft can be inserted. (d) After a shot of pattern weft, the weaving sword is pushed back to allow the ground-weave harnesses to open. Several shots of the same pattern can be woven (alternating with ground weave) before the next row of pattern is selected.

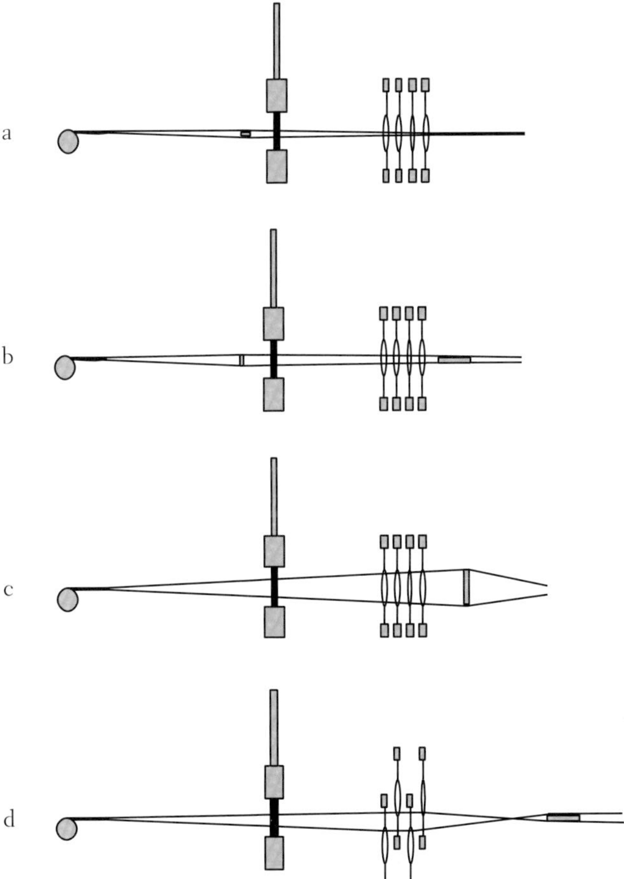

For a design that was symmetrical about a horizontal axis, the first half of the pattern was often stored row by row on pattern rods at the back of the loom. These rods were then brought forward in reverse order when the second half of the pattern was to be woven (fig. 10.25). If a pattern was to appear several times throughout the weaving, the pattern rods in the back of the loom were often replaced by half-heddle rods. Pattern warps were picked up for each row of pattern and attached to the half-heddle rods with small slings, one rod for each row of pattern. When the desired half-heddle rod was lifted, the weaving sword could be inserted into the opened pattern shed and then brought forward in the loom (fig. 10.26). An assistant who manipulated the pattern rods or half-heddle rods at the back of the loom and brought the pattern shed forward when necessary was of great help in this process. Such an assistant was often found in the person of the weaver's daughter. Many Norwegian girls began their weaving experience at the age of eight or nine by helping their mothers with this task.

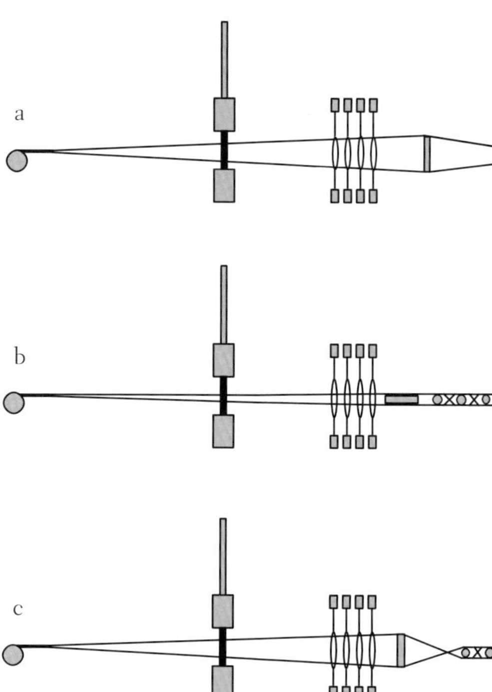

10.25 Storing picked-up patterns at the back of the loom: *(a)* The shed opened by the weaving sword is saved on a pattern rod at the back of the loom. *(b)* In a pattern that is symmetrical about a horizontal axis, several rows of pattern are stored in this manner. When the middle of the pattern is reached, the process is reversed and the weaving sword is inserted into the shed stored by the last pattern rod. (c) When the weaving sword is turned on its side, it opens a shed for weaving a row of pattern.

10.26 Using half heddles to store rows of pattern: *(a)* Selected pattern warps are picked up by small slings, usually made from extra string heddles. *(b)* The desired row of pattern is selected by lifting the appropriate half-heddle rod at the back of the loom. A weaving sword is inserted into the opening. *(c)* The weaving sword is turned on its side to bring the opening forward, and a second weaving sword is inserted. (d) The second weaving sword opens a shed for weaving a row of pattern.

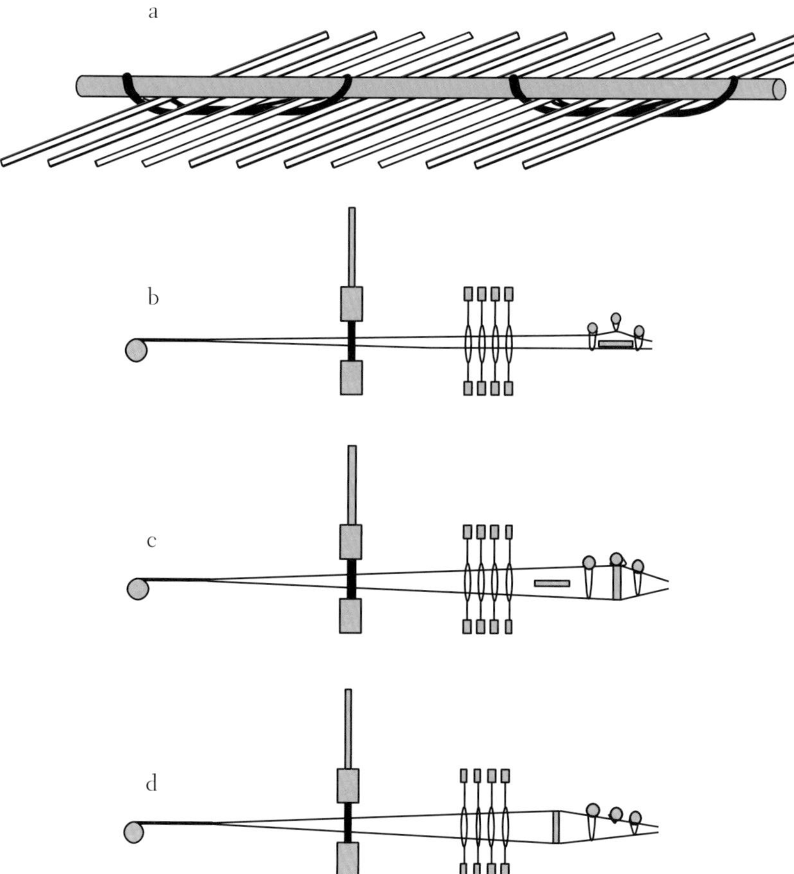

The second method for weaving skillbragd (Nordland's and Telemark's weaves) was considerably faster, since patterns were loom-controlled instead of being picked up on a weaving sword, but much of the flexibility of creating designs during the weaving process was lost. Patterns were threaded through two sets of harnesses, one set for the ground weave and the other for the pattern weave. Extra long heddles on the pattern harnesses allowed the ground-weave shed to come forward through the pattern heddles (fig. 10.27). Usually Nordland's-weave patterns consisted of four rows, corresponding to the four pattern harnesses, but patterns of eight rows, requiring eight pattern harnesses, were not uncommon. Telemark's-weave patterns were typically composed of three rows, or three pattern harness (although today this technique is usually woven as a three-block weave with six harnesses and five treadles, similar to the two-block monk's-belt technique). Individual pattern elements in both variations were usually four warp threads in width, and although the pattern was often "squared" in height, the weaver could freely elongate or truncate the basic pattern by varying the treadling sequence.

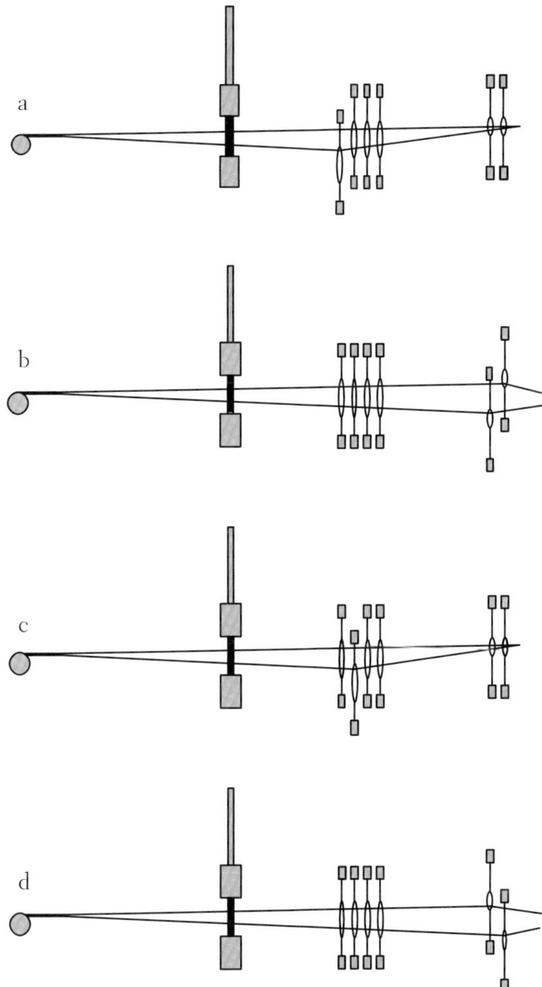

10.27 Nordland's and Telemark's weaves. The warp is threaded through two sets of harnesses, the pattern harnesses closest to the beater and the ground-weave harnesses further back. The ground-weave shed is able to pass to the front of the loom through the extra long eyes of the pattern harnesses. (a) The first pattern harness is selected for a shot of pattern weft. (b) A ground weave shed is opened for a shot of ground weave. (c) The second pattern harness is selected for a shot of pattern weft. (Several repetitions of one pattern harness are needed, each followed by a shot of ground weave, to complete a row of pattern. In this case the second pattern harness is selected to begin a new row.) (d) The alternate ground weave shed is opened for the next shot of ground weave.

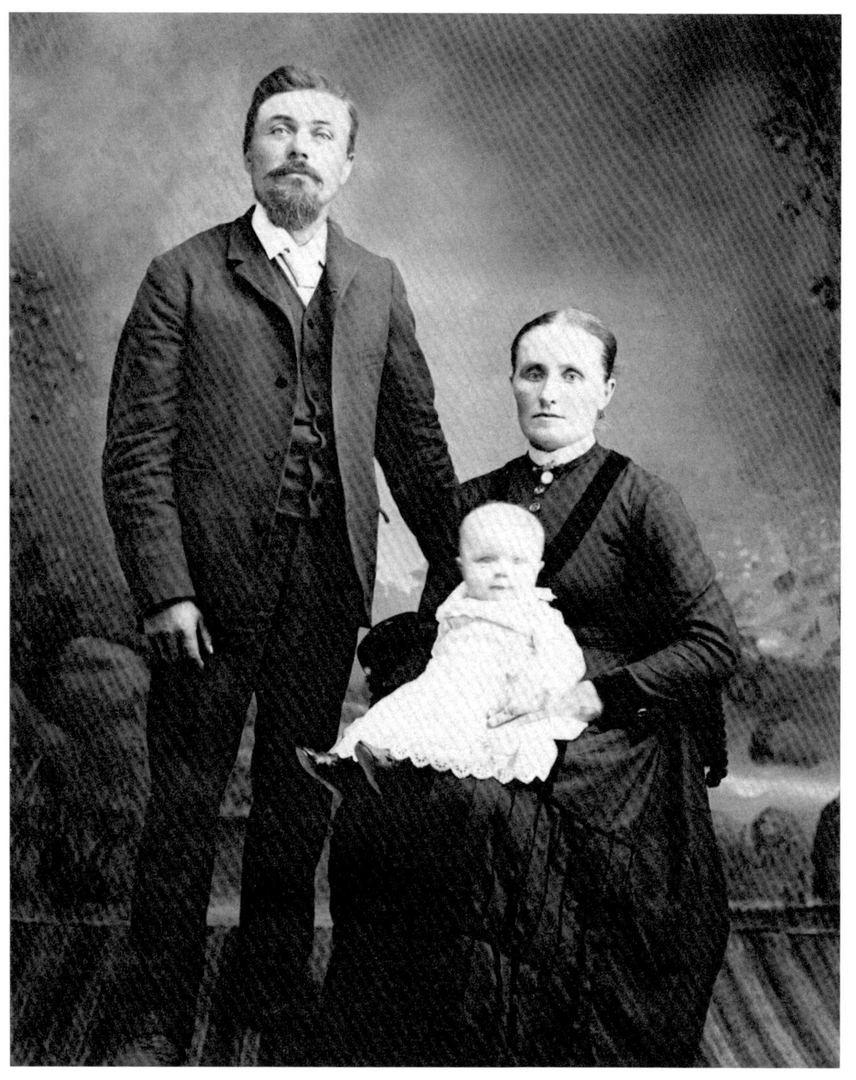

Peter Christian and Maren Kristin Peterson of Vega, Nordland, ca. 1880. Like many Norwegians of their generation, the Petersons emigrated to America and became home-steaders in Dakota Territory.

Afterword

Many of you may have pictures such as this in your family album: a young couple, poised to embark on their journey to America. There is nothing particularly exceptional about this couple. They produced no presidents, became neither tycoons nor desperadoes, were never war heroes. In fact, nothing distinguishes them from the thousands of immigrants who came before and the thousands who would follow after, except in the eyes of their descendants. We each have these ancestors in our family history, and to each of us they represent the beginning of the American dream.

This young couple happen to be my great-grandparents, Peter Christian and Maren Kristin Peterson. Looking at their serious expressions, I have often wondered what their thoughts might have been when they made the decision to emigrate. No doubt necessity was a major factor, enhanced by glowing reports of opportunity and prosperity in the new world. A sense of adventure may have entered into the decision as well. But did they realize they were leaving more than family and friends behind, that gradually the customs and traditions that made them Norwegians would be lost to their children and grandchildren? Perhaps settled in their strongly Norwegian communities in the Midwest, this was not readily apparent. Perhaps their first inkling of how the future might look came when their children adopted English as quickly as possible, not wanting to sound like they were "fresh off the boat." My grandfather, their first child to be born in America, never spoke a word of Norwegian to me in the sixteen years he lived with us, even though Norwegian was his first language. No family heirlooms were passed down from either side of my family, and my parents' knowledge of exactly where in Norway their families had come from could be characterized as "somewhere around this area. . . ."

When I went to school in Norway thirty years ago, I was looking for the land my great-grandparents left behind — a Norwegian Brigadoon. Reality soon dashed my expectations, however, for although steeped in tradition, Norway is a vibrant and progressive member of the modern world. Ultimately, the fortunate chance that led me to study weaving provided the link with the past for which I was searching. Here were traditions I had never known existed, and, of particular relevance to me as a woman, traditions that had been central to the lives of my grandmothers.

I find the coverlets of Norway interesting from many standpoints. As a weaver, I enjoy the variety of structures, from delicate tapestries to shaggy ryas; as one who appreciates art history, I feel a deep resonance with the timeless motifs preserved in the coverlets; as a social historian, I believe the survival of this folk art from a preindustrial tradition makes a significant contribution to the study of women's history; but most important of all, on a personal level, the coverlets of Norway reestablish a connection with a heritage that was lost to me, and perhaps to many of you. They tell me the things my great-grandmother might have said if only her photograph could speak.

Alas, the photograph remains mute, but the coverlets speak volumes.

Appendix

Table of Equivalent Terms

STRIVING TO AVOID INCONSISTENCIES IN THE USE of terms, especially when translating from one language to another, I have consulted numerous sources on the subject of textile terminology. Even within the English language there are differences, however, starting with the proper term for that most basic of interlacements, over-one/under-one. In referring to this weave structure, the term *plain weave* is preferred over *tabby* by Irene Emery: "It is not possible . . . to justify continued use of many different terms for precise designation of the plain-weave structure"(Emery 1966:85). In contrast, *tabby* is preferred over *plain weave* by Dorothy Burnham: although plain weave is synonymous with tabby, its meaning is imprecise, and therefore "tabby is recommended as a more specific term." (Burnham 1980:101). Given such discrepancies, it appears that the best course of action is to make reasonable choices, give clear explanations, and present the alternatives in a form that allows easy cross-referencing.

Many techniques used in the creation of the Norwegian coverlets already have well-known English names (tapestry, brocading, double weave, overshot). In addition, a number of techniques are commonly referred to in English by technically or structurally descriptive names (pick-and-pick, supplementary-weft patterning, voided pile). Where English equivalents are available I have used them. Where they are not, the task of properly identifying the Norwegian techniques is complicated by the fact that a number of Swedish textile terms have been used to some extent in English. The Norwegian and Swedish techniques are generally identical, but as this is a book about Norwegian textiles, I have made the following choices:

KROKBRAGD I have opted to use the Norwegian term *krokbragd* instead
of either of the English equivalents, boundweave or bound rosepath.
Although the term boundweave is commonly used to describe this technique in English (along with a variety of other weft-faced weaves), most
authorities on textile terminology feel it is too imprecise and therefore
do not use it. The term bound rosepath, on the other hand, is a translation
of the Swedish term *bunden rosengång* and connotes the rosepath threading
in which these Swedish textiles were often woven. This is not typical of the
Norwegian coverlets, and since the term krokbragd has had some usage
in English already, it seems a logical choice to describe this technique.
However, bound rosepath, the translation recommended by *Nordisk
Textilteknisk Terminologi* (NTT) (see Table of Equivalent Terms, p. 180),
provides the English equivalent for the title of chapter 6.

MONK'S BELT The Norwegian *tavlebragd* technique is well known in
English as monk's belt. This comes from the Swedish *munkabälte*, which
happily translates into recognizable English words, and thus is the obvious
choice for this technique.

RYA The Scandinavian knotted-pile technique is fairly well known in
English by the Swedish term *rya* (pronounced "ree-yah"). Because this is
nearly identical to the Norwegian word *rye* ("ree-yeh") and appears closer
to the approximate pronunciation in English ("ree-yuh"), I have opted to
use the Swedish term.

SKILLBRAGD When referring to the combination of monk's-belt and
skillbragd coverlets (pronounced "shill-bragd"), I have used the general
term overshot. However, when referring to the latter only, I have chosen to
use the Norwegian word *skillbragd* instead of the Swedish word *opphämta*.
Although *opphämta* has been used to describe this technique in English
and is the recommended NTT translation, its use would seem as inappropriate as *rölakan* (above) in a book about Norwegian weaving. Additionally,
a direct translation (*skillbragd* = shedpath, shed weave) does not seem particularly informative in this case.

SQUARE WEAVE I have chosen to use a direct translation of the Norwegian term *rutevev* (*rute* = square, *vev* = weave). Although the Swedish
term *rölakan* (or sometimes "Norwegian *rölakan*") has been used to describe
this technique in English, it would appear out of place in a book about Norwegian weaving. *Rutevev* is also referred to variously as interlocked tapestry
weave, square interlock technique, and geometric tapestry. These descriptive
alternatives each indicate two of the three key elements of a technique that
is probably best described as interlocking geometric-patterned tapestry. All
of these options are rather unwieldy, however, and although less technically
accurate, the direct translation seems the most straightforward. (Other Nor-

wegian terms that have been translated directly into English are "Danish weave" and "lightning weave.")

WEAVING SWORD The term "weaving sword," used in English translations of several Swedish books, is an apt description of an object that resembles the blade of a broadsword. In fact, the Norwegian and Swedish terms for the object (skillblad, skälblad) both translate as "shed blade." Another implement, used to beat the weft into place on a warp-weighted loom, also translates as "weaving sword" from both Swedish and Danish (vävsvärd, vævesværd). To distinguish between two similar implements with different functions, NTT recommends "sword beater" as the English term for the weft-beating implement, and "pattern board" for the shed-opening device. However, the latter term seems inexact, and since the more descriptive term "weaving sword" has been used previously in English, I have chosen to use it. See Johansson's *Damask and Opphämta with Weaving Sword and Drawloom*, and Cyrus-Zettersttrom's *Manual of Swedish Handweaving*.

In an effort to minimize confusion over terminology, the table on page 180 lists equivalent terms for each of the major Norwegian coverlet techniques in English, Norwegian, and Swedish, and gives the recommended translation from Strömberg et al., *Nordisk Textilteknisk Terminologi: Förindustriell Vävnadsproduktion.*

TABLE OF EQUIVALENT TERMS

ENGLISH	NORWEGIAN	SWEDISH	NTT*
tapestry	*billedvev*	*flamskväv*	tapestry
square weave** geometric tapestry interlocked tapestry square interlock	*rutevev*	*rölakan*	tapestry type: *rölakan*
bound rosepath boundweave	*krokbragd*	*bunden rosengång*	bound rosepath
pick-and-pick weft-faced color and weave	*kjerringtenner*	*tvist*	
	grene (Sami: *rátnu*)	*rana*	
lightning weave**	*lynildvev*	*viggrölakan* *diagonal rölakan*	
brocading	Vestfoldsmett	*krabbasnår*	brocaded tabby type: *krabbasnår*
	blokkvev	*halvkrabba*	brocaded tabby type: *halvkrabba*
supplementary-weft pattern	*lansert innslag*	*lanserad inslag*	pattern weft
Danish weave** skip plain-weave weft substitution	*dansk brogd*		
double weave pick-up double weave double-cloth weave	*dobbeltvev* *flensvev*	*finnväv* *dubbelväv*	pick-up doublecloth
knotted pile weave	*rye*	*rya*	pile rug type: *rya*
voided pile weave	*halvfloss*	*halvflossa*	voided-pile fabric
monk's belt	*tavlebragd*	*munkabälte*	monk's belt
overshot	*skillbragd*	*opphämta* *upphämta*	weft-patterned tabby type: *opphämta*

*From Strömberg et al., *Nordisk Textilteknisk Terminologi: Förindustriell Vävnadsproduction*, 1979.

**Direct translation from Norwegian

Notes

1 / The Yearly Cycle of Textile Production

1. *Engelstad*, "Håndarbeid i Norge før 1875," 23.
2. *Ryssdal*, "Husflid og handarbeid i tida ca. 1850–1940," 4.
3. *Drabløs*, Soga om smalen, Jubileumsskrift Norsk sau-og geitalslag, 1947–97.
4. *Larson* (trans), *Speculum Regale*, 84.

2 / Of Spinning Wheels and Looms

1. *Hauglid*, Hus, peis og billedvev, 5.
2. *Geijer*, A History of Textile Art, 15.
3. *Barber*, Prehistoric Textiles, 93.
4. *Herodotus*, The History, 145.
5. *Hoffmann*, The Warp-Weighted Loom, 23–140.

4 / Tapestry Coverlets

1. *Appeared in the* Oslo Morgenbladet, *12 August 1907; cited in Sjøvold*, Norwegian Tapestries, 7.
2. *Kielland*, Norsk Billedvev, *vol. 1, 121.*
3. *Ibid., vol. 3, 111.*

5 / Square-Weave Coverlets

1. *Nylén*, Swedish Handcraft, 151.
2. *Kostveit*, Kors i kake, skurd i tre, 91.
3. *Kielland*, Norsk Billedvev, *vol. 3, 31.*
4. *Wang*, Ruteåklær, 81–85.
5. *Ibid., 147.*

6 / Bound Rosepath Coverlets

1. *Petersson and Jansson*, Bunden rosengång, 11.
2. *Forbes*, Studies in Ancient Technology, *vol. 4, 208.*

7 / Other Weft-Faced Coverlets

1. *Collingwood*, The Techniques of Rug Weaving, 122.
2. *Sveinall*, Øyslebø Gard og Ætt., 352.

8 / Double-Weave Coverlets

1. *Arlenborg and Feltzing*, Finnväv, 7.
2. *Engelstad*, Dobbeltvev i Norge, 36.
3. *Kielland*, Norsk Billedvev, *vol. 3, 27.*
4. *Ambroz*, "On the Symbolism of Russian Peasant Embroidery of Archaic Type," 23.
5. *Hoffmann*, The Warp-Weighted Loom, 186–87.

9 / Knotted-Pile Coverlets

1. *Ytreberg*, N. A., Nordlandske handelsteder, *Bruns Forlag, Trondheim, 1942, 67, as cited in Kjellmo*, Båtrya, 83.
2. *Engelstad*, Norske ryer, 53.
3. *Ibid., 27.*
4. *Barber*, Prehistoric Textiles, 212–13.
5. *Engelstad*, Norske ryer, 11.
6. *Geijer*, History of Textile Art, 199, 204–5.
7. *Engelstad*, Norske ryer, 25.
8. *Kjellmo*, Båtrya, 44.
9. *Ibid., 43.*

10 / Overshot Coverlets

1. *Ryssdal*, "Husflid og handarbeid," 34.
2. *Erlandsen and Petersen*, Fell-åklær fra Rana-distriktet, 9.
3. *Barber*, Prehistoric Textiles, 253.
4. *Collin*, Skånsk Konstvävnad, 7–8.
5. *Hjeltnes*, "Telemarksteppe," 12.
6. *Walterstorff*, "Svenska vävnadstekniker och mönstertyper," 160.

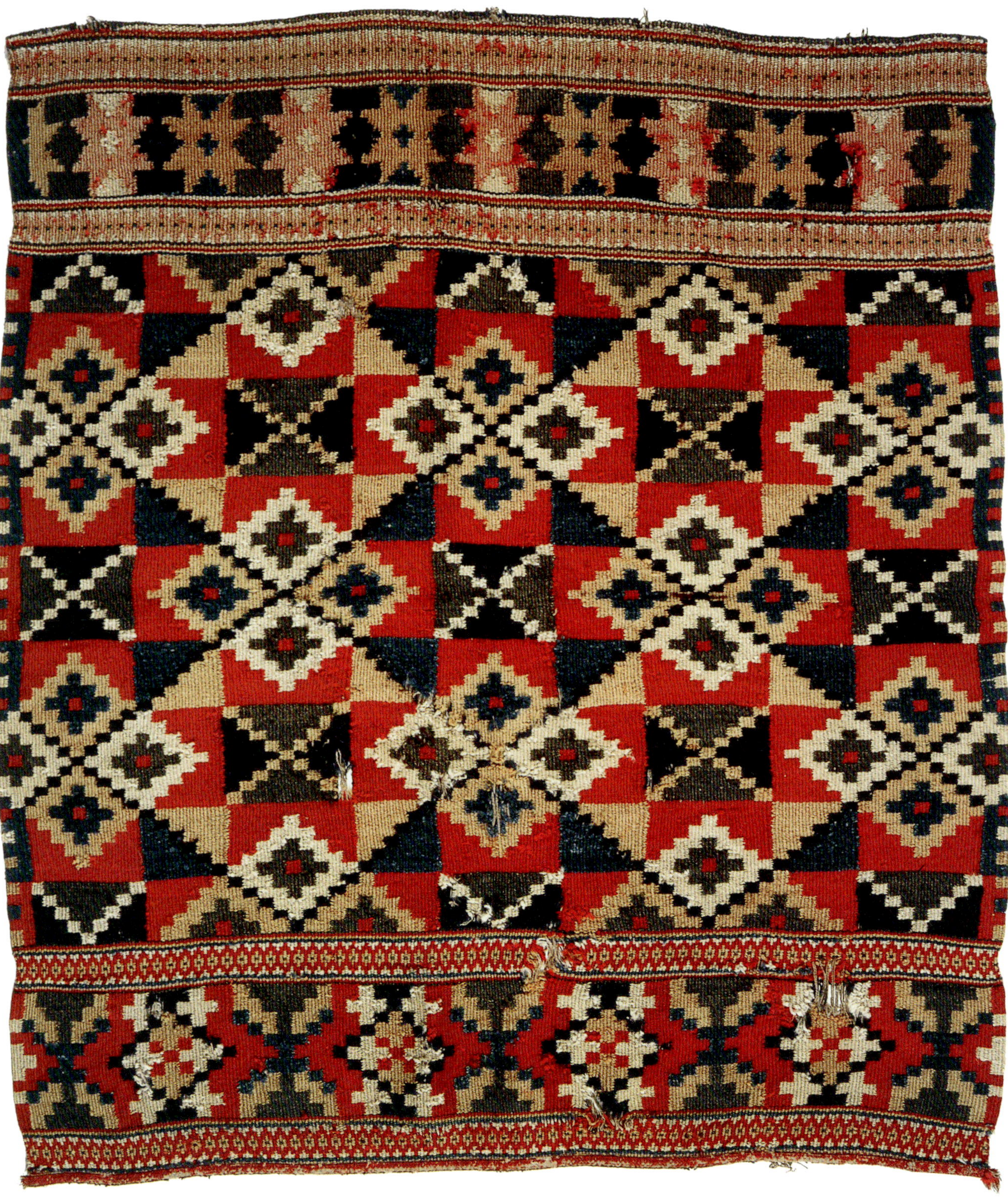

Glossary of Textile Terms

The eight-petaled rose and diamond motifs in
a pleasingly balanced color scheme decorate
this square-weave coverlet from Hallingdal.
Historical Museum, University of Bergen.

BALANCED WEAVE A weave structure in which the warp and weft
threads appear in equal proportions on the surface of the fabric.

DISTAFF An implement for holding combed flax or wool fibers for
spinning.

DOVETAILING A tapestry technique for joining two areas of weft in
which neighboring weft threads are alternately woven around a central
warp thread.

DROP SPINDLE An ancient spinning implement consisting of a stick
fitted with a weighted whorl.

ENDS PER INCH A measurement indicating the number of warp
threads per inch in a fabric.

FLOAT A length of weft thread that skips over several warp threads (or warp
thread that skips over several weft threads), "floating" on the surface of
the fabric.

GROUND WEAVE An underlying weave structure to which supplementary pattern threads are added

HALF-HEDDLE ROD A rod to which small slings are attached that lift
selected warps to create a pattern shed. The half-heddle rod rests on top
of the warp threads behind the ground-weave harness.

HARNESS A frame or two horizontal sticks to which heddles are attached
for manipulating the warp threads on a loom; also known as a shaft.

HEDDLE A device that is attached to a harness and through which a warp
end is threaded; can be made of twine, wire, or steel.

HORIZONTAL LOOM A cube-like loom, usually of four or more
harnesses, on which warp threads are strung horizontally for weaving;
not to be confused with the "basse-lisse," or horizontal tapestry loom.

INTERLOCKING A tapestry technique for joining the weft threads of
neighboring areas.

MORDANT A fixing agent used in dyeing to bind the coloring agent
to the fibers.

PATTERN ROD A rod placed through the warp threads to preserve
a pattern shed behind the ground-weave harness.

PICK-UP STICK A flat stick used for selecting and lifting appropriate
warp threads for pattern weaving.

PILE, KNOTTED Supplementary weft threads that are tied to the
ground weave of a fabric, producing a tufted surface.

PLAIN WEAVE A weave structure in which the weft travels over one,
under one warp. Also known as tabby.

SHED An opening in the warp created by raising and lowering selected
threads in order that the weft may pass through.

SHOT A pass of the weft thread through the open shed of the warp. Also
known as a pick.

SWORD BEATER A flat implement of bone, wood, or iron used to beat
the weft into place on a warp-weighted loom.

TWILL A weave structure in which the weft thread travels over or under
more than one warp thread at a time in a sequence that shifts to the side
at every row, creating a diagonal pattern.

WARP The threads strung on a loom into which the weft threads are woven.

WARP-FACED WEAVE A weave structure in which only the warp
threads are visible on the surface of the fabric.

WARP-WEIGHTED LOOM An ancient weaving implement consisting
of a three-sided frame upon which weighted bundles of warp threads
were hung.

WEAVING SWORD A wide, flat wooden stick used to transfer selected
pattern warp threads between the front and back of the loom in the
skillbragd technique; sometimes referred to as a pattern board.

WEFT The threads that are woven across the warp threads to create a fabric.

WEFT-FACED WEAVE A weave structure in which only weft threads
are visible on the surface of the fabric.

Bibliography

Alver, Brynjulf. *Dag og merke*. Bergen: Universitetsforlaget, 1970.

Ambroz, A. K. "On the Symbolism of Russian Peasant Embroidery of Archaic Type," *Soviet Anthropology and Archeology* 4, no. 2 (1966):22–37.

Anker, Peter. "Norwegian Folk Art," *Norwegian Tapestries, An Exhibition*. Smithsonian Institution, 1959.

Archer, Karin Fagelund. "De gamle vestfoldteppene," *Norsk Husflid*, 1975–3:8–10.

Arlenborg, Ingrid, and Ulla Feltzing. *Finnväv*. Stockholm: LTs Förlag, 1973.

Arnøy, Rigmor. "Vosseryen," *Norsk Husflid* 3 (1975):10–11.

Asbjørnsen, P. Chr., and Jørgen Moe. *Samlede Eventyr, Jubiliums utgave 1840–1940, første bind*. Olso: Gyldendal, 1940.

Baines, Patricia. *Linen, Handspinning and Weaving*. London: B. T. Batsford, 1989.

Barber, E. J. W. *Prehistoric Textiles*. Princeton: Princeton University Press, 1991.

———. *Women's Work, The First 20,000 Years*. New York: W. W. Norton & Co., 1994.

Black, Mary E. *The Key to Weaving*, 2d rev. ed. New York: Macmillan Publishing Company, 1980.

Bremnes, Gunn. "Om fargebruk i 'Døvlet-teppet,'" *Vestfold Minne*. Tønsberg: Vestfold Historielag, 1979.

Bringsdal, Kathrine. "To gamle åklær fra Vest-Agder," *Norsk Husflid* 6 (1976):14.

Buchanan, Rita. *A Weaver's Garden*. Loveland, Colorado: Interweave Press, Inc., 1987.

Bugge, Astrid. "Ryene på kjerringøy handelssted i Nordland,"

By og Bygd, Norsk Folkemuseums årbok XIX. Oslo: Tanum, 1966.

Burnham, Dorothy K. *Warp & Weft: A Dictionary of Textile Terms*. New York: Charles Scribner's Sons, 1980.

Casselman, Karen Leigh. *Craft of the Dyer*, 2d rev. ed. New York: Dover Publications, 1993.

Christophersen, H. O., Nils Christie, and Kaare Petersen, eds. *Eilert Sundt, Verker i Utvalg, Om renligheds-stellet i Norge*. Oslo: Gyldendal Norsk Forlag, 1975.

Clayhills, Harriet. *Det store lappeteppet*. Oslo: Det Norske Samlaget, 1984.

Collin, Marie. *Skånsk Konstvävnad*. Lund: A. B. PH. Lindstedts Univ. Bokhandel, 1924.

Collingwood, Peter. *The Techniques of Rug Weaving*. London: Faber and Faber Ltd., 1968.

Cootner, Cathryn. *Flat-Woven Textiles*. Washington, D.C.: The Textile Museum, 1981.

Cyrus-Zetterström, Ulla. *Manual of Swedish Handweaving*. Translated by Alice Blomquist. Stockholm: LTs Förlag, 1984.

Dedekam, Hans. *Hvidsøm på Nordmøre*. Trondheim: Bruns, 1914.

Drabløs, Dagfinn. *Soga om smalen, Jubileumsskrift Norsk sau- og geitalslag 1947–97*. Oslo: Norsk sau-og geitalslag, 1997.

Dybdahl, Audun. *Fra ull og lin til klær*. Steinkjer Museum, 1988.

Ekstrand, F. E. *The Ancient Norwegian Calendar Stick*. Seattle: Welcome Press, 1984.

Emery, Irene. *The Primary Structures of Fabrics*. Washington, D.C.: The Textile Museum, 1966.

Engelstad, Helen. *Norske ryer*. Oslo: Kunstindustrimuseet i Oslo, 1942.

———. "Håndarbeid i Norge før 1875," *Statens Kvinnelige Industriskole 1875–1950*. Oslo: H. Aschehoug & Co., 1950.

———. *Refil, Bunad, Tjeld, Middelalderens billedtepper i Norge*. Oslo: Gyldendal Norsk Forlag, 1952.

———. "Plantefargings historie i Norge," in Kielland, Thor B. *Norsk Billedvev, Vol I*. Oslo: Gyldendal Norsk Forlag, 1953, 103–11.

———. *Dobbeltvev i Norge*. Oslo: Gyldendal Norsk Forlag, 1958.

———. "Norwegian Art Weaving," *Native Art of Norway*. Oslo: Dreyers Forlag, 1965.

Eriksen, Erling. "Gammel vevkunst i Vestfolds bygder," *Vestfold Minne*. Tønsberg: Vestfold Historielag, 1955.

Erlandsen, Lillian, and Brynhild Petersen. *Fell-åklær fra Rana-distriktet*. A/S Oslo: Landbruksforlaget, 1987.

Fiske, Patricia L., W. Russell Pickering, and Ralph S. Yohe, eds. *From the Far West: Carpets and Textiles of Morocco*. Washington, D.C.: The Textile Museum, 1980.

Forbes, R. J. *Studies in Ancient Technology*. Vol. 4. Leiden: E. J. Brill, 1956.

Galløe, Olaf. *Natural History of the Danish Lichens*. Parts 5 and 7. Copenhagen: Munksgaard International Publishers Ltd., 1936, 1947.

Gauslaa, Torbjørg. "Linbrett," *Norsk Husflid* 3 (1976):16.

———. "Tjukkåkle," *Norsk Husflid* 2 (1985):14–19.

Gauslaa, Torbjørg, and Tove Østby. *Åkleboka*. Oslo: Landbruksforlaget, 1977.

Geijer, Agnes. *A History of Textile Art*. London: Pasold Research Fund Ltd, 1982.

Gjerdåker, Johannes. *Arbeidet i bygdene, Årsrytmen på Voss før landbruket vart mekanisert*. Voss: Vestanbok Forlag, 1980.

Graabræk, Elin. "Tepper—til pryd og varme," *Tepper i Vestfold*. Tønsberg: Vestfold Fylkesmusuem, 1989.

Grieg, Sigurd, ed. *Norsk Tekstil*. Oslo: Johan Grundt Tanum, 1948.

Gudjánsson, Elsu E. "Forn röggvarvefnaður," *Árbók hins íslenzka fornleifafélags*. Reykjavik, 1962.

———. "A Note on Mediaeval Icelandic Shaggy Pile Weaving," *CIETA Bulletin*, nos. 51–52 (1980):41–45.

Halvorsen, Caroline. *Den Norske Husflidsforenings Håndbok i veving*. 9th ed. Oslo: J. W. Cappelens Forlag, 1950.

Haugen, Anny. *Samisk husflid i Finnmark*. Oslo: Norsk Folkemeusum, Landbruksforlaget, 1987.

Hauglid, Roar. *Hus, peis og billedvev*. Oslo: Foreningen til Norske Fortidsminnesmerkers Bevaring, 1956.

Herodotus. *The History*. Translated by David Grene. Chicago: University of Chicago Press, 1987.

Hjeltnes, Torunn. "Telemarksteppe," *Norsk Husflid* 3 (1982):12–13.

Hoffmann, Marta. *En gruppe vevstoler på vestlandet*. Oslo: Norsk Folkemuseum, 1958.

———. *The Warp-Weighted Loom*. Oslo: The Norwegian Research Council for Science and the Humanities, 1974.

———. "The Looms of the Old World," *Looms and Their Products: Roundtable on Musuem Textiles*, 1977 Proceedings. Washington, D.C.: The Textile Museum, 1977.

———. "Manndalen Revisited: Traditional Weaving in an Old Lappish Community in Transition," *Studies in Textile History*. Toronto: Royal Ontario Museum, 1977.

———. *Studiehefte no. 3: Tekstilarbeid*. Department of Ethnology, School of Cultural Studies, University of Oslo, 1989.

———. *Fra fiber til tøy*. Oslo: Landbrukset, 1991.

Huxley, Anthony. *Green Inheritance: The World Wildlife Fund Book of Plants*. New York: Four Walls Eight Windows, 1984.

Johansson, Lillemor. *Damask and Opphämta with Weaving Sword or Drawloom*. Translated by Susan Jones. Stockholm: LTs Forlag, 1984.

Julius Bårdsen. *Krossåkle frå Suldal*. Sand, 1975.

Kielland, Thor B. *Norsk Billedvev*, vols. 1–3. Oslo: Gyldendal Norsk Forlag, 1953–55 (English summary).

———. "Norwegian Textiles," in *Norwegian Tapestries, An Exhibition*. Smithsonian Institution, Washington, D.C., 1959.

Kjellberg, Anne. "Brodert vevnad eller vevet broderi?" *By og Bydg, Norsk Folkemuseums Årbok XXVII*. Reprint, Oslo: Tanum, 1979.

———. "Rutevevde tekstiler fra Vest-Agder," *By og Bygd, Norsk Folkemuseums Årbok XXXI*. Oslo: Tanum, 1985–86.

———. "Et skillbragdteppe fra Lardal i Vestfold," *Tepper i Vestfold*. Tønsberg: Vestfold Fylkesmusuem, 1989.

———. "Tepper i skillbragd og tavlebragd fra Budalen," *By og Bygd, Norsk Folkemuseums Årbok XXXIII*. Oslo: Tanum, 1991.

Kjellmo, Ellen. *Båtrya i gammel og ny tid*. Stamsund: Orkana Forlag, 1996.

Koppen, Maria Brekke. *Innføring i billedvev*. Oslo: Universitetsforlaget, 1974.

———. *Videreføring i billedvev*. Oslo: Universitetsforlaget, 1981.

Kostveit, Åsta Østmoe. *Kors i kake, skurd i tre: tegn og symboler i folkekulturen*. Oslo: Landbruksforlaget, 1997.

Krafft, Sofie. *Pictorial Weavings from the Viking Age*. Oslo: Dreyers Forlag, 1956.

Larson, Laurence Marcellus, trans. *Speculum Regale—Konungs Skuggsjá—The King's Mirror*. Scandinavian Monographs, vol. 3. New York: The American-Scandinavian Foundation, 1917.

Lexow, Einar. "Gammel vestlandsk vævkunst," *Bergens Museums Aarbok*, Nr. 2, 1914.

Lightfoot, Amy. "Ullseil i tusen år," *SPOR-fortidsnytt fra midt-norge* 2 (1997):10–15.

Lincoln, Louise, ed. *The Art of Norway, 1750–1914*. The Minneapolis Institute of Arts and The Regents of the University of Wisconsin, 1978.

Lund, Juel. *Primstaven, eller Messedagsstaven og Runestaven*. Oslo: Fonna Forlag, 1944.

Lunde, Dagmar. "Forsøk med korkje," *Årbok 1972–75, Kunstindustrimuseet i Oslo*. Oslo: Kunstindustrimuseet i Oslo, 1975.

Lundell, Laila, Inger Molin, Hilkka Råbergh, and Elisabeth Windesjö. *Vevingens Farger, Form og Materialer*. Translated to Norwegian by Anna Crælius. Oslo: Teknologisk Forlag, 1979.

Lundin, Judy D., and Liv Gjelsvik. *Norsk—Engelsk, Engelsk—Norsk Ordliste for veving, Norwegian—English, English—Norwegian Weaving Glossary*. Oslo: Statens lærerhøgskole i forming Oslo, 1986.

Mattera, Joanne. *Rugweaving: Techniques for Two-Harness*. New York: Watson-Guptill Publications, 1979.

Midbrød, Arvid, and Lisabet Ris, eds. *Rogaland i Nær Fortid*. Oslo: Det Norske Samlaget, 1983.

Mohr, Emily. "Gammel vestlandsk åklevev." Reprinted in *Bergens Tidende*, 11 January 1936.

Nordby, Ragnar. "Vestfoldteppe," *Yrke* 2 (1948):29–34.

Nordhaugen, Rolf. *Norsk Flora*. Vols. 1–4. Oslo: H. Aschehoug & Co., 1970.

Nygaard, Turid. Voss Husflidskule, personal communication.

Nylén, Anna-Maja. *Swedish Handcraft*. Translated by Anne-Charlotte Hanes Harvey. New York: Van Nostrand Reinhold Co., 1977.

Peesch, Reinhard. *The Ornament in European Folk Art*. New York: Alpine Fine Arts Collection, 1982.

Petersson, Inga Lisa, and Birgit Jansson. *Bunden Rosengång från Jämtland och Härjedalen*. Stockholm: LTs Förlag, 1983.

Rasmussen, Reidunn Strand. "Skillbragdveving i Nordfjord," *Norsk Husflid* 2 (1984):8–10.

Roth, H. Ling. *Ancient Egyptian and Greek Looms*. Halifax: Bankfield Museum, 1913.

Rud, Mogens. *The Bayeux Tapestry and the Battle of Hastings 1066*. English language ed. Translated by Chris Bojesen. Copenhagen: Christian Eilers, 1988.

Ryssdal, Marie. "Husflid og handarbeid i tida ca. 1850–1940," *Soga om Gloppen og Breim*. Sandane, 1979.

Seiler-Baldinger, Annemarie. *Textiles: A Classification of Techniques*. Washington, D.C.: Smithsonian Institution Press, 1994.

Seland, Kari. "Rik tekstilkunst på utstilling," *Norsk Husflid* 4 (1983):16–17.

Sjøvold, Aase Bay. *Norwegian Tapestries*. Translated by Elizabeth Seeberg. Oslo: C. Huitfeldt Forlag, 1976.

Steen, Sverre. *Langsomt ble landet vårt eget*. Oslo: J. W. Cappelens Forlag, 1967.

Stewart, Janice S. *The Folk Arts of Norway*. New York: Dover Publications, 1972.

Strömberg, Elisabeth, Agnes Geijer, Margrethe Hald, and Marta Hoffmann. *Nordisk Textilteknisk Terminologi: Förindustriell Vävnadsproduktion*. 3d ed. Oslo: Tanum-Norli, 1979. (Originally published in 1967.)

Sveinall, Paul. *Øyslebø Gard og Ætt*, vol. 2. Sogenemnda i Marnardal, 1976.

Thomassen, Ella. "Krokbragd på Vestlandet," textile history lecture, Statens lærershøgskole i forming Oslo, Sept. 23, 1957. Mimeograph.

Thomson, F. P. *Tapestry: Mirror of History*. New York: Crown Publishers, 1980.

Thorrud, Laila Emma. *Tepper og ryer i Vestfold, Mønsterhefte*. Tønsberg: Vestfold Historielag, 1992.

Walterstorff, Emelie von, ed. *Swedish Textiles*. Stockholm: Nordiska Museet, 1925.

———. "Svenska vävnadstekniker och mönstertyper," *Nordiska Museets Handlingar*. Vol. 11. Stockholm: 1940.

Wang, Marit. *Ruteåklær*. Bergen: Universitetsforlaget, 1983.

Weibel, Adéle Coulin. *Two Thousand Years of Textiles*. New York: Pantheon, 1952.

Wiklund, Doris. *Gamla Svenska Vävnader från norr til söder omkring 1850–1950*. Luleå: I-Tryck/Grafiska Huset, 1996.

Wille, Hans Jacob. *Beskrivelse over Lillejords Præstegield i Øvre-Tellemarken i Norge*. Copenhagen: Gyldendahls, 1786.

Wilson, Kax. *A History of Textiles*. Boulder, Colorado: Westview Press, 1979.

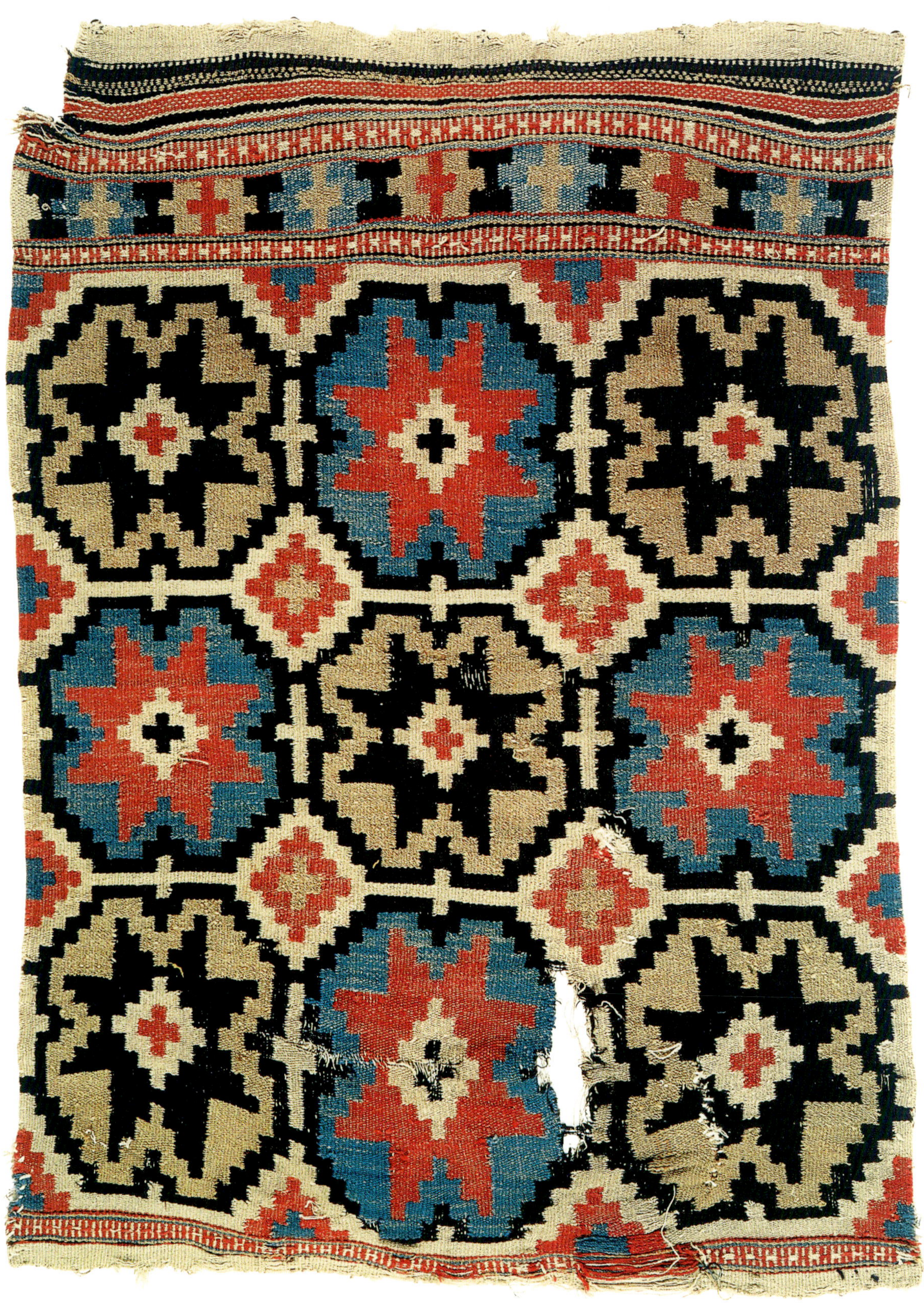 A regular array of the eight-petaled rose motif decorates this square-weave coverlet. A mistake in the pattern (right center) draws attention to the weaver. A busy mother? An inexperienced young girl? *Historical Museum, University of Bergen.*

Index

weave, 136; in rya, 152; in tapestry, 56. *See also* sheep, primitive
Gudbrandsdal, 41, 44, **45**, **49**, **51**, **53**, 80, 92, 115, 119, 120, 121, **121-29**, 136, 141, **144**, 160, 165

Hackling, 10, 10, **11**, **12**
hakketechnique. See dovetailing technique
half-heddle rod, 172
Hallingdal, 89
halvfloss, 180. *See also* voided pile
halvkrabba. See brocading: in Vestfold coverlets
Hardanger, 67, 77
hearth house, 17, **17**, **32**, 33–34
Heddal, **45**
heddle rod, **29**, 83, 84
heddle, 20, 171, 173; long eye, 171, 173; rigid, 100. *See also* half-heddle rod
Hedmark, **15**, 17, 42, 44
hemp, 7, 88
homes, improvements in, **24**, 25–26. *See also* hearth house
Hordaland, 20, 29, 84, 92, 97, 112

Icelandic textiles, 137, 142, **142**
inscriptions: in double weave, 115, 121, 130–32; in square weave, 64; in tapestry, 48
interlocking, 85, **85**

Jølster, 96, 107

Kjerringtenner, 180. *See also* pick-and-pick
knitting, 4, 5, 7, 9; balls of yarn for, 15; wool for, 12
knotted pile. *See* rya
korkje, 18–19, **19**
krabbasnår, 180. *See* brocading: in Vestfold coverlets
kristnaåkle. See christening blanket
krokbragd, 178, 180; colors, 88; in combined technique coverlets, 112, **113**; in Danish weave, 108, **110**; history, 87; looms, 88, **92**; materials, 88; pat-

terns, 88, **88**, **91**; weaving technique, 93, **93**

Lightning weave, 102, **103**; in combined technique coverlets, 112, **113**; in square weave coverlets, 64, **65**
Lofoten, 22, **23**, 139, **146**
loom, four-harness, 20–21, **22**, 24, 25, 26, **30**; in double weave, 136; history, 30–31, 30*n*; in krokbragd, 88; in overshot, 169, 171, 173; parts of, **21**; in rya, 152; in square weave, 83; warping, 20. *See also* heddle: rigid; loom, upright; loom, warp-weighted
loom, upright, 56, **58**, 83, **84**, 137; parts of, 83. *See also* loom, warp-weighted
loom, warp-weighted, 28–31, **28**, **31**; double weave, 136; with four sheds, 137; krokbragd, 88, **92**; parts of, **29**; Sami, 98; variations, 56, 83, 84; warping, 20, 100, **101**, **102**

Magical symbols, 70, 117, **118**
monk's belt, 157, 178, 180; colors, 159; materials, 168; patterns, **158**, 159; weaving technique, 170, **170**. *See also* overshot
motifs: non-reversible double weave, 130–34 passim, **130**; reversible double weave, 123–29, **123**; square weave, 70–75, **70–71**; tapestry, 48–56 passim. *See also* inscriptions; magical symbols; patterns

Natural dyes. *See* dyes and dyeing
nettles, 7
Nordfjord, 21, **156**, **163**
Nordhordland, 113
Nordland, 87, **147**, **149**, 160, 174
Nordland's weave, 36, 164, **164**, **165**, 167, **168**, 169, 173. *See also* skillbragd
Nord-Trøndelag, **134**, 141, **150**

Opphämta, 178, 180. *See also skill-bragd*; Swedish textiles
Oseberg: brocaded textile, 41, **42**, 104; motifs, 70, **117**; textile tools, 7, **16**
overshot, 37, 157, 177, 180; ends per inch,

168; history, 158; loom, 169, 171; materials, 168; weaving techniques, 169, **169**. *See also* monk's belt; *skillbragd*

Pattern rod, 172, **172**
patterns: brocading, 104, **105**; Danish weave, 108, **110**; grene, 98; krokbragd, 88, **88**, **91**; lightning weave, 102, **103**; monk's belt, **158**, 159; pick-and-pick, 95, 96; rya, 145; skillbragd, with weaving sword, 162, **162**; skillbragd, loom-controlled, 164, **164**, 166. *See also* motifs; inscriptions
pick-and-pick, 95–96, **96**, 97, 177, 180; in combined technique coverlets, 112; in Danish weave 108; in square weave coverlets, 64; with supplementary pattern weft, 104, **106**, 107. *See also* grene
pillows, 23, 35; in tapestry 44, **45**, 56, **57**; in voided-pile, 126, 142, **144**
plain weave, 21, 36–37, **36**, 177, 180; in brocaded coverlets, 104; in Danish weave coverlets, 108; in double weave coverlets, 136; in grene, 100; in krokbragd, 93; in monk's belt coverlets, 170; in overshot coverlets, 169; in pick-and-pick, 95; in rya coverlets, 153; in square weave, 85; in tapestry, 56
primstav. See calendar stick

Rags, 5, 35; in rya, **147**, 152
Rana, 157
reel, 15, **16**
Renaissance, influence of: on tapestry, 41, 44–47, 48; on double-weave, 120, 132, 134
retting, 7–10 passim
rigid heddle, 100
ripple, 7, 9, 10
Rogaland, 20, **71**
rölakan, 178, 180. *See also* square weave
rutevev, 178, 180. *See also* square weave
rya, 178, 180; colors, 145; double weave used in, 145, **151**, **126**; ends per inch, 152; history, 141–142; looms, 152; materials, 152; patterns, 145; technique,